W9-CPF-006

CANADA

Warning to Users of Radio

All Radio Receiving Sets MUST be Licensed

Penalty on summary conviction is a fine not exceeding $50.00

License Fee $1.00 per annum

Licenses, valid to 31st March, 1930, may be obtained from: Staff Post Offices, Radio Dealers, Radio Inspectors, or from Radio Branch, Department of Marine, Ottawa.

A. JOHNSTON,
Deputy Minister of Marine

SIGNING ON

THE BIRTH OF RADIO IN CANADA
SIGNING ON

BILL McNEIL
and
MORRIS WOLFE

Doubleday Canada Limited, Toronto, Canada
Doubleday & Company, Inc. Garden City, New York
1982

Library of Congress Catalogue Card Number: 82-45257

ISBN 0-385-17742-9 cloth
      0-385-18379-8 paperback

Copyright © Selection and arrangement 1982
              by Bill McNeil and Morris Wolfe

All Rights Reserved

Cover Art: David Craig

Design: Lamont Cranston with Irene Carefoot

Typeset: ART-U Graphics Ltd.

Printed and bound in Canada by
T. H. Best Printing Company Limited

First Edition

for our parents
from whom we learned
a love of radio

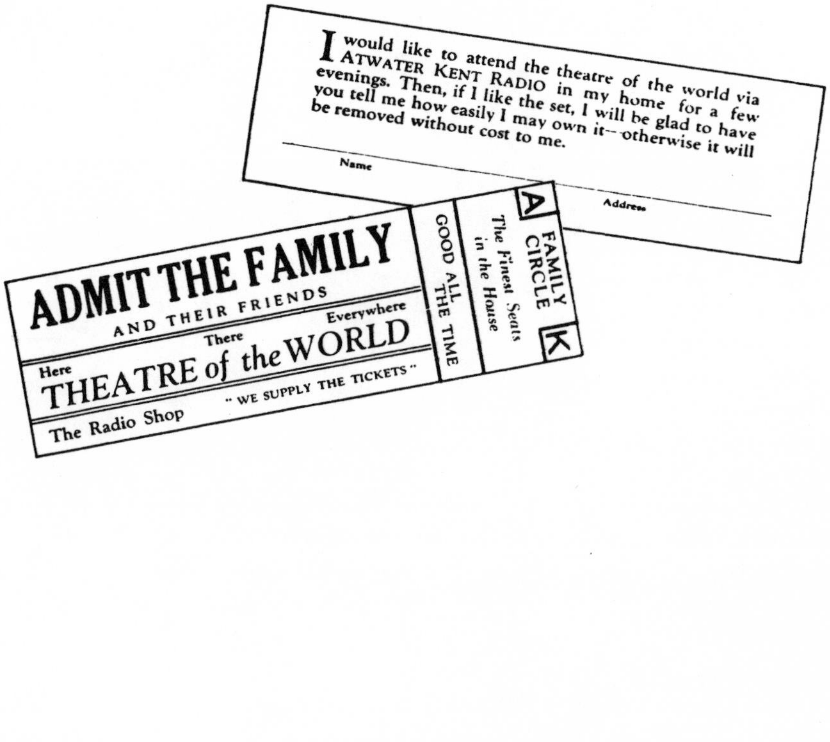

I would like to attend the theatre of the world via ATWATER KENT RADIO in my home for a few evenings. Then, if I like the set, I will be glad to have you tell me how easily I may own it—otherwise it will be removed without cost to me.

Name _____

Address _____

ADMIT THE FAMILY
AND THEIR FRIENDS

Here   There   Everywhere

THEATRE of the WORLD

The Radio Shop   " WE SUPPLY THE TICKETS "

GOOD ALL THE TIME

The Finest Seats in the House

A

FAMILY CIRCLE

K

Introduction 10
Acknowledgements 21

A 1924 article in <u>Maclean's</u> declares that the businessman of 1975 "will need no chauffeur, for radio controls will operate the car at his will; table service will be automatic. When the soup is finished, you say merely 'bring in the fish' and the fish comes in from the kitchen by himself."

Introduction

In 1932, following years of discussion and delay, public radio officially arrived in Canada. *Signing On* celebrates a half century of Canadian public broadcasting. But it does more than that. Almost always omitted from histories of the development of Canadian radio is the story of the important pioneering work done by *private* broadcasters—especially in the years *before* 1932. This book attempts to correct that omission.

Signing On contains one hundred and twenty-five interviews with broadcasters, producers, technicians, entrepreneurs and ordinary listeners. Those included come from all ten provinces and represent both private and public broadcasting. Some of their names are well known nationally (Lorne Greene and Mary Grannan); some are well known regionally (Bert Hooper); others aren't really known outside the communities they served. Some began broadcasting early in the period we're looking at (Foster Hewitt); others much later (Max Ferguson). We've tried to balance all these factors in deciding which of the more than two hundred interviews available to us to include. We've divided the material in *Signing On* into seven chapters—three devoted to private broadcasting, three to public, with a final brief chapter on the coming of television in 1952, when this book ends.

The following chronology lists some of the major events in Canadian radio history that *Signing On* touches on:

1901 Marconi, in St. John's, Newfoundland, receives first transatlantic 'wireless' signal from Cornwall, England.

1906 First wireless voice broadcast by Reginald Fessenden, a Canadian working for Edison in the U.S.

1912 Titanic sinks. Wireless credited with saving hundreds of lives.

1919 XWA (later CFCF) Montreal signs on. XWA, operated by the Marconi Wireless Company, is widely regarded as the oldest station in the world. KDKA Pittsburgh doesn't sign on until some months later.

1922 CKCK Regina signs on.*

1923 CNR network begins broadcasting. Unofficial beginning of public radio.

1926 Canadian Association of Broadcasters organized. At first it includes all broadcasters. Later CAB becomes the official organization of the private sector.

1926 CHNS Halifax signs on.*

1927 July 1, Diamond Jubilee Broadcast. First coast to coast network in North America.

1927 CFRB Toronto signs on.*

1929 Aird Commission recommends creation of a public body to regulate private broadcasters and to broadcast its own programmes.

1932 Canadian Radio Broadcasting Commission (CRBC) established.

1936 Moose River Mine Disaster. All of Canada and U.S. tune in to CRBC broadcasts.

1936 CBC replaces CRBC.

1939 Second World War begins. Public broadcasting comes of age.

1951 Massey Commission recommends CBC go into television.

1952 CBC television begins.

*We have decided to pay particular attention to one private station in each of the three geographical regions represented in the book.

CIRCULATION LARGER THAN THAT OF ANY OTHER RADIO PUBLICATION

RADIO PHONE
WRNY
STATION

RADIO NEWS
REG. U.S. PAT. OFF.

25 Cents

FEBRUARY

Over 200
Illustrations

Edited by HUGO GERNSBACK

"WIRELESS"
RADIO DANCING
SEE PAGE 1120

RADIO'S GREATEST MAGAZINE

EXPERIMENTER PUBLISHING COMPANY, NEW YORK, PUBLISHERS OF
THE EXPERIMENTER
MOTOR CAMPER & TOURIST
SCIENCE and INVENTION

Some Canadians preferred American
radio magazines such as *Radio News*.

Signing On isn't just an oral record of the early years of Canadian radio; it's also a visual record. Included are over four hundred illustrations—advertisements, licences, photographs, radio listings, rate cards, etc.—most of which have not appeared in book form before. The visual material is drawn from public archives and private collections and from the back files of newspapers and magazines from across the country. Some of the material is old and brittle; we have reproduced it here as best we could.

It was a particular treat in researching this book to discover and read some of the radio magazines that flourished in the 1920s—magazines such as *Canadian Radio, Radio News of Canada, Canadian Wireless* and *The Radio Bug*. Nowhere does one quite feel the excitement of the early days of radio as in the pages—especially the advertising pages—of these early magazines. We've tried to capture some of that flavour in the design and layout of this book.

Radio, some people assumed, was going to transform the world. And it wasn't just the radio magazines that said that. The headline of a 1924 article in *Maclean's* declares: "Radio May Remake Our Lives: Our Business and Leisure Fifty Years Hence May Be Conducted In Amazingly Different Manner." According to the article that follows, the businessman of 1975 "will need no chauffeur, for radio controls will operate the car at his will....no stenographers or typewriters will be needed, because all his correspondence will be done by radio....table service will be automatic. When the soup is finished, you say merely 'bring in the fish' and the fish comes in from the kitchen by himself."

Unlike *Maclean's* and the radio magazines, newspapers were far more restrained in their enthusiasm for radio. That's one of the recurring themes in this book. Newspapers saw radio as a potential threat. At first some papers tried owning stations themselves as a way of controlling the competition. When that didn't work, they tried ignoring radio. Newspapers refused to list radio programmes or to review them. Radio wasn't mentioned in news stories and the call letters of stations were eliminated from news photographs. Joseph Sedgwick, lawyer for the Canadian Association of Broadcasters, wrote in the early 1940s: "The press of Canada...has maintained a conspiracy of silence concerning radio. The most insignificant concert merits a column of criticism;

THE WIRELESS BALL

Four Microphones arranged to give a dance
And Broadcast invitations in advance;
    The Circuit of their friends, the Wireless Parts,
    Was very large; and these with happy hearts
Assembled on the evening of the ball.
Loud Speakers, many of them, in the hall
    Where the Receiving Set, the Microphones,
    Received their guests and spoke in pleasant Tones.
Were hung with flags. "So grand!" an Anode said.
    The Wireless Beam was beaming with delight,
    A Jigger jigged, vowed he could dance all night!
The hall looked gay: the Aerials o'erhead
The band Conductor soon Relayed an air,
    A pretty young Electron with her hair
    In Waves, who had a most Magnetic face,
    Then Oscillated with Undamped grace,
Watched by admiring Batteries of eyes,
The while a Diode praised her to the skies.
    The Dull Emitter quite cheered up and bounced
    About Watt-Hour the supper was announced.
He put a Pancake Coil upon his Plate,
For Beverage (Aerial) he had to wait,
    And, as his thirst he wanted to assuage,
    He soon began to Choke with utter rage!
A Wander Plug then wandered to his side,
Bringing some Currents, and these Amplified
    Their meal. The guests enjoyed the ball, no doubt;
    They danced until the stars all Faded Out!
                                    —Leslie M. Oyler

Joseph Sedgwick, lawyer for the Canadian Association of Broadcasters, wrote in the early 1940s: "The press of Canada...has maintained a conspiracy of silence concerning radio."

Major F. S. McPherson
Officer Commanding

2nd Company, 2nd Battalion Canadian Corps of Signals

invites you to attend

at

The Armouries
(University Avenue, Toronto)

on any

Friday Evening

so that he may bring to your attention the work of the young
Canadian in Radio Wireless, Line Telegraphy
and Telephony.

(Watch for the man with the blue
and white band on his arm.)

Advertisement in *Radio News of Canada*, November, 1923. ▶

Unidentified Canadian radio manufacturing plant in mid-1920s. Note Canadian and American flags and coil winding machines. ▼

the cheapest dramatic effort is viewed and professionally appraised; most papers of any importance carry motion picture review departments; but radio, presumably because it competes with the press, cannot even be mentioned." One of the first regular broadcasting columnists on a Canadian daily, Frank Chamberlain, appeared in the *Globe and Mail* three times a week courtesy, not of the *Globe*, but of Simpson's, which paid for the space.

In the years before the Second World War, there were occasions when Canadians saw clearly what public radio could do and what its possibilities were. Unfortunately, those occasions were all too rare. For example, all of Canada was joined together by radio for the first time on July 1, 1927, in order to celebrate the Diamond Jubilee of Confederation. Thousands wrote to Ottawa to express their delight at the achievement. One Saskatchewan farmer described the Jubilee broadcast as "a miracle" which only a poet could adequately describe. And poet Wilson MacDonald, always ready to oblige, responded with these mortal lines:

> A silence there, expectant, meaning,
>   And then a voice clear-pitched and tense;
> A million hearers, forward-leaning,
>   Were in the thrall of eloquence.
>
> A pause, a hush, a wonder growing;
>   A prophet's vision understood;
> In that strange spell of his bestowing,
>   They dreamed, with him, of Brotherhood.

Or in April 1936, Canada was again glued to the radio during Frank Willis's sixty-nine hours of suspense-filled broadcasting from the Moose River Mine Disaster, where two men were rescued after being buried alive for ten days. Willis's reports were carried not only by fifty-eight Canadian stations but by six hundred and fifty in the U.S.

But with the exceptions of Jubilee broadcasts and Moose River Mine Disasters, Canadians weren't overly impressed with what public broadcasting offered them in its early years. One criticism was that public radio wasn't distinctive enough. (In the late 1930s the CBC's prime listening hours were largely filled with American programmes.) People wondered whether it was worth the licence fees they had to pay. One member of Parliament

Do You want to Earn Good Money in Your Spare Time?

Just the Thing for Boys--- Join Our *Young Hustlers Club!*

NO MATTER WHERE YOU LIVE IN CANADA, YOU SHOULD APPLY

The work will not interfere with school duties, in fact will supplement them by giving you actual practice in keeping your small accounts. The best boy in each district will be appointed Captain and given more important work to do.

The easy work of securing and looking after customers for Radio News of Canada and the Radio Log Book is attracting some of the finest Canadian Boys, many of whom are now making real money.

In Addition There Are Prizes For Everyone

You can earn prizes from a Flashlight to a Beautiful Bicycle. Your friends will help you.

BOYS, FILL IN AND MAIL THIS COUPON

To Radio News of Canada
7 Jordan Street,
TORONTO, ONT.

I would like to join the Young Hustlers Club and earn a regular income. Please send me a free start in business and complete information as to how I can win the prizes offered.

My Full Name Is ....

Address ....

Town ....Province..................

My Age Is ....Date..................

Signature ....

A number of Canadian radio magazines sprang up in the early 1920s—magazines such as *Radio News of Canada, Canadian Wireless,* and *The Radio Bug.* They competed with one another for readers.

15

ALWAYS THE FIRST ORDER OF THE NAZI INVADER

"SEIZE THE RADIO STATION!"

MAKE NO MISTAKE, Hitler knows the power of radio.

But in his hands, it is a power for evil — a force to smash men's liberty.

We, as free men, will listen tonight to programs of our own choosing — because brave men are fighting that we may remain free.

And so that these fighting men may have ample resources of vital equipment, Rogers Majestic has converted its factories and its research laboratories 100% to war purposes.

On that triumphant day when the peoples of the conquered lands once again control their radio stations, we shall provide Canadians with revolutionary new Rogers, Majestic and DeForest Radios.

H P Mackenzie

PRESIDENT

ROGERS MAJESTIC (1941) LIMITED
AND AFFILIATED COMPANIES

Manufacturers of Rogers, Majestic and DeForest Radios and Rogers Long-Life Fully Guaranteed Radio Tubes. A Tube for Every Purpose.

told the House of Commons in 1938: "If the Canadian Broadcasting Corporation cannot do better it might as well fold up. If it was fewer United States programmes we wanted, we are getting more; if it was less booming of United States products through United States programmes, we are getting more; if our object was to cut down on this United States invasion, the new policy, with its accompanying increase in the licence fee, is bringing us still more and more of the United States influence."

The Second World War changed that. Widespread criticism of public broadcasting evaporated overnight; it was now clear to everyone that the CBC had an important part to play in Canada's war effort and had the will and the resources to do so. During the War, for instance, the CBC finally began its own news service. "You had the feeling," says Harry Boyle of the war years, "that come ten o'clock every evening *every* radio in the country was tuned in to the CBC to find out what was going on." And it was during the War that the CBC's farm broadcasts began. And the "Stage" series. And much more. Those achievements are reflected in the chapter on the CBC.

Signing On, as we've indicated, is an oral history. The advantage of using the raw material of oral history is that it has the colour and flavour and rough edges of real life; it allows one to experience the past in a more immediate way. Sometimes that results in insights that the neat perspectives of more formal approaches to history fail to capture.

Nowhere, for example, is it made so clear as in the pages that follow, the extent to which radio pioneers *accidentally* stumbled on broadcasting as a way of making money. Pioneer broadcasters started stations so those to whom they were selling radios would have something to listen to. But the money was to be made from the radios, not the broadcasting; *that* was a kind of loss leader.

Or it's assumed that the radio pioneers were all brilliant scientists and engineers like Marconi. In fact, most of them hadn't the faintest idea how radio functioned. One operator tells of going over and kicking the transmitter every time someone phoned to complain that the station wasn't coming through clearly. He didn't know what else to do.

It's two minutes to five. Two minutes to five in Normandy, and the sun hasn't risen yet, over us or over the Germans, 800 yards away. It will rise on a fearful scene, because at five o'clock precisely, the Canadians are going to attack. And they'll attack with the most enormous concentration of fire ever put down on a small objective. The morning is as soft and beautiful as a swan gliding down a quiet river.
I am in a stone barn with a company of western Canadian machine gunners who are going to be in battle soon....In front of me, not half a mile away, is the powerful German strongpoint of Carpiquet village and Carpiquet airdrome, two or three miles west of Caen. That position has been a thorn in our side. We can't get Caen until we get Carpiquet. And now we're going to get it.
We can see Germans moving from time to time in the half light. We won't see them when the barrage begins. Little white rabbits and baby ducks are playing at my feet. They don't know that this barn will soon be shelled and machine-gunned....The attack will come across, right in front of us and toward us. I've never had a better observation post for a battle. And I dread what I'll see through this door.

Partial text of a Matthew Halton broadcast in July, 1944, one month after D-Day.

One member of Parliament told the House of Commons in 1938: "If the Canadian Broadcasting Corporation cannot do better it might as well fold up."

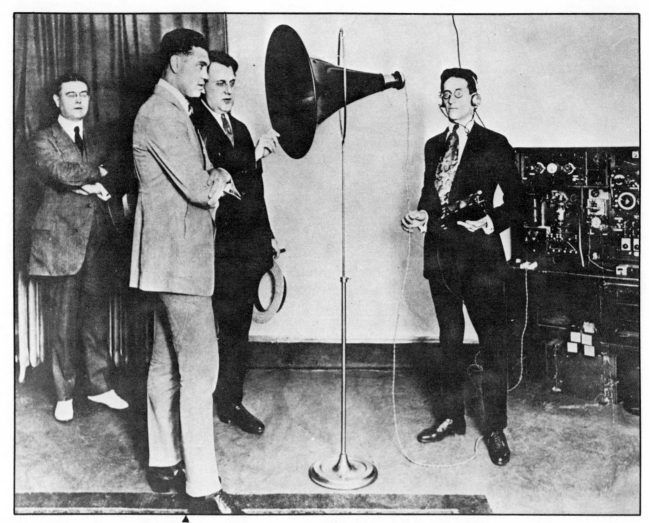

World Heavyweight Champion, Jack Dempsey, interviewed at station CFCF (formerly XWA) Montreal in 1922.

RADIO RIBS . . . . . . G. Harkled.

"Remember, sister, when television comes, you're out."

It was assumed by men in countless cartoons such as this one that the way they looked was fine.

Attitudes towards women in broadcasting are revealed here in a sharper and more personal way than in any other account of Canadian radio. Jane Gray complains to a station manager in London, Ontario in the 1920s because there are no women on the air. "He looked at me," she reports, "as if I had said a dirty word. 'Women on the air!? There never will be either by the grace of God!'" Miss Forrest becomes an announcer at CHNS Halifax in 1942 only because all the men have gone off to war. And our award for most sexist ad in *Signing On* goes to CKNX. (See page 108)

One final example. The comments of the listeners included here add yet another—sometimes funny, sometimes poignant— dimension to the story. Some listeners are incredulous about radio; they assume there's some trick involved. Surely voices can't just come out of the air. Others couldn't care less. "Who wants to hear a dog bark in Italy?" asks one woman. Some become obsessed by radio, turning their dials (DXing) into the wee hours of the morning. And the isolation of those living in remote northern communities in the days before radio, now seems unimaginable. Several listeners describe in touching personal detail how their lives were transformed by radio.

The world of the early years of Canadian radio seems long ago, now. It comes as a something of a surprise, therefore, to recall that anyone over the age of forty is certain to have memories of the days before television when people played bridge by radio, gave radio tubes as Christmas presents, or went to an early movie because they knew they'd be able to hear "Amos 'n' Andy" over the PA system in the theatre before their screening began. Whether you are over or under age forty, whether you are remembering or just now discovering the early years of Canadian radio, we hope *Signing On* gives you something of the pleasure the preparing of it gave us.

Morris Wolfe
Bill McNeil
August 1982

The isolation of those living in remote northern communities in the days before radio, now seems unimaginable.

Letters of Appreciation to Radio Stations

To encourage fans and facilitate the despatch of letters of appreciation for programmes heard, we print below ten coupons for this purpose. Just fill in the details and mail in an envelope direct to the Station, the call letters and name of town being sufficient address.

LETTER OF APPRECIATION

I heard your Station ....

on .... at ....a.m............p.m.
and particularly enjoyed your programme.

Name ....

Address ....

Date ....

Radio News of Canada.

LETTER OF APPRECIATION

I heard your Station ....

on .... at ....a.m............p.m.
and particularly enjoyed your programme.

Name ....

Address ....

Date ....

Radio News of Canada.

LETTER OF APPRECIATION

I heard your Station ....

on .... at ....a.m............p.m.
and particularly enjoyed your programme.

Name ....

Address ....

Date ....

Radio News of Canada.

LETTER OF APPRECIATION

I heard your Station ....

on .... at ....a.m............p.m.
and particularly enjoyed your programme.

Name ....

Address ....

Date ....

Radio News of Canada.

LETTER OF APPRECIATION

I heard your Station ....

on .... at ....a.m............p.m.
and particularly enjoyed your programme.

Name ....

Address ....

Date ....

Radio News of Canada.

LETTER OF APPRECIATION

I heard your Station ....

on .... at ....a.m............p.m.
and particularly enjoyed your programme.

Name ....

Address ....

Date ....

Radio News of Canada.

LETTER OF APPRECIATION

I heard your Station ....

on .... at ....a.m............p.m.
and particularly enjoyed your programme.

Name ....

Address ....

Date ....

Radio News of Canada.

LETTER OF APPRECIATION

I heard your Station ....

on .... at ....a.m............p.m.
and particularly enjoyed your programme.

Name ....

Address ....

Date ....

Radio News of Canada.

LETTER OF APPRECIATION

I heard your Station ....

on .... at ....a.m............p.m.
and particularly enjoyed your programme.

Name ....

Address ....

Date ....

Radio News of Canada.

LETTER OF APPRECIATION

I heard your Station ....

on .... at ....a.m............p.m.
and particularly enjoyed your programme.

Name ....

Address ....

Date ....

Radio News of Canada.

Acknowledgements

This book would not have been possible without the assistance and co-operation of a number of individuals and institutions across Canada. We are particularly grateful to Professor Kenneth Bambrick of the School of Journalism at the University of Western Ontario. Bambrick spent the academic year 1976-1977 interviewing radio pioneers—men and women who had begun in broadcasting before 1936. Those interviews have become the Bambrick Collection at the Public Archives of Canada and approximately half the interviews in *Signing On* derive in whole or in part from that collection. Ernie Dick and Jacques Gagné of the Public Archives of Canada provided us with valuable leads and advice. Sylvie Robitaille, also of PAC, cheerfully handled numerous details. All of the material we've collected will be deposited in the Public Archives.

We are grateful to Ernie De Coste of the Museum of Science and Technology who had periodicals in his collection available nowhere else; to Judith McErvil of Eaton's Archives; to Patricia Kipping of the Nova Scotia Archives; to Ruth Peachell of CFRB; to CKCK; to CFCO; to the Canadian Association of Broadcasters; to the Beaton Institute, College of Cape Breton; to the Ontario Archives; to the C.N.R. Archives; to Robarts Library and the Toronto Public Library.

Peter Herrndorf cut through CBC red tape by giving us access to their libraries and archives across the country. Included in *Signing On* are photographs from the CBC Collection at the Public Archives and the CBC Design Library. Liz Jenner and her staff at the CBC Reference Library were friendly and helpful through several weeks of combing through their programme schedules and files. Ivan Harris, enthusiastic Curator of the CBC's (homeless) Broadcast Museum, gave us access to the scrapbooks of Canada's first full-time radio critic, Frank Chamberlain. And (as always) Dido Mendl and her associates at the CBC's Program Archives were a joy to work with as we audited several hundred hours of interview material in their collection. (Nine of the interviews in this book come from that source.) Listeners' comments are from open line segments of the CBC programme "Fresh Air."

Some of the photographs and other visual material included in *Signing On* come from the collections of individuals—Bill Baker, Harry Boyle, Jack Brickenden, Foster Hewitt, Jim Kidd, Robbie Robertson, Joey Smallwood and Graham Spry. Michael Drainie provided us with a cassette of a television interview his father, John Drainie, had done in the 1960s.

Eileen McNeil, Jennifer Wolfe and Ann Wilson typed and re-typed the manuscript as it was slowly reduced to manageable proportions. Almerinda Travassos (in the spring of 1981) and Paul Gibson (in the spring of 1982) provided part-time research assistance. Barbara Balfour was an invaluable 'advance' person in the spring and summer of 1981 checking out the holdings of various archives (and other sources) and assisting in a preliminary selection of material. Bryan Gee was equally invaluable during the spring and summer of 1982 doing last minute research, gathering visual material for the designer, assembling shot lists and preparing the index. We're indebted to Garfield Reeves-Stevens whose simple and effective design has allowed us to include a vast amount of material in *Signing On* without making our pages too busy. Irene Carefoot assisted with design decisions and with paste-up in the crucial final stages of this project. The co-ordination of so much graphic material and its accompanying copy required many last minute additions and deletions. Roxshana Khambata and the staff of ART-U Graphics, as well as Eric Burt of T.H. Best were enormously helpful, and enormously patient. Finally, we would like to thank our editor, Dean Cooke, who except for fleeting—and God knows, understandable—moments of panic, was a cheerful and gracious guide throughout the complicated process of assembling this book.

MW
BM

The first outstanding use of wireless. Survivors of the *Titanic* credited Marconi's invention with saving their lives. The Toronto *Globe*, April 15, 1912. ▶

Marconi at Signal Hill, St. John's, Newfoundland on the occasion of the first overseas transmission. 1901. ▼

VOL. LXIX., NUMBER 19,416.

TITANIC COLLIDES WITH AN ICEBERG

CARRIES THIRTEEN HUNDRED PASSENGERS AND BIG CREW

The Giant White Star Liner, on Maiden Trip to New York, Sends Out Wireless Message for Assistance—Allan Liner Virginian Reports That She is on Her Way to the Titanic—The Message is Received in Montreal.

(Canadian Press Despatch.)

MONTREAL, April 14.—The Allan Line office here to-night received a wireless message from the captain of the company's steamship Virginian stating that he had been in wireless communication with the White Star Line steamship Titanic, which had been in collision with an iceberg and requested assistance. The Virginian's captain reported that he was on his way to the Titanic.

The Virginian sailed from Halifax this morning, and at the time the is reckoned to have been about abeam of gers on board, but can accommodate 900

As she is not far from Halifax the re- any great amount of discomfort.

ginian's captain was sent by wireless to cable to Halifax and then by wire to Hals here expect to hear further news at

nic, the largest vessel afloat, left South- voyage for New York. She is a vessel of es long, and displaces 66,000 tons.

Southampton had about 1,300 passengers the first cabin. Among these latter are resident of the Consolidated American bald Butt, military aide to President Taft, and Trunk Railway; J. Bruce Ismay, Chair- he White Star Line; Henry B. Harris, the W. T. Stead, Mrs. Isador Straus, Mr. and d Mrs. Geo. D. Widener, Benjamin Gug- rry Widener. The crew would probably

The Maritimes

Melvin Rowe

I started work as a cable operator in Hearts Content, Newfoundland in 1920. Newfoundland at that time was a centre of world communication. Marconi had done his early work there, establishing direct contact between Cornwall, in Great Britain, and Signal Hill on December 12, 1901. Marconi intended to set up a radio station in Newfoundland. Unfortunately, the Anglo-American Telegraph Company held the franchise. So it wasn't until 1904, after the franchise ran out, that the Canadian Marconi Company built a wireless station at Cape Race.

But what really gave radio a boost was the sinking of the *Titanic.* A fellow named Godson was at Cape Race at the time and he intercepted the SOS call. He got in touch with the *Carpathia,* and she was responsible for saving the majority of the passengers and crew. People then started to realize that radio was really something.

On July 25, 1920, the first attempt to span the Atlantic by voice was made from Signal Hill. The Canadian Marconi Company erected a temporary transmitting station. They contacted the S.S. *Victoria* and had a two-way conversation. That was the beginning of broadcasting as we know it. And the first person to speak over the radio was the prime minister of Newfoundland.

As a result of the sinking of the *Titanic* the British admiralty set up a wireless receiving and transmitting station at Mount Pearl, outside St. John's, during the First World War. Operators and naval personnel came over from England to man the station. Its purpose was to advise and warn the Allied naval powers of icebergs. The station was phased out around 1923.

In 1925, a United Church minister, Dr. Joyce, thought it would be a splendid idea to establish a radio station to carry church services to people living in remote communities. That's

Marconi Wireless Schools
AT
Toronto and Montreal

AMATEUR AND COMMERCIAL CLASSES

Write for particulars:
THE MARCONI WIRELESS TELEGRAPH CO.
OF CANADA, LIMITED
11 ST. SACRAMENT ST., MONTREAL

Mark Telegrams to Great Britain and Foreign Countries

"Via Marconi"

GREATER ACCURACY—BETTER SPEED
"MORE WORDS FOR LESS MONEY"

Ask at any telegraph office, and tell the clerk it MUST be sent
"VIA MARCONI"

All Equally Good !

This Book is All Important

It is supplied with every Marconi Outfit. Written in non-technical language, it clearly explains the whys and wherefores of modern radio. How to install your set; how to operate it; how to get the best possible results. Its possession assures each purchaser of Marconi Apparatus of the best that Radio offers.

You take no chances when you buy a Marconi Radio Outfit—our test room standards take care of that.

First, each little accessory is individually tested; next, each component part; then each unit; and finally each complete receiver is examined for structural and electrical defects and tested out on actual long range reception. And our test room standards are high—none higher.

This is just one of the reasons why thousands of our receivers are giving absolute satisfaction in all parts of the country; working regularly, day in and day out, and operated by people who are not radio experts but who want the best that radio offers without fuss and bother.

The nearest Marconi Dealer will be glad to put you on the high road to the joys of real radio. An enquiry will not obligate you in any manner.

New Complete Catalogue on Request

THE MARCONI WIRELESS TELEGRAPH COMPANY OF CANADA LIMITED
MONTREAL

MARCONI RADIO

Complete Installations

$55.00 $57.50 $60.00 $100.00 $105.00

how VOWR, the Voice of Wesley Radio, got started. It was a tremendously popular station. Then, around 1932, the Seventh Day Adventists got into it.

The first real broadcasting outlet in Newfoundland, VOGY, followed a few months later, in November 1932, by VONF. They only broadcast in St. John's and coverage was rather limited. Things continued like that until around 1939. Coming events cast their shadow and the government felt there was a need to get to the people. Remember there were no roads as we know them today. What the coastal areas depended on for information was the steamship and that was a very irregular operation. They took over VONF. Again the Canadian Marconi Company entered the picture. They built a transmitter at Mount Pearl and used the towers the British admiralty had put there in 1916. From the very start, though, VONF carried BBC news. We didn't start getting Canadian news until after the Canadian Armed Forces were stationed here. When we started broadcasting in 1939 we had a fellow by the name of Joe Smallwood with us. He called himself "The Barrelman" and told tales of Newfoundland.

Shortly, after we joined Confederation in 1949, a bunch of fellows walked into the studios. They turned out to be CBC officials down to arrange the takeover of the Newfoundland network, which by then extended to Corner Brook. We had VONF, VONH and Gander, which we'd taken over from the Canadian Armed Forces. We went to Corner Brook in 1941. Reception wasn't too reliable because it was all done by galvanized wire, especially through the interior where everything had to be strung up. That situation continued until microwave came in. When the CBC started in 1949 they shot the signal from Cape North in Cape Breton to Red Rocks. This is how we tied into the Canadian network.

A WIRELESS ALPHABET

A is the Anode glowing bright red,
B is the Battery, sure to be dead ;
C the Condenser that always leaks,
D the Detector that only squeaks.
E the Electron that hateth man,
F is the Filament "also ran."
G is the Grid that is touching the plate,
H the High Tension that won't actuate.
I the Inductance, much too long,
J is the Jigger, always wrong.
K is the Konstant whose value we sight for,
L is the Licence we didn't apply for.
M is the Mutual, wound the wrong way,
N is the Novice who worries all day.
O is the Office where cockroaches crawl,
P is the Patent that's no use at all ;
Q for the Questions, which rise thick and fast,
R the Resistance which beats us at last.
S is the Starter that never will act,
T the Transformer whose casing is cracked.
U the Unknown that ruins the test,
V is the Vacuum, doubtful at best.
W the Worries which chase us all night,
X's will never let signals come right.
Y the Young Helper who gets in the way,
Z is the end of this rhyme—hurray !

J. A. S.—in "*The Aerial.*"

Oscar Hierlihy

My mother had a piano in the living room and I had an old telephone microphone installed inside it. I'd get her to play and we'd transmit that over the air.

The first time I ever heard wireless was around 1915. My father had a business on the coast of Labrador and we travelled down and back in summertime by ship. The first year the ship had a radio, I would sit outside the wireless room and listen to the dots and dashes of the Morse code. It fascinated me so much that I had to see how it operated. That is where I first heard about wireless, which later became my teenage hobby.

In 1926 when I was sixteen, I was experimenting with short-wave receivers. I had a little receiver and it had a short circuit in it. I used to play records for my own amusement. I had a pickup that I made myself out of headphones and part of an old gramophone. Anyway, I was playing some records and a friend came over to see me and said, "It's a funny thing, but I'm hearing the records you're playing on *my* radio." I got him to play some records and I went down to his house, and sure enough, my station was on the air.

That prompted me to wire in a microphone and we used to broadcast to people around the neighbourhood. That was my first experience with broadcasting. I don't think it was illegal because there wasn't any department set up in St. John's to issue licences. My mother had a piano in the living room and I had an old telephone microphone installed inside it. I'd get her to play and we'd transmit that over the air. There weren't many radios. I can count them up on my fingers, there were so few. The furthest distance I ever got with that little transmitter was seven or eight miles from where I lived.

Shortly afterwards I left home for St. John's and went to work at Ayre and Sons, a music and radio shop. They had the franchise for RCA Victor sets, so I built a little radio station there so we could demonstrate the radios that were in the showroom.

The LYRADION
The Radio Set Supreme

Dependable - Powerful - Beautiful

Lyradion Sets Are Attracting the Best Trade Everywhere

Table Models, Period Furniture, Suitcase and other Portables. All equipped complete with 5-tube Lyradion Receiving Set, Amplifying Horn, 90-volt Dry Battery, Phone Jack and Aerial Equipment.

Responsible Dealers, Write for Attractive Proposition

VAN GELDER & COMPANY
CANADIAN DISTRIBUTORS
Ryrie Bldg.   Yonge & Shuter Sts.   Phone M. 2491   TORONTO

Eventually they got a commercial licence and became VOAS, the Voice of Ayre and Sons. But in 1930 Ayre and Sons dismantled VOAS and threw it out. I can't understand why they didn't see the potential they had there. They were doing their own advertising and they had a mail-order business that you wouldn't believe. All day long we had two stations on the air, but VOAS was on more consistently. The other station would only come on for a couple of hours in the middle of the day and sign off. Still another station was VONA, the Voice of the North Atlantic. It too was started by a minister, Pastor Williams of the Seventh Day Adventists. When Pastor Williams got a transfer in 1932 he asked me to take it over, operate it commercially and broadcast his services on the weekends. I did that for several years.

Around 1934 the man who'd built VONA originally, George Stevens, decided to build a high power station. While he was in the process of putting VONF together, he offered me a job if I closed down my station. He said I'd be foolish not to accept this because when he got on the air he was going to put me out of business anyway. I thought it over. I wasn't making enough money to support myself and run a car. The commercial side of the business was pretty slack. So I decided maybe it was a good idea to join up with him. I stayed with VONF until 1937 when the Avalon Telephone Company, which owned it, decided that they would sell the station to the government. Avalon was going into the radiotelephone business and wanted me to stay full-time with them as an engineer in charge of equipment. So I gradually phased out of radio as we got busier with the telephone. Up to the time they sold VONF to the government I was dabbling in both, but when the government took VONF over I ceased having anything to do with broadcasting until 1945 when Geoff Stirling came along and offered me the job of chief engineer at CJON.

New Marconi, 1929

BATTERYLESS RADIOS AND COMBINATIONS IN STOCK

Terms of Payment Arranged

———

BRUNSWICK RECORDS

———

HARDMAN GRAND PIANO
Used in CFCF Studio

SOLE AGENTS

WM. LEE COMPANY
LIMITED
1450 St. Catherine St. W.
MONTREAL, QUE.

Radio- Meeting every taste

¶ In a world of mirth and gaiety many people do not find time to attend those services where music of another order soothes mind and body. The deep and full tones of an organ echoing through the nave of some stately cathedral, the clear, high notes of a boy choir, are perhaps rare joys in their lives.

¶ RADIO has time for everything, and sacred music is one of the mediums of beautiful expression which it has not overlooked.

¶ To transmit the best in music the best RADIO set is required and your customers will be glad to know that they may listen to organ recitals, with

THE NORTHERN ELECTRIC RADIO TELEPHONE RECEIVING SET

(The set with the famous Peanut Tube, eliminating the charging Batteries)

FOR SIX DAYS A WEEK - AND SUNDAY

Manufactured in Canada by

Northern Electric Company
LIMITED

| Montreal | Quebec | Toronto | | Windsor | Regina | Edmonton |
| Halifax | Ottawa | Hamilton | London | Winnipeg | Calgary | Vanconver |

Dealers apply to Nearest Branch Houses for Prices and Discounts.

Studio Slang—A Colorful New Language

The early pioneer days in radio broadcasting created many new expressions, some vagrant, some unpopular. Many of them were short lived. But there are many slang words and phrases now recognized, widely used and readily understood by production men, announcers, and studio engineers.

Here is an interesting list of some of the words, each with its singular meaning:

"Adenoid tenor:" one with a "tight" voice.

"Announcer's delight:" sarcastically applied to the announcer's control box in the studio, a complex instrument with rows of lights.

"Birdie:" the tweet-tweet sound occasionally encountered on long-distance transmission lines.

"Blasty:" the blasting sound, too much volume.

"Bug juice:" a term describing carbon tetrachloride.

"Bugs:" trouble in equipment caused by something not immediately obvious.

"Cans:" headphones.

"Corn fed:" when the performance of either a singer or instrumentalist lacks culture.

"Cross-fire:" Morse telegraph codes picked up by program lines.

"Cross-talk:" conversation picked up from a foreign source.

"Cross-tone:" foreign tones picked up.

"Down in the mud:" a very low reproduction volume.

"Electrical transcription:" broadcasting a program recorded on a record.

"Fade in" or "fade out:" gradual reduction or increase in volume, respectively.

"Fighting the music:" lacking ease in singing.

"Fill in:" those who stand by to go on the air in case a program change must be made.

"Final shot:" the last test of a program originating outside the main studio.

"Fuzzy:" a voice lacking in clarity.

"Gelatine tenor:" one with vibrato or tremolo in his voice.

"Haywire:" relates to equipment in poor condition.

"Hold it down:" an order directed to studio engineer to reduce the volume.

"Hot switch:" a rapid program transfer from one point of origin to another.

From *RCA Radio Parade,* 1931.

Studio Slang—A Colorful New Language

(Continued)

"Killie loo bird:" a flighty coloratura soprano who sings with a florid style.

"Line hits:" when overhead transmission wires contact accidentally, usually during storms.

"Lock jaw:" the voice of one who sings as if tired.

"Nemo:" programs originating outside of studio.

"Nervous baritone:" one who over-emphasizes the dramatic effect.

"Old sexton:" a bass with a sepulchral voice.

"On the beach:" out of a job, unemployed.

"On the log:" an entry in the studio record, complimentary or otherwise.

"On the nose:" a radio program executed according to schedule.

"On the pipe:" answer the telephone.

"Peaks" or "kicks:" the maximum point of the needle swing on a volume indicator.

"Riding gain:" keeping program volume within practicable limits.

"Scratches:" a noise caused by faulty equipment.

"Scooper:" A singer, usually a contralto, who slides up and down the scale without distinguishing clearly between notes.

"Short voice:" one with a limited range.

"Standby:" a warning to get ready to take the air.

"Standbys:" alternatives for programs on the air.

"Sour" or "blue:" voice or instrument off pitch.

"Talking in his beard:" a muffled voice.

"The King:" the engineer on duty at the master control desk who supervises all operations.

"Thick:" when the individual instruments in a group selection are not distinguishable.

"Throne:" master control desk.

"Town crier:" one who sings too loud.

"Up three miles:" indicates very high amount of units or volume of reproduction.

"Wooden voice:" lacks clarity and expression.

"Woof:" a word used frequently in making tests, but having no meaning.

The Ring of Truth in a Babel of Claims

Exaggerated or unusual claims are never permitted in Sterling advertising. The famous Sterling "Baby" Loud Speaker definitely offers the following advantages: 1. Ample volume for ordinary sized rooms and a reproduction that is consistently faithful and pleasing in tone. 2. Perfect finish and graceful design. 3. Splendid value for money — capable of proof by comparative test at radio dealers before purchase. There, in simple language, are the reasons why the Sterling "Baby" is accepted as a really perfect loud speaker the world over.

The Sterling "Baby" Loud Speaker is supplied in black or brown tinted finish (2,000 ohms resistance) complete with flexible cord.

TO THE TRADE.
Write for particulars of this popular loud speaker and of the whole range of Sterling radio apparatus including Lightweight Headphones and "Dinkie" "Audivox" and "Primax" Loud Speakers.

Advt. of
STERLING TELEPHONE & ELECTRIC Co. Ld.
Manufacturers of Telephones & Radio Apparatus, etc.
210-212, Tottenham Court Road, London, W.1. Eng.

Sterling Agents for the Dominion of Canada:
MARCONI WIRELESS TELEGRAPH CO. OF CANADA LTD. *Head Office:* 11, St. Sacrament Street, Montreal. *Branches:* Toronto, Winnipeg, Vancouver, Halifax & St. John's.

Menjie Shulman

VOCM was an independent station in St. John's and people said the call letters stood for, Voice of the Common Man. VOCM came on at eleven in the mornings and went off at two, came on again at six and went off at ten at night. The big feature on VOCM was a sponsored programme called "Harvey's Terranova News." Harvey's, the sponsor, was headed by Sir Leonard Outerbridge and his brothers. They were typically British.

The news came on at one-thirty in the afternoon for fifteen minutes, was repeated at six-forty-five and nine-forty-five. It was always done by J. L. Butler, the owner of the station. He had a BBC voice with a Newfoundland intonation. One time when he was away on a trip he asked me if I would do the news in his absence. This was an honour. But I came on with "Good afternoon. Here is 'Harvey's Terranewva Nose Bulletin.'" I realized right off what I'd said and I tried to correct myself. I had to repeat it three times before I finally got it right. Well, I got calls from Sir Leonard and the Outerbridges because of this travesty. Despite that, I got a year's contract for the station's first morning show. The station would come on at eight o'clock and I would come on with the news at eight-fifteen. Nothing can ever equal the acceptance of the early morning broadcasts by the public. Not even man's visit to the moon. It was overwhelming! This would be around 1946.

Before Newfoundland came into Confederation stations took part in the debate on whether the Island should become part of Canada or form an economic union with the United States. Joey Smallwood, for example, would come stomping into the studio and say that he was going to make a speech. The station facilities were always open and available. There are no words to describe that era in Newfoundland and the process we went through. Part of the reason the doors of VOCM were wide open was because we were four steps behind the rest of the world. We even did sidewalk interviews by dropping the microphone out the window.

At that time there were no stations in other parts of Newfoundland. Only in St. John's. And we were exploiting radio to its

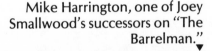

We even did sidewalk interviews by dropping the microphone out the window.

Mike Harrington, one of Joey Smallwood's successors on "The Barrelman." ▼

fullest. We were trying everything and anything. Newspapers were big before radio. But when radio came in the fishermen in the outports tuned in to VONF, the government station. It had "Doyle's News Bulletin" and "O'Leary's Barrelman" with Joey Smallwood. On it you heard a ship's bell and then the "Barrelman" would come on with stories about the people of Newfoundland. It was quite a feature—as Newfoundland as codfish.

Slowly radio became part of every Newfoundlander's life. In the outports he listened to the radio for the news. He didn't get his newspaper until three days later. On the radio he got the weather, which he depended on. He also got personal messages through "Doyle's News Bulletin." For example, you'd hear, "To John Smith. Mary is leaving the hospital. Will meet you at the Brigus Railroad Station on Tuesday when the train comes in." You see, radio not only took the place of the newspapers, it was the telephone too. It became as essential as breathing. There were little outports with no electricity but they had battery operated radios and that was their means of communication with the outside world.

When Joey Smallwood says that God created radio just for Newfoundland, he's not just being inane, because radio does come out of the sky and the Garden of Eden was the name of Marconi's little place on Signal Hill, from which we sent the first signal. I don't think it's possible for a person who had only lived in a big city to realize what this thing called radio must have meant to a country like Newfoundland. It was not only vital to our well-being, it became the cultural centre of the home. Home and church were the important things to the people. You had books, radio, and your neighbours.

I remember when we first got Reuters and United Press. This was about the time of Confederation. To go in there and tear off the news! It was one of the wonders of the century to get the news from other parts of the world so quickly. Of course, Newfoundland didn't have "Amos 'n' Andy," and a lot of other popular shows in the early days, so in the late 1960s I got a bunch of old recordings and played them. They were blockbusters.

F. Walter Hyndman

I became interested in amateur radio before the First World War ended. There'd be something in the odd magazine we got our hands on, but what I really learned I got off the ships. I would go down and make friends with the wireless operators and little by little I picked up things. By 1920, I had an amateur licence and was all set up with a station. Actually, I'd been operating illegally a little before that like a lot of the fellows.

I think it was during 1920 that I heard the first radio telephone message in P.E.I. It was reported in the newspapers. I was walking down the street one day and I heard a woman say as I passed, "That's the fellow that thinks he hears the angels singing." People thought I was crazy, but it was a broadcast from a ship going upriver on her way from England, and the Marconi people were testing. The next time I heard it, it was Western Electric on a ship in the Hudson River near New York. Then we began to hear it more. I think it was 1921 that we heard the first radio broadcasting voice. SBZ was our favourite station here. We got it better than any of the others. We didn't hear KDKA as well, although that came in too.

Three of us boys were building sets and selling them. First it was crystal sets, and then it was tube sets, because you couldn't really hear anybody with just a crystal set. We built these sets, and sold them, and earned a little money. Then I built a small transmitter using a couple of tubes that an operator from an American warship gave me. You couldn't buy these things, you know. I later sold that to a fellow named Walter Burke. He was intrigued because he'd been listening on one of these home-built sets. He asked me about a year later if I could build a more powerful station. He was a devout Methodist. The one ambition in his life was to broadcast the services from Trinity Church which was then Methodist. He said, "If I find the money, will you do it?" I said I would, and I built the station for him. I got all the parts from the United States, and I never charged a cent. It was a labour of love. The cost was several hundred dollars. It was a twenty- or thirty-watt station whose coverage would surprise you because there was no interference.

Keith Rogers had the franchise for Deforest Crosley Radio Receivers. He was selling these at a great rate. So he went to Burke one day and said, "If you will allow me to advertise over your station, I will maintain it for you. I'll replace the tubes and so on." These were very expensive in those days. It was a good

I was walking down the street and I heard a woman say as I passed, "That's the fellow that thinks he hears the angels singing."

Brandes

His first taste of music!

The truly modern young person gets his first taste of music by Radio—and a Brandes. Catchy melodies and charming bed-time stories come to him clearly through a Brandes *Matched Tone* Headset.

Mother lets him wear only a Brandes because it's so much lighter in weight and won't catch in his curls. And she knows that his little ears will be trained to true harmony by the *Matched Tone* qualities of Brandes.

Distributed by Perkins Electric, Limited, Toronto, Montreal and Winnipeg.

CANADIAN BRANDES LIMITED, Toronto and London.

New Price-*Superior* - $7.00

Matched Tone
Radio Headsets

scheme, and that was the first radio advertising on the Island. This would be the latter part of 1923 or early 1924. By then I had the job of part-time radio inspector—collecting licence fees and monitoring stations to see if they were on frequency.

Programming was very simple in the beginning. Mostly it was records and bits of news. But I didn't have a very great interest in programming at that time. My interest was always more in the building than it was the operating. The early microphones, for example, were just telephones. It was the only thing we had. We put a bit of a horn on the front of a telephone because there was nothing else. You had to make almost all of your own parts. I still have the first tube that came here—an Audiotron. I got that in late 1920 or early 1921. They cost a fortune in those days—around nine dollars—for one tube. For a young fellow that was a lot of money, and tubes burned out very quickly.

A Listener

In the early 1920s I was in training in a religious school for nursing. We all had to attend chapel every morning before going on duty. Then along came radio and here is where I sinned. A patient had given me a crystal set. It was so marvellous to have that set on my pillow and listen to a good sermon on station KDKA on Sunday mornings that I would just stay in bed. It simply boggled the mind to realize you could hear so distinctly from so many miles away. Lights had to be out by ten every night and again I felt like a sinner, listening to the delicious tunes of the famous bands.

Nightingale RADIO
A·BIRD·OF·A·LINE

The Sets with the Golden Contacts

In every Nightingale receiving set the best quality of material is used—and expert workmanship. An outstanding reason for perfect reception is the use of Golden contacts—one demonstration will prove this.

A 2-Tube Set $34   A 4-Tube Set $45

Prices exclusive of Tubes and Batteries.

WRITE FOR ILLUSTRATED FOLDER AND PRICE LIST

CYCLE SUPPLY CO. LIMITED
218a King St. E.   Toronto, Ont.

Then along came radio and here is where I sinned.

WANTED

Junior Radio Electrical Engineer for the Department of Marine and Fisheries, Ottawa. Initial salary $1,680 per annum plus bonus, maximum $2,040 per annum. Candidates must be graduates in electrical engineering from a recognized university with two years' experience in radio or electrical engineering work, or have four years' experience in radio or electrical engineering work. They must be British subjects with at least three years' residence in Canada. Apply to the Civil Service Commission, Ottawa, not later than November 22nd, 1924.

RADIO BRANCH
Department of Marine and Fisheries
WARNING

OWNERS of unlicensed radio receiving sets are hereby warned that on and after 1st July, 1924, the Department of Marine and Fisheries will take steps to seize any such unlicensed apparatus and to prosecute the owner thereof.

The penalty on summary conviction is a fine not exceeding $50.00 and forfeiture of all unlicensed radio apparatus to the Government.

Broadcast listeners are accordingly advised to obtain their licenses immediately.

The license fee is $1.00 per annum. Licenses, valid to 31st March, 1925, may be obtained from: Radio Branch, Dept. Marine & Fisheries, Ottawa, Departmental Radio Inspectors, Post Offices and authorized Radio Dealers.

A. J. JOHNSON,
Deputy-Minister

Department of Marine and Fisheries

The Most Marvellous Musical Instrument Since the Beginning of Time!

The GOLD MEDAL Radio Phonograph

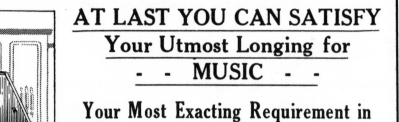

AT LAST YOU CAN SATISFY

Your Utmost Longing for

- - MUSIC - -

Your Most Exacting Requirement in

Radio

—Both for the Price of One High Grade Set.

4-tube Federal Radio Frequency Radio Receiving Set.

Standard Gold Medal Phonograph Equipment—Loud Speaker an integral part of Ivorite Horn. Designs and Trade Mark Registered 1923—Patents Pending, Canada and U.S.A.

Cabinet in Mahogany and Walnut.

Scientifically Built as a Complete Unit.

$350.⁰⁰ Delivered, including one set Earphones and Plug. Tubes, Batteries, Antenna, etc., ready to instal, $65.00 extra.

Your Music or Radio Dealer Can Procure a Set For You or Write Direct to the Manufacturers.

Gold Medal Radio-Phonograph Corporation
Limited
UXBRIDGE - ONTARIO

FULL INFORMATION UPON REQUEST

DEALERS: We are jobbers for Federal Standard Radio Products, Amplion Loud Speakers, Eveready Radio Batteries, etc. Have you Cuts and Prices of Our Radio Tables and Radio Furniture?

~ Announcing ~

The Famous QUADRODYNE 4-Tube Receiver

(Patents Pending, 1924)

$110.00

Equal in Value to a $200 Set

Simple—all stations can be logged.

Dependable—in all seasons and anywhere.

Powerful—Will operate loud speaker with clarity of tone and volume.

The Quadrodyne set, complete, with the following extras ready to erect aerial and operate, F.O.B. any dealer's store East of Winnipeg, $170.00. Winnipeg and West, $175.00.

EXTRAS:

4 UV Radiotron tubes.

67½ volts tapped Eveready B Batteries.

WD80 Eveready 6-volt storage A battery.

100 feet 14-gauge antenna wire.

50 feet lead-in 14-gauge wire.

75 feet indoor 18-gauge antenna.

Leads and clips.

2 insulators.

1 set 2,200-ohm. Federal phones.

1 plug.

Instructions go with every set.

Note:

Cost of extras shown above cover the best and most expensive equipment — suitable additions for this splendid set.

Champion Radio Table

Finishes: Mahogany, Walnut, or Oak.
Room for all Batteries in Compartment.

Amplion Loud Speaker, $45.00
(ILLUSTRATED)

The best dealers can obtain this set and table for you, or write direct to us.

Dealers: Write for proposition.

Distributors required in Maritime Provinces and Western Canada.

Gold Medal Radio-Phonograph Corporation
Limited
UXBRIDGE - ONTARIO

Distributors of Federal Standard Radio Products

Marianne Morrow

My mother said, "Good heavens, what's happened to the children?" Dad said, "Good heavens, what's happened to my transmitter?"

CFCY went on the air in 1924. Dad had been broadcasting before that on amateur station VE10AS. It was in the room next to my bedroom when I was a little girl and I went to sleep to the snap and crackle of the telegraphy key.

Some of my first memories are of the development of CFCY. My father had to sell radios to make radio broadcasting a business. It was the chicken and the egg. For example, to demonstrate the radios he was selling, my mother had a booth at the Prince Edward Island exhibition grounds. Dad would be at home playing the records that were being broadcast on our gramophone. Once when he was anxious to find out what was going on at the booth, he left my older sister and I in charge of this rather precarious operation. All we were supposed to do was change the records which were picked up by the microphone from the Victrola speaker. There were wires all over the place. Betty and I changed the records religiously. Then we put on a record you could dance to. Being youngsters we started to dance and we toppled the whole affair over with a crash. Over at the other end of the line at the exhibition grounds, my mother said, "Good heavens, what's happened to the children?" Dad said, "Good heavens, what's happened to my transmitter?" I don't ever remember any terrible consequences and eventually it all got put together again.

We called our home "The Bayfield Street Studios" and many broadcasts were made from there. Country music and old-time fiddling was what people wanted. And the old-time fiddlers used to come and set themselves up in The Bayfield Street Studios in our living room. Mother would play the piano and the fiddlers would saw away. Many, many people took part musically. There was no money to pay people and the thought of being paid didn't really occur to anyone. It was the honour of being on a broadcast that motivated them. And friendship. Charlottetown was a pretty small town.

My sister did the first "Sleepy Town Express" children's story show, a programme that was introduced by a recording called Sleepy Town Express. She went away to school when I was thirteen and I took over reading the bedtime story. By this time Dad had a small studio and transmitter in downtown Charlottetown. I can remember running to do this broadcast and as I was running I could hear radios playing my theme song on them, and I wasn't even there. I would run in and breathlessly start to tell my children's story. I read the stories out of books, but I read them in what I felt was a dramatic way.

At that same time we did plays for Dr. Lambert's Cough Syrup. The Dr. Lambert's Cough Syrup people sent us the plays and we didn't have to pay any royalties on them. Now as a thirteen- to fifteen-year-old girl, here I was playing leads in these plays opposite the most famous hockey player in Charlottetown. His name was Harry Richardson. He was in his twenties and I thought these were the most thrilling moments a young girl could have, playing in these dramas.

When Dad started out there were no regulations. Then regulations began to come in. They'd come around and inspect the station and say that he was infringing on someone else's fre-

quency. Eventually he had to build a new transmitter a couple of miles outside Charlottetown. When Dad started that building he had no money and the bank considered it a foolish idea. So he used the trade and barter system. He would say to a manufacturer of shingles, I will give you X number of minutes on CFCY for X number of shingles. He got many of his building materials that way. It served a double purpose because he was also trying to break down the resistance of firms to radio advertising. He also got bread for the house, and milk, other things. Advertisers weren't convinced of the value of radio and of course the newspapers fought radio all the way. It was amusing that the local newspaper never printed the word 'radio,' and they certainly never printed radio schedules. Radio was never mentioned in the *Guardian.*

I went away to school at Mount Allison and when I came back I did a children's programme and a women's programme. My Santa Claus was so good that in all my years since, I have never heard anyone to match him. He was a local man who adored being Santa Claus. He was on once a week at the start of the Christmas season but as it got closer and closer, he was on three or four times a week. One of the things that especially thrilled me about Santa Claus were the letters that came in. I had a letter from a woman on the west coast of Newfoundland, where CFCY was probably the only radio station they got, and this woman said, "My little boy listens to your programmes every night." He walked half a mile down the road to a neighbour's radio to listen. Now, she said, "He wants a pony for Christmas and he believes he's going to get one. There's no way that we can get him a pony for Christmas." This bothered me and I wrote a line for Santa to speak to this child. Santa told him there was no way he could carry a live pony around in his sack in the clouds and cold. He explained to the little boy how he couldn't have a pony. I got this wonderful letter back from the mother saying how

A RADIOGRAM *from* SANTA CLAUS

Dear Daddy:

Do you remember how, when you were a boy, you used to be awake nights just before Christmas and wonder what Santa was going to bring you?

Your boy will be doing the same thing a few weeks from now, and perhaps a little suggestion from me will help a whole lot.

Radio has a great fascination for every red-blooded Canadian boy, and there is nothing you could get that would give him more lasting pleasure than a good Radio Set.

Maybe he is already a radio fan; if he is, then there are dozens of things he needs in order to enlarge and improve his set.

Let him experiment; it will teach him many things that are not taught at the schools—patience, accuracy, logical reasoning. And the beneficial result of successful experiments will never be lost on the young mind that you are so anxious to develope along right lines.

With a good set in the home, your boy will be able to listen to University Extension courses, operas, beautiful readings from good authors; your whole family will benefit; your home will never be lonely during the long winter evenings, for you have but to tune in, and the whole world will come to you on the wings of the night.

My sleigh will be loaded with sets, loud speakers, tubes, transformers, headphones, batteries, and everything. Find out what your boy wants, and with your help I'll do my best.

Yours very truly,

SANTA CLAUS.

Don Messer and the Islanders in the mid-1930s shortly after they changed their name from "Don Messer and his New Brunswick Lumberjacks." In the centre, with guitar, is Charlie Chamberlain. Messer is second from the right.

excited the child was. It made me feel all my time and effort was worthwhile.

Don Messer and the Islanders got their start as national people at CFCY although they'd been at a station in Saint John before that. They were "The Lumberjacks." But CFCY was called the "Friendly Voice of the Maritimes." So they identified themselves as the Friendly Voice of the Maritimes. Eventually they became identified as Don Messer and his Islanders. Messer became fantastically popular. Charlie Chamberlain was a great big lumberjack from the north woods. I can remember going and watching him while he sang sad ballads or religious songs, which were really out of character for him. He would wink at me in his sadness and have a great big grin on his face. Charlie had a lovely voice. When my father died of a heart attack in the middle of winter, the Islanders were still at CFCY. I woke up the morning of the funeral and there had been a big blizzard during the night. But every drop of snow had been removed from our driveway and steps and verandah. And all up and down the street. Charlie Chamberlain had come and shovelled it all.

Dad was called a practical idealist. He felt very strongly that radio was going to change people's lives for the better. It would bring the world closer together. And in those days anybody who had a message Dad felt would help the people of Prince Edward Island got free time to discuss their ideas. We didn't feel the threat of American radio to the extent people in Ontario did. Prince Edward Island was unique in that it was naturally isolated from the rest of the world. CFCY was with the CBC from the time it was established. The CBC was not a great organization with its own facilities everywhere. Rather it was made up of a few key stations plus affiliates. As an affiliate, Dad lost some of his autonomy. I can remember Frank Willis coming to tell him he was going to be affiliated with the Dominion network. That upset Dad at the time, but it worked out to everyone's advantage.

Hugh Trueman

I have a pretty good memory of the first time I was on the air. I was twelve years old and it was 1931. What happened was that they had started a kids' radio show in Saint John with kid talent. I used to organize backyard shows. We'd sell tickets on the street for a couple of cents each. I was sort of impresario. When the people at the show asked me what *I* did, whether I sang or tap-danced, I had to admit that I didn't do anything. So they said, "You can be the announcer and introduce the talent." That's how it started. I've been in the broadcasting business ever since. Of course, at twelve, I was still going to school, but I had this kids' programme for what must be some kind of record. I had it for thirty-six years. I was Uncle Bill. It was CFBO when I started out. Then it became CHSJ. When I became manager of CFBC, I transferred the "Uncle Bill Show" over there.

I've tried several times to explain to younger people what radio was like in the early days, and it's difficult. It's amazing when I stop to think of all that's happened in my lifetime. Radio wasn't taken seriously. People used to ask my brother—in spite of the fact that I had finished school and was on the air full-time—when I was going to get a job. They'd say, "You know, I hear your brother on the air all the time. When is he going to get a job?"

Radio stations in a good many places had been set up by newspapers as a means of killing off any possible competition and the stations were sort of kept as stand-bys. No money was pumped into them. And they weren't looked on as a source of profit. At CHSJ we had a hundred watt transmitter in the corner of the control room, and every so often the phone would ring and someone would say, "I can't hear anything, and I don't think it's my radio, I think it's your transmitter." The chief engineer would walk over to the transmitter and kick it. Then he'd go back to the phone and say, "Can you hear us now?" The person on the other end would say, yes, they could hear it. It was never taken apart to find out where the loose connection was. It was much easier to kick it.

One Saturday we were practising, getting ready to go on the air with my children's programme. Some men were putting in a new ceiling. I think they'd just discovered soundproof ceilings or something. Anyway, they were hammering away. I found this rather annoying and finally, I told these fellows that they'd have to be quiet for the next half-hour because we'd be going on the air. They said, "We've got to finish this job. We weren't supposed to work this Saturday and we're just doing it as a favour. We'll have to keep going." So what I did was go on the air. It didn't seem an extraordinary thing to do in those days. I went on and explained what the noise was. I said, "Periodically, you'll hear bang, bang, bang through the show." I'm sure there weren't any phone calls with complaints. That was acceptable, as long as it was explained.

We had steel needles. Nobody ever cued a record. I saw a fellow cue one in 1934, and I was impressed. He put his thumb under the record and he'd count the number of turns around, and then he'd back it up. You could see the shellac shoot right off the end of the needle. Later on we got to counting the number of turns, feeling the vibration with our thumbs, then running it in again

The chief engineer would walk over to the transmitter and kick it. Then he'd go back to the phone and say, "Can you hear us now?"

UNCLE BILL, the oldest feature in Canadian Radio, originated on CKNC in 1929 and is still going strong over CFRB. From children of all ages, Uncle Bill has received over a quarter of a million letters.

and stopping one turn back. Announcers in the old days had the turntables on all the time. They'd say, "Now here's a selection by Paul Whiteman" and at the same time they'd be lifting the needle over to drop it on the record. Then they'd bring the volume up. If the music happened to be playing, that was fine. If the groove was dead, that too was fine. Nobody cared about this.

One dear soul who worked for us had a women's programme. She was the typical sort of blue-haired lady. Very proper. She called all the fellows at the station "my boy." She used to give recipes. She'd give one ingredient and then would pause to give the audience a chance to write it down. One day we opened her studio window (studio windows could be opened in those days), got a handful of snow and the next time she paused we lifted the back of her dress and dropped the snow down her back. She bravely tried not to make a sound.

I used to do the eight o'clock newscast, and I formed the very bad habit of turning off my microphone and clearing my throat and coughing after every item. Of course, although my microphone was off the speaker was on and the guy in the control room, who was a real scamp, would open *his* mike and burp! It sounded to the listening audience as if at the end of every item I belched. One dear old soul asked me to phone her after the newscast and she went on with friendly advice about trying a little Bromo Seltzer before I went on the air to stop my belching.

Another time, I had a laughing jag during the weather forecast. Remember, in the Maritimes, the weather can be rather important with fishermen and so on. Anyway, I had a real laughing jag, and I just couldn't stop laughing at some tomfoolery going on in the station. Finally, I told the audience that they'd have to wait. I'd play a record until I could get hold of myself. There were no complaining phone calls. Nobody seemed to mind it. They would simply say, "You know, you seem to have a good time up there."

DEMAND Complete Coverage

In 7 months from April 1st. 1948, more radio licenses were sold in Fredericton than during the previous 12 months. No other Maritime city can make that claim!. Is there more buying power in Fredericton, or do the listeners get greater enjoyment from CFNB programs?

Either way, more radios mean more Complete Coverage!

CFNB
FREDERICTON, N.B

THE DOORWAY TO NEW BRUNSWICK

People didn't listen to radio very much in the morning in those days. It was unthinkable. But I hit on the idea that people might want to be advised of the time as they were getting dressed. We would be a kind of musical clock. There was no such thing as traffic reports, but I knew they'd be interested in the weather. Not just marine weather, but weather in human terms. Whether or not the kids should wear their overshoes. That sort of thing. I went to the management of CHSJ. I was about sixteen-years-old at the time. What they said was that if I sold 'spots' at that impossible hour I could have forty percent of what I sold. For about three years, I secretly made a huge amount of money, and about once a month I was made to promise that I'd never tell anyone how much money I was making. That was because the manager of the station was making about eighteen dollars a week, while I was making about thirty-two, which was a fortune in those days. It's startling to think that all of this happened in one man's lifetime. A whole industry growing up.

Nathan Nathanson

The first time I ever heard of radio, it seemed like a fable that people would be able to hear entertainment and talking from distant points. We had heard of telephones, but this radio coming through the air without a wire connection was something we couldn't imagine. My feeling was that it just couldn't be done, and that the whole thing was something somebody had dreamt up. You know, people weren't even thinking of getting off the ground in those days.

We were in the music business. We were selling gramophones and sheet music and eventually these 'radio boxes' came on the market, and we were asked to sell them. We didn't want to. We were afraid of it. But eventually we were forced to admit that radio was a reality. We needed a local radio signal that could be heard, because outside reception was a very indifferent thing. One day it came and the next day it didn't. A local station would fix that. So I ventured into a fifty-watt transmitter. It took quite a while to get the Department of Transport to give us that privilege, but eventually it came, and that was the start. We now had something for people to hear on the radios we wanted to sell them. The only reason I started a radio station was to give people something to hear with the boxes they were buying. What happened when that signal became steady, poor as it was, was unimaginable. People were mystified and excited about this new thing they had in their homes. When the station started on Valentine's Day, 1929, the ability to hear a signal during daylight hours was something that even those who owned a radio set didn't believe possible. Until we started, reception only came in during the dark hours. Now people could hear it in the daytime too. Sales of radios soared unbelievably. People who still didn't have one would block the streets in front of homes where there was a radio, listening to the sounds. And the sidewalk was so congested with people wanting to buy radios that a policeman would make them line up so others could get by.

At that time I didn't really see the potential of broadcasting. I

The first electric sets were $300, $350. We also sold a good many at $500 and, in one or two instances, for $600 and $700.... They cost as much as an automobile.

Nate Nathanson, founder of CJCB in Sydney, Nova Scotia. He started his station so people could hear something on the radios he was selling.

saw it just as a way to sell radios—nothing else. We had faith that it would keep itself going, but we didn't think it could develop beyond that. I was wrong. At first, the station didn't earn any money. There was no commercial advertising at that time. That came later. Our first sale came from a milliner who agreed to pay five dollars for a week's announcements. Six announcements, one a day, for a five-dollar bill. The next Monday morning the lady came in to tell us that she would take five dollar's more. That was the start of advertising for us.

National advertising was more of a battle. Those who were in big business had made their success in other ways. They couldn't understand what a message over the air could produce. The earliest businessmen that used radio were producers of medical preparations. They took a chance, and the results they got were real eye-openers. That was the origin of national advertising on radio.

By 1932 or '33, I realized radio was going to be a giant, that it was going to be more than just a toy. In those days everybody talked radio, radio, radio. When you met someone on the street, they would ask if you had heard "Amos 'n' Andy" last night, or "The Jack Benny Show." Jack Benny's latest joke was the joke of the day. Everyone waited for Sunday night to hear him. You must remember that in those days electric sets hadn't come into being. There were only battery radios. People paid for radios when they couldn't pay for something they needed more. But radio became the prize thing in the home. A battery set was expensive. It was just a little box, seven or eight inches by twelve, and all the cables and coils and batteries were either on the table or under it. And there were headphones. This was before the days of the loud-speaker. If two people, or three, wanted to listen together they all had to wear headphones. This set cost $200 for just a small one. A bigger one ran $300 and even $400. The first electric sets were $300, $350. We also sold a good many at $500 and, in one or two instances, for $600 and $700. They were *very* expensive. They cost as much as an automobile.

My first transmitter at the station, the fifty-watter, was twenty-five inches wide by about thirty-five inches high, and about thirty deep. It was set on a table, and it had a B battery under the table. I think it was 360 volts total. It was all enclosed in a cage on one side of the waiting room. Then we had the studio in another room adjacent to this one, which was hung with curtains to stop rebound of sound. The ceiling was also covered with draperies, and we had the old carbon microphones. Big ungainly things that hissed and crackled. Of course, that was part of radio then. If it was a record, you had the scratching of the record. Also we had the old generator motor out in the hall and the sound of *that* could always be heard on any programme. That wasn't only the case here in Sydney. That was broadcasting everywhere in those days. Hissing and whining and static sounds were part of the whole thing. One difficulty was in getting ice off antennas when it stormed. It always seemed to happen on the night of a hockey game. That really was trouble. Getting up there in stormy weather to clear the ice off was treacherous.

Then there was the Sunday morning the operator overslept; he came rushing into the studio late, got the transmitter going, and suddenly remembered that he hadn't had breakfast. Well, there was a restaurant across the street, so he put a hymn on the turntable, rushed down the hall and across the street, got a sandwich, and dashed back to the studio and put on his head-phones. Remember, there were no loudspeakers. And he heard "Jesus Christ, Jesus Christ, Jesus Christ," over and over again. The needle was stuck in a groove. We had a lot of complaints about that. These sorts of accidents happened all the time.

At first, our station used to sign on at noon until one or one-thirty. Even that took a lot of effort for a small staff. Then we'd sign on again at five-thirty and stay on until seven or seven-thirty, and we'd hope that after those hours there would be good reception from the outside stations. Sometimes there was. Often there was not. That was the extent of our efforts in the early days. There was no network at the time. Each station was on its own. The networks came two or three years later. Sundays we just had church services in the morning and filled up most of the other time with record music. We also had news, of course. I don't recall if there was anything more special than that. Local talent, such as singers or fiddlers, always found us receptive. We'd put them on the air. People in those days used to keep logs of what they heard on radio. As the months and years went by, their logs would become quite lengthy, and they'd compare them with other listeners' to see who had the longer log.

The number of service calls that had to be made to help people tune their sets was a big job in those early days. That kept you on the road night and day. I often took the family with me, because I'd be away so much that I'd never see them otherwise. It was an unending task. The price of a tube for a radio then was ten or fifteen dollars. If you blew five or six tubes, that was a real bill, and the howls of the customers were terrific. You couldn't blame them. And tubes blew all the time. However, for the most part, people took it in stride because they were getting so much out of it. They found the money somehow.

About thirteen miles from here, out in Glace Bay, the great Marconi sent the first wireless message across the Atlantic. I never met him personally, but we had the benefit of his engineers in keeping us on the air in those early days. They actually helped us change our fifty-watter to a hundred watts, and they saved us many a call to Montreal for service. My station used a Marconi transmitter, so there was no difficulty in getting co-operation.

RADIO SERMON

FIRST TIME EVER PLAYED ON THE SABBATH WITH A CLEAR CONSCIENCE.

BETWEEN SHOTS

CAN WE EXPECT THIS?
—Zero in the New York Evening Post

49

Robbie Robertson

I was working with Nate Nathanson in 1926 at his bookstore which also sold gramophones and records. By 1927 we were selling the odd radio receiver too. Now, when you sold a radio you were expected to service them too—something you preferred to do in the daytime. The problem was that when you were working on a radio and tried to tune in a station, you couldn't find a signal coming into Cape Breton in the daytime. Half the time all you'd get was noise. The American stations boomed in at night, so we had to do most of our servicing after dark.

Mr. Nathanson got the bright idea of starting a small station in Sydney so that we could at least have something to tune in while we were fixing sets. That was why CJCB was started. At first we were only on for two hours, from noon till two and from about five to eight in the evenings. CJCB was just an adjunct to Mr. Nathanson's music and book store—something to help the business along. We had to carry radios because people were beginning to ask for them. I was a clerk, moving back and forth between the books, the music and the radios.

Up to this point I'd been making twelve dollars a week, but when the radio station started, my pay went up to sixteen dollars because I now had the combined job of clerk, announcer, technician and everything else. As we began to sell more radios, Mr. Nathanson could see something of what the future was going to be. People were going wild for all these programmes that were coming in from American and Canadian stations. It became increasingly clear that if you were going to sell radios, a local station was needed to keep the people happy. It was especially important when we took a set out for demonstration. When we first went into radio we needed someone who knew something about it, so Mr. Nathanson went out to Glace Bay where Marconi himself had set up a station called VAS, the Voice Of The Atlantic Seaboard, from which they broadcast weather reports. They were very co-operative and sent us a little five-foot man by the name of Jones who really got things going. I remember after we got our 'portable' equipment—everything, batteries and all, in a box with a rope on it—Mr. Nathanson asked Jones to move it to some remote point where we were to do a broadcast. Jones said, "Mr. Nathanson, my name's Jones, not Samson."

That's how I got involved. I can't begin to count how many times I lugged that box around. It must have weighed between 75 and 100 pounds. I started off setting up in churches and dance halls or wherever and then my job gradually enlarged into everything else. One Sunday morning after setting up at the Presbyterian church we got word that the announcer was sick. Nathanson called and told me to read the opening and closing. It must have been all right, because after that, he got me reading stock reports and other things. It just kept growing. But even after I started announcing, I had to lug that equipment around. We used to do a Saturday night dance and I'd drag that box up three flights of stairs, set it up, broadcast the dance, then lug the box over to one of the churches where we'd be doing a broadcast on Sunday morning.

The 'J' in CJCB was for his wife, Jennie, and the 'CB' was for Cape Breton.

◄

Marconi (third from left) and his staff outside their wireless telegraph station in Glace Bay. October 1907.

◄

Robbie Robertson, a clerk in Nathanson's store. One of his duties was to play records so something would come out of the radios his boss was selling.

"Cotter's Saturday Night," a network programme broadcast on CJCB in the 1930s.

We played a fair amount of recorded music but we also put on a lot of local groups from our studios. We played an awful lot of Scottish music because Cape Bretoners never seemed to get enough of that. In the 1930s we had a Scottish programme that went out over the CBC network. It was called "Cotter's Saturday Night," and consisted of music, dancing and storytelling. We were the CBC affiliate in Cape Breton. In fact, we were the only commercial station on the Island—the only station of any kind really, apart from Marconi's VAS. We had a tremendous audience and were involved in everything that was going on.

One time I remember taking our remote equipment up to Antigonish, about 120 miles away on the mainland, to do a hockey game. I went up alone by train, got a taxi, lugged all this stuff into the rink and set it up. I called the game, did the commercials, and all the colour commentary for the whole game and two overtime periods. Then I packed everything up again, loaded it back into a taxi and caught the midnight train home. I didn't mind that. It was fun.

Mr. Nathanson wasn't an 'on air' man himself. He had an asthmatic condition that caused him to choke a lot. But if there was a dramatic announcement to be made such as a disaster in the coal mines, or the death of the King, he wanted to announce that himself. The rest, he usually left to the staff unless he heard us do something he didn't like. Then he'd come into the studio and do it over again the way he thought it should be done. It was his station and it was run the way he wanted. The 'J' in CJCB was for his wife, Jennie, and the 'CB' was for Cape Breton.

Radios were relatively expensive when we started out. A six-tube set was about $150 and the combination Marconi sets that came out around 1932, 1933 were $475. They were beautiful things with a great massive cabinet and we sold them for a dollar

CJCB's staff in the late 1930s. Seated on the left in the front row is Clyde Nunn who later started his own radio station, CJFX in Antigonish. Second from left in back row is Robbie Robertson.

down and a dollar a week. I was selling these radios at the same time I was doing all the other things at the station. I would deliver and install them and set up the outside aerials.

As we went along, the station got bigger and more powerful and we grew from a staff of two or three to upwards of thirty. We had some wonderful 'on air' personalities who became local celebrities even though Mr. Nathanson didn't believe in on air staff using their own names. Terry MacLellan, our women's commentator, for instance, was known as Ann Terry. Lloyd McInnis and Bill Loeb did a morning show called "Dishpan Parade" using fictitious names and fictitious country accents. When they held a once a year get together with their listeners there was hardly a place in Sydney big enough to hold their fans. They would do Cape Breton stories, give news of things that were happening around the Island and sing Cape Breton songs their listeners had composed. Some of those songs were very, very funny and usually they poked a bit of fun at Cape Breton idiosyncrasies, like the habit of having nicknames for just about every family. All of our on air people became famous even though they didn't use their own names. People found out who they really were. Mr. Nathanson would not bend this rule. He'd say, "Who cares who you are? Just do a good job!"

Those were the days when talent came free and there was never any shortage. People jumped at the chance to perform on radio and we had a waiting list of groups and artists who wanted to display their talents. It made sense, too, because that's the only way they could get known. Anyway, how could the station afford to give them even four or five dollars when we were only getting two dollars for a commercial? Most of them would have been willing to pay to get on the air. And most of us on staff felt the same way.

A Listener

I remember when I was very young and I was walking to school this day and some of the other kids were talking about this marvellous new invention called radio which did all kinds of wonderful things, like playing music, and talking and one of the kids said, "It will even tell you the time." I didn't have any idea what they were talking about as I'd never even heard of radio, so I said, "Do you mean you can ask for the time, and it will tell you?" I remember how they all laughed at me. That's one of the most embarrassing moments of my life.

Major William Borrett

I became interested in telegraphy and wireless during the First World War when I was in the army. I decided that when the war was over I was going to have equipment of my own. In 1919, I gathered some junk together and got a licence. In 1922 or so a group of us formed a club called The Halifax Radio Listeners Club. We'd gather at each other's homes and talk about radio, about how to get better reception and of new stations we'd picked up. But there was never any thought then of starting a radio station. In the first place, nobody thought of it as a way of making money. How could you?

In 1925 there was a conference of experimenters and amateurs in Paris and I was selected to represent Canada. When I came back I got a lot of publicity. But to tell the truth, I still didn't really know anything about broadcasting. When Bill Jones, the manager of Northern Electric, read about me, he asked me if I would run a station for him if his company sent some equipment to Halifax. I said, "Sure."

A couple of fellows from the radio club and myself formed a committee to run the equipment. We opened up in the Carlton Hotel. I was handed a microphone and told to go to it. Luckily I had the gift of the gab and we did just fine. But at the end of the year Jones' company sold all our equipment to a Vancouver outfit. That's when I took the bull by the horns. I was a government employee at the time but I quit my job, even though everybody thought I was crazy. I bought equipment from Jones and opened up $30,000 in debt.

We'd come on the air at eight in the morning, sign off at nine, do the office work and then go out and sell. Sometimes we'd sign on again at noon and sign off again at six or we might even stay on until eight. Gradually it got so we were on the air all day. CHNS became the first commercial station in Nova Scotia. Our first broadcast was in May 1925. An ad cost about two dollars and sometimes only one dollar. You could buy a half-hour programme for thirty dollars.

When we first started out in the old Carlton Hotel everybody thought our call letters stood for Carlton Hotel Nova Scotia. It was just a coincidence. After that we went to the Lord Nelson—rent free. They knew it would be good advertising for them, and it was. We'd say, "From the Lord Nelson Hotel in Halifax, Nova Scotia, this is radio station CHNS." People would check into that hotel just to see the station on the air or get a glimpse of the

A hungry-looking little fellow came in one day with a guitar and asked for a chance to sing. He was pathetic looking. It was Hank Snow.

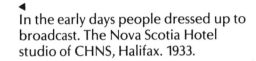
In the early days people dressed up to broadcast. The Nova Scotia Hotel studio of CHNS, Halifax. 1933.

◄
Early radio stations were very often converted homes. Here in the 1930s is Major Bill Borrett, founder of CHNS, Halifax, in his living room-office-studio. Taking dictation is his daughter.

announcers, who by this time had become personalities around the town.

We had no trouble getting people, no matter how important they were, to come on the air. I still have men and women come up to remind me they were once on "Home Laundry Minstrels" or some such thing. Sometimes people would just come in off the street. One of them, I remember, was a hungry-looking little fellow who came in one day with a guitar and asked for a chance to sing. He was pathetic looking. I auditioned him and he surprised me. I could tell right off that this fellow really had something. I put him on the air and he was a natural. It was Hank Snow. Although he became a multi-millionaire, he never forgot where he got his start.

There were only seven thousand sets in all of Nova Scotia when we started, all of them homemade. But by 1926 radio was changing from being a 'toy' to something people felt they had to have. Manufacturers were building radio sets and crystal sets were being used by children or were relegated to drawers in workshops.

Radio was a prestigious business as far as we were concerned

A new announcer, Miss Forrest replaces Mr. Clare who has gone overseas with His Majesty's Forces.

and we dressed to suit the part. We wore morning suits and progressed through other changes during the day to tuxedos at night. We wouldn't think of appearing in front of a mike unless we were properly attired. I loved to go on the air myself. I read the news, announced music programmes, etc. But the best thing I ever did was a weekly show called "Tales From Under the Old Town Clock," which referred to the clock on Citadel Hill, Halifax's trademark. I thought up this idea of telling stories—most of them true—about Halifax and Nova Scotia. I felt that people should have more pride in their city and their province. That programme became an immediate hit and it went on for eighteen years.

We dressed up but we were folksy too. When you had to stop to change a needle, you'd tell the listeners what you were doing. We broadcast our records from an old gramophone—a coffee grinder type of thing. Our first slogan was "CHNS Halifax, Nova Scotia—The Front Door of Canada—Always Open." We were referring, of course, to Halifax Harbour. But I remember one young listener saying, "It must be awfully cold in that radio station with the door always open."

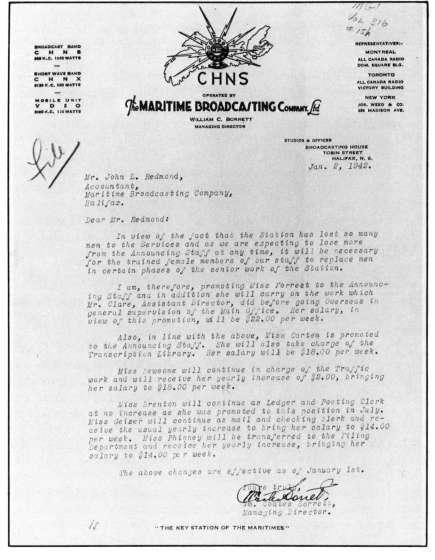

Hugh Mills

Stand beside your radios, raise your right hand, and repeat after me, "I pledge myself to safety first."

My involvement in radio goes back to Bill Borrett's little station, CHNS, in Halifax. It's not 'little' today but at that time it had the most primitive equipment and it seemed to be made mostly of old tin cans and bits of wire. I was something of a church basement amateur actor and I guess my big talent was being able to do a lot of different voices and accents. There was a group of us and we'd do anything from singing badly to putting on plays. When Bill Borrett asked us to do something for his station, we said, "Why not?" Not many people had sets at the time, and we figured if we made a mess of it, who would know?

We got a book of plays and we'd meet at CHNS to do them in front of a microphone which was just a big horn off a phonograph. When your line came up, you'd step up in front of this thing, and let go. It seemed to work out all right because the people who were listening in those days weren't doing it for high quality entertainment, but rather for the thrill of hearing a human voice coming out of the air. Nonetheless we took it all seriously, and always tried to do a professional job. We experimented with sound effects, and came up with some extremely good ones. Being Maritimers, one of the first we worked out was the sound of the Atlantic Ocean. After a lot of fooling around we came up with a piece of canvas nailed to long handles; this rig was filled with pebbles. When rolled and tipped back and forth, it gave us the sound of the Atlantic rolling in on the shore. Frank Willis later used that sound effect on "Harmony Harbour" and "Nocturne." Frank and his brother Austin were two of the actors in our CHNS group. "Mr. Canada," John Fisher also got his start with us.

One day I got a call from Senator Dennis who owned the Halifax *Herald and Mail.* He also had some money invested in CHNS. He asked me to come down and see him. I was excited because I thought he was going to offer me a job reading the news. But when I got there, he said, "I want you to read the comics from my newspaper on the air every night. You've got all these different voices and you should be able to do a good job." You could have knocked me over with a feather. I didn't know whether to be insulted or to laugh. Me, the great actor, reading comics on the air to kids?! He went on to explain that to follow me as I read the comics, the children who were listening would have to have a copy of his newspaper in front of them. It was a gimmick to increase circulation. I was to be called "Uncle Mel."

I was doubtful about all this. For one thing I hadn't even glanced at the comics in years. Nonetheless I agreed and went on the air as Uncle Mel, describing the latest adventures of "Popeye," "Mickey Mouse," "Red Ryder," and all the others. The reaction was immediate. Kids loved the show and the newspaper's circulation shot up. Pretty soon everyone was talking about Uncle Mel. I added a safety pledge. After the programme opened with a song, I would say, "Good evening boys and girls (knock knock), the meeting will come to order. Stand beside your radios, raise your right hand, and repeat after me, 'I pledge myself to safety first—on the streets or wherever I may be, at all times.'" Every kid in Halifax knew that pledge by heart in no time. And Uncle Mel's Safety Club was the biggest thing on radio. Five days a week.

◄
Uncle Mel (Hugh Mills) of CHNS, Halifax.

A Quarter Century of Service

IN MAY, 1925, the "Voice of Halifax" was first heard in the Maritimes—the pioneer station that then, as now, stressed service to the public as its first objective.

The intervening years have brought constant improvements—in equipment, facilities, staff and coverage until today, in the face of all competition, CHNS rates first for results in the Halifax area.

1925 —— FIRST IN HALIFAX —— 1950

CHNS operates on both AM and FM and Short Wave Transmissions are carried over CHNX

CHNS

Studios and offices at Broadcasting House, Tobin St., Halifax; Transmitter at Bedford, N.S.

MARITIME BROADCASTING CO. LTD.—Wm. C. Borrett, Man. Dir., HALIFAX, N.S.

CHNS
THE VOICE OF HALIFAX

960 on the Dial
FIRST in NOVA SCOTIA

We decided that on Saturdays the children should have a chance to show their own talents and we put on singers, tap dancers, piano players, trumpet players, accordionists—everything you can imagine. By now, sponsors were flocking to us and we were beginning to make a bit of money. We had an 'official' brand of milk for the club, 'official' everything from syrup to bread and peanut butter. People didn't yet understand what advertising on radio was all about so when they heard me refer to a brand of peanut butter, they thought I mentioned it because I liked it. We were advertising milk from the Maple Leaf Dairy, for example. A friend who owned the Oxford Dairy called me one day, wondering why I couldn't say something nice about *his* milk, as it was just as good as Maple Leaf. He said, "Anyway, I thought you were a friend of mine." He told me that his own grandchild was refusing to drink Oxford Dairy milk because he wanted to drink only 'official' milk.

When we began advertising Schwartz Peanut Butter, the children had to mail in a label to get a badge from Uncle Mel's Safety Club. Schwartz Peanut Butter was disappearing from grocers' shelves so fast that it was never there long enough for the oil to come to the top as it will with all peanut butter. People saw this and said, "Schwartz Peanut Butter is better because the oil doesn't come to the top." This was nonsense, of course, but we were becoming aware of the power of advertising.

"Uncle Mel's Talent Show," on Saturday afternoons was a huge success and went on for fifteen or sixteen years. When the war started in 1939, I took the programme all over the province and played before sailors, soldiers and airmen stationed here—many of whom had children back home. It was wonderful to watch those men as the children performed; tears would be rolling down their faces and you knew their thoughts.

I still have grown men come up to me today and begin the conversation by reciting the safety pledge. Most people call me "Uncle Mel" and I'm sure a lot of them forget that my real name is Hugh. I don't mind at all because I have so many great friends and wonderful memories of my eighteen years as Uncle Mel.

MARITIME BROADCASTING CO. LTD.
RADIO STATION

Location
Lord Nelson Hotel,
HALIFAX, N. S.
Canada.

C H N S

Associated with
The Halifax Herald and The Halifax Mail
Wm. C. Borrett, Station Director.
500 Watts output Power—329.7 Meters—910 KC.

Operated Daily
**National Rate Card
No. 5**
In Effect Jan. 1st, 1931

Associated Station, Trans-Canada Broadcasting Company
Associated Station, Canadian Broadcasting System

Associated Station, Maritime Chain Radio Stations
Associated Station, Canadian Pacific Radio Chain

1—General Goodwill Advertising.

a. **Musical Programs.**
    Per hour.........................$40.00
    Per Half Hour.................... 25.00
    Per Quarter Hour................ 15.00
    The above musical program rates are for the facilities of the station only; talent is extra.

b. **Announcements and Talks.**
    Per minute.......................$ 1.00
         (Minimum $10.00)

Discounts.

c. One Programme per week.
    For 13 consecutive weeks..........10%
    For 26 consecutive weeks..........15%

d. Agency Commission.................15%

e. No extra charge will be made when announcements are given by station staff.

f. All proposals subject to prior booking of time.

g. Minimum time sold, 10 minutes for talks.
    " " " 15 minutes for Musical Programs.

h. No blanket contracts accepted.

i. No contract accepted for longer than one year. All contracts subject to the station owner's approval and governmental regulations. The station reserves the right
                 (over)

▶ A contestant on one of Uncle Mel's talent shows.

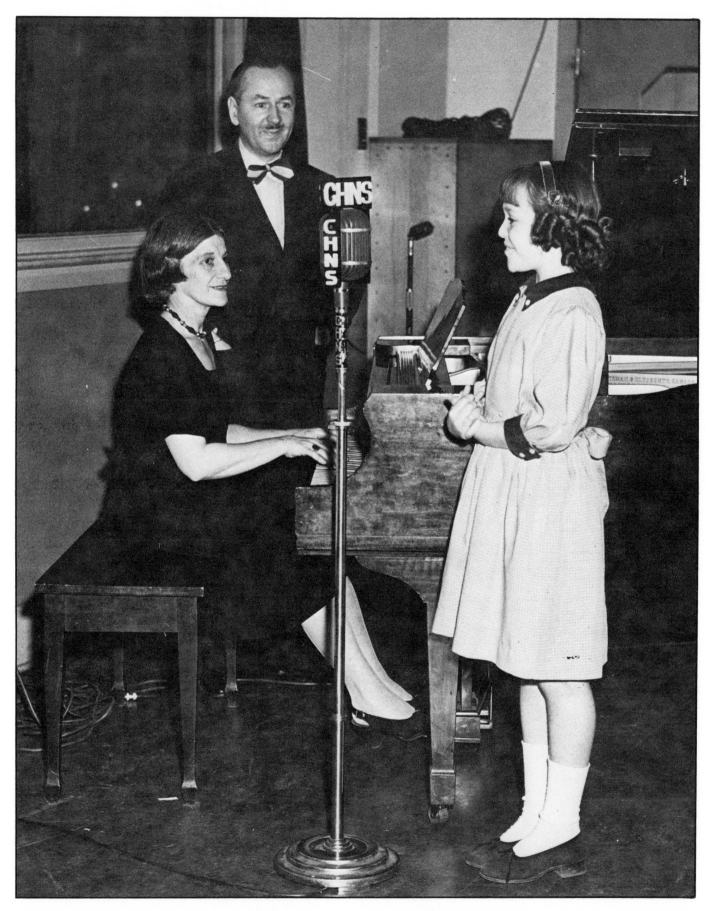

Jerry Redmond

I was educated at Dalhousie and I joined the Nova Scotia Department of Education in 1930. I'd known Major Bill Borrett and the men associated with CHNS when it was established, so it was an easy step to arrange to do some broadcasts. I had the idea to broadcast to schools, something very new and different. I planned the programmes and secured the services of specialists from all areas. We did English literature, French, history, music.

The programme was intended to supplement the work of the classroom teacher. Time was provided free by the station. Programmes ran for two hours, from two to four, every Friday afternoon. We'd open with a classical, or semi-classical, selection. Then we'd have our first speaker. Then some more music, and then into the next speaker. And so on. It was an early example of a magazine format. Performers weren't paid, although at the end of the year those who had appeared in a regular series as instructors or actors would get a very modest honorarium.

We did a lot of drama. Helen Creighton, for example, wrote historical scripts. The American networks were doing geography dramas, using a family. A mother and father and two children were depicted visiting different countries and cities every week. We were able to get these scripts on an exchange basis and have local dramatic talent do them. Halifax had a very active theatre during these years, the Theatre Arts Guild of Halifax, and actors like Hugh and Jean Mills and Frank and Austin Willis came to us saying, "If you're going to do drama for the schools, count us in." So week after week, they came down and rehearsed their scripts and did a half-hour 'live' drama. It was all wonderfully experimental, and remember, throughout that time I was employed by the Department of Education. I didn't join the full-time staff of CHNS until 1945.

One of the most humorous things that happened during my years in broadcasting took place during a 'near' hurricane. The winds were 100 miles an hour, and our thousand-watt transmitter, which was located at the head of Bedford Basin, came down. We were in the middle of a musical programme at the time. It was a quarter past nine in the evening. The tower was completely blown over. The transmitter house and everything was gone. We'd been off the air for about ten minutes when one of the members of our Board of Directors called and said, "Jerry, did you know you're off the air?" I said, "Yes, sir." He said, "I was enjoying the programme very much. How long will it be before you get it back on again?" I said, "I'm awfully sorry, but the tower has collapsed and we may be off the air for days or weeks." "Well," he said, "if that's the case, you're certainly going to have an awful lot of disappointed people tonight. Why don't you go on the air and tell them what's wrong?" He had absolutely no idea how things worked! And in those days, not many people did. Most accepted it as a kind of magic.

There was no network in the early days. All we had was our own thousand-watt transmitter—the one that came down in the hurricane. It covered a good deal of the south shore, perhaps seventy-five to eighty miles in either direction. It covered up-country pretty well too. We also used to send some of our school broadcasts on discs to Yarmouth and to Cape Breton. CHNS played a very big role in pioneering educational programmes on radio, and we're proud of that.

Actors like Hugh and Jean Mills and Frank and Austin Willis came to us saying, "If you're going to do drama for the schools, count us in."

A Report on John Fisher
COMMENTATOR LECTURER

All Canada knows John Fisher and John Fisher knows all Canada. Through his national CBC broadcast "John Fisher Reports," in addition to several dominion-wide sponsored series, hundreds of thousands of listeners recognize his voice and distinctive style. He receives over 500 requests annually to appear as guest speaker at conventions, service and study clubs in Canada and U.S.A. Gathering material for his broadcasts has taken "this wandering observer and story teller" from the isolated Magdalen Islands on the Atlantic seaboard to the equally isolated Queen Charlotte Islands on the Pacific coast; from the bush-plane-lands of northern mining camps to south of Mason-Dixon. He has logged 137,000 miles in Canada and the United States.

Nor is his compass restricted to North America. John Fisher last winter made an extensive tour of European countries. In the United States there is an increasing demand for his broadcasts and personal appearances. As a Canadian he has the double advantage of understanding and dispassionate observation of the great neighbour. His knowledge of French enables him to interpret the Old World and the New.

John Fisher's career is Canada, her people, her way of life, her relationship in the world.

"Here is one speaker we'll invite back"
"Truly an observer with comprehensive candor"
"John Fisher is always aware of human values,
the unusual bleeds with the next-door-neighbour reality,
and hard facts come alive . . . and lively!"
"Canada without tears"

Lawyer, newspaperman, writer, broadcaster, all describe John Fisher. Born Sackville N.B. 1912 . . . graduate Dalhousie University . . . member of the Bar of Nova Scotia . . . worked on the Rowell-Sirois Commission. Winner of the Beaver Award for "best Canadian commentator," John Fisher has also twice been awarded the La Fleche Trophy for "distinguished contribution to Canadian radio." He has been given the freedom of Canadian cities . . . made appearances in legislatures . . . pulpits . . . factories . . . even the Winnipeg Grain Exchange. John Fisher has become a Canadian institution.

John Fisher, 'Mr. Canada,' was a protégé of Hugh Mills.

62

TIME MARCHES ON!

- - - has your radio kept abreast of the times?

DeFOREST CROSLEY

NO MATTER what type of radio you now own—the time has come to trade it in on one of the new radio models by De Forest Crosley— with the sensational NO-STOOP, NO-SQUINT Sloping Tuning Panel—METAL-type Dual-Purpose Tubes and Guaranteed Foreign Reception.

To those who paid a big price for their radio years ago but now find it obsolete, we say that here is the answer to your radio problem.

A score of new 1937 features challenge your interest. Get rid of your old radio, and take advantage of present liberal trade-in allowances being made by De Forest Crosley dealers.

**The Original and Exclusive
"No-Stoop, No-Squint"
Sloping Tuning Panel**

"Jupiter" model (illustrated) gives 17-tube performance and creates an entirely new conception of radio. Don't be without a modern De Forest Crosley All-Wave Radio another day!

METAL Spray TUBES

The Jupiter

DeForest Crosley Limited

TORONTO and MONTREAL

RADIO CABINETS
All Sizes and Designs Made to Order

NEUTRODYNE CABINETS A SPECIALTY
Celoron Panels and Base Boards
Cut to Suit

THE MONTREAL PATTERN WORKS
(Just below St. Catherine St.)

242 Clarke Street - - Montreal

Telephone: Plateau 0524

Message Announcing President's Death Heard by Radio

The message announcing the death of President Harding, transmitted Thursday night, at 12 a.m., by Station WDAP, Board of Trade, Drake Hotel, Chicago, was distinctly heard on our honey-comb receiver by Lieutenant C. McPherson, Manager of the Main Radio.

The diagram and parts for this receiving set can be bought at either of our stores.

1—43 Plate Variable Condenser	$2.95	1—75 Turn Honeycomb Coil	1.05
1—23 Plate Variable Condenser	1.95	30-Ohm Rheostat	1.25
2—3-in. Dials	.70	1 Switch Lever	.15
1—5 Ohm Rheostat	.85	2 Contact Points	.02
8—Binding Posts	.32	2 Stops	.02
1—3 Coil Honeycomb Mount	2.50	1 Grid Leak and Condenser	.15
1—35 Turn Honeycomb Coil	.95	1 Socket	.60 or..1.00
1—50 Turn Honeycomb Coil	.95	1 Vacuum Tube	6.00
		1 Pair 2,000 Manhattan Phones	4.00

Main Radio and Audio Supplies
WHOLESALE AND RETAIL

Open till 11 p.m. on Saturday
86 ST. JAMES STREET, MONTREAL
(Near Place d'Armes)

Main 5396   283 Bleury St.
Lieut. C. McPherson, Manager

Can You Light a Match?

If so, you have brains enough to save one hundred dollars on that receiving set of yours!

New idea, proven to work splendidly
Write for particulars, to the

CANADIAN SCHOOL of TELEGRAPHY and RAILROADING

314 St. Catherine West, Montreal, P. Q.

Canada's Biggest and Best Equipped School of its Kind

WIRELESS

Be a wireless expert. Wonderful Opportunity for those desiring to get in on the ground floor of an industry that will furnish employment for thousands, and amusement and convenience to thousands of others Study at home. Write to-day for full particulars. International Correspondence Schools Canadian, Limited, Dept. 1841, Montreal, Canada.

Ontario-Quebec

B. H. Smith

When I came to Canada I was part of the Pacific Cable Board, which consisted of Canada, the U.S., Australia, New Zealand and England. When you handed in a cable in London to go to Australia it had to go first to Waterford, Ireland by landline. From Waterford it came to Canso, Nova Scotia by submarine cable. From Canso it was transferred to the CPR, who relayed it to Montreal, and from there to Australia. We had the one direct line. It was all those re-transmissions that took the time. This cable stuff is all pre-radio, really, while the First World War was on. We had special lines for the armed forces. Soldiers flooded our company with messages. There were so many messages coming from soldiers we couldn't get them all sent. The poor fellows were back at the front getting killed before their messages were delivered.

This cable business led me to radio in the 1920s in Winnipeg. James A. Richardson had started a freight business to the Arctic Circle from Winnipeg and for this purpose he established a series of short wave stations. I operated one of these stations from Winnipeg. He also had stations in The Pas, Calgary and Vancouver. He established them all with the aid of the Marconi Company. I was with him for no more than three years when the crash came. It left James A. almost bankrupt.

Soldiers flooded our company with messages. The poor fellows were back at the front getting killed before their messages were delivered.

I took a correspondence course in radio, got my diploma, and from 1929 on worked in Montreal at CFCF, the Marconi station. The job at CFCF was rather simple. I was in charge of the telegraph wire which linked Montreal with the American networks in New York. When a programme came on and there was to be a break at a certain time, they sent you a message saying that at so many hours, so many minutes, so many seconds, there'd be a pause following the words such and such. Then we were to cut in with whatever local announcement we had. At that time there were very few local announcements.

A Listener

My memories of radio go back almost to the very beginning. A fellow down the street had built a radio that ran on batteries and he traded it at my father's general store for groceries. It had three knobs and we brought in programmes on that from all over the world. We then moved up to an Atwater-Kent, and later on to an old Philco. I was an instant fan. Radio replaced lollipops as the object of my affection. I especially remember a great twosome of singing comedians who came on with, "We're the interwoven pair. We're Billy Jones and Ernie Hare. How do you doodle doodle doodle do?" They were really good. And there was a newscaster at the time who sang the opening words of his broadcast, "I see by the paper..." and he'd launch into the news which was just a series of headlines. There wasn't much I didn't hear because I was glued to the set. I even sneaked away from school a few times just to get my ear up to that radio. It had a tremendous impact on my life.

There was a newscaster at the time who sang the opening words of his broadcast.

How do you do, every-body, how do you do?
Gee it's great to say hell-o to all of you;
I'm Billy Jones,
I'm Ernie Hare,
And we're a silly-lookin' pair;
How do you doodle-doodle-doodle-doodle-do?

▲

The opening lines of "The Happiness Boys" show.

▶

Maclean's, April 1, 1925

Diamond·F

CONDENSITE

CELORON

RADIO PANELS, KNOBS, RHEOSTATS, DIALS, SOCKET BASES.

Condensite Celeron supplied in Sheets, Rods, Tubes or machined to any specifications.

Diamond State Fibre Co. of Canada
Limited
235 Carlaw Avenue .. Toronto, Ont.

Used by
THE MARCONI CO. OF CANADA

ATWATER KENT RADIO

TO OWN an ATWATER KENT—what a wonderful, delightful difference it makes—just think what it means—in one evening the thrills of a lifetime are crowded into a few short hours.

Set its dials and the melodies of a famous orchestra flood your home; another touch and you hear a lecture from miles away—turn again and you have the news of the day or the sweet voice of a renowned singer generously broadcasting for your entertainment.

Choose whatever program you will, with an ATWATER KENT you are master of the air.

There is an ATWATER KENT well within your means: it combines every feature that assures radio satisfaction for years to come—Any ATWATER KENT dealer will help you in your selection.

Interesting literature on request.

CANADIAN DISTRIBUTORS:

McKee Sales & Service Co.
22-24 King St., Sherbrooke, Que.
Motor Car Supply Co.
10621 Jasper Ave., E.
Edmonton

John Millen & Son, Ltd.
321 St. James St., Montreal
Canadian Fairbanks-
Morse Co.
300 Princess Street, Winnipeg

Bowman Brothers, Ltd.
234 20th St., E., Saskatoon
Bowman Brothers, Ltd.
1827 Cornwall St., Regina
Crowell Brothers, 81 Upper Water St., Halifax

Keyes Supply Co.
282 Sparks St., Ottawa
Bennet & Elliott, Ltd.
71 Wellington St., W.
Toronto

Motor Car Supply Co.
514 11th Ave., Calgary
Canadian Fairbanks-
Morse Co.
758 Beatty Street, Vancouver

THINK WHAT IS BACK OF IT

Canadian Broadcasting Stations

List Corrected to July 15th, 1924

Call Signal	Owner of Station	Location of Station	Wave-length (metres)	Power inputt (Watts)
CFAC	The Calgary Herald	Calgary, Alta	430	2000
CFCA	Star Publishing & Printing Co.	18 King St. W., Toronto	400	2000
CFCF	Marconi Wireless Telegraph Co. of Can. Ltd.	Canada Cement Bldg., Phillips Sq., Montreal.	440	2000
CFCH	Abitibi Power & Paper Co. Ltd.	Iroquois Falls, Ont.	400	500
CFCK	Radio Supply Co. Ltd.	10229-101st Street, Edmonton, Alta.	410	250
CFCL	Centennial Methodist Ch.	Victoria, B.C.	400	500
CFCN	W. W. Grant Radio Ltd.	708 Crescent Rd. N.W., Calgary, Alta.	440	1000
CFCQ	Radio Specialties Ltd.	791 Dunsmuir Ave., Vancouver, B.C.	450	40
CFCR	Laurentide Air Service Limited.	Nickle Range Hotel, Sudbury, Ont.	410	200
CFCT	The Victoria City Temple	1110 Douglas Street, Victoria, B.C.	410	500
CFCU	Jack V. Elliot Ltd.	123 King Street W., Hamilton, Ont.	410	20
CFDC	Sparks Company	Wallace and Fitzwilliam Sts., Nanaimo, B.C.	430	50
CFHC	Henry Birks & Sons Ltd.	708 Crescent Road N.W., Calgary, Alta.	440	1000
CFLC	Chas. Guy Hunter	551 Adelaide St., London, Ont.	430	100
CFQC	The Electric Shop Ltd.	144 Second Ave. North, Saskatoon, Sask.	400	200
CFRC	Queen's University (Dept. of Electrical Engr.)	Fleming Hall, Queen's Univ., Kingston, Ont.	450	1500
CFXC	Westminster Trust Co.	Columbia and Begbie Sts., New Westminster, B.C.	440	50
CFYC	Victor Wentworth Odlum	Mercantile Building, 318 Homer St., Vancouver	400	20
CHBC	The Albertan Publishing Co. Ltd.	708 Crescent Road N.W., Calgary, Alta.	410	500
CHCE	Western Canada Radio Supply Ltd.	919 Fort St., Victoria, B.C.	400	20
CHCM	Riley & McCormick Ltd.	708 Crescent Road N.W., Calgary, Alta.	440	1000
CHCS	The Hamilton Spectator	Spectator Bldg., Hamilton, Ont.	410	2000
CHNC	Toronto Radio Research Society	46 Lauder Ave., Toronto, Ontario.	350	200
CHXC	J. R. Booth, Jr.	28 Range Rd., Ottawa, Ont.	435	1200
CHYC	Northern Electric Co. Ltd.	121 Shearer Street, Montreal, P.Q.	341	2000
CJBC	Jarvis St. Baptist Church	Toronto, Ont.	312	4000
CJCA	The Edmonton Journal Ltd.	Journal Bldg., Edmonton, Alta.	450	500
CJCD	The T. Eaton Co. Ltd.	Queen St. W., Toronto, Ont.	410	100
CJCE	Sprott Shaw Radio Co.	Room 1604, Tower Bldg., Vancouver, B.C.	400	150
CJCF	The News Record	39 South Cameron Street, Kitchener, Ont.	295	300
CJCK	Radio Corporation of Calgary, Ltd.	1731 College Lane, Calgary, Alta.	316	500
CJCM	J. L. Philippe Landry	Mont Joli, P.Q.	312	2000
CJGC	London Free Press Ptg. Co.	440 Richmond St., London, Ont.	430	200
CJSC	The Evening Telegram	81 Bay St., Toronto, Ont.	430	500
CKAC	La Presse Publishing Co. Ltd.	Cor. St. James St. and St. Lawrence Blvd., Montreal, P.Q.	430	2000
CKCD	Vancouver Daily Province	142 Hastings Street W., Vancouver, B.C.	410	2000
CKCE	Canadian Independent	Wallace Ave. and Ward St., Toronto	450	2000
CKCI	Le "Soleil" Limitee	C. W. Lindsay Bldg., cor. St. John and St. Eustache Sts., Quebec, P.Q.	295	200
CKCK	Leader Publishing Co. Ld.	Regina, Sask.	420	2000
CKCO	Dr. G. M. Geldert	282 Somerset St. West, Ottawa, Ont.	400	200
CKCX	P. Burns & Co. Ltd.	708 Crescent Road N.W., Calgary, Alta.	440	1000
CKLC	Wilkinson Electric Co.	2119 Seventh Ave. N.W., Calgary, Alta.	400	200
CKY	Manitoba Telephone System.	Sherbrook Street, Winnipeg, Man.	450	2000
CNRC	Canadian Nat. Rys.	Calgary, Alta	440	1000
CNRE	Canadian Nat. Rys.	Edmonton, Alta.	450	500
CNRM	Canadian Nat. Rys.	Montreal, P.Q.	341	2000
CNRO	Canadian Nat. Rys.	Ottawa, Ont.	435	2000
CNRR	Canadian Nat. Rys.	Regina, Sask.	420	2000
CNRS	Canadian Nat. Rys.	Saskatoon, Sask.	400	500
CNRT	Canadian Nat. Rys.	Toronto, Ont.	400	2000
CNRW	Canadian Nat. Rys.	Winnipeg, Man.	450	2000

PAYETTE MONTREAL 910 BLEURY ST. RADIO PARTS

Aurèle Pelletier

I started at *Le Soleil* in the advertising section working for a man, Mr. Ti-Vierge, who was doing radio at night as a hobby. When he decided to quit *Le Soleil* and start *Le Journal* he asked me to go with him. We worked at the newspaper during the day and broadcast at night. We didn't have a regular broadcasting schedule. We operated mostly at night from six on. If we had material for an hour, we were on for an hour. If we had nothing, we'd sign off. Then one day in 1930 he said to me, "I'm quitting the newspaper business and going into radio full-time. Do you want to come along?" I said, "Yes." I was earning seven dollars a week at the newspaper but he said, "All I can afford to give you is five dollars." I said I didn't care. I liked the business and I thought there was more future in radio than in newspapers. I was seventeen and I had nothing to lose.

CHRC covered quite a large territory—three or four hundred miles—because the frequencies weren't as crowded as they are today. The station was heard from Three Rivers down into the Gaspé. I was a part-time announcer, part-time operator and part-time copy writer. It wasn't easy to sell radio then but we did have a few sponsors. I was assigned to broadcast the Chateau Frontenac Orchestra and the Victoria Hotel Orchestra a half-hour daily. We also covered lunch speakers from the various service clubs. I also broadcast hockey.

When the Canadian Radio Commission was established they didn't have a station in Quebec City so we were their link in both French and English for a few years. And we originated a lot of bilingual programmes too. One time we broadcast Christmas Mass from St. Dominic right across Canada through the CRBC and the United States through NBC.

Another time three men escaped from the local jail and Mr. Ti-Vierge got very involved in this story. After a few days the prisoners were located on St. Jean Street and the whole police force went off to capture them. Ti-Vierge called me and said, "Lad, go and get that story." I went there and I had to go down in a cellar where it was very dark. There was a gun fight and one prisoner and one policeman were killed. I went back home where I proceeded to get sick. After an hour or so Ti-Vierge called and said, "What the hell are you doing at home? Where is my story?" He ended his tirade by firing me. The next day I went to the station and told him I'd been afraid. So he said, "OK, come on back and get to work." He never mentioned it again.

The station was heard from Three Rivers down into the Gaspé.

Paul L'Anglais

I started at CHLP Montreal in 1932. CHLP opened in the fall of that year. I saw an ad in the paper saying that they were looking for talent. I called an old McGill classmate, Lawrence Hart, and said, "Are you game to go down and audition?" He said, "Yes," and we both went. Larry was hired as a part-time pianist. I was hired as a salesman. We had our first show on CHLP a month or so later. I sold it to Ed Michaud of Michaud Hats. He lived in Outremont. The show was called "Les Chansons du Pierrot." In addition to selling it, I announced it, wrote it and sang on it. Larry accompanied me on the piano. I got a very nice notice in the Montreal *Herald*. Unfortunately, Michaud cancelled after four weeks because the station was so weak that it didn't reach as far as Outremont for him to hear it himself.

We used to get a lot of fake mail at CHLP in those days from artists and groups who appeared on the station to prove their popularity. One time we booked Hal Jones and his Cowboys, or some such group. They were to be on at seven o'clock on a Saturday night which, in those days, was a very good time. Well, on Saturday morning a guy came in with cold cash wanting to buy the half-hour from seven to seven-thirty. The boss took the cash and cancelled Jones and company. When they arrived at quarter to seven to play, they were told they'd been cancelled. Nonetheless, on Monday morning we received thirty-five or forty letters congratulating Hal Jones and his Cowboys for their wonderful show on Saturday. They'd sent the mail and they couldn't get it back. A lot of that kind of thing went on. It was fairly easy, though, to spot the fake letters. Sometimes they'd all be in exactly the same handwriting with exactly the same wording.

Eventually I left CHLP to become sales manager of Julio Romano's Canadian Broadcast Company. He used to buy time on stations. It was a common practice then to buy blocks of one hour and fill them with music, skits and, of course, commercials. Then, in the spring of 1934, I started my own business, Radio Programme Producers. We had only one account when we started, but by the fall of 1934 we'd sold a series of contracts on CKAC. In those days, CKAC was a bilingual station. It was the CBS outlet in Montreal. CFCF, the Marconi station, was the NBC outlet, and it too was bilingual. Both stations were highly competitive. My firm produced as much English programming in Montreal as it did French, at least until the CBC began. Afterwards, they let the centre of English production move to Toronto; that was the virtual end of English production in Montreal.

We used to get a lot of fake mail at CHLP in those days from artists and groups who appeared on the station.

Yves Bourassa

One night in 1933 I was listening to the radio and I figured I could do as good a job as those announcers were doing. One had to be bilingual because Quebec stations were neither totally French nor totally English. I called the manager of CKAC, Phil Lalonde, and asked for an audition. He said, "Sure, come on down." My audition consisted of reading an article in English from the front page of the Montreal *Star* and another in French from the front page of *La Presse*. Phil said, "I like the way you read. When can you begin? I'll give you twenty dollars a week plus anything you can make on commercials."

That was it. I became an announcer in September 1933. That meant that I worked seven days a week doing anything from cataloguing the record library to sweeping the floor. Seven days a week from nine in the morning to one in the morning. Many times we slept over at the station because there was no time to go home. I did this for two years but my real interest was programme direction. I was disturbed at the haphazard way programmes were being produced. In 1935 I was made Programme Director and I must have driven everyone crazy because of the way I kept buzzing around. They nicknamed me "the hornet."

We became intensely involved in the crises leading up to the war. There were direct broadcasts of Hitler's speeches and CBS, which we were affiliated with, had a commentator named H. V. Kaltenborn doing simultaneous translations. When the war broke out I had gone for the weekend but I'd left instructions for the station to remain open. I got a phone call that the war looked certain. That's when we became true broadcasters. There was no news in French from the Canadian Press and we couldn't take time to translate it properly. We'd just tear the English copy off the machines and translate it on the air as we went along. I relieved the guy who'd been there since Saturday morning at Sunday noon and stayed at it until Monday evening. We had all the newspapers, a pot of glue and the stuff that was coming in on the wire. It was hectic. On the first night of the war the *Athenia* was sunk and without thinking we put the news on the air immediately. What a mistake that was! We were deluged with calls from people who had relatives on board and we didn't realize that next of kin hadn't been informed. We spent the rest of the night apologizing.

This period could, I suppose, be described as an ordeal, but it wasn't really. It was one of the most thrilling times of our lives. We were totally involved. We talk about the long hours but there were always a lot of one or two hour hiatuses where we had a lot of fun. We were young. We had a certain aura because we were broadcasters, with an attraction to the public, including some lovely girls. We all had little black books and it was no problem to get some beautiful young thing to come up to the station and help us spend the lonely hours between eleven and one in the morning while waiting to sign off.

We all had little black books and it was no problem to get some beautiful young thing to come up to the station and help us spend the lonely hours.

WE'RE *"Tout oreilles"* IN QUEBEC...

What's Your Message?

"Yes—we're definitely 'all ears'. My name is Yvette Dupré... I live in a large town... I must admit that I take pride in my appearance, as all girls do, and I love nice cosmetics. But it's risky to buy any but the best beauty-aids, so I rely on the quality brands advertised on CKAC..."

JUST as French Canada's young girls are noted for their beauty, French Canada as a nation is noted for its devotion to radio. The radio, in fact, is the centre of Quebec's family life, and the station with family coverage and overwhelming dominance is CKAC. To advertise your product over CKAC is to bring it to the attention of an eager, responsible audience, and an enormous market spending annually over $800,000,000. Write today for details of CKAC's dominance, markets, and programme planning.

CKAC La Presse, MONTREAL
Affiliated with CBS

Canada: C. W. Wright.
REPRESENTATIVES: Victory Building, Toronto, Ontario.
United States: Adam J. Young, Jr., Inc.

Harvey Dobbs

I first heard radio on a crystal set as a youngster growing up in Montreal. It was thrilling to sit there scratching this crystal and finally hearing something in your earphones. The germ was born there because by luck or good management I was able to become a part of radio and spend my whole life in it. I started in 1929, the year the stock market crashed, at Canada's first commercial station, CFCF in Montreal. I took an audition and was chosen to be the singing M.C. of an hour-long Saturday night programme called "The Informal Studio Party."

Radio was coming into its own at the time. Everybody was listening. I can remember walking down the street and as I strolled I could hear the radio coming out of every open window. I could hear every word of "Amos 'n' Andy." Those were the days when you invited people in to listen to Jack Benny, Eddie Cantor or Fibber McGee and Molly. You'd really look forward to these shows and everyone would sit around "shushing" anyone who dared make a noise.

That job with CFCF only lasted for a couple of months but it was enough to get me enthused about making radio my career. After Montreal, I worked as an announcer at different stations around the country. In the late thirties I worked for Nate Nathanson at CJCB. I started a show there called "The Havelock Home Reporter" in which I used the phone to carry on two-way conversations with listeners. As far as I know this was the first time anything like that had been done. I'd phone and ask a simple question. Then I'd send a case of Havelock beverage for the person's courtesy in talking to me. It worked great and became the talk of Cape Breton. Then somebody told Nathanson that this was an invasion of privacy and against the law. He got scared and took it off the air. We were years ahead of anyone in using the phone as part of the broadcasting pattern.

I moved from Cape Breton to Toronto in 1939 and by this time I was getting pretty experienced at doing game shows, which were in their heyday then. I did a lot of those, including one on CKCL, which later became CKEY. The show was called "Criss-Cross Clues." I also started the first recorded quiz show in Canada, "Did I Say That?" Another thing I did was start one of the first broadcasting schools in the country in partnership with Ralph Snelgrove. A big problem in those days was that you couldn't get hired without experience and there was no place to learn. This would be from 1939 on, because in the early days the problem didn't exist—nobody had any experience. But as the industry grew there was a need for schools to teach the art of broadcasting. So we started what we called The Grenville School, with me as teacher and Ralph as technician. A lot of young people went directly from there to jobs in radio.

A big problem in those days was that you couldn't get hired without experience and there was no place to learn.

They're the "Amos 'n' Andy" of 3,000,000 French Canadians

Nazaire et Barnabe

show you how to reach "A Nation within a Nation"

● Religiously each Friday evening Jean Baptiste's family gather round the radio on the red-checked kitchen table. While in their sumptuous *vivoirs*, Quebec's *élite* are chuckling over the same program—*Nazaire & Barnabé*—on CKAC.

Actually, Nazaire & Barnabé mean more to 3,000,000 French-Canadians than Amos & Andy in English-speaking radio history. French-Canadians listen to radio in a 3 to 2 proportion compared to English-speaking people. *Proportionately, CKAC audience figures are astronomic!*

CKAC's tremendous popularity as the *family station* of French Quebec makes it the key to the $600,000,000 family spending of this great compact market. Write for details of CKAC's market coverage and suggestions for programme planning.

CKAC MONTREAL
affiliated with CBS

A Listener

I bought my first set in the winter of 1925—a Westinghouse. A four-tube set with earphones. It was the first set in my small village between the towns of Carleton and Maria on the Gaspé. We were bothered with static and fading. The nearest stations at the time were CHRC in Quebec and CKAC in Montreal but they weren't powerful enough to reach us, so we had to wait for darkness to get anything. Because of this my favourite stations were WGY Schenectaday, WJZ New York, WOR Newark, and KDKA Pittsburgh. Sometimes I even tuned in WENR from Chicago.

Harry Swabey

I was in the Boy Scouts and had learned the Morse code. I got interested in wireless because of the *Titanic,* which was about the first time wireless was used for rescue. I was going to Sunday school at the Anglican Church, but the Baptist Church had a better Sunday school paper. They nearly always had articles like "How to Build a Radio Transmitter." So I changed religion right then. I built all these things that had anything to do with radio.

By this time, I was working in a millinery shop and I was fed up. Someone told me to go see a man at Independent Telephone, which was part of Standard Radio. They were doing telephone work and radio then—making headphones and crystal sets. I was taken on. We assembled headphones and I mostly did the soldering. You had to solder a wire finer than a human hair Then Ted Rogers' dad bought him the company. That was in 1922.

I went from there to a company in Toronto that was producing Rogers Majestic radios. Then I went to the tube plant where we started to make the world's first AC tubes. It was two years before the United States brought one out.

In 1927 I went to CFRB. Ted Rogers, who invented the radio tube, owned the station, but he didn't go down to the studio. He wasn't interested in that part. He stayed home and listened. We shared frequencies then with CKGW, the Gooderham and Worts station. My job was to keep the transmitter on the air and to maintain it. I had a pretty high salary at that time. I was getting eighteen dollars a month, but that was cut to fifteen dollars during the Depression. Around that time we went to what we called "the Bedstead Transmitter"—a wooden frame with water-cooled tubes. If it rained you had to retune. The inspectors would phone and say, "You're sliding." So we'd have to retune the whole thing. The government monitored the stations closely.

The American influence was strong. For example, when the quintuplets were born, I was astonished to hear Callander being talked about on the air from New York. It hadn't dawned on me that this quint business was so big. The fact that Callander was on the air from New York was the thing that impressed me.

Ours was the first station in the world to be batteryless. When we brought out the AC tube you didn't have to have a car battery in your living room, or the big B battery, or the C battery. That really was a big step forward, along with the fact that our programming was good. We used more 'live' talent than any

The Baptist Church had a better Sunday school paper. They nearly always had articles like "How to Build a Radio Transmitter." So I changed religion right then.

station in the country during our evening broadcasts. We only played records in the daytime.

Radios were expensive when you consider how low wages were. The average set was around $100, but if you wanted a more elaborate cabinet that made a difference. I remember an $800 model and it was beautiful. Radio was the centrepiece of the home in those days. So people got the best one they could afford. The big ones not only sounded better, they looked better. People took more pride in their radios in those days than they did in their cars.

The fact that Callander was on the air from New York was the thing that impressed me.

A Listener

My mother bought our first radio during the Depression. We were living in the Ottawa Valley. Money was very scarce but somehow she found the two dollars down and two dollars a month. When dad came home and found out what she had contracted for he was furious. Where was this two dollars a month going to come from? But he soon found out that what it gave us—that connection with the outside world—was worth it. That first radio was a second-hand floor model—quite a big radio—either an R.C.A. or a Phillips. I'm not quite sure. It was quite a thrill for all of us when we heard our very first programme—"Major Bowes Amateur Hour." Then of course, there was "Amos 'n' Andy." On Saturday nights the whole family would gather around to listen to Foster Hewitt's hockey broadcast and the big barn dance programme, which came from Nashville. That radio made us feel part of what was going on. My father never complained again about the two dollars a month.

Bill Baker

Until 1936, CFRB did most of the big shows in Canada.

When I was at Riverdale Collegiate in 1924 I flunked my second year because my only real interest was radio. So I went to work for the Independent Telephone Company, which was making radios. The next year Rogers' Batteryless bought them out and began making radios on a larger scale. The batteryless radio made an amazing difference; its quality was so much better. Then we bought the rights for the American company which made Majestic and we bought out Deforest, so we made Rogers Majestic *and* Rogers Batteryless. The name of the company became Standard Radio.

CFRB started on February 19, 1927. I remember the first broadcast as if it were yesterday. We made it from the Uptown Theatre. We had about forty artists on the show and it lasted for three hours. All the top soloists in the city performed. I have the script of our first broadcast. It was handwritten by Charles Shearer, who was our manager for years. Standard Radio had to sell radio sets and CFRB programmes were done to sell them.

In the early days advertisers got call letters too. Carnation Milk used the letters CKOW, for example. CFRB, Rogers' Batteryless, were on the same channel as CKGW, the Gooderham and Worts liquor distillers station. Sometimes we'd finish our part of the broadcast and sign off and an advertiser would frantically call, saying that their transmitter wasn't working and could they feed their stuff to us. So we'd stay on the air for them. In those days there was a great deal of co-operation.

Until 1936, CFRB did most of the big shows in Canada. We had "The CN Hour," which broadcast the Toronto Symphony, and we had Reginald Stewart and the "CIL Opera House of the Air." We also had "The Imperial Oil Hour;" they brought The London String Quartet over and a quartet from Russia. World famous people were on these shows. This was before the CBC was formed. And we broadcast the hockey games sponsored by General Motors. CFRB remained the key hockey station for twelve years because even after the CBC was established the sponsors stayed with us. Foster Hewitt was the commentator from the very beginning and he did a great job. Sometimes people who went to see a game were disappointed because they said his broadcasts were better than the real thing.

On Saturday nights we had a programme called "Around the Town," which included every dance band working in Toronto. We had studios set up in places such as The Royal York, The King Edward, Columbus Hall, The Embassy, The Old Mill, The Silver Slipper and The Palais Royale. The show would start with maybe Fred Cully and his Orchestra at The Royal York, who'd play two numbers and then we'd say, "I wonder what's going on at The King Edward?" Then we'd swing over there and on to the other hotels. That made quite a bit of complicated work for us. Another popular programme was Kay Stokes at The Uptown or the downtown Loews', where she would play the organ. We'd get letters from all over the world about her show. There was a time we even had a Wurlitzer in the studio, but nowadays we don't have a studio big enough. The studios then were much bigger because we had to have room for a full orchestra. Some of the other shows

THE ROGERS "BATTERYLESS" RADIO
is not only a Master Development
— it is a PROVEN SUCCESS !

No
"A" or "B"
Batteries

RADIO RECEIVING SETS

No
Aerial

"Just plug in - then tune in"

So great is the public interest in this newest advance in radio (the invention that utilizes electric current instead of storage batteries) that we have prepared a pamphlet explaining in the most simple manner the "WHY" of the Rogers Batteryless Set—how it operates and why its construction makes it so economical. Every intending owner of a radio set should get this pamphlet. Among other valuable information, this pamphlet tells why—

—the A/C Tubes in the Rogers Set have longer life than ordinary tubes in sets operated from batteries.

— why line voltage fluctuations cannot affect the operation of the Rogers.

— why the power required from your electric light system is less than the addition of a 60-watt lamp and the cost of current is less than 5c a week.

What About the Rogers Performance ?

As the pamphlet explains the "WHY" of the Rogers Set, these remarkable testimonials tell about its success in operation:

(a) A letter from the Maritime says: "While our local broadcasting station was operating, we picked up 25 other stations on loud speaker without any interference. One was CKCL, Toronto. The first time this year that this station has been heard here."

(b) A Government Engineer, after severe tests, states: "Without hesitation, I would recommend this apparatus to the most exacting radio enthusiast."

(c) "In August last, under worst atmospheric conditions, secured transcontinental stations seldom heard in summer."

(d) A dealer writes: "The elimination of battery and tube troubles is a blessing both to the public and dealer. We have had wonderful results in tone quality, volume and selectivity. I can furnish you with names of many customers who are great Rogers boosters."

This New Pamphlet Answers All Your
Questions ~~ Write for FREE Copy.

Whether you now own a radio set or not, you will want to read this specially prepared pamphlet, which covers in complete and concise terms every feature of this latest development in the science of radio reception. Write for your copy to-day. Address nearest distributor.

Rogers Radio Receiving Sets are manufactured under the DeForest Canadian Radio Patents, the E. S. Rogers Radio Patents, and the Canadian McCullough A/C Radio Patents by

STANDARD RADIO MANUFACTURING CORPORATION LIMITED, TORONTO
Owners of the De Forest Canadian Radio Patents.

DISTRIBUTORS –
Q..RS. Music Co. Canada, Ltd., 590 King St. West, Toronto -   - for Ontario and Quebec
Radio Corporation of Winnipeg Limited, 290 McDermott Ave., Winnipeg   - for Manitoba
Canada West Electric, Limited, Regina - - - - - for Saskatchewan and Alberta
Radio Corporation of Vancouver Limited, 605 Dunsmuir St., Vancouver - for British Columbia

Santa's radio programme, 1936.

Jack Frost Stand over closer to the microphone, Santa (Claus) so

all the boys and girls can hear you.

SANTA CLAUS: All right, Jack Frost! I'm so excited I don't know
what I'm doing! This is a surprise for jolly old
Santa Claus.

(GROUP SING - "FOR HE'S A JOLLY GOOD FELLOW")

...US: Hello, hello, hello, all my dear, little friends!
My dear, little girls and boys -- the little folk I
love so well! Imagine how surprised I was to know
you were waiting to hear me. Hello, hello again,
boys and girls! It's your own, jolliest, chuckling
friend, Santa Claus, talking to you again. Why, I've
waited a whole, long year...just think of THAT! But
just you wait till I get down to Eaton's Toyland with
all my grand, new Christmas toys. My, my! They're
better and better than ever. You never did see such
wonderful new toys...lots and lots of new ones that
you never saw before. Yes sir! My little gnome toy-
makers have been working like beavers, thinking up
brand new toys for you. (LAUGH) You didn't know
about my gnome thinkers, did you, boys and girls?
Well, I have six, bright little fellows, and all they
do is sit and think and think and THINK of just the
kind of toys that boys and girls will like best, and
...fter they think all about it, they tell the little
...nome workmen, and the gnome workmen make them just
...or you. (LAUGH) Oh, tickle my toes, but isn't that
...citing! And you should just see my toy workshops
...here at the North Pole! Why, in our very busiest
...ason, we use lots and lots of forest trees to make
...all the lovely sleds, and toy furniture for little
...ls' doll houses, and rocking horses, and building
...cks -- gracious me! -- and hundreds more special
...prises, too. And the forest gnomes worked night
...day cutting down all those trees, and little
...es tunneled below the ice and snow at the North
...to get to the deep mines to find the iron to
...shiny runners for all the sleighs, and for meccano

"Leaving the North Pole Ice Palace."

Characters:
Santa Claus
Radio Engineer
Jack Frost
Tito
Toyland Engineer
Eaton Beauty
Toyland Airman
Fairy Queen
Story Book Lady
Mrs. Santa
Safety Brigade Captain
Bandmaster
Creepy Old Weather Man
Bluffy Bluster the North Wind

Music: Chorus - "Jingle Bells"
Chorus - "For He's a Jolly Good Fellow"
Song - "Wouldn't You like to Peep in Santa's Workshop?"
Solo - "Little Toy Engine"
Lullaby Land"
Chorus - "Sing a Song of Toyland"
Chorus - March music.
Record - "Ho, Ho, Ho, Who Wouldn't Go?"
Song

ANNOUNCER: This is Station C.F.R.B. in Toronto, ~~Canada~~. Hello,
boys and girls! Do you know what night this is? Why,
it's almost as important as Christmas itself...it's the
very night when Santa Claus starts from his big Ice
Palace at the North Pole on his long journey down to
Eaton's big Toyland in Toronto and Hamilton, and the
Canadian Department Stores throughout Ontario. Yes sir,
that's what night it is, and all year, dear old Santa
Claus and his loyal friends (you remember lovely little
Eaton Beauty, and Jack Frost, and the Toyland Engineer,
and the Fairy Queen.....oh my, such a lot of special
"Christmas" friends).....well, they've been as busy as
can be up there at the North Pole, making thousands and
thousands of wonderful toys for you. Oh, just think
of it, boys and girls, to-night they start on their way
to bring them to you! Just wait till you see them all
bright and shiny and gay in Eaton's Toyland in the big
store in Toronto, and Eaton's in Hamilton, and all the
Canadian Department Stores throughout Ontario. Santa
hasn't started on his way yet. He's still up in his
Ice Palace at the North Pole, enjoying a big, farewell
party -- and we've made special arrangements to have him

that began on CFRB were "Take a Chance" and "Treasure Trail."

Remote broadcasts were especially hard because there were times when we didn't know if they could hear us back at the studio. I remember one day Foster Hewitt and I were at Varsity Stadium to do a college football game. It was a terrible day. I got all the equipment set up but I had no way to get in touch with the people back in the studio. I didn't see how Foster was going to be able to do a broadcast in all that rain, snow and wind, but we went ahead. When we got back to the studio the engineer on duty said, "What happened? We got you guys for a couple of minutes and then you conked out. There was no way of getting in touch with you, so we filled with music." That's the way things were then.

We always had 'star' personalities at CFRB, people like Jim Hunter, who was our top news man for years. You can't imagine the appeal he had. Everyone dropped what they were doing to listen to him read the news. And during the war there was an announcer called John Collingwood Reade, who was English. When news from the front seemed to indicate that Britain was finished, John would come on with his Churchillian voice and would say, "We're going to come through." Everyone could go to bed with an easy mind because we believed him.

And wonderful people like Claire Wallace started their careers in radio on CFRB. Claire did a column in the Toronto *Star* called "Over the Tea Cups" and we wanted her. She was loath to try broadcasting but we talked her into it. She knew how to write but she wasn't sure that she could project over a mike. For three months before she went on the air she came in every day and rehearsed as if she were actually broadcasting. She was a great broadcaster. Bert Pearl began with us. He came from Winnipeg with a show called "Crushy Swingers" sponsored by Orange Crush. Gordon Sinclair had a show called "Ontario Panorama." We would have an advance man go to a town and find six people worth talking to. Alan Savage would do three and Gordon would do three. People would crowd in to see the broadcast and some would be turned away. It was during this time that Sinclair got the idea of wearing colourful clothing. We used to set up at noon and go for a walk. In one town we came across a pair of pink trousers and a yellow hat and Gordon just had to have that outfit. He bought it and wore it up the main street. You can imagine the reaction he got.

When the Dionne Quintuplets were born, I went to Callander to install the equipment. We fed New York three five-minute shows a week by Doctor Dafoe right from his home. We left a fellow up there for two years and all he had to do was these three five-minute shows. The scripts were written in New York and Dafoe would change the odd word to make it sound more like he really spoke. The fellow we left up there was Dick McDougal, who later became host of the T.V. show "Tabloid."

I was in broadcasting for almost fifty years on the technical side and the programme side. But if you ask me the greatest thrill of all, I'd say it was the day I came from the factory to the station. How could one person be that lucky!

In one town we came across a pair of pink trousers and a yellow hat and Gordon just had to have that outfit. He bought it and wore it up the main street.

SANTA CLAUS
HAS PROMISED
THE MARCONI CQMPANY
that he will speak on
Christmas Eve by

Wireless Telephone

to every house within
200 miles of Montreal
equipped with a suitable
wireless receiver.

LET THE KIDDIES LISTEN

to his songs, rhymes and
stories. He will com-
mence promptly at 7.30
P.M., and will continue
until 8.30 P.M.

TUNE SHARPLY TO 1200 METRES

SCIENTIFIC EXPERIMENTER LIMITED
33 McGILL COLLEGE AVENUE

The Rogers Radio Broadcasting Company, C F R B

Pay homage to their most gracious Majesties,

King George Sixth

and

Queen Elizabeth

🍁 🍁 🍁 🍁

Long May They Reign

Radio advertising was influenced by the major radio broadcast of 1937, the coronation of King George the Sixth.

CORONATION ON C. B. C.

Canadian Broadcasting Corporation
May 12, 1937 CRCY

(All times given are Eastern Daylight Saving Time.)

A.M.	Program
5.00- 5.15	Carillon from Peace Tower, Ottawa. C.B.C.
5.15- 5.30	Commentary — from B.B.C.
5.30- 6.00	Their Majesties leave Buckingham Palace. B.B.C.
6.00- 8.40	The Coronation Service. B.B.C.
8.40- 9.15	Their Majesties leave Westminster Abbey. B.B.C.
9.15-10.10	The return procession at Constitution Hill. B.B.C.
10.10-10.20	Their Majesties return to Buckingham Palace. B.B.C.
10.20-10.30	Interlude — Bells from Christ Church Cathedral, Victoria. C.B.C.
10.30-11.00	Children's Chorus directed by Arthur Putland — from Fort William. C.B.C.
11.00-12.00	Songs of Empire — from Toronto. C.B.C.

P.M.	
12.00- 1.00	Fairy Coronation — Children's Play, from Vancouver. C.B.C.
1.00- 1.15	Premier Patullo officially welcoming first Canadian cruiser to B.C. waters from Vancouver. C.B.C.
1.15- 1.30	Ottawa Ladies' Choir: director, Wilfred Coulson, Ottawa. C.B.C.
1.30- 1.45	Canadian Press News Bulletin — from Toronto. C.B.C.
1.45- 2.00	Peter Dawson, Australian bass-baritone, from B.B.C.
2.00- 2.10	Royal Salute of twenty-one guns from Winnipeg. C.B.C.
2.10- 2.20	Message from His Excellency, Lord Tweedsmuir, Governor-General of Canada. C.B.C.
2.20- 3.00	The Empire's Homage. B.B.C. and C.B.C.
3.00- 3.10	His Majesty, King George VI. B.B.C.
3.10- 3.30	Army and Navy Veterans' Band; director, Eugene Hudson—from Winnipeg.
3.30- 5.45	Rebroadcast of the Coronation Service, Ottawa. C.B.C.
5.45- 6.00	Bruce Hutchison — comments on the Coronation—from London. B.B.C.
6.00- 6.45	The C.B.C. presents a British Radio Party — from New York. N.B.C.
6.45- 7.00	John Masefield, Poet Laureate—from London via N.B.C.
7.00- 7.30	Recital by Percy Grainger, the distinguished Australian pianist — from Montreal. C.B.C.
7.30- 7.45	Poems in Praise. Reading by Frank Willis, Halifax.
7.45- 8.00	Dr. Stanley Russell, Toronto. C.B.C.
8.00- 9.00	Operetta, Montreal. C.B.C. Countess Maritza.
9.00- 9.15	Beverly Baxter. B.B.C.
9.15- 9.30	London Scenes, Halifax.
10.00-10.50	Repeat of Empire Homage

Radio's Crowning Achievement

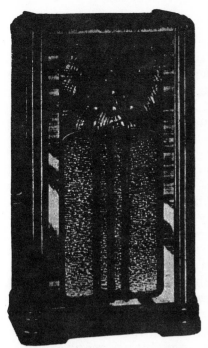

The "Buckingham" Model 721
A 7-tube A.C. Long and Short Wave Console of the highest quality. Tuning meter on Black Aeroplane lighted dial. **$109.95**

The "Edinburgh" Model 420
Battery-operated companion set to the Balmoral. **$39.95**

The "St. James" Model 520
A 5-tube A.C. Long and Short Wave Table Model of particular beauty, in the new modern style —Illuminated gold dial. **$49.25**

Northern Electric "Coronation Series"

The brilliant, new 1937-38 Northern Electric radio receivers—the Coronation Series—have been built with but one thought in mind: to make it possible for you to hear this—the greatest broadcast of all time—in all its beauty either through your local station or direct from London more economically than ever before. It has been our aim to establish entirely new standards of value in the low and medium priced fields. These sets have been designed and built by the organization that is "Supreme in Sound". They embody every worthwhile improvement yet developed. See your Northern Electric dealer now.

Northern Electric Company Limited

The "Windsor" Model 521
A 5-tube A.C. Long and Short Wave Console Model in beautiful colour and design, with Magna Dial tuning on 31 meter band. This model typifies the new trend in furniture. Illuminated gold dial. **$67.95**

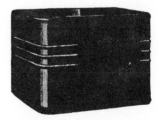

The "Glamis" Model 320
A 3-tube A.C. Standard Wave Personal Set in Black with Gold Trim. Edge lighted gold dial. **$24.45**

The "Balmoral" Model 422
A 4-tube A.C. Standard Wave Personal Set, with edge lighted gold dial. **$34.45**

Northern Electric RADIO

Foster Hewitt

I took an arts course at university because I wanted to go into the newspaper business. One summer I took a radio engineering course and even worked in a factory making radios. After university I tried selling radio equipment. But I could see that everybody was selling radios. Even grocery stores had them. So I decided to get out of that in a hurry.

I got a job at the Toronto *Star* just when they started their radio station, CFCA. There was no such thing as a job title then. Everyone did everything. I was the announcer, and did the news and the musical shows. I relieved the engineer on his day off.

After the first two or three years, we were on fairly consistently during the day and at night until about ten-thirty. Then, often we would pick up dance programmes from Chicago and run them until around twelve or one. We did the first hockey game in 1925 and from then on we did football and horse racing. We had the "Hour of Good Music" with Reginald Stewart, a well-known musician in the city. We also had a dance band.

CFCA closed in 1932. The *Star*'s original intention was to have the station as a novelty. It was something new and exciting. And the *Star* was great on promotion of that type. Nobody knew how long it would last. But it had only a limited life, according to Mr. Atkinson. When they put up a new building on King Street I designed the studios for a radio station on the seventeenth floor. But that never really came to light. At that point the *Star* got mixed up with the Ottawa *Citizen* in a discussion on the future of radio. The story I got was that the *Citizen* and the *Star* felt that radio was going to compete with newspapers and the best thing to do was get rid of it. The best way to do that, they felt, was to give back their licences. And they did that.

As I said, I started doing sports in 1925. My father was well known in sports, and I had always taken an active interest in it. So it was just a logical move. But I didn't want to go into the sports department of the *Star* because my father was the sports editor. So I went into radio at the *Star*. And I was a regular reporter as well. But I was taken off regular reporting after two or three years to do just radio.

The conditions for broadcasting sports weren't terrific. I had a piano box on the roof of Varsity Stadium with a heater in the back. It was very cold up there. The main thing was to try to protect the carbon mike from the wind, which made quite a roar. I used to have a blanket. And I'd pull it over me and I'd lie on the roof in the piano box and talk that way. Until one time there was a terrific gale blowing at Varsity, and the wind caught the box and lifted it off the end of the roof and onto Devonshire Place. Fortunately no one was hit. But that was the last time I ever had a box up there. We worked in the open from then on. But that was quite a scare.

I remember doing a game in Kingston. Queens and Varsity were playing at Richardson Stadium. We had to go up on the roof there too, but it was more difficult because you had to go up the outside of the wall on a ladder. To climb up there carrying our radio equipment was quite a trick. Another chap and I did it but we had to make about four trips. Then the roof had a strong slope

When they pulled on the wire to get me back up, I was frozen stuck. Finally, they got me loose, but I left the whole seat of my chinchilla coat on the roof.

to the front. The only way we could manage properly was that I had a wire wrapped under my arms, and my partner lowered me down until my feet were in the eavestrough. There was a flagpole in front of me and I had a box on which I put the microphone. It started out as a beautiful day. But then it started to rain. By half-time, it was freezing. Then the snow came. Of course, I had to stay put through the whole game. When it was over, I could hardly move, I was so cold and stiff. When they pulled on the wire to get me back up, I was frozen stuck. Finally, they got me loose, but I left the whole seat of my chinchilla coat on the roof. They pulled it right out.

There was no money paid to teams in those days. You simply got permission to do the games. Either they allowed you, or they didn't. It was publicity for them. We never really had any problems getting the rights to do games. I used to do the Argo games and nothing was paid to them. The only thing was, we could only do the games away from home so that we weren't hurting home attendance in any way. As for me, I was paid by the *Star* as an announcer, or, I should say, as a reporter. You didn't get extra money for doing radio work.

FOSTER HEWITT RETURNS FOR NEW HOCKEY SEASON

With his usual cheery greeting—"Hello Canada, and hockey fans in the United States and Newfoundland"—Foster Hewitt will inaugurate a new series of Saturday night hockey broadcasts on November 4, at 9.00 p.m.

These broadcasts, which will originate in the Maple Leaf Gardens, Toronto, will bring to listeners play-by-play accounts of all *Saturday* night home games of the Toronto Maple Leafs throughout the winter months.

Foster Hewitt is a veteran hockey announcer and his vivid commentaries during the past years have gained for him a host of admirers from coast-to-coast. Speaking from the gondola, high above the playing surface, Hewitt will call the play as the Maple Leafs meet the Boston Bruins in their first official National Hockey League game of this season.

Foster Hewitt broadcasting a baseball game from the roof of Maple Leaf Stadium, Toronto, in the mid-1920s.

GENERAL MOTORS
HOCKEY BROADCAST NEWS

PUBLISHED BY GENERAL MOTORS PRODUCTS OF CANADA, LIMITED, OSHAWA, ONT.—MAY, 1934

GM HOCKEY BROADCASTS HANG UP NEW HIGH MARKS IN QUALITY AND COVERAGE

Listening Audience Grows Thousands to Millions in Three Winters

33 STATIONS IN GROUP

More Games Carried Each Year More on National Network

Another season of General Motors Hockey Broadcasts has ended, setting up a record of more broadcasts, better broadcasts and a much wider coverage than ever before.

In November, 1931, General Motors went on the air with the first dressed hockey broadcast. It was carried by a small stations with a combined output of 600 watts.

On March 30th, this year, General Motors "signed off" its third season of hockey broadcast carried by 33 stations with a combined output of more than 40,000 watts.

The audience on the first broadcast was probably less than 100,000 listeners. On March 30th last, the Canadian audience alone was

FOSTER HEWITT

variously estimated all the way from 1,500,000 to 3,000,000—to say nothing of unknown hundreds of thousands (possibly even millions) of additional listeners in the dense populations south of the American border.

In broadcasting, as in everything else, General Motors has been operating with "an eye to the future —an ear to the ground." Or perhaps in this case it should be "with an ear to the sky." The progress has been steady, rather than rapid.

On the second game of the 1931-32 season, a 4,000-watt station was added. Later in the season, certain of the games were "piped" to Montreal, and broadcast over stations in that city.

Real Progress Began in 1932-33

The following season, all games of Montreal teams in Toronto were carried to Montreal. Early in January, 1933, in response to a persistent demand from dealers, a national network was added, bringing the total of stations in use on Saturday nights to 20.

Telephone tests made in various parts of Canada during February, 1933, showed an audience, on ordinary schedule games, of just under a million listeners. In the play-offs, of course, it was larger.

Network Continues to Grow

Last fall, General Motors began its first Quebec season, broadcasting the Saturday night games played in the Montreal Forum. A five-station Quebec network was hooked up for these broadcasts. Three French and three English announcers were engaged, Canadiens' games being broadcast in French, and Maroons' games entirely in English.

At the beginning of the 1933-34 season, the Quebec, Ontario and National networks totalled 24 stations. But still other districts wanted the broadcast. Wherever the requests seemed justified, and where the line costs were not prohibitive, new stations were added, until by the end of February, the three networks carried a total of 33 regular stations.

What the Stations Think

Radio stations know a good attraction when they hear it. Eleven Canadian Radio stations thought so highly of General Motors Hockey Broadcast, during the past winter, that they

51 Games Broadcast During Past Season

When the bell rang to end the final game of the National Hockey League championship series on March 30th, the curtain fell on the 51st General Motors Hockey Broadcast for the season 1933-34.

A total of 29 Maple Leaf games were broadcast in Ontario. Twenty-two of these were also carried through Western Canada to the Pacific Coast. Twenty-one were carried to the principal stations of the Maritime Provinces. Four of the Toronto games were broadcast over one or more stations in the Province of Quebec.

In addition, twenty-two home games of Canadiens and Maroons were carried over a Quebec network consisting normally of five stations. Ten of these were Canadiens' games—in French. Twelve were Maroons' games—in English.

Of the 51 games broadcast, 43 were schedule games and eight were play-offs.

Of the eight play-off games, three were carried on the national network; five were confined to Ontario or Quebec provincial networks.

offered their station time free if we would feed them the broadcasts.

On the last broadcast of the season, three new stations were added to the network. At the same time, however, three Quebec stations were dropped. Consequently, the total for the final game remained at 33 stations.

More Games Each Year

Meantime there has been a steady increase in the number of games broadcast.

In 1931-32 there were 30 broadcasts—all of Leaf games, three of these being away-from-home.

In 1932-33 there were 41 broadcasts, of which 40 were Leaf games, ten being away-from-home.

In 1933-34 there were 51 broadcasts, made up of 29 Leaf games, 10 Canadien games, and 12 Maroon games.

More National Broadcasts

Similarly, there has been an increase in the number of "national" broadcasts. In 1931-32 no games were broadcast nationally. In 1932-33 fourteen games were carried over the national network. In the season just ended, the total of national broadcasts was raised to 22. This, however, is about as high as it can go, as there are only 19 Saturdays in the regular schedule season.

When General Motors first went on the air with a full schedule of Toronto home games, this was an entirely new venture in broadcast advertising. But when the broadcasts proved their value in two successive seasons, and over a national network as well as in Ontario, they were no longer an experiment.

Montreal Likes to Listen

The company then turned its eyes to Montreal, a city long famous for its love of hockey. And last summer the Forum franchise was purchased.

Naturally there was much curiosity concerning the size of our new audience.

Consequently a telephone test was made in Montreal on February 3rd. Twelve girls with twelve telephones rang number after number in quick succession for the full hour-and-a-half of the broadcast. And this is what they learned: Of the people who were at home, and using their radio sets, 74 per cent. were listening to General Motors Hockey Broadcasts—only 26 per cent. to all other programmes combined!

Luigi Romanelli (left) and Bob McIntyre just leaving the studio after a rehearsal. From the expressions on their faces, the rehearsal must have gone rather badly that day

CRIPPLES, INVALIDS, ENJOY BROADCASTS

Deaf Men Among Our Listeners; Blind Men Watch Play; All Enthusiasts

Blind men who "see" the games with their ears—deaf men who "hear" the broadcast with their eyes—hopeless cripples, lying motionless on white hospital cots, who mentally hurl themselves into action beside Howie Morenz, Hooley Smith, or Chuck Conacher . . . These are some of the miracles of human resourcefulness in which all of us have had the good fortune to share through the medium of our Hockey Broadcasts.

The Most Grateful

In literally dozens of hospitals, and sanitariums, General Motors Hockey Broadcasts are followed with the keenest enjoyment by practically the entire body of patients. Testimonials have been received from such places bearing, in some cases, several hundred signatures. Individual letters arrive in almost every mail from invalids and cripples, or from their nurses or relatives.

From the tone of the letters, we can say quite definitely that the most enthusiastic and most

(Continued on Page 3)

RADIO SET IN HOME IS YOUR ADVANTAGE

Three Listeners In Every Four Enjoy Saturday Evening Hockey Broadcast

3-TO-1 "EDGE" FOR YOU

Majority Not Sport Followers But Look on Hockey as Gripping Drama

If you're hunting for prospects whose goodwill has been won by our hockey broadcasts, you don't need to confine yourself to the regular sport fans.

Some of the most grateful members of our audience are people who have never seen a game of hockey in their lives. How do we know? . . . Because they've written to tell us.

Thousands of such people have written; and for every one who writes there are dozens who don't—folks who have never seen hockey, but who never miss our broadcast.

When these letters first began to come in, two years ago, we couldn't figure it out. It didn't add up to make sense that anyone would bother listening if they didn't know the game.

Do You "Throw" Forward Pass?

Some of these writers wanted to know whether the "blue lines" are hurdles that had to be jumped —whether a puck looks anything like a basketball—whether hockey sticks resemble baseball bats or tennis racquets—whether a forward pass is thrown by hand. We heard of missionary meetings and lodge meetings breaking up early so that members could get home in time for the broadcast. Most amazing of all—listeners who had been blind from birth seemed to be among our most enthusiastic fans.

It was all very puzzling. We hardly knew how much of it to believe.

Then a radio man provided the answer.

"They're not sporting fans," he told us. "They're drama fans. Radio drama has a big following—but where can you get a thrill out of Fu Manchu to compare with the thrill that lifts you off your seat in a close game when the winning goal is poked in?"

That seems to be the explanation.

In any event, telephone tests have shown us that three out of every four listeners are tuned in on General Motors Hockey Broadcasts—any night we're on the air.

Three to One in Your Favor

That means that when you see a radio in a prospect's home the chances are 3 to 1 that the family listens more or less frequently to our broadcasts—3 to 1 that there's some feeling of gratitude toward General Motors dealers and salesmen for helping to sponsor this thrilling

(Continued on Page 2)

This Is Important!

Turn to the editorial at the top of page 2.

The Editor has a special message for you—and a special question to ask you. They are both important.

Please!—before you lay this aside, take your pen and some paper . . . answer his question frankly . . . answer it as fully as you can . . . and answer it RIGHT NOW.

It is highly necessary to have the answer to this question at the earliest possible moment. It is necessary—in YOUR interest.

You are the only man who can give us the answer so far as your territory is concerned.

So please turn to the editorial on page 2. It is really important.

Foster Hewitt broadcasting a hockey game. 1920s.

A Listener

In 1921 all the boys on my street were making crystal sets. We got the parts together—some from the store, and some from the kitchen. There'd be a round salt box, a bar for a slider, a piece of crystal and a wire we'd call a tickler. You'd adjust the bar on the slider and you'd use the tickler to scratch the crystal. All I needed after that was the earphones and when I asked my father for the five dollars to buy them, he was a bit doubtful. Anyway I persuaded him and finally got an aerial up on the roof and into my bedroom where the set was. When I called my father and he put the earphones on, the first words he heard were, "This is CFCA, the Daily Star, Toronto, Canada." He slapped his knee and just couldn't believe it. From there on, he was as big a fan as I was.

A Listener

I remember a famous hockey match in the 1930s when overtime ran into the early hours of the morning. My father was listening and at the crucial moment our radio went off. Looking out the window and seeing our neighbour's lights on, Dad grabbed his coat and tore up the road to hear the rest of the game. On nights when the Leafs were losing my father would relieve his annoyance by stoking the box stove. One night when the Leafs were getting a really bad pasting, an uncle called to ask if our house was on fire.

One night when the Leafs were getting a really bad pasting, an uncle called to ask if our house was on fire.

S.M.S.

Model No. 409.—Renaissance
Design, made in Gumwood,
finished Walnut. Equipped with
Radiola III-A Receiver, $175.00.
Other models from $60.00 to
$425.00.

SmS
RADIO
CABINETS

MANUFACTURED BY
THE STRATHROY FURNITURE
COMPANY LIMITED.
STRATHROY, ONT.

The RADIO BEAUTIFUL

RADIO outfits in the early days of its use, were in-efficient, unsightly, expensive, and unsatisfactory.

To-day, you can have your first experience with radio in your own home under very different conditions.

An S.M.S. Radio Cabinet equipped with Westinghouse apparatus, gives you the utmost in reproduction quality and handsome appearance.

Every day you are without radio is a day lost in joining the millions who nightly listen to the finest possible pro-grammes of music, song, story, plays, lectures, sports, market information and world events.

Write us direct if your dealer cannot supply you.

This Horn is Exclusive in S. M. S. Cabinets

NOTE.—S.M.S. Cabinets are the only ones in
which you can obtain Westinghouse equipment,
the Baldwin Concert Grand Loud Speaker unit
and our own specially-designed wood-fibre horn.

The STRATHROY FURNITURE CO. Ltd.
STRATHROY - ONTARIO

Jane Gray

I became interested and involved in radio in 1924, the year my last baby was born. My husband bought me a radio and that was fine, except there was nothing to listen to except static and a bunch of stuff that couldn't be heard. I told my husband I couldn't be bothered with that 'thing' and that the only thing I'd found out was that there were no women broadcasters. He said, "Thank God for that."

The London station was being run at that time by the London *Free Press*. I got a neighbour to look after the children and I made my way down to see the manager of the station to ask for a job. On my way there I met our minister and told him of my plan. He said, "Go back and look after your bairns. They won't give you a job. You lisp and you have an English accent." I thanked him for his advice and kept on going. When I got to the station the man asked me what I could do. I told him I'd been trained for the stage, but that what concerned me was that there were no women on the air and I wanted to do something about that. He looked at me as if I had said a dirty word and said, "Women on the air!? There never will be either by the grace of God!" I asked him if he would at least test my voice and explained what I could do. I figured I knew what people liked to hear and if I could get a chance, they wouldn't be sorry.

I was put in a room which was draped in black and a voice came from nowhere commanding me to "Say something." I suddenly remembered a schmaltzy poem titled "It Takes A Heap of Living to Make A House A Home" by Edgar Guest, a popular poet of the time. I recited and the manager came in and said, "You know, I can't figure out what it is, but you have something. You lisp and you have an English accent, but I like the way you did that poem." I said I had lots of poems and he said, "OK, let's try some poetry with an organ background." And that's what we did. I didn't get paid for it and it actually cost me money. It was a nickel then to use a pay telephone and I spent a dollar and a half phoning all my friends to listen in. Then I spent another dollar

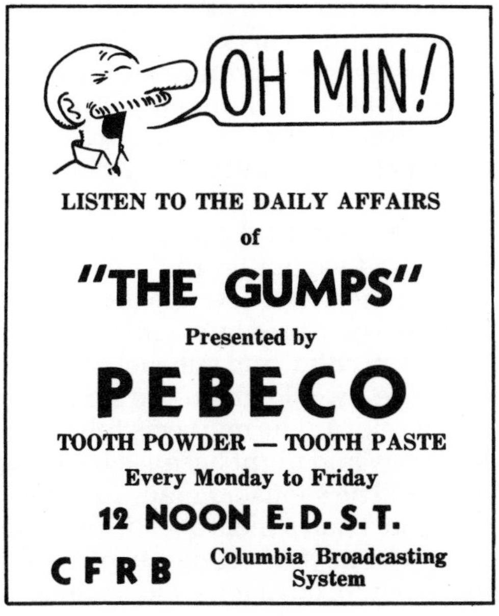

I told my husband...the only thing I'd found out was that there were no women broadcasters. He said, "Thank God for that."

OH MIN!

LISTEN TO THE DAILY AFFAIRS
of
"THE GUMPS"
Presented by
PEBECO
TOOTH POWDER — TOOTH PASTE
Every Monday to Friday
12 NOON E. D. S. T.
CFRB   Columbia Broadcasting System

and a half phoning them back to find none of them had heard me. It's not very auspicious but that's the way I got started.

When we moved to Toronto in 1928 I began looking around for radio work and was told there were going to be auditions at CFRB for a woman to do a cooking programme. Now that's a far cry from poetry reading but I thought I'd give it a whirl. Next morning I walked into the station to find all these women there ahead of me. But not one of them was an actress. The reason was that in those days radio was considered beneath an actress's dignity. Radio was just a dirty word. I considered myself an actress too, but radio didn't bother me.

Ninety other women tried out for the job and we all had to do something. I did my schmaltzy poem again and when the auditions were over the man who'd conducted them spoke to each of the contestants. Their voices were too high or too strident or something. Then he came to me and said, "You have an English accent and you roll your Rs, but you've got something." They offered me twenty-five dollars a week which was fabulous. Men at that time were only getting fifteen dollars a week at Eaton's. I was all set to accept the offer, when one of the salesmen slipped over and said, "Look, you can make more than that." He said I should buy a half-hour of time from the station and go out and sell the spots myself. He kept talking and finally I agreed.

I went back and told the sales manager and he said I was crazy since that half-hour would cost me twenty-eight dollars—in advance. I wasn't deterred. The salesman was waiting when I came out. He told me to go to my butcher, my baker, my dry-cleaner, anybody I could think of and offer them a spot at a low price—something like three dollars. He said I could always raise my prices later. I followed his advice and sold enough spots to fill the half-hour for the first week. I either made three dollars or lost three dollars; I'm not sure.

But when I went back to the station to buy another half-hour, they said, "Sorry. If you can sell time in that slot our salesman should be able to do it too." They wouldn't sell me the time. They offered me a job as a salesman instead. I said "No thanks." I swallowed this and moved on to other stations and other places but that was the low point in my career. I don't know that I was *the first* woman on the air in Canada but I was one of the first. I know that I'd already been working for years when Kate Aitken and Claire Wallace came on the scene and became the best known of women broadcasters nationally. They did a lot to prove that women had a place in broadcasting.

As for me, I've done it all. I had a drama group called the Jane Gray Players and we put on radio plays, most of which I wrote myself. One time I was even passed off as the Indian princess Mus-Kee-Kee sponsored by a 'real Indian medicine' made of seneca root, pine needles and alcohol. A lot of alcohol. As Princess Mus-Kee-Kee I would go on the air and solve the problems of those who wrote in. The mail was fabulous. I had to wear an Indian costume day and night because I was supposed to be a real Indian Princess. The sponsors made me move into the Ford Hotel in Toronto where I had a nice room at ten dollars a week and was warned never to let anyone see me out of my Indian costume. One did *anything* in those days for a programme.

Listen to Kate - Thousands do!

Kate Aitken HAS MOVED TO 1010 ON YOUR DIAL!

Now 50,000 watts — a new high in good listening!

1010

YES, Kate Aitken, and all your favourite CFRB programs and favourite radio personalities, have moved to *1010 on your radio dial!* There you hear them over CFRB's powerful new 50,000-watt transmitter . . . a new high in good listening! Listen to Kate every morning at 9.15 a.m. on CFRB! Follow *all* your radio favourites to 1010 on your dial—CFRB!

Follow your favourites to 1010 on your dial CFRB

HYDRO IS YOURS...USE IT!

YOUR RADIO DEPENDS ON HYDRO!

When you tune in your radio, you do not hear the sound of rushing water . . . yet far away . . . perhaps hundreds of miles . . . Hydro power is being generated. It is this power that enables the radio studio to fill the air with the finest the entertainment field affords, and this same power permits your radio set to efficiently transform these studio transmitted programs into enjoyment for the entire family.

As you sit in the comfort of your home it is well to consider that hundreds of trained Hydro men are working—watching, day and night, to ensure that nothing will interfere with the continued enjoyment and pleasure you obtain from your radio.

Radio is just one of many services made possible by your Hydro which has made, and is making, life more enjoyable for yourself and family.

The
HYDRO ELECTRIC POWER COMMISSION
of Ontario

G. Lovatt

I sort of slid into radio. A group of us had a little orchestra which played on all the early Toronto stations. Just for the fun of it, of course, because there was no money involved. Marconi's station was first, and then came others like Gooderham and Worts, and the Metropolitan Motors on King Street. They had a radio station on the second floor and an automobile showroom on the main floor. They'd set the orchestra up with one of the telephone microphones with a little cardboard horn stuck on it, and that was it. I remember one night when we got a phone call from Port Credit, which was ten miles away, and we just thought that was marvellous. To think that we were going all the way from Toronto to Port Credit.

In about 1929 I began to do remote broadcasts for CFRB and we would get two dollars a broadcast and two car tickets. Our equipment was all delivered and picked up, so all we had to do was go to the place and come back. We broadcast all of the dance bands around the city, from the Silver Slipper and The Embassy, for example. And we had all sorts of church services too. Finally I was taken on at CFRB as a permanent employee.

At that time CFRB was interested in doing some recording, and there wasn't any equipment available for it. I had a lathe and all that sort of thing and I said I'd try to build something. And I did. An advertising agency came over, made a few tests on my equipment and we recorded for them. We made a whole pile of soft discs that went all over the country. CFRB was into the business then. Later, commercial equipment became available on the market for this sort of thing. But I built CFRB's first recording machine. Discs were made of lacquer, with a lot of plasticizer in it, and they were on an aluminum base. When talk of the war became rampant they went to glass. The glass discs were all right, but were pretty breakable and hard to handle. As long as you didn't skip the playback needle across them you were fine. You could get quite a number of playings out of them. Still later, we had recordings pressed by a company in Montreal.

I was always on the technical side and a lot of funny things happened. One day I was on a remote down at the King Edward Hotel. They had about 120 stations on that hook up from the Crystal Ballroom. Romanelli's Orchestra played for these shows. Andrew Allan was the announcer. Andrew had been sitting with some of the people at one of the tables in the room. It was close to the microphone, and they were having a good time and maybe a little too much to drink. Anyway, Andrew went up to the mike and signed the show off five minutes early. The wires were buzzing. I told Romanelli, "Keep the theme going, no matter what." We had to have the theme over and over for five minutes. As you can imagine, we had a big meeting about *that* the next morning.

It was a big honour to appear on radio in those years, and sometimes when someone was on it was hard to get them off. I remember a woman named Ann Adams who had a cooking school. She would always run over. She just wouldn't get off the air. Many a time we had to put the theme record on and close her off in midstream. Would she be mad! But then, everybody tried to chisel an extra minute or two.

If Dad came in he'd raise a row.
He'd warm their little seats, and howl
They'll take the chance and hear
   the game--
Their old man's doing just the same.

It's "Hockey Night", and far and
   wide,
In city, town and countryside,
Both young and old, as you can see,
Are tuned in to CFRB.

860 KC   CFRB   TORONTO
10.000 WATTS OF SELLING POWER!

She thought that all the broadcasters were talking to her personally and were really visitors in her home.

Yes, you now hear Jim Hunter with his hot-off-the-wires news at *1010 on your radio dial!* At 8:00 a.m. and 6:30 p.m. Monday thru' Saturday, Jim brings you the latest news over CFRB's powerful new 50,000-watt transmitter! Listen to him today on CFRB. Follow *all* your radio favourites to 1010 on your dial—CFRB!

Now 50,000 watts — a new high in good listening!

1010

Follow your favourites to 1010 on your dial CFRB

A Listener

My grandmother, who was in her late seventies or early eighties at the time of early radio, never quite understood it. She thought that all the broadcasters were talking to *her* personally and were really visitors in her home. Jim Hunter of CFRB was her great favourite. One day the housekeeper, who was probably having a bad day, walked over to the radio and flipped the off switch while Jim Hunter was talking. Grandma was not as upset by the interruption as she was by the discourtesy to Mr. Hunter. When relating this incident she would exclaim: "Annie turned it right off in his face!"

Cy Strange

When I was about eight in 1922 we lived in the country about twenty-five miles from London and there was a man near where we lived who had a battery radio. I remember going over to his house and hearing all sorts of squeaks and squawks and occasionally a burst of music. I was so fascinated that my brother and I built little crystal sets using the round box Quaker Oats came in. You'd wind very fine wire all around it and mount it on a board. Sifto Salt boxes were also used.

It wasn't long after this that we got a real radio, an Atwater-Kent. The first station we heard was WWJ Detroit but it didn't take long before stations were going on the air by the dozen and you could pick them up all over the place. But we still got a great deal of noise. The most important thing in those days was an outside aerial, which was simply a wire attached to the radio and strung from the chimney to a tree, or across the top of the house. Reception in summer was bad, so most of your listening was done in winter when you had to really work for your listening pleasure—keeping the batteries up, scraping the ice off the aerial, and so on. Radios had to be grounded too, in case of an electrical storm. I remember one time my father coming home with a long coil spring, which he strung from one corner of the room to the other. An indoor aerial, would you believe, and the music came in just as good as it did with the outside one.

I liked music and as I got older I sang as a means of making a bit of money. I played banjo and guitar. Some of the shows where I sang with a band were broadcast locally. I thought I'd like to get into announcing. I auditioned for anyone I could get to. I knew I wanted to be in radio. Eventually I auditioned for Roy Thomson and Jack Kent Cooke, who had stations in northern Ontario. By gosh, they hired me and I was sent to Timmins in the autumn of 1940. I was there for about a year at CKGB. Also on the staff at that time were Gordon Keeble and Vic Copps, who also wrote sports for the Timmins *Daily Press*. Dennis Braithwaite was another who did broadcasting as well as writing for the paper.

When Jack Kent Cooke made the rounds of his stations we would all get geared up to approach him for money, but he was the world's greatest salesman. I went into his office one day to ask for a raise and I came out walking ten feet off the ground. I'd been promoted. It took three days to realize I had a title, three times as much work to do and not one more cent. But he made me feel good! You hear all sorts of stories about Jack Kent Cooke and Roy

Thomson and of how tight and mean they were to their staffs. That's simply not true. They were two very hard-working men who devoted every waking hour to the success of their stations and newspapers. Roy Thomson was not a very exciting personality, but in his own quiet way he could inspire you. If we were short of staff he'd be there, doing station breaks, news and weather forecasts.

Thomson and Cooke along with the Davies family later opened CHEX in Peterborough and CKWS in Kingston. I was transferred to Kingston for about a year and then I joined CFRB in 1943. Radio was well established by this time. Stations were being programmed by libraries like Thesaurus, Transworld and Standard, which were transcription services. They would send a sixteen-inch disc with six or seven cuts on each side of the Mills Brothers, for instance. Every month there'd be a new issue, scripted and timed.

Back then we were more than just announcers. At CFRB the salesman would go out and sell a series of spots and if I was announcing it, I had to write the commercials. Then the salesman would take your copy back to the merchant for approval. If he didn't approve you'd have to rewrite it. Then you would deliver the copy on the air yourself. You could also pick the music and figure out the theme. Immediately after that you might do a newscast or a sportscast. In the morning if the minister didn't show up you would do devotions as well.

The people that made money were the salesmen. The station depended on what they brought in locally. But all the stations across the country also had national 'reps.' They'd go to advertising agencies and sing the praises of various local stations and the benefits that could be derived for Lever Brothers, etc., in using these stations to advertise. Locally the salesman were out constantly, talking to local merchants, pushing the benefits of advertising on their station. The sales people and the announcers would get together every so often and the salesman would say he thought he could get a certain businessman to advertise if we could come up with a programme of sports stories, say. So we'd work and work and put a package together and get the businessman up to the station to listen. Or we'd have contests or little giveaways or have a lucky letter chosen.

The soaps in the afternoons were a tremendously popular brand of programming. "Big Sister," "The Romance of Helen Trent," "Ma Perkins." They were all produced in advertising agencies and sold to people like Lever Brothers or Ogilvie Flour Mills. All the soap operas, with the exception of three or four done during the war, were produced by the agencies. "Soldier's Wife" was written and produced at CFRB and there were a couple of other local shows, but all the rest came from New York or Chicago daily, and live. I was the announcer on "Lucy Linton's Stories From Life" and I was known as Sonny. The reason was that the sponsor was Sunlight Soap. The thing necessary for that stint was boyish enthusiasm, as all the commercials were done in Aunt Lucy's kitchen in a typical small town. Sonny Rogers, the boy next door, was always in and out looking for some of her cakes and cookies. It was simple-minded, but we sold Sunlight Soap like you wouldn't believe.

Cy Strange and Kate Aitken.

Time now for "The Romance of Helen Trent"…the real-life drama of Helen Trent, who—when life mocks her, breaks her hopes, dashes her against the rocks of despair—fights back bravely, successfully, to prove what so many women long to prove in their own lives: that because a woman is thirty-five, and more, romance in life need not be over; that the romance of youth can extend into middle life, and even beyond…

There was one soap opera which was broadcast live from CBC Toronto every day, five days a week. It was "Brave Voyage" and starred Beth Locherbie and John Scott. It was sponsored by Rinso. I was the producer. The budget was pretty rigid so that you could have the principal performer on for five days a week, but the next principal would be on only four and a half days a week and the lesser performers were on maybe one day a week. This meant that the script had to be written so that your talent budget would not exceed X number of dollars, which meant they would write an actor into the show for so many weeks and then have him take a trip somewhere for two or three months. The cheques for all of those people came from the advertiser. We performed at CBC but were hired by the agency, which paid the Corporation for studio facilities, the use of the Hammond organ, and so on.

I worked at just about everything in those days and for a time I owned a company that produced programmes and spots. But all the time I was doing these other things, I was still doing a great deal of commercial announcing. Each audition you won was a small triumph. There were 'cattle calls' at which dozens of people would audition for the same commercial. One of the programmes I was chosen for was with Kate Aitken, who was an institution across the country. Horace Lapp played the organ and Kate and I did the talking.

Funny things happened. One time up in Kirkland Lake there was an announcer who was a fun kind of character. He was the sort of fellow who, instead of reading the temperature, would throw open the window and holler to someone on the street, "How cold is it out there?" Someone would answer, "Jeez, it's really cold." The announcer would come back on the air and say, "A guy down there says, 'Jeez, it's cold.'" Or he'd ask someone what time they had and they'd answer, "The same time you have." He'd tell his listeners, "The time now is the same time you have." Just before the "National News" with Lorne Greene the local stations had a thirty-second spot. That was prime time. You couldn't sell the news, but you could sell the adjacent times. A merchant in Kirkland Lake who owned a men's wear shop called Seymour's Men's Wear had that spot and his advertisement always ended with, "If Seymour's clothes don't fit, Seymour won't let you wear them." Then the "National News" would come on. Well, one night this chap had had it up to here with the station and with Seymour and he said, "Remember, if Seymour's clothes don't fit, Seymour doesn't give a shit. And," he continued, "neither do I." He had joined the army. With that he walked out of the station, went to Toronto with the Queen's Own Rifles, and eventually wound up as a prisoner of war. Jack Kent Cooke said at the time, "I hope the Germans shoot him, because if they don't, I will."

Another time I was with CFRB. Jack Dennett was there too. Jack was one of the best broadcasters this country ever had. Anyway, I did commercials on his newscast quite often. Sometimes after I'd finished the opening commercial I'd turn my mike off before he turned his on, and in that brief second, he'd say, "Would you get me the weather, Cy?" I would get him the weather, but really, it was his job to get it. So one hot evening in August I went through the file of weather forecasts and dug out one he'd read the previous January. He always finished the news with,

"Remember, if Seymour's clothes don't fit, Seymour doesn't give a shit. And," he continued, "neither do I."

"After this brief word from our sponsor, I'll return with the weather." Usually I handed him the weather at that point so he had a chance to look it over while I did the commercial. But this particular time I held it back and when I was finished I plunked it in front of him and he read it. He didn't know what to make of it because it was full of talk about snowstorms and zero temperatures. He never asked me to get the weather for him again.

One time John Collingwood Reade was doing the news. Hugh Bartlett was the commercial announcer. When John was away, Hugh filled-in and read the news. There was a big desk in the studio at CFRB. Hugh didn't usually have much time to get the news ready. It was typed on flimsy sheets, and Hugh, as he was wont to do, was into the sauce a bit. I read the opening commercial and went out of the studio to chat with the operator. All of a sudden we noticed there was no sound coming out of the studio. We looked in and there was no announcer. What had happened was that the piece of paper Hugh was reading had slipped out of his fingers and had floated under this big desk. He had gone under to retrieve it and couldn't quite make it back up. His head was thumping the bottom of the desk. It was a while before he got himself reorganized. In the meantime, the operator put on a record. It was very funny.

1945.

Toronto's New Station

CHUM

is on the air!

Toronto's new Radio Station — CHUM — hit the airwaves on Sunday, October 28th and instantly made a host of friends in the Toronto listening area.

Here is why you should spot time on CHUM for your clients — CHUM is predestined to make and hold its audience because of the tried-and-true program policy of giving listeners the programs they want and the variety they want. CHUM will hold its advertisers because it individualizes and personalizes every show and because of the merchandising aid it offers.

Latest Western Electric equipment ensures a blanket coverage of the entire Toronto trading area.

1000 WATTS   CHUM   *The Friendly Station*   1050 on the dial

YORK BROADCASTERS LIMITED — 21 DUNDAS SQUARE
TORONTO

Representatives: Radio Representatives Limited — Montreal
Adam J. Young Jr., Inc., New York, Chicago

THE BEST RADIO BOOKS

Radio has come into its own—to-day it speaks and sings, entertains and educates—and all as free as the air.

But the man who wants to take up Radio for the first time finds himself in a maze of technicalities, mathematical and electrical problems. To fill this need for Radio information, we recommend the following **selected** books by authorities on the subject:

THE HOME RADIO, How to Make and Use It

By A. HYATT VERRILL. With 60 Illustrations. Cloth, 85c.

Intended and designed particularly for the use of amateurs and those who wish to know how to make, use or adjust wireless-telephone instruments. Written in simply explanatory style, illustrated by diagrammatic figures. (Postage, 6c.)

RADIO FOR EVERYBODY

By AUSTIN C. LESCARBOURA, Managing Editor "Scientific American." 352 pages, 125 expanatory illustrations, and many clear diagrams. Cloth, $1.65.

An authoritative book on Radio, understandable to every amateur, written and backed by the authoritative reputation of "Scientific American." It takes the reader from the very beginning and goes step by step—with diagrams, illustrations and complete explanations—throughout Radio, from the aerial set-up to the final adjusting and listening in. (Postage, 10c.)

THE RADIO AMATEUR'S HAND BOOK

By A. FREDERICK COLLINS, Inventor of the Wireless Telephone. 320 pages, exceptionally well illustrated. Cloth, $1.65.

A complete, authentic and informative work on wireless telegraphy and telephony, written by the inventor of the Wireless Telephone. Fully illustrated with original drawings and diagrams made especially for this book. Gives the reader a complete grasp of this fascinating new science with a working knowledge of how to hook up and operate his own set. (Postage, 12c.)

THE MUSSON BOOK COMPANY, LTD.

Publishers   265 Adelaide St. West   TORONTO

Tom Darling

Mr. Thomson was driving to Toronto that day and when he heard me on the air he turned around and drove back to North Bay to get me off the air before I wrecked his station.

Eaton's Good Deed Club Observes Its Tenth Anniversary

Membership Has Grown to 75,000 During Years of Activity

In February, 1933, an idea was born—an idea that youngsters from six to 16 years of age should be given an opportunity to show their talents to the public, that some kind of club should be organized giving those with talent their opportunity and those without particular talents something worthwhile to strive for and enjoy. Thus the good deed idea was born in Hamilton, and the Good Deed Club launched.

To-day the Eaton Good Deed Club is recognized as the largest of its kind in Canada. Since its inception, the total club membership grew to 75,000; meaning that no less than 75,000 good deeds were performed during this time.

Every week a 15-jewel wrist watch is awarded for the best good deed of the week—as well as a gold star pin, which is the highest honour to be attained in the Eaton Good Deed Club. At the tenth birthday celebrations to-day, L.A.C. Brian Coleman, who won the first good deed award in 1933, will present the award for the best good deed this week.

The *Hamilton Spectator*, March 6, 1943. The "Good Deed Club" was a popular radio programme across the country.

In 1930 I was working at the Royal Bank in North Bay as a ledger keeper at a salary of sixty-six dollars a month. Roy Thomson owned a business in town, Northern Supplies Limited, and he was one of our customers. One day he came in and told me he'd received a licence to operate radio station CFCH in North Bay. He offered me a job at Northern Supplies at a salary of thirty-five dollars a week. He said the job might eventually lead to something in radio. I had no hesitation in accepting. After all, it was almost double the money I'd been making.

A couple of weeks after I started at Northern Supplies one of the announcers at the radio station got sick, so I volunteered to take his place on the morning programme. Mr. Thomson was driving to Toronto that day and when he heard *me* on the air he turned around and drove back to North Bay to get me off the air before I wrecked his station. He finished the shift himself.

Thomson was barely making ends meet at that time and he was working harder than anyone else at keeping things going. I got thirty-five dollars a week only the first week. The second week I got thirty dollars and by the third week my cheque was only twenty-five dollars. And I couldn't find Mr. Thomson anywhere to ask him what was going on. My salary kept going down at the rate of five dollars a week until I was getting nothing. That was the week the bailiff locked up Northern Supplies and most of the employees were let go.

Because I'd stayed until the bitter end Roy said, "Come over to the radio station and I'll give you a job there." It was a bitter time. Salaries ranged from eighteen dollars a week down to ten or twelve dollars and sometimes to nothing at all. But it was a job and I was lucky to have it.

The Thomson chain of stations gradually expanded to include Timmins and Kirkland Lake. I worked at both places during the ten or eleven years I was with Roy and I got the best training I could have got anywhere. You had to do every job that had to be done but you learned the business inside out. That little station in North Bay was the beginning of the Thomson empire which eventually embraced hundreds of newspapers all over the world plus radio and television stations. CFCH propelled Roy Thomson from an almost bankrupt in 1930 to the status of multi-millionaire and lord of the realm.

After working up north I moved to CHML Hamilton. All the live programming of those days was tremendous fun. We broadcast all the orchestras playing at local hotels like The Royal Connaught and the Alexandra Ballroom. We broadcast shows from The Brant Inn on Saturday nights and we did the Hamilton Concert Orchestra. We also did all kinds of small groups from around town, including a lot of country and western stuff. For one such programme, called "Main Street Jamboree," I picked a guy named Gordie Tapp. At first he didn't want it. Needless to say, he finally took it and created the "Cousin Clem" character. We put that show on in auditoriums all over Ontario. It made for great radio and it went on for years.

Ken Sobel, the man who later hired me at CHML, was indirectly involved in a terrible goof at Thomson's station in Timmins.

96

Our very first network show was to be "The Ken Sobel Amateur Hour," which originated in Toronto and was broadcast nationally. We were proud and excited that our station was being added to the network of stations across the country carrying it. Because it was our first crack at the network, we didn't want anything to go wrong. For weeks we kept ironing out the details. We spoke to the minister who was doing the church service that preceded the show and asked him to be sure to be off the air on time. We rehearsed our engineer and everyone else concerned to be sure that nothing went wrong. Finally the big day arrived. As the clock ticked towards twelve-twenty we could see that the minister was going to run overtime and that we'd have to pull the plug on him if we were going to join the network on time. At twelve-thirty, exactly, the announcer's voice from Toronto came on with the opening, "The Royal Canadian Tobacco Company…" (followed by an appropriate pause) and to our utter horror, the next thing we heard was a loud and clear "JESUS CHRIST" spoken by our minister. Our engineer—in spite of all our rehearsing—had forgotten to pull the plug. We were still connected up to the church. We had a lot of explaining to do.

…the Shadow Knows!!*

… and Gillies Coy. Limited, Hamilton's BLUE COAL Dealer knows too that HAMILTON is Canada's 4th largest market. To cover HAMILTON you need a Hamilton station

and **CKOC** is that Hamilton Station with Local and National Advertisers who want RESULTS in the Hamilton Market THE ALL CANADA STATION

*The Shadow—Sunday on CKOC at 9.00 p.m.

Radio test car for CKOC, Hamilton.
▼

Ramsay Lees

One of our salesmen got a brilliant idea. He went out and sold fifteen minutes of blank air to one of the lumber companies. We signed off so people could hear "Amos 'n' Andy."

I began in the late 1920s. I was in high school and the announcer at CHML in Hamilton wanted Saturday nights off and the station was looking for a substitute. I got the job. Then in the early thirties I went to CHML on a permanent basis. It didn't seem like work because it was so much fun.

There was a man in Toronto who played the piano very fast. He called himself "Flying Fingers Boyd." He was remarkably rapid, but he wasn't that accurate. We had a player piano in our studio and I found that by getting the lever that rewound the thing to about halfway, it would play at two or three times the average speed. One day we decided to have some fun. We announced that we had found competition for "Flying Fingers." We said we had the contender in our studio, that he wished to remain anonymous and that he would prove his ability here and now. So away went the player piano at three times normal speed. Poor old "Flying Fingers Boyd" was in the next studio just shaking his head saying, "It's impossible! It can't be done!"

When the big network shows in the U.S. began, our local audience went way down. There were complaints, too, that while CHML was on they couldn't get "Amos 'n' Andy" on WBEN Buffalo, a programme everyone wanted to hear. One of our salesmen got a brilliant idea. He went out and sold fifteen minutes of blank air to one of the lumber companies. We signed off so people could hear "Amos 'n' Andy." It was incredible how much good will that provided. And the lumber company thought it was great because it seemed as if *they* were sponsoring "Amos 'n' Andy." WBEN, you see, was 930 on the dial and we were at 900, but back then there was a thing called 'wandering' signals.

At first there were no professional radio writers. They were primarily newspapermen. A lot of mistakes were made because the material we were given was written by people who didn't know how to write copy that was to be read aloud. Many of these bloopers can't be repeated in polite company. For example, one of the announcers was given this to read, "These days when you sit shivering beside your radiator..." But that's not what came out of his mouth.

Henry Gooderham owned CKCL and he was a real gentleman. One night the phone rang while I was on duty. A man said, "What's that dreadful programme you have on now?" I said, "That's 'Old King Cole.'" "Well," he said, "I have heard some dreadful programmes in my time but that is one of the most asinine." I said, "It's for children, sir." He said, "I don't care what it's for. Between those screaming singers you have on at night and those gawdawful religious programmes, you're a disgrace. Who owns that station?" I said, "Henry Gooderham owns it." The caller said, "Well, I know Henry Gooderham and believe me, I'll tell him a thing or two." The next morning, I waited until I saw Henry and I told him of the caller. He said, "Did he sound as if he might have had an extra drink or two?" I said I hadn't noticed. Mr Gooderham said, "If he did, it might have been me." That's a true story.

Campbell Ritchie

I started as a singer at CKOC in Hamilton in 1934. My introduction to broadcasting was on a programme called "Eaton's Good Deed Club." Subsequently while still at school I became a part-time announcer and singer at CHML, which was then a little fifty-watt station. I hung around CHML until they got so tired of seeing me that they hired me.

In those days there was no place you could go to get any training. You just had to learn on the job. There were the two stations in Hamilton and each had its own audience. Ramsay Lees, the grandson of the jeweller who owned the station, was an announcer there. He gave me my first chance. A shift was usually four hours long and people must have gotten awfully tired of hearing the same voice between selections and programmes for that long.

In 1936 I went to CKLW in Windsor. I started as a singer but then one of the announcers left town in a hurry and they needed one fast so I became an announcer too. I went to Windsor to be there for a year or two but it wasn't until thirty-five years later that I finally left. I had to open the place up, announce, sing, act as control operator and manager—everything at the same time. In our spare time we were salesmen. You'd go out and sell spots and programmes. My first client was the Royal Oak Dairy. I sold them a half-hour programme of recorded concert singers. It cost something like ten or fifteen dollars for a half-hour. You sold it, wrote it and announced it.

When the war came along I joined up and eventually took over the Canadian Forces Network. In 1945 I came back to CKLW in Windsor and took up where I'd left off in 1939. For many years we had a staff orchestra of eleven or twelve men and we did one or two programmes a day using the orchestra. We also had a staff pianist and a staff organist. For musicians those were the good old days. The major show I sang on was "Quiet Sanctuary," a programme of inspirational words and music with organ accompaniment. That went on from 1936 to 1958 and the only reason it went off the air was because the organist died. Before I went overseas I recorded a lot of the hymns on glass transcriptions and these were played on "Quiet Sanctuary" while I was away. People were very loyal to their favourite programmes and performers in those days. Certain performers and programmes became habits that the audience didn't want to break.

I hung around CHML until they got so tired of seeing me that they hired me.

Amos: Andy, listen, the man is just about to say it!
Andy: Yeah, let's everybody listen.
Announcer: Rinso, the new Rinso with solium, brings you the Amos 'n' Andy show. Yes sir, Rinso, the soap that contains solium, the sunlight ingredient, brings you a full half-hour of entertainment with the Jubellairs, Jeff Alexander's orchestra and chorus and radio's all time favourites—Amos 'n' Andy.

"Tops in Canada"

A Listener

Remember Orson Welles's *War Of The Worlds?* That was in 1938. It started off very innocently, "The programme originally scheduled at this time is not available, and instead we take you to…" In a few minutes the programme was interrupted for a special news bulletin. Everyone knows what happened after that. I realized after the second or third 'newscast' that the whole thing was fictional. But I was amazed at the end of the broadcast when the announcer came on in a state of extreme agitation to say that it was only a play: "Don't call the police. Don't call the station." I would love to hear that announcer again. And they broke into several programmes later that evening trying to tell people it was only a play.

As Marshall McLuhan put it, Hitler then, "gave radio the Orson Welles treatment for real."

Hugh Bremner

I started at fifteen dollars a week as an announcer with CKPC in Brantford in 1936. Although I was hired as an announcer there was no such thing as that kind of specialization. Everybody pitched in and did what there was to do. For example, I was always expected to get in a half-hour or so before signing on in the morning to put a heater under the turntables. This was to soften up the grease that lubricated them so they would turn at the proper speed.

We did very little local news in those days. But eventually we made an arrangement with the Brantford *Expositor*. They sent over a fairly good summary of local news for the noon newscast. They would only do that after their paper was out safely on the streets. We did have wire stories but it used to come in on a long ribbon-like roll of paper. When it came time to do the sign on news at ten to eight in the morning, there'd be miles of this ribbon on the floor to go through. You were supposed to put it through a glass tube with water in it and over a little felt pad and stick it on a sheet of paper so it could be read normally. You could manage this if you had lots of time but most often you didn't. You'd go on the air reading straight off the ribbon, which you'd be pulling through your fingers. In the meantime you'd be going crazy as it would be tying itself in little knots. One of the things we did then was stand up at a lectern to read the news. I still believe that was a better way to do it as you can get much better projection.

We did all of our commercials 'live' and many of them were done with sound effects. I remember one we had for a coal dealer in Brantford which started off with the slogan, "Just another load of McDonald coal." The announcer would then pour a small bucket of coal down a tin chute into another bucket. He had to do this while he was reading.

All of us young fellows in the business kept looking around for heroes to imitate. That was the only way one could learn. I was always more interested in news than anything else and I made it a point to never miss Jim Hunter's newscast on CFRB from Toronto. He did the news with a dramatic style in a 'newspaper' kind of way because he was a newspaperman. He started his newscast with a hunting horn. Others I listened to were Kaltenborn and Lowell Thomas. They also had a unique style.

Radio people in those days, as they do now, have a tendency to move from station to another always looking for a better deal. But I stayed with CKPC from 1936 to 1954.

The announcer would then pour a small bucket of coal down a tin chute into another bucket. He had to do this while he was reading.

Stuart Clark

So few stations were on the air in those days that through 'skip waves' even a small station could be heard almost anywhere in the world.

Fibber McGee and Molly.

When I was growing up in Chatham in the 1920s radio was an exciting and mysterious thing and I can't remember a time when I wasn't involved with it. I was totally fascinated. I built crystal sets as a young boy. When I delivered papers to the building where Jack Beardall had his transmitter, I'd stand outside the window looking in at him working, thinking how much I'd like to get in there with him and get my hands on that transmitter. At the time I already had my own little transmitter but I didn't have my amateur licence. Jack was also the radio inspector for the area and one day I was summoned to his office and told that I was in for it.

On the day I was to appear, I put my transmitter in a bushel basket and carried it down there. He sat me down and we talked at great length about the technical aspects of radio and before I left I was offered a job. That's how I began working for him. Beardall was typical of the kind of people who got into radio in the beginning. They frequently had no technical training and radio was just a hobby. Jack, for example, was a butcher. He started this hobby in the early twenties and had broadcast regularly with no financial return because there were no commercials then. His first call letters were 10BT, a non-commercial broadcast station. But he applied for his commercial licence and started CFCO in 1927. Up to that time, he'd used money from his butcher shop to run the station.

In 1929, when I was fourteen, I got my amateur licence. I was the youngest amateur in Canada at the time. That entitled me to build and operate equipment for the amateur band. There was a tendency for radio stations to hire licenced amateurs because there wasn't a very big pool of technical talent anywhere else. After all, there were no schools. So the same year I got my licence, I went to work for Jack Beardall at CFCO Chatham.

In those days nearly all transmitters were homemade, and I built the one Jack used until 1948. There weren't many stations who could afford to walk into RCA or Western Electric to buy ready-made equipment. And even if they could, not many broadcasters were willing to invest heavily in equipment because radio was still a shaky proposition. The Depression didn't help.

That's why stations had so few staff. In Chatham there was only Jack Beardall and me. We shared both the operating and announcing functions and usually only one of us would be there at a time. But sometimes Jack would announce from the studio while I operated from the control room. I remember one time I threw the toggle switch the wrong way and instead of picking up what *Jack* was saying, the control room mike was picking up what *I* was saying. I was looking at Jack, who seemed to be talking, but I couldn't hear anything. So I yelled, "Come on, you so-and-so! Say something!" But it was no use, he couldn't hear me. I yelled even louder. Of course, when I realized that it was *my* mike that was on, I was horrified. I knew the listeners had heard everything I'd said. I never mentioned it to Jack and he never said a word about it either, although I'm sure he knew.

Radio stations then, as now, had assigned frequencies which they had to stick pretty close to. You weren't permitted to wander

"The Triolettes" performing on CRCW, Windsor. 1930s.

off more than seven cycles and you were monitored pretty closely by government inspectors to see that you did what you were supposed to be doing. When it was in the interests of the government, however, they made their own rules. At CFCO in 1930, for example, during the federal election, I got a call from the Windsor inspector who said that he wanted us to move our frequency for the night so the people of Windsor could hear the election results better. He told me to keep turning the frequency knob until he told me to stop. I did what I was told. Finally he said, "That's fine. Just leave it there for tonight." That sounds weird now, but those kinds of things happened then.

So few stations were on the air in those days that through 'skip waves,' late at night, even a small station could be heard almost anywhere in the world. CFCO could quite easily reach the west coast and when we put on a DX programme where listeners would write to say that they were hearing you, we got letters from Britain and other far-off countries.

When I moved on to CJGC, I continued to do everything including announcing. But I was no announcer. I remember getting a call one night from Harry Link, the station manager. He was very concerned with diction. He said, "Stuart, from now on you are to say 'Lundon,' not 'Lunnen.'" I'm afraid a lot of early announcers were like me—technicians who sometimes talked.

CFCO
CHATHAM ONT. *Offering*

CONTINUOUS PUBLIC
SERVICE
to a
WORTHWHILE
WESTERN ONTARIO
AUDIENCE

JOHN BEARDALL
MANAGER-OWNER
STUDIOS IN THE WM PITT HOTEL

SHORT-WAVE STATIONS RECEIVED

Date	Time	Call	Location	Frequency	Dial

Page 132

Heintzman Presents Two Aristocrats

NORGE
Rollator Refrigerator

All Porcelain - No Extra Cost

Porcelain! Gleaming radiant beauty that will never fade, discolor, scar, burn, tarnish or wear out! Such are the new 1937-38 Norge "all-Porcelain" Refrigerators. Outside as well as inside—top, sides and front—no paint, no lacquer, no varnish—but beautiful, sanitary, life-time porcelain.

While all good Refrigerators have a porcelain-lined food compartment, porcelain exterior has heretofore been available only at extra cost. Now, Norge offers this genuine expensive, exclusive, luxury-finish—AT NO EXTRA COST!

SEE THE NEW NORGE WITH ALL-PORCELAIN AND FAMOUS ROLLATOR AT HEINTZMAN'S.

ROGERS
RADIO
No Stoop Tuning

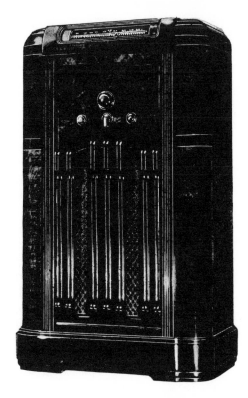

Here is the radio that made history—with the greatest advance yet made toward better, easier and more convenient tuning. With Rogers "No Stoop" Target Tuning, you can tune in your favourite program accurately and easily without squatting, squinting or stooping. Standing or sitting, young, old or near-sighted people can tune with the greatest simplicity—so easy to read is the Rogers Target Tuning Dial. Illustrated is Model 1175, an unusually striking cabinet design. It features "No Stoop" Tuning, 3-way bands, 8-tube performance from 7 tubes, 12" improved dynamic speaker, Chladni disc for eliminating cabinet "boom" and other features. The price is sensationally low—the value high. Only $129.95.

**SEE THE BEAUTIFUL ROGERS
WITH "NO STOOP" TUNING
AT**

HEINTZMAN & Co.
195 YONGE ST. - - TORONTO

Open Evenings   *Elgin 6201*

Guy Lombardo

Without a wire into a radio station, you couldn't make it into the 'big time.'

The big band sound can thank radio for its popularity. Both started about the same time and, without radio, the bands wouldn't have had the big audiences that they needed. We listened to them over the American stations that boomed into London, Ontario and they inspired us to try it ourselves. We were very lucky, and very proud of the fact that the nine of us who left London stayed together through all of those Depression years. We added a few more members, but the original nine, who had left London and gone to Cleveland and had a lot of success, stuck together, and after that we went on to New York and the Roosevelt Hotel.

I think, though, that the thing that gave us the idea that we might be able to get into the 'big time' was that we were hired to perform at Port Stanley in Ontario. Before this, they always hired a 'name' American band, but here we were, the first Canadian band to break through that barrier. That was in 1923, I think. I was only twenty years old at the time—the others were only fifteen or sixteen—and I believe we sold ourselves the idea that we were pretty good. We had no more right to think we were good than the man in the moon. We found that out when we got to Cleveland. The city was loaded with big bands! It seemed there was one on every street corner. We landed a job at the Claremont and that's what started the whole career. We were with a man who knew the band business, and the first thing he taught us was to play soft and to put in some harmony. Then he taught us the 'medley,' going from one song to another, and that became a big part of our style. The other thing that helped us was that we were on radio from the Claremont. People out there could hear us in their homes. They got to know our music and they got to know our names.

This went on for about a year and a half, and we decided to try Chicago. When we got there we found that nobody knew us. There was no network broadcasting in those days, so although radio had made us well known in Cleveland, we were unknowns in Chicago. There was a man who had a little café who had heard us and liked us when we were in Cleveland, and he thought we'd be right for him. He hired us, but we didn't even draw flies. Nobody came for four or five weeks. Finally, I said to the owner, "You'll just have to get a wire in here, or we'll have to pack it up and go back to Cleveland." He fought it, of course, but he finally gave in. He went to downtown Chicago, to all the radio stations, and eventually got WBBM to agree to come out and give us fifteen minutes of air time a night. That didn't sound like much because most bands were on for an hour. After all kinds of delays, they put those telephone lines in on the fifteenth of November, 1925. At nine p.m. we had all the waiters and staff gathered near the microphones to make noise, and I stepped up to the mike and announced, "Now, from the Granada Café, Guy Lombardo and his orchestra." We had these fellows applaud, and we did the first number. Before our fifteen minutes were up, the man who owned WBBM phoned and said, "Tell them to play all night." Well, we were delighted! We played until five to ten, took a five-minute break, and by midnight the café was crowded with people. We

The Guy Lombardo Band in the 1930s.

were just playing the way that we always did, but it was brand new to the people of Chicago. New tempos. New combinations of instruments. It was the radio that was doing it, bringing *our* sound to them for the first time. We were an overnight success, and from that moment on the Granada Café was crowded every night. A critic named Aston Stevens wrote a beautiful column about us in which he said, "Truly, the sweetest music this side of Heaven." We decided that was such a good phrase that we adopted it. That was how it all started. It was radio that did it for us and for the other big bands that made good. Without a wire into a radio station, you couldn't make it into the 'big time.' There were lots of really good bands playing all over the country, some of them better than the ones that made it; but they didn't have that *wire.*

Doc Cruikshank

Before the licence, I was calling the station JOKE because that's all it was to me up to this time—a private joke.

What a wonder radio was in those early days! There were few people who knew anything about it, and what they did know they gained from magazines like *Popular Mechanics*. One day back in 1921 I was leafing through a copy of *Popular Mechanics* in Wingham, Ontario when I saw a plan for a radio transmitter. I had heard about radio, but that's about all I knew about it at the time. Using my mother's fifteen-inch breadboard as a base, I got busy and built one. The trouble was that even though I had a transmitter to send sounds out, nobody had receivers to pick those sounds up. There were no radios available, so I had to make them myself if I was going to sell them. The first three or four I made I was able to sell in just a few minutes, and that gave me the idea. Why not represent some firm that manufactures radios? So I got a company in Hamilton that was making them to supply me with these receivers and I went out and sold them myself for one hour a day.

I could have sold a lot more of them if I had more time, but I didn't. You see, I worked in a foundry ten hours a day, seven days a week. And I ran the projector in the picture show for about four hours a night. There was one hour left over between seven and eight o'clock in the evening where I had nothing to do. That's when I sold radios.

Nobody worried too much about studios in those days. Just about any place at all would do to put on a programme. On Sunday we always did a service from one of the churches. At that time it meant we had to connect up all the churches in town with a telephone line. We got a lot of wire and strung it on top of buildings and everything else from the studio over to one of the churches. We did that for years before anyone thought there was any other way of doing it.

On Sunday after church service we had a little programme from my home. I'd carry the transmitter under my arm down to my house and we'd do an hour broadcast from there, a programme of music, hymns and that sort of thing with local people along to sing and play the piano. There was recorded music available, but it was of no use to me because I didn't have a turntable to play it on. I only had one microphone and everything was done through that.

We didn't even know that you had to have a licence for broadcasting. Somebody tipped me off that I had to have one and, by golly, I enquired and, sure enough, I was supposed to have a licence. It was very simple to get though. All I did was write a letter and pay ten dollars. Before all this business of the licence, I was calling the station JOKE because that's all it was to me up to this time—a private joke. And a lot of fun.

But you know, depending on atmospheric conditions, that little station with one tube was being heard, some nights, all around the world. Of course, that was before the airwaves were all cluttered up with hundreds of thousands of stations. When you got a good night, why, my goodness, the world wasn't big enough for you. Lots of other nights, though, we couldn't even get outside of town.

Up to this point I had been running the station with whatever little money I had to spare out of my own pocket. There were many times I became so discouraged about the station not bringing in money and taking so much of my time that I'd decide to quit—*today* would be the last day of broadcasting. Every time I'd say that somebody would come along and encourage me to keep it going and we'd try it again. One day we hit on the idea of the spot advertisement and we found it wasn't a bit hard to sell them, at least not at the price we were charging. Fifty cents! I would sell the ad and write it up and put it on the air and then go out and collect the money. Many times I had to take groceries instead of money, but I was glad to get anything. Anyway, I survived and eventually the station, now called CKNX, became a vital part of the farming community. People started to depend on us for news of the world, for farm reports and entertainment. In time our equipment improved and so did our programming. Finally, I was able to give up my job in the foundry and the other part-time jobs and give all of my time to running the station.

I did everything from sweeping to announcing. Then one day I heard a recording of my own voice. It was a shock! I couldn't believe that I was forcing people to listen to this kind of voice. I said, "That's it," and I never went on the air again. I turned the job over to my son Bud, who was now old enough to take part in the business.

A Listener

The first radio I remember was an old Stewart-Warner, an early one. I was born about the same time that radio was in 1920, so the early days, especially the thirties, are very clear in my memory. I was raised around Windsor, Ontario, right across the river from Detroit, so my memories are mostly of WXYZ, WJR, WWBA and WABC. There was a great sportscaster at the time named Ty Tyson and even to this day, I can't think of anyone better. He brought those baseball games right into our home and it was even better than being there.

One of the major programmes that we listened to, believe it or not, was the religious programme with Father Coughlin, a Catholic priest who gave hell to the Protestants and of course this was answered in another programme by the Rev. Shields of the Baptist Church, broadcasting from Toronto. Coughlin broadcast from near Detroit and it was amazing the amount of controversy those two men stirred up. I used to do a great imitation of Father Coughlin when I was in high school. Almost everybody was going around imitating the characters they heard on the radio, from Amos 'n' Andy to Foster Hewitt.

Gosh, the great people they had on in those days. Bert and Marge, Singin' Sam, Joe Penner, whose catch phrase was, "Wanna buy a duck?" Half the people in North America were trying to imitate Joe Penner. I had a crystal set then and I'd have it and the earphones under the bedclothes, listening, when I should have been asleep. Radio made much more of an impact when it came in than TV ever did because radio came suddenly, while TV sort of 'sneaked' in gradually, and we knew for years that it was coming. Radio didn't just become part of life. For a lot of us it was practically our *whole* life. It was pure magic. Nobody knew how it worked but suddenly there it was.

Then one day I heard a recording of my own voice. It was a shock! I couldn't believe that I was forcing people to listen to this kind of voice. I said, "That's it," and I never went on the air again.

Just Expressing
the
Christmas Wish
of
A Well-filled Stocking
for you
from
C K N X
The Voice of the Community

One of the major programmes was the religious programme with Father Coughlin, a Catholic priest who gave hell to the Protestants.

Harry Boyle

I was born in a little community called St. Augustine, north of London, Ontario. It was a farm community and life was quiet. My father owned the general store and people came to the store to catch up on what was happening. The big thing that started to change all that happened around the mid-1920s.

There were two fellows who were always into everything. Always trying something new. They were brothers; one was tall, and the other was short, and they were interested in everything—except farming—as a way to make money. One day they came to my father and persuaded him to try out a radio at the store. They knew little or nothing about it except what they'd read in some magazine or other. Anyway, the word got around that the Martin brothers were going to demonstrate this new marvel in our store. That evening they came in with their radio. They placed it on the counter and took the covers off. It had a great big horn and batteries. Wires hung out from everywhere. They sent me across the street to climb the church steeple to attach the wire they called an 'aerial.' It had to go as high as possible, so I hooked it around the belfry, which was as high as you could get. The whole community was there for the demonstration of this fantastic thing which the Martins said would bring the whole world to our town. The trouble was that the Martins didn't have a clue what they were doing. They fiddled around from about seven o'clock on, with everyone watching their every move. They twisted dials, changed wires around and everything. But there was nothing. Finally about ten-thirty, amidst all the squeals and noise, an announcer came on and we heard the words "KDKA, Pittsburgh, Pennsylvania." Everybody cheered and yelled. There were congratulations all around and that was it. We just got more noise after that. Finally everybody went home satisfied. At least we now knew it was possible.

Shortly after that there was a priest in Stratford who was making radios. They were beautiful things of rosewood with four legs that stood on the floor. Father bought one and it worked just fine except that you had to be perfectly still in the room when you got it going. If you disturbed it at all, it would stop. Then you'd have to send for the priest and he'd come and fiddle around.

Radio was something that came from somewhere else—Pittsburgh or London or Toronto—during most of my years of growing up. And it might still be that way if it weren't for a wonderful character in Wingham, W. T. Cruikshank, who was known by everybody as "Doc." He got the name because he used to chauffeur around a lady doctor. Anyway, Doc was a ham operator. Then he decided he wanted to build his own transmitter. So he got a bunch of guys together and they each put in a dollar and formed a radio club. They got a licence to operate an amateur radio station. After they got it going, they started to sell advertisements until somebody from Ottawa said, "You can't sell ads on an amateur station." Doc asked them what he had to do to make it legal and they told him he had to have a certain kind of transmitter. So he picked up a copy of *Popular Mechanics,* built the transmitter and applied for a licence. The fellow in Ottawa who gave out licences nearly went crazy because a town of 1,300

They sent me across the street to climb the church steeple to attach the wire they called an 'aerial.'

wasn't supposed to have a radio station all for themselves. The local MP got in on the act and put the pressure on. He said, "What harm is it going to do? The station probably won't last a year." So Doc got his licence in 1926 for CKNX and it's still going strong today. I started to work for Doc in 1936 and stayed with the station until 1941.

Before going to CKNX I had been working in the newspaper business and had seen how they established a network of local correspondents. So I set about forming a network of radio correspondents for Doc's station. We had a lot of competition for listeners between three and four in the afternoon because Detroit and Toronto were booming in with soap operas which everyone was listening to. To counteract this, I had two high school students come in every afternoon and do a programme in which they read all the personals from the weekly newspapers. "John so-and-so was in London this week." Or, "Mr. and Mrs. Brown visited their daughter, who now lives in Toronto." It worked like magic. People left the soap operas to hear these two kids reading the names of people they knew on the air. Of course, they also hoped to hear their own names.

Quod Erat Demonstrandum

as the Latins used to say, means "that which has been proved," and this certainly applies to CENTRALAB. An ever-improving line of radio parts manufactured since 1922 justifies this quotation.

To add a touch of class to radio in its early days, advertisers frequently used bits of Latin.

Bill Anderson

Up until 1958 radio in the North was simply a 'sometimes' thing. There'd be an occasional programme on shortwave from southern Canada or Russia, or programmes put together by people with amateur sets, but for the most part there was nothing—certainly nothing in the daytime. If you lived in the North and had a shortwave radio you could get something from the 'outside' late at night, but most people were starved for news. Magazines such as *Maclean's, Time* and *Newsweek,* were flown in, of course, and people would be there at the airports waiting for their copies. This was the only way that people in the North could capture the feeling that they were in touch, or a part of the events that were going on in the rest of the country and the world.

Before the CBC established its Northern Service the people themselves put together volunteer stations in the different communities. Housewives, businessmen, trappers and, in fact, anyone who wanted to help was welcome. They'd pick up their news from conversations on the street and turn it into a newscast. Someone would phone in and say that Mrs. So-and-So had her new baby, or that old Grandma Donaldson was in hospital after having a fall and was suffering from a broken hip. Someone else would call in with something they had heard on a shortwave broadcast late last night. All of those things would be put together by one of the volunteers and it became the noon or evening news. It may not have been much but it was something and when you're in total isolation you welcome anything at all. Someone else might have a collection of jazz records. They would bring them in and play them on the air. Another person might have symphony records or western music. Same thing. They'd bring them in and play them and do the announcing too.

Nobody got paid of course. I used to go on the air every morning until two in the afternoon. Then a group of housewives would take over for two hours and then from four till seven, some of the teenagers took over. After that you'd have the older people doing the things that they wanted to do.

When there was a fire somewhere in town people always used to rush to their phones to find out where it was and the lines would get jammed up. This wasn't good because if someone needed a doctor or there was some other emergency they couldn't get through. So we made it known around town that the phone company would no longer give this information and that the only way they could get it was to turn on their radios. So that solved that situation. The phone company would tell *us* and we'd keep repeating it on the air. Now, our little station wasn't very professional but it sure filled a need in the community.

Even before the community stations people found a way of hearing the human voice in communication. The bush pilots when they first started coming in here, in the thirties, had radios aboard their small craft and sometimes while they were on the ground, they would put on a little programme of news about things they had picked up in their travels. Everybody would be tuned in as if it were a high budget show from Toronto.

Later on, the Armed Services came in—a special branch of the Canadian Corps of Signals—and Dawson became one of the

Arctic Nights

aren't so lonely now!

Photo courtesy Canadian Westinghouse Co., Ltd. and Hudsons Bay Co.

BURGESS aids the northward course of civilization

RADIO . . . the marvel of the age . . . is breaking the centuries-old silence of the Arctic. No trading post or mounted police station is now considered fully equipped without a receiving set.

Burgess Chrome-built Batteries, the better radio batteries with the familiar black and white stripes, are serving Canada's northland just as efficiently as they serve radio listeners in older parts of the Dominion.

This photograph, taken at a post at Pond's Inlet on Baffin Land, shows Eskimos listening in to a concert, through the aid of Burgess Batteries.

Here again Burgess leads. In the Arctic there is no store "just around the corner". The hardy pioneers choose all their supplies and equipment carefully. Because of their superior performance, staying power and all-round dependability Burgess Batteries meet the exacting requirements. In the far north—and here at home, Burgess gives longer and better service.

BURGESS BATTERY COMPANY
Niagara Falls, Ontario

BURGESS DRY CELLS, LIMITED,
Winnipeg, Man.

RADIO·FLASHLIGHT·IGNITION·BATTERIES

From CNR Magazine, May 1931.

first places in the North to have broadcast radio. One of the R.C.M.P. boys had about a hundred pounds of records that he would take from one community to another as volunteer stations kept springing up. There was never a shortage of volunteers and in fact, one problem was trying to decide how often any one person was going to be allowed on the air in any one month. Some of the volunteers showed natural ability and, of course, others showed none at all. It was a very difficult problem to keep the inept ones off the air, and to do it diplomatically. But those who were good, were very good, and the women especially, would sit up half the night going through magazines for recipes and interesting articles, and auditioning the records they would use on the next day's programme. Of course it was 'hit and miss' radio. If a volunteer who had been scheduled to do a programme on a particular night suddenly found himself invited to a big party at the same time, it was usually the party that won out.

Studios were just empty corners in some building, usually in the basement, and it was something we didn't pay for. The technical work was donated by someone who knew something about it and in some communities, like Whitehouse, it was the army signal boys who set it up.

We also had people all over the North in tiny little communities who would provide news as to what was happening there, how the weather was, who was sick, who had died, and so on. We had Eskimo and native people who would broadcast in their own language, sending messages and things like that. It's really amazing when you think about it, how well it all worked, but it was a necessary thing and for a lot of people it made life in the isolated North, bearable.

This went on for a long time and it wasn't until 1958 that the CBC was able to tie us in with the rest of the country when they established the Northern Service.

J. D. Soper and David Wark at the radio in Cape Dorset, Baffin Island, N.W.T. 1928.

Manitoba High School Orchestra in
CKY studio. Winnipeg, 1937.

The West

Tony Messenger

I made my start in 1927 at CJRW, a station with studios in Winnipeg and a broadcasting tower in Fleming, Saskatchewan. The reason was that the Manitoba government wouldn't sanction another station in Manitoba. Therefore James Richardson built the tower in Fleming, just across the border. I did a number of broadcasts on a Monday through Friday basis and three days a week I went over to CKY to do shows there. My programmes were about furs and fur-bearing animals and trapping. I would broadcast the market prices plus a talk on wild animal life.

About 1931 I had a bad accident and lost my right arm. I felt quite sorry for myself and I didn't go to work for four or five years. But at the end of that time I got tired of living on hamburger and I applied to the All-Canada organization, who had their headquarters in Calgary. At the time people didn't believe in advertising in the summertime. Some people actually put their radios away in the summer months. Anyway, Guy Herbert of All-Canada told me that he appreciated my letter and call, but they didn't have any openings in the sales staff at that time. I gave him a pretty good argument so he decided to hire me after all, and I got the magnificent salary of seventy-five dollars a month, which he promised to boost if I could show any results. I presume I must have shown good results because I did get a raise a few months later.

At first we couldn't mention prices on the air. We'd say, "Northwest Laundry are doing wet wash for the price per pound of an ice cream cone." We had different ways of getting around it, until one year at the Western Association of Broadcasters we moved that the matter be taken up by the Canadian Association of Broadcasters and brought before the CBC Board. Everybody was surprised when it was okayed.

Some people actually put their radios away in the summer months.

115

Our Latest---
Vox Humana

(Meaning Human Voice)

--- wonderfully selective, terrific volume, pleasant tone, the very newest in radio frequency circuits, employs 5 tubes, equal in performance to any super-heterodyne.

Vox Humana, Console model, with built-in loud-speaker, compartments for batteries and phones.

Price only
$125.⁰⁰

Eliminate
Body-Capacity

The worst enemy in the radio world to-day is body-capacity and re-radiation. These two evils are entirely eliminated by the use of our

NEW NON-CAPACITY INDUCTANCE

for building the latest non-capacity and non-radiating receiving sets. Total cost of parts less than $25.00. So simple a child can operate it. Range unlimited. Price of special non-capacity inductance, complete with building instructions, wiring diagram, blue prints and panel lay-out $3.00.

Specialists in the Art of Radio.

Receiving Sets Repaired, Rewired and Exchanged.

Everything in Radio Built to Order.

Winnipeg Radio Exchange

Conducted by J. F. Boumont
226 Smith St., Winnipeg
Phone: A 7155

It was a freewheeling kind of time, getting radio going, and you could try just about anything. For example, when I was commercial manager at CKY they opened the station at eight, which was considered early. I approached the manager and asked if he would open the station at seven. I said that we could fill the time with advertising inside a month. To please me he said we'd try it for a month but if we didn't get any sales we'd go back to eight o'clock. We did sell, of course. And eventually they opened at six in the morning and the air was still filled with commercials.

You could do a lot of things but one thing you *couldn't* do was use off-colour language on air. I remember one time they sent an announcer out to the transmitter with a couple of hundred records so he could keep the station on the air all day. They also gave him commercials to read. After a few hours he got sick and tired of it and asked for some relief. He wanted to have something to eat. About three o'clock in the afternoon he finally got through to Winnipeg over some line but he forgot to cut his mike. He said, "Look, I need some help out here and I need it now. No horseshit about it either." The thing went out on the air. The phone commissioner complained and the man had to resign. When it came to language that's the way it was in those days.

PROGRAMME
of
The T. Eaton Co. Radio Show

ON the morning of October 18th the curtain will raise on Western Canada's first all-radio show to be held on the seventh floor of The T. Eaton Company's store at Winnipeg.

From all over the world have come radio manufacturers to exhibit to both the public and the trade the very latest and best in radio equipment—a truly remarkable display of all the finest that radio can show.

Commencing on Saturday, October 18th, and continuing until the following Saturday, October 25th, Western Canada's first all-radio show will entertain the thousands of radio fans from both the city and country.

Opening at 8.30 o'clock in the morning, the show will continue—one round of radio splendor—until 5 o'clock in the evening, with the exception of Saturday, when the show will close at one o'clock noon.

Everything will be seen at this gigantic radio show—radio sets, parts, loud-speakers, demonstrations, lectures, tableaux—both inspirational and educational.

At 10 o'clock each morning a half-hour talk on some popular radio topic will be delivered by some well-known authority on the subject. Don't miss these interesting talks as the speakers are well worth hearing. The lectures will be both educational and informative.

On Saturday, October 18th, Mr. L. V. Salton, B.A., M.I.C.E., radio engineer for The T. Eaton Co., will speak on "The Construction of Simple Crystal Sets."

On Monday, October 20th, Mr. R. D. Lister, editor of "The Radio Bug," will speak on "What Type of Radio Set Shall I Buy?"

On Tuesday, October 21st, Mr. F. E. Rutland, former announcer of Station CJNC, will speak on "The Construction of a Business Aerial on a Sloping Roof."

On Wednesday, October 22nd, Mr. L. V. Salton, B.A., M.I.R.E., radio engineer of The T. Eaton Co., will speak on "Aerials; Their Purpose and Construction."

On Thursday, October 23rd, Major F. J. North, M.C., commanding wireless officer 10th Signal Co., will speak on "Wireless Development During the War."

On Friday, October 24th, Mr. D. R. P. Coates, announcer, Station CKY, will speak on "Some Broadcasting Problems."

Saturday, October 25th. — The speaker for this day has not yet been appointed.

All lectures will be broadcast by CKY.

The daily programme is as follows:
8.30 a.m.—Show opens to the public.
10.00 a.m.—Lecture of the morning.
12.30-1.30.—Musical programme by Earle C. Hill's Capitol Theatre Orchestra.
3.30-4.30 p.m.—Musical programme by the orchestra.
4.00-5.00 p.m.—CKY will broadcast their afternoon programme direct from the radio show.

In the afternoons, from 4 to 5 o'clock, CKY will broadcast direct from the platform in full view of the public. Earle C. Hill's Capitol Theatre Orchestra will play standard and popular music twice daily.

Wonderful tableaux—"Radio in the Home"—"Radio in the Sick-room" "Radio in the Camp"—will be on view during the entire 8 days of the show.

It is expected that 75,000 of the radio public will attend Western Canada's first all-radio show—you are invited to come and see this wonderful display.

A Listener

In the very early 1920s I was teaching school in a rural district a few miles from my home town. My father and a good friend had worked together to make the first two radios in the town of Deloraine, Manitoba. I recall their talk about 'crystal sets' and 'peanut tubes.' My most vivid memory is of seeing members of the family fastened to the set with earphones which resembled huge earmuffs. When the static was bad or the signals faded it was amusing to see the heads lean in towards the set as though by so doing they could hear better. Here's an entry from my diary for January, 1922 after I'd spent an evening at the home of one of my school trustees: "We listened to radio tonight in a new and exciting way. A set of earphones was placed inside a cut-glass bowl which magnified and echoed the sound so we were all able to sit around the table and hear the programme."

A set of earphones was placed inside a cut-glass bowl which magnified and echoed the sound so we were all able to hear the programme.

A Listener

My earliest memories of radio go back to about 1922 when I lived in Winnipeg. A friend of my father's was very keen on his new "toy" and stayed up until all hours of the night exploring the air waves. Eventually my father got a 'cat's whisker' set too. It came in a safety razor box. But my mother dismissed the whole thing by saying, "Who wants to hear a dog bark in Italy?"

But my mother dismissed the whole thing by saying, "Who wants to hear a dog bark in Italy?"

Darby Coates, early Winnipeg broadcaster, with 1906 telephone.

117

A Gift
for the
Radio Fan
useful for 365 days
— and a —
constant reminder
of good will
Westinghouse
Radio Tubes

Radio for the Farm

ISSUED BY
EATON'S FARM NEWS SERVICE
WINNIPEG, CANADA

THE MODERN ALADDIN'S LAMP

Almost as fanciful as the old fairy tale is the magical story of one of the greatest discoveries of science—radio. Even though one is located in the wilds of our northern Canada or in the more settled sections of prairie land, at the snap of a switch we are transported at will to New York, Florida, Chicago or California, picking and choosing as we go, and once the "distance fever" is over, the real joy in the possession of a radio set is ours.

According to our mood, we can listen to the finest of instrumental or vocal music, dance until the small hours, or listen enthralled to the words of some famous speaker or lecturer. Consider the thousands who live in homes more or less isolated and remote

in this great Dominion of ours. Think what the best in music, news, literature and religion must mean to them.

Radio has made it possible for us to have at our finger tips the latest market reports and quotations, enabling us to sell our products to the very best advantage. Help and instruction on modern scientific and more business-like methods of farming is now available to every farmer who has a radio set. He may listen to a regular course of lectures by agricultural college professors, or may take a course with the Radio Farm School by the simple process of "tuning in" on the lectures. On Sundays, too, we can have our choice of perhaps half a dozen different church services right in our own home. This is not offered as an excuse for not attending church, but to point out what a splendid thing it is to be able to enjoy a church service at home when the weather is rough and the roads impassable.

The kiddies are not overlooked either, but may enjoy their own special programmes and bedtime stories. Many a little heart has beaten faster at the voice of its very own Santa Claus issuing from the loudspeaker or headphones.

Right here let us say that the artists and station operators who entertain us are very human and appreciate applause just as much as do the actors in a theatre. Drop them a postal card now and again and let them know that you appreciate their efforts. They are very anxious to please their invisible audiences, and the only way they have of knowing whether they are doing so or not is by the number of appreciations, or criticisms, as the case might be, they receive through the mail from their audiences.

For the dweller on the farm who is not yet the fortunate possessor of a radio set, the following notes regarding cost and operation may be of interest.

The Cost may be regulated to suit one's pocket-book, varying from about $30 for a modest 2-tube table set to as high as $350 for an elaborate console model. Splendid loudspeaker results may be obtained from a good 5-tube set, which can be purchased complete for very little over $100.

Once the set is installed, the air is free, with the exception in Canada of a yearly license fee of one dollar. Licenses may be obtained from radio dealers or post offices, and must be renewed each year after March 31st.

Operating Cost is very slight, consisting of charging costs for storage battery, replacement of "B" batteries—at the most three times a year—and occasionally the replacement of a worn-out tube.

Installing a Radio Set is very simple if the instructions supplied with the set are followed, the hardest part perhaps being the erection of the aerial, as the results obtained depend to a large extent upon how good the aerial installation is.

Results Obtained will vary according to size and location of aerial, class of radio set used, location of set in regard to electrical interference from outside sources, and, last but not least, atmospheric conditions. As yet there does not seem to be any way
[OVER

Dave Robertson is hep
to Winnipeg's teeners

OVER 8000 LISTEN
TO HIM DAILY . . .

Dave's programs keep the teen-agers listening . . . and merchants know that this group is an important buying group tool Get on the bandwagon and reach this lively group of shoppers!

CJOB

See our reps . . .
Radio Representatives
Limited
Toronto, Montreal
Winnipeg & Vancouver
Donald Cooke, Inc.
U.S.A.

WINNER OF
John J. Gillan Jr. Award
G.E. On the Air Award
Billboard Award

A Listener

Our first radio was made by my father and a friend. He subscribed to scientific journals and from them he got plans and diagrams. They made every part except tubes, dials, jacks and wires. My mother's empty darning spool was wound with wire, varnished, and then mounted so that it swivelled inside a large cardboard tube, which was also wire-covered for tuning. I remember words like "reostat," "amps" and "grid." This last was a block of graphite implanted on the front panel. We scribbled on it sometimes with a soft lead pencil to enhance reception. The panels were sawed from black hard rubber that had once encased old car batteries. The triumphant finale came when the row of dials were installed on the smooth front panels. A completed radio was at least three feet long. It had a place to plug in a jack which was attached to a cord leading to the earphones. Under the table were A, B and C batteries for power. We became very popular. Folks came crowding into our garage to take their turn at the headset. We "DXed" around, as we called it, to see how many stations we could bring in. One thrilling night Papa got Havana and called us all in to hear. By 1926 Papa and his friend had added a big-horned Magnavox speaker, so that the headset wasn't needed. The gathered crowd heard the Dempsey-Tunney fight together.

My grandpa and some of his friends travelled some distance just to hear this thing. The night they came there was a big lightning storm and all they heard was static. "Just as I thought," said grandpa, "It doesn't work." Later when grandpa heard another radio we had he was convinced that there was a phonograph in there. He said it was nonsense that one could hear sounds coming from far away. On the other hand, one of my uncles believed all the stories were *real* situations and involved living persons, and that we were secretly listening in to their conversations.

Radio grew, and was perfected. We got rid of the B and C batteries and owned one that could be run on just one A battery. We put the set by the window and ran the cord to the battery in our car. We could listen in the afternoons and evenings until the battery was exhausted. But we were selective. We marked our Radio Guide with red to indicate what we most wanted to hear, and saved the battery for the best.

One of my uncles believed all the stories were real situations and involved living persons, and that we were secretly listening in to their conversations.

OWNED AND OPERATED BY ITS LISTENERS

C K S B

ST-BONIFACE, MANITOBA

1000 watts   1250 kilocycles

The only way advertisers can reach the FRENCH speaking population of Manitoba effectively is by using **THEIR** station.

CKSB blankets an expansive and entirely new territory via 55,000 French speaking listeners **who buy products advertised on THEIR station.**

WESTERN CANADA'S FIRST FRENCH LANGUAGE STATION

C. W. Wright - Canada
        Adam J. Young Jr. Inc., U.S.A.

His Majesty George VI broadcasting a
Royal Message to the Empire.
Winnipeg. May 24, 1939. ▶

The Red River Flood Winnipeg, 1950. ▶
The reporter is Maurice Burchell.

Eve Henderson

It's funny the way I got into radio. I went and auditioned for a stock theatre company. I'd done a lot of amateur acting and I sang. So I went and auditioned. I didn't want a lead or anything. I wanted to do character roles. I could do dialects. Instead of taking a play to read I just made up my own little dialogue of different characters. There were two Scottish ladies talking at a bus stop, and a Cockney woman on the bus, and a Swedish girl asking the bus driver how to get to Victoria Station, and so on. The manager of the CBC in Winnipeg, whom I'd met socially, said, "Eve, I didn't know you could do all those voices. Why aren't you on radio? I'm sending a boy out with an application and you fill it in." This was on Tuesday. On Thursday night I was on "Woodhouse and Hawkins" doing two different characters. One was the wife of the Duchess of Calgary and the other was Alfie's daughter, a Cockney girl.

The first thing you know they asked me to be on the farm broadcasts. I was the poor downtrodden Mrs. Brown whose husband was a shiftless farmer, and we were next door to the Kirbys who were very clever. Some of the sound effects that were used on these farm broadcasts and on the evening shows were amazing. There was one scene where this girl was supposed to kill a man by splitting his head with a hatchet. To get that sound effect, they ended up with a big butcher knife and a cabbage, a good hard cabbage. It sounded terrible. One time we were rehearsing and Charlie Wright was directing us from the control room. Tommy Tweed said, "During the next scene, when he gives us the cue, let's all mouth the words, but not make a sound." Well, we watched Charlie in the control room fiddling away with the controls and looking at the wires. They thought something had gone wrong.

The St. Lawrence Starch Company wanted me to do a show for them. They called me "Betty Beehive." I was to discuss women in the news and news women would be interested in. It was a ten-minute show. But Waldo Holden, the manager of CJRC, offered me a half-hour programme for women. And they had a morning show that I did the commercials on. There was a theatre in the studio and every Saturday morning it was packed with women because the station gave away food baskets from different firms. Jack Wells and Waldo Holden used to do everything under the sun to make me laugh when I was doing a commercial. One Saturday that crazy Jack Wells took his trousers off. He had put on a pair of white shorts with red hearts all over them. The women just screamed, and here was me trying to do a commercial.

There was one scene where this girl was supposed to kill a man by splitting his head with a hatchet. To get that sound effect, they ended up with a big butcher knife and a cabbage.

Bert Hooper

**I said, "Where's Regina?" He said,
"In Saskatchewan." I said,
"Where's Saskatchewan?" He said,
"In the middle of Canada."**

The reason I went into radio was that I had been a wireless operator for six years on ships sailing all over the world and I was sick and tired of it. At the end of one trip in 1922 we had just pulled into Vancouver when the Marconi Company sent me a message to report to the office first thing in the morning, which I did. The manager closed the door and said, "Do you want to be on the sea all your life?" I replied, "No, as a matter of fact I'm ready to quit." "Well," he said, "Regina wants an engineer-announcer." I said, "Where's Regina?" He said, "In Saskatchewan." I said, "Where's Saskatchewan?" He said, "In the middle of Canada." And he pointed to it on the map. I said, "How far is that from deep water?" He said, "About a thousand miles." I said, "I'll take the job." He said, "You haven't got it yet. I want you to go to Victoria this afternoon and meet George Bell, of the Regina *Leader-Post*."

I went to Victoria and met Mr. Bell, who told me he wanted to audition me. He said, "I want you to go to the store, buy a newspaper and phone this number. I'll answer the phone." I did this; he answered the phone and said, "I want you to read the New York stocks and bonds to me." *That* was my audition! He asked if I'd be willing to go to Regina on the following Tuesday, as there was an Exhibition there and they were going to open the station the same day as the Exhibition opened. When I told my dad I had quit he said, "Oh, you fool! You're going to Regina? That place is so cold in winter you have to put one thermometer below the other to get a reading." Anyway, I went to CKCK. The only other Regina station was CHWC. We used to call it Can Hear the Water Closet. It was next door to a toilet and every time it was flushed the flush could be heard on the air.

It was a busy job, especially at night when we had to answer phones for requests and do announcing, plus putting on live shows. I would put a mark on the floor where the artists were to stand and they would sing into this horn. The studio was padded. One woman put her head right in the horn and sang as loud as she was able. I asked her why she did this and she said she had a sister listening in Ontario and she wanted to be sure she could hear her.

One time I was broadcasting a church service from the studio. A minister borrowed a choir and came in on Sunday nights to do the programme. He had a soloist and when I announced, "The next hymn will be by Mrs. So-and-so," the minister said, "No, no, correction." Listeners thought he had said, "Collection," and somebody sent in a twenty-dollar bill. After that, he wanted to say, "Correction" every time he went on the air. Another time a Miss Smith was accompanying an artist who was singing his heart out, when all of a sudden the piano stool collapsed and Miss Smith landed on the floor with her legs outstretched. The artist, who was quite a good-looking fellow, was also an optometrist and he was singing for publicity purposes. Anyway, he saw quite a bit of Miss Smith's legs. He must have liked what he saw, because three weeks later they were married.

"*throat-easy*" says Radio Announcer

"The dual portfolio of operator and announcer entails considerable anxiety and strain," writes A. W. (Bert) Hooper, popular radio operator and announcer — Station CKCK, Regina, Saskatchewan.

"To broadcast regularly four times a day, requires that I pay careful attention to my throat. I find that I can smoke Buckingham cigarettes without fear of any ill effect."

Bert Hooper

Mr. Hooper is the best known and one of the most popular radio announcers in Western Canada, winning a silver cup in the competition sponsored by The Western Producer. Mr. Hooper has the distinction of being the first individual to broadcast from the first radio broadcasting station erected in Saskatchewan—the world's wheat bin.

Buckingham CIGARETTES

BY SPECIAL APPOINTMENT.
PHILIP MORRIS & CO. LIMITED
ESTABLISHED OVER 60 YEARS

Buckingham TWENTY CIGARETTES

20 for 25c
No Coupons
All Quality

A Listener

Radio was a real lifesaver for my husband and me during the four years we lived and taught school in the Doukhobor settlement of Thunderbird, northeast of Yorkton, Saskatchewan. We were there from 1930 to 1934 and doubt we could have survived without the two-battery wet-cell radio we had there. We started the day with Don McNeill's morning show. We went to bed when "Amos 'n' Andy" was over. I remember the weekly long-distance contacts with Admiral Byrd at the South Pole. One of the men on his expedition had to have an appendix operation—the first in Antarctica—and the whole world listened in. Ahh, the good old days of radio! Not that today's programmes aren't umpteen percent better. But those old days were days of magic.

Andy McDermott

I was in high school in Regina in 1922 when CKCK came on the air and everyone wanted to listen to this new thing. We built crystal sets and sneaked them into school. We would roll wire tightly on round Quaker Oats boxes and then shellac them, which gave a good pickup. We'd hide them in our desks and have a wire running up our sleeves. There were always two or three fellows reporting to everybody else what was going on; how the World Series was doing and so on. Those were the days when you could hear stations from all over the continent.

While I was in high school, I was writing sports for the *Leader*—later the *Leader-Post*—where I took a job as assistant sports editor when I finished school. I was there until 1928. Somewhere in that period the Regina *Star* began to publish. It was a Conservative paper and the *Leader* was Liberal. CKCK had been started by the *Leader,* just as the Toronto *Star* had started its own station. But like the Toronto *Star,* and a lot of other papers, the Regina *Star* didn't realize the value of radio and they leased the station out to different individuals. Bert Hooper was the first to take it on. He was the engineer, the announcer and everything else. Around 1928, CHWC came on the air and shared the frequency with CKCK. CHWC came on at eight in the morning and ran until three in the afternoon. Then CKCK would take over. At ten CHWC would come back and run until midnight or whenever they decided to shut down. I went from the *Leader* to the *Star* about the end of 1928. At that time, interest in radio had become terrific so I started a column in the *Star* writing about what was going on in the radio world. It eventually grew to be a full page, the first full page of radio news anywhere in Canada.

Those were the days of entrepreneurs like Horace Stovin. Horace was an amateur radio operator and he convinced the *Leader* that he should take over their station and run it. He would pay them for the privilege of doing so. This, to the *Leader,* was a great way to get rid of what they considered a nuisance and an expense. So they turned the station over to him. He inspired all kinds of local talent. Eventually he went on to join the CRBC and became its western Canada director.

I got into radio indirectly through the column I was writing. The *Star* was looking for promotion and they proposed that I do

The newspaper lobby was very powerful. After a lot of newspapers jumped into radio and discarded it, they found they'd made a mistake. So they fought radio.

an eight o'clock newscast on CHWC—fifteen minutes every morning. (In those days you never thought of a newscast being anything less than fifteen minutes. I think Jack Kent Cooke of CKEY was one of the first to use a five-minute newscast.) He wanted a whole new style at the station. In making up my newscasts, I took the items that were in the *Star* and clipped and pasted them up. On my way down to the station I would grab a copy of the *Leader* and I'd rewrite some of their stories. Half the time there wasn't enough news in the two papers for a decent newscast. I also helped CHWC promote an amateur hour, which ran on Saturdays at a local ballroom. It was supposed to be an hour long but it ran on sometimes to three hours depending on how much talent there was. People paid ten cents to come and stand there while the amateur show was on. But CHWC was mostly forced to play records. They didn't have the money to attract talent that CKCK had. And CKCK was on a network, which made it very attractive for talent. You weren't going to get network on CHWC so if you had any talent at all you hustled over to CKCK, which was the production centre for that part of the prairies. Eventually CHWC owed so much money to the *Leader* that it took over the station and CHWC disappeared.

Radio prospered in the thirties at the expense of newspapers because the railways cut down on their service from a train a day to maybe two a week. A combination of the Depression and the terrible drought meant there were no crops for the trains to carry. The whole week's newspapers would arrive in one bundle. By the time the farmer got them the news was old. So he came to depend on radio and daily newspapers declined in circulation. The *Leader,* which at one time had 60,000 readers, dropped to 14,000.

The newspaper lobby was very powerful. After a lot of newspapers jumped into radio and discarded it, they found they'd made a mistake. So they fought radio and actually came close to pushing private radio right out of the picture at one point. They pushed hard for the CBC and, of course, they wanted a CBC without commercials so advertising would all go to them. When the first networks began the papers urged that the CRBC take them over. When the CBC came on the scene in 1936 and was given regulatory control over private stations the private people protested loudly that it was wrong for a competitor to regulate the competition. They demanded a separate regulatory body. But a lot of them later wished they hadn't because the CBC was like a benevolent father who gave in a certain amount. The ones who had hollered the loudest realized after the Board of Broadcast Governors came in that they'd probably bought a pig in a poke.

"We're Ridin' High"

BRIDGE *by* RADIO

Third Season Begins
Week of October 31

HAVE your cards and players ready and tune in with your nearest station broadcasting the Bridge Games. You will have the pleasure of playing the most fascinating Bridge hands imaginable just as played by the recognized experts, Work and Whitehead and others of Canada and the States.

To get the utmost help from the games, look for advance announcement of hands in newspapers or Saturday Evening Post, play them your own way, then compare your bidding and playing with that of the experts.

Every bid and play is broadcast in detail so you can follow the game at your own card table, point by point. Card players who have listened-in the past two years say the broadcast games are not only delightful recreation but a liberal education in the correct playing of Bridge. The 1927-28 series will be the most interesting of all.

Tune in with any of the following stations.
See newspapers for time of broadcasting.

CFAC	Herald	Calgary
CFLC	Radio Ass'n	Prescott
CFQC	Electric Shop	Saskatoon
CHNS	Northern Elec. Co.	Halifax
CHXC	J. R. Booth, Jr.	Ottawa
CJCA	Journal	Edmonton
CJGC	Free Press	London
CJRM	Jas. Richardson & Sons	Moose Jaw
CKAC	La Presse	Montreal
CKCD	Daily Province	Vancouver
CKNC	Canadian Nat. Carbon Co.	Toronto
CKY	Manitoba Tel. System	Winnipeg

The games will be broadcast also from many stations in the States including the following

Every Tuesday, 8:30 P. M., Pacific Time
KFI, KFOA, KGW, KHQ, KOMO, KPO, KGO.

Every Tuesday, 10 P. M., Eastern Time
WEAF, WSAI, WEEI, WJAR, WTAG, WTIC, WGR, WCSH, WTAM, WWJ, WGN, WGY, and many others.

To get the utmost pleasure from the radio games or any other game of cards use fresh new Bicycle or Congress Cards. Their big indexes, splendid finish, beautiful printing and snappy quality are a delight to every card player. You cannot get equally good cards for less money.

The U. S. Playing Card Company
Windsor, Canada.

Auction Bridge Magazine, 30 Ferry St., New York.
Milton C. Work and Wilbur C. Whitehead. Editors

Bill Speers

He could get words off a page like nobody I ever heard. Unfortunately, he didn't know what the words meant.

I had been in the grain business but in October 1929 the bottom fell out of the market, so I was out of a job. I worked at a lot of jobs for two or three years. A gang of us used to gather in a confectionery store in Regina every night about five o'clock. We'd read the help wanted ads. One time there was an ad for a radio announcer at CHWC. One of the guys bet me two dollars I couldn't get the job, so I went over and auditioned. There were 167 other guys who applied but I got the job. It was 1932. It was a split licence between CHWC and CKCK, so we were only on the air part time. There were two announcers, Jack Kemp and me. We got to imitating each other's mannerisms and nobody could tell which of us was which. If Jack made a mistake he'd just say, "This is Bill Speers speaking." Some time later we hired an announcer named Charles Bussey. He was a darned good announcer. He could get words off a page like nobody I ever heard. Unfortunately, he didn't know what the words meant. One day I got a piece of his copy and wrote in, using the same typewriter, "This is Fishface Bussey announcing." He read it on the air.

The reason two stations shared a frequency was that there was a shortage of frequencies. Receiving equipment was so imprecise that you couldn't put radio stations too close together on the band. What they did was take a frequency and assign it to an area. If there were two applications, they split the time. We were 980 kilo-cycles at CHWC, and CKCK was on the same frequency. We were both a quarter kilowatt. Finally we amalgamated the two stations and increased our power to a kilowatt.

I did everything from moving pianos to writing copy to acting. I started out at ten bucks a week. When they decided to cut expenses, since I was the last man on staff, they fired me. However, the fellow who was running the station hired me back on a fee basis to do a couple of programmes. One of them was "Magazine of the Air" in the mornings. Another was with organ and violin, with poetry reading and that kind of jazz. It was on in the evenings. In total, I was getting fifteen bucks a week for these programmes, so they decided it would be cheaper to have me on staff, and they put me back on.

I don't think I'd ever heard a complete radio programme in my life when I got my first job at CHWC. Not long after I got there, my boss said to me, "You go over to the lobby of the Metropolitan Theatre. You'll find a group called Jeff Germaine and his Band there. The equipment is there. You just have to turn a button. You put on a headset and when you hear, "We take you now to the lobby of the Metropolitan Theatre," you put these guys on the air." I said, "What do you mean, put them on the air?" He said, "You turn the switch, and you announce the programme." I really didn't know what I was doing. I turned the switch, and I heard the cue, and I said, "Good evening, ladies and gentlemen," as if I knew what I was doing, and I quickly dreamed up a set of cliché phrases like, "Our next selection is..." and "Now we're going to hear..." The next day, I'm sitting in the studio and this same guy leaned over my shoulder and said, "Now we bring you the five o'clock news," and he handed me a copy of the *Leader-*

Post. So I read the first two paragraphs of every story on the front page and then signed off ten minutes later.

Because so many of our programmes were 'live' there were a lot of goofs. One night we were broadcasting the Saturday night hockey game out of Toronto. The guy in the control room flipped a switch down, instead of turning his monitor down. His mike was on and he was talking to his girlfriend on the telephone in the control room. They were having a pretty sexy conversation. He was all alone in the building, and since he was using the phone there was no way to reach him. Over Foster Hewitt's voice with his play-by-play Regina could hear the most lurid conversation. I got in my car and tore down to the station and flipped his mike off. Only then did he realize what he'd done. He and his girlfriend had been on the air for twenty minutes or more.

Buy Your Radio Set Now or During

Radio reception will be at its best during the next few months, and for this reason the entire radio industry is concentrating its efforts on securing your interest in this wonderful, magic thing—called Radio.

Manufacturers, dealers and distributors are co-operating with the Canadian Radio Trades Association to make Canada's Second National Radio Week a great success from every angle.

Owners of receiving sets and prospective purchasers will be welcomed by every radio store throughout the Dominion. Special concerts will be on the air each night.

Buy your Set or other needs during Canada's National Radio Week, February 2-8.

CANADA'S NATIONAL RADIO WEEK

Offices:

257 Adelaide St. W., Toronto - Phone Adelaide 0300

17 Main St. East, Hamilton - Phone Regent 8686

Wilf Collier

I started with CKCK Regina in 1931. Although they'd been on the air since 1922, they didn't go commercial till 1929. That's when Horace Stovin came in to run the station. Horace had been a druggist in Unity, Saskatchewan but it seems he was born to be a broadcaster. He had lots of original ideas which he put to work at CKCK before he became a force on the national scene.

In those days stations operated in a minimum of space. Our control room, which also housed the transmitter, was roughly nine by twelve. Everything was squeezed into that space, including two seventy-eight r.p.m. turntables. The studios were bigger. They occupied the room where the editorial staff and reporters had their 'office' space. All the walls were lined with straw pressed into bales about four inches thick with drapes hanging in front of them. This was both for soundproofing and for taking out any 'hollow' sound from the room. Of course with all that straw the place smelled a bit like a stable and it also made a perfect place for mice to set up housekeeping. Once two sisters were playing twin pianos. The announcer was introducing them when a mouse decided to join the act. Suddenly the girls went into hysterics and the whole place was in pandemonium—all going out on the air.

Newspapers like *Leader-Post* certainly didn't make money on their stations. My theory is that they saw this big bad thing called radio coming along and they were scared of having their papers run out of business and got the stations just so they could control them. I remember when Bert Hooper was at CKCK he had a hard time getting money from the *Leader-Post* even to buy new tubes to keep us on the air. They wouldn't give him money to buy anything, and it wasn't because they didn't have it. All of that changed around 1936 when the All-Canada group took over and turned CKCK into a real commercial operation.

I left in 1949 and went to CJNB in North Battleford as manager and I never regretted it. But I enjoyed the pioneering of CKCK. I know for a fact that they put on the very first church broadcast in the world. The date was February 11, 1923 and they broadcast two services that day from the Carmichael Church. The minister was J. W. Whillans. They arranged it with the Department of Telephones who were interested in radio at the time. It wasn't until a year later that a church service was broadcast in the British Isles.

All the walls were lined with straw pressed into bales about four inches thick with drapes hanging in front of them.

Fred Usher

They didn't have thirty-three and a third on the turntable, so the guy was turning it with his finger.

At Central Collegiate in Regina we formed a quartet in my senior year, the Freshmen Quartet. We auditioned for a station, no longer in existence, CHWC. The Freshmen Quartet sort of copied the Mills Brothers style, "four boys and a guitar." We used to have a lot of fun imitating those orchestra sounds of the Mills Brothers. We got very ambitious for our ages and decided that we were ready for bigger and better things. So we went up to Horace Stovin's office at CHWC. He was on one of the upper floors of the Saskatchewan Hotel and he agreed to listen to us. He said, "All right, boys—sing." We sang about fifteen numbers. He said, "Some more." So we did a couple more. He said, "Some more." We said, "There ain't no more." He said, "Boys, I like what you have to offer. Go home, keep practising, and when you've got a hundred numbers down as well as the ones you've just auditioned for me you come back, and I'll put you on the network." So we went away for six months and got the numbers down pat. Then we went back to Stovin and said, "We're ready." He said, "Good. Let's go." He was as good as his word, and he put us on the air.

We lasted from 1934 to 1938, on a western regional network. We did really well. We alternated with Mart Kenney's trio, Three Of A Kind, who played at the Saskatchewan Hotel. At that time I was working at Massey-Harris. It was the hungry thirties and I was well paid. I was getting a dollar a day. But I was making more for singing fifteen minutes on the network than I was for working all week at Massey-Harris. Let's face it—I was rich. I had two suits in the closet. But eventually the whole thing finished and we went our different ways. One thing I regret is that in those early days there were few transcriptions made and as a result I have no actual record of the singing. I have the scrapbooks, but nothing on tape.

I met up with an old chum, Bob McGill, who used to sing with me when we were kids. We had a morning show on CKCK. Bob and I would roar down on my motorcycle and our show went on after the great Al Smith on the piano. Al was known all over Saskatchewan. It was a very free and easy show, an informal type of thing. We used to kibbitz a lot with announcers.

Then 1939 came along, and we gave up our jobs. We phoned the station and told them we were hopping on Fred's motorcycle and driving out to Victoria to join the army. We thought we'd rather start our soldiering where we didn't have to jump snowbanks in the wintertime. We joined the engineers, got into entertaining, and we did some radio work on the old Victoria station. The equipment was really primitive. I can remember going in one night and they didn't have thirty-three and a third on the turntable, so the guy was turning it with his finger. Can you imagine? During the war, I continued to entertain in the army. Organizing shows and things like that.

In October 1945 I went to work at CJVI in Victoria. I went into the sales side of it, but I did a bit of announcing and some work as an entertainer too. I didn't do any singing commercials until I came to Victoria. It was one of the first that was to emanate from the West, and it was for Lyons Tea. That was a feather in our cap, because something had come out of little Victoria.

The pranks that used to take place in radio were a joy to me. I can remember one of our announcers, Barry Woods, standing in the studio at CKCK in Regina, doing a newscast, and the boys snuck in and set fire to his script. Another time Barry was doing his newscast, reading it as it came off the wire. He was right in the middle of some battle the Chinese were fighting when suddenly the teletype stopped dead. There was nothing coming. Barry never batted an eye. He made up the rest of that whole battle, and did a beautiful job.

Those were the days when people used to send you things. They'd send you cakes if you happened to mention it was your birthday, or they'd knit you a pair of socks. I remember announcers, as well as the entertainers, receiving all sorts of gifts, particularly during the Christmas season. People were so enthused about what we were bringing them on radio. They were grateful.

Radiola
Super Hetrodyne
(Second Harmonic)

Music from Across the Continent without the Aid of Aerials or Wires

Radiola IIIA, complete with four Radiotrons, ear 'phones and special Radiola Loud Speaker, complete except Batteries and Antenna.........$115.00

NO longer is it necessary to have unsightly batteries, ground connections or aerials, in order to enjoy radio reception. The Radiola Super Heterodyne, illustrated above, contains a loop antenna, concealed in the back of the cabinet, which will receive far distant stations without further connections of any description. Provision is made, however, for a larger external loop should one be desired.

The Radiola Super Heterodyne is non-radiating, and will not interfere with any other receiving set, however close it may be. It can be used in close proximity to powerful broadcasting stations, and yet will easily tune them out in favor of more distant stations.

In tuning the Super Heterodyne, the various stations are picked up at exactly the same spot each time. It is as simple to operate as a gramophone.

The six Radiotrons are operated by dry cells, and the set may be carried with perfect ease. The cabinet is beautifully finished mahogany, equipped with a leather handle for carrying from place to place.

Radiola Super Heterodyne, complete with the exception of Batteries....................$350.00

General Merchandising Dept.
Canadian General Electric Co., Limited, Toronto, Ont.

Please send me illustrated folder and particulars regarding Radiolas.

Name ....
Address ....

"Made in Canada" by
Canadian General Electric Co., Limited
HEAD OFFICE — TORONTO
Sales Branches in all Large Cities

Art Crighton

Radio was the cultural centre of the whole community. The only other cultural outlet was the movies.

Radio came to Regina about 1928, and when I started in 1942 the early pioneering work was all done. I joined CKCK while I was still in high school. In 1942, radio wasn't that new. It was pretty sophisticated already. I mean, we were on the air eighteen hours a day seven days a week. One of the reasons I got my job at CKCK was that everyone else went to war—all the guys who were old enough to fight. I was getting to that age myself by the time the war ended, but in 1942 I was still not old enough. The station didn't have any other choice than to hire kids going to university, and even high school kids who were interested. It didn't pay that much so you *had* to be fairly interested, I'll tell you. I was just about fifteen years old when I first started working there. I really can't say why I chose a radio station. Perhaps if I'd been in Toronto I wouldn't have because there was so much other work to do. But in a city like Regina, with only 28,000 or maybe 30,000 people, there wasn't much else to do. There was no live theatre, no symphony. There were no jobs of any kind in the arts. And after all, that's what radio is—a member of the arts community. A great many people in western Canada went into radio because they were inclined towards the arts.

CKCK was very rich. We had a salesman. All he had to do was *accept* orders. He didn't have to go out and try to sell radio time because we had every time slot sold. They even had the church services sold. They went to a church and said, "If you will buy the line from the church to the station, we will put you on the air on Sundays." So they had the same church service every Sunday because that particular church was willing to pick up the expenses. Mind you, it was an amateurish pickup. We put an unattended amplifier in the church under the seat where the minister sat. We told him to turn on the amplifier when he came in to start the service. There was a microphone at the pulpit. As long as the mike and the amplifier worked we had ourselves a church service. It didn't cost us a penny. We weren't going to sell anything on Sunday morning between eleven and twelve anyway.

Radio was the cultural centre of the whole community. The only other cultural outlet was the movies. And no one could afford to go to the movies every night. We were the station that carried the NHL hockey games on Saturday nights, and everybody had the station on. You'd walk down the street and you'd see nobody. They were all at home listening to the hockey game.

Odd as it may seem, the major difficulty in operating a station in Regina was in getting staff. No matter how wealthy a station is, even today, they don't pay very well. This station was no exception. During the war there were munitions plants in Regina and they were paying a fair amount of money. As a result, high school and university kids were going there. That's where the money was. You really had to have a love of radio to stay in it.

We couldn't put on CBC "Stage," but still we did some dramas. Small ones, mind you, using the staff as announcers, actors, and sound effects technicians. We had a photographer in Regina who travelled around the world. He had all kinds of stories to tell and several of us dramatized these things. The photographer was a man by the name of Dick Bird. Bird's Camera Store was the sponsor for these programmes, which we put on for fifteen minutes on Sunday afternoons. That was great! Bird gave us the stories, paid for the commercials and he got a good audience. We had another chap in town, another photographer, who loved reading poetry. He had a deep bass voice. We sold him fifteen minutes with organ music played behind his reading. At the end of his broadcast the announcer would say, "This programme has been presented by Wilf West, and if you want your photo taken, come down and Wilf will do it." He was his own talent. That station was making a lot of money out of Regina, but we were also contributing a lot to the life of the community. We were giving them something that they couldn't get anywhere else, and we were showing them that there was talent in the town.

We didn't do much on provincial and federal affairs because we didn't have the staff, but we could, and did, cover the city council. It was just down the street. We covered any other thing that was going on, such as hockey and football. Sometimes, if a hockey game was running late we had to take the news down to the arena for the announcer to read it from there because we were so short of staff and all the equipment was at the arena. That was fun.

When you walked down the street everybody greeted you because you were part of the radio station. That was tremendous. And it was fantastic to be asked to M.C. a dance because you worked in radio.

How They Stand

The following appeared in the current Elliott-Haynes Reports as the top ten national programs, based on fifteen key markets. The first figure following the name is the E-H Rating; the second is the change from the previous month.

DAYTIME

English

Ma Perkins	18.1	— .3
Happy Gang	17.1	—1.9
Big Sister	16.4	— .6
Pepper Young	16.0	— .8
Life Can Be Beautiful	14.5	— .9
Laura Limited	13.9	— .2
Claire Wallace*	13.2	—1.7
Road of Life	13.1	— .7
Household Counsellor	12.7	—1.0
Lucy Linton	12.4	— .8

* 3 a week (all others 5 a week)

French

Rue Principale	26.8	+3.6
Jeunesse Dorée	26.3	+1.2
Joyeux Troubadours	22.3	+1.0
Quelles Nouvelles**	19.5	+4.9
Tante Lucie	18.7	+ .5
L'Ami du Consommateur	15.0	+ .9
Le Quart d'Heure*	14.0	+1.4
Madeleine et Pierre	12.7	+ .3
Pierre et Pierrette	10.1	+1.8

* 2 a week (all others 5 a weekQ
** Change of Time

EVENING

English

Charlie McCarthy	40.6	+1.9
Lux Radio Theatre	37.5	+ .6
Fibber McGee & Molly	36.1	—1.5
Fred Allen	29.3	+4.4
Ozzie & Harriet	28.9	+1.0
Amos 'N' Andy	25.5	— .3
Alb. Familiar Music	23.9	+2.4
Duffy's Tavern	21.6	+4.6
NHL Hockey	21.5	+ .2
Take It or Leave It	21.4	new

French

Ralliement du Rire	43.8	+5.4
Un Homme et son Pêché	42.7	+2.3
Talents de Chez Nous	39.4	+5.1
Enchantant dans le Vivoir	38.6	—2.3
Métropole	36.5	+2.5
Juliette Beliveau	33.9	new
Nazaire et Barnabé	33.4	—1.0
Radio Carabins	31.0	—3.6
Café Concert	30.7	—1.2
Tourbillon de la Gaieté	30.2	—4.3

This precursor of the Nielsen Ratings indicates that times haven't changed. The most popular English-language programmes are almost all American.

133

R. H. Hahn

I remember people sitting around with crystal sets at our homestead in northern Saskatchewan listening to the World Series.

Around 1930, when I was seven or eight, I remember people sitting around with crystal sets at our homestead in northern Saskatchewan listening to the World Series. Only one person at a time could hear the thing. They'd share this little ear plug. I was never important enough to get a turn. There'd be a group of maybe twenty grown men at these gatherings, each taking a brief moment to hear what was going on and then reporting it to everyone else. In 1936 we left the homestead in a homemade trailer to try our hand as a musical family. We figured anything was better than starving.

Our first experience in broadcasting was at CFQC in Saskatoon. CFQC was in the back of a service station. They put me and my family in there and turned us on. I remember getting a phone call from someone who owned a Chinese restaurant in another town wanting to know if we could sing Chinese songs. We couldn't. But eventually we got to the town he'd called from, met him, and he taught us a Chinese song. We performed it for him later on another station.

That fall we got into Regina and played at a Rotary Club luncheon. One of CKRM's owners was there and afterwards he asked if we were interested in appearing on his station. We ended up with a Friday and Saturday programme on CKRM, which also ran on CJRC. I remember marvelling at the fact that we were on a two station network. Our programmes were supposed to be a half-hour long, but they just went on and on. We'd play until we couldn't think of anything else.

Listeners would phone in requests and when I think of it, it must have been pretty bad radio, because we'd argue about keys and who was going to sing and how we'd do it, etc. However, we had a fantastic mail response. I remember lighting our fires in the trailer for months and months with the fan mail that we got.

"Prairie Schooner" was a popular network programme from the West. Emil Magnacca, Jimmy Gowler, Pete Couture and Ted Komar.

We were living in our trailer. When government authorities stopped us leaving Regina because they were afraid we'd get stuck on the road that time of year, we parked the trailer, hooked up some electrical things and were really quite comfortable. 'We' consisted of my mother and dad, my brother Lloyd, my sister Kay and my sister Joyce, who later became well-known when television began. At that time she was only five. Kay was eight, I was fourteen, and my brother was fifteen. When we went on at CFQC in Saskatoon we were introduced as "Hahn and his Kids." Someone phoned to say this didn't sound very nice, that we should change our name to "The Harmony Kids." That's how we got the name.

We sold postcards of ourselves at ten cents apiece or three for a quarter. My dad used to make them with some kind of a photographic thing and an inverted beer case. We had cards of Joyce, some of Joyce and Kay, and some of the whole group of us. When the tremendous mail response started we ended up making about a hundred dollars a week just selling postcards. In the middle of the Depression, that was an awful lot of money.

From the point of view of sheer excitement, I don't think I've ever been involved in anything as satisfying as the literally hundreds of letters that flooded into CKRM Regina every week. The station then went out and sold our programme to an advertiser and gave us a raise of ten dollars to twenty a week. Our sponsor was a detergent called OGD or "Out Goes Dirt." "OGD, the wonder cleanser, presents The Harmony Kids." It was a big production. Then the sponsor decided it would be a great idea if he put a picture of "The Harmony Kids" on the box of detergent. There went our $100 a week selling postcards, and we were back to twenty.

Meanwhile, we had developed musically and we began to put a show together based around magic illusions, which always ended with a musical number. We started getting bookings in some of the northern states, working further and further out of Regina, until one week we decided that twenty dollars a week wasn't any great hell, so we just kept driving. We did a couple of programmes from Winnipeg. Then, somewhere in northern Ontario, we heard Gabriel Heater's "We, the People." They had a family on not unlike ours, a musical family which claimed to be the most trailer-travelled family in the world. Dad wrote these people a nasty letter asking why they didn't check their information before putting it on the air. When our mail caught up with us there was a nice letter asking if we could come to New York. My dad answered with another letter. Weeks later after our mail caught up with us again, we were transplanted right to the heart of New York. What a bunch of hayseeds we were! We went to New York on a one-week permit, to appear on "We, the People." Then we did "Major Bowes Amateur Hour" and won. Other bookings came with that and we stayed in New York for almost three years.

We carried on as a family until the war when my brother and I went into the air force. My dad went to work in an aircraft plant. When the war was over my brother decided that he didn't want to be a musician any longer. My sister Kay married. That left Joyce and me. We kept going in different ways until 1952, when Joyce moved into television and I went into the jingle-writing business.

.... CKRM
Regina

W. V. Chestnut

Mr. Sponsor arrived with Mrs. Sponsor and all the little Sponsors to watch their programme.

I was training for the navy in World War One and a good deal of my training had to do with communications. But I ran away from naval college in Halifax when I was fifteen and went overseas as a signalman. When I returned in 1919 I took a course in radio telegraphy and got my certificate. I was sent from Halifax to western Canada to work on an air patrol for forest fire prevention. It was operated by people fresh out of the service.

When the man in charge, Bill Grant, became involved in building CFCN, he asked me to join him and we became the two-man staff. I was chief engineer, programme director, copy writer, announcer and janitor. Bill Grant built it all. Eventually I became a sort of doctor for sick radio stations. Whenever my outfit, Taylor-Pearson-Carson, acquired the rights to operate a new station they sent me to get it started up. Which was a bit frustrating because just as the thing was getting rolling and there was time for a little golf or something, I was shifted somewhere else.

I didn't always know what I was talking about. I remember they had a certain programme at CKCK in Regina. The first time I heard it when I took over, I thought, "Give it the axe." Then I discovered that it had the highest rating of any programme at the station. It was a Sunday morning amateur hour. All ethnic stuff. There were Hungarians and Romanians who played different instruments. People would attend church on Sunday mornings and afterwards they'd go to the homes of those who had radio sets and they'd listen to this two-hour amateur show. Anyway, I quickly realized it wouldn't be wise to axe that one.

Mostly we had to rely on records for our programmes. I think it was at CFAC Calgary that we got the idea of putting records together in a cohesive fashion. We built programmes around imported gramophone records. There was "The Blighty Show," a typical English music hall affair complete with recorded applause. And "Café Franz-Josef," with Viennese waltzes and German singers. We even hired an announcer with a German accent. His accent was so thick nobody could understand him. But our ethnic audiences loved it.

There were embarrassing moments. A new retailer started up in town selling rugs and drapes. Our salesman tried for months to get him to take a programme and finally he said yes, he would sponsor a programme. But he didn't want our usual spot announcements, he wanted a live programme, something like they had in the States with an orchestra and a singer. He wanted a half-hour a week show. We didn't quite know how to go about producing this but we did our best. When the time came for this big programme to go on the air everybody involved was terribly on edge. Mr. Sponsor arrived with Mrs. Sponsor and all the little sponsors to watch their programme. This made the announcer all the more jittery. You could see him shaking. When the red light came on he turned to the microphone and said, "Ladies and gentlemen, the following programme comes to you through the courtesy of the Calgary Drug and Papery Shop." That was the last piece of advertising we got from that firm. The irony is that that was the best advertising that firm ever had. Listeners heard it and talked about the store much more than they would have had the announcer not made that mistake.

Another time in Regina we had a big semi-final game coming up. Regina was playing the Blue Bombers for the right to meet the East. The day before that game our sports commentator had to go into hospital for emergency surgery and we had to scramble for a replacement. We had nobody on staff who could do it, but the young manager of the motion picture theatre used to do all his own commercials and was accustomed to the microphone. He was also an ardent football fan. The day of the game it rained and by game time at two o'clock the playing field was Saskatchewan gumbo. It was a mess. You couldn't see the numbers on the players' uniforms, and they couldn't get going in the mud. Our substitute announcer was doing his best but nothing was happening. The programme was sagging. Suddenly one of the Regina men, who in real life was a motorcycle policeman, got the ball and went down the field. Larry came to life and shouted, "Vic Murdoch has the ball and he's going down the field. He's made ten yards, fifteen, twenty…He's going to make it! *Jesus Christ, he dropped it!*" Back at the studio the telephones began ringing off the walls. There was an awful uproar. The Ministerial Association even tried to have our licence rescinded.

I began to lose interest in radio when the race for ratings began and it became clear that in order to get a good rating you actually had to degenerate your programmes to the lowest common denominator of human intelligence. In other words, we had to come down to the masses. These days I often thank God for the CBC, but we hated those bastards then and we fought them tooth and nail. I know now that it was the CBC that kept the spark alive and did broadcasting for minority audiences.

These days I often thank God for the CBC, but we hated those bastards then and we fought them tooth and nail.

We're HOME ON THE RANGE

THE days of the rip-snorting, gun-toting range have faded beyond the horizon of the modern "West". Oil wells, wheat fields, coal mines and modern cattle ranches have grown up where once the deer and the antelope played.

But out here, where the hand-shake is a little firmer, friendly Albertans, busy putting their shoulders behind the wheel of war, are ready to welcome your sales messages, bringing them news of the goods and services they need in the course of their busy lives.

From the modern city of Calgary, we'll broadcast your message to more friendly listeners throughout Alberta than any other medium can offer.

10,000 WATTS
1010 KC

CFCN

CALGARY ALBERTA
The Voice of the Prairies

Contact
RADIO REPRESENTATIVES LTD.
Toronto and Montreal
Winnipeg—H. N. Stovin
In the U.S.—HOWARD H. WILSON COMPANY

What's on the Air Tonight
Programmes of Canadian Broadcasting Stations
Sept. 15 to Oct. 12

HOW TO USE THIS PROGRAMME

THIS is a condensed programme of what Canada's broadcasting stations are doing every night in the week during the period of September 15th to October 12th. The hours specified are central standard time. If you live in the Maritime Provinces, add two hours to the time specified. If you live in Quebec or Ontario, add one hour; Saskatchewan or Alberta, subtract one hour; British Columbia, subtract two hours. This enables you to find out what time a station comes on the air without knowing its exact location or change of time.

Monday

CFAC, 430 meters, Calgary, Alta. 2.00–2.30 p.m., news, grain and market reports; 2.30–4.30 p.m., music and vocal; 8–9 p.m., studio concert, vocal and music.

CFCH, 400 meters, Iroquois Falls, Ontario. 7.00–7.05 p.m., weather report; 7.05–7.15 p.m., forestry talk; 7.15–8.00 p.m., dance musical selections; 8.00–9.00 p.m., dance programme.

CFQC, 400 meters, Saskatoon, Sask. 1.15–2.00 p.m., livestock prices, grain report, latest news, phonograph selections; 8.30–10.00 p.m., bedtime story, studio concert, vocal and instrumental.

CHBC, 410 meters, Calgary, Alta. 8.45–10.00 p.m., studio concert, instrumental and vocal, news items.

CHNC, 350 meters, Toronto, Ontario. 8.30–11.30 p.m., high-class vocal and instrumental programme, 15-minute talk on radio subjects.

CJCA, 450 meters, Edmonton, Alta. 1.30–2.15 p.m., crop and weather report, latest news items; 8.30–9.00 p.m., bedtime story, news items, acknowledgements; 9.30–10.30 p.m., studio concert, vocal and instrumental numbers; 10.15 p.m., additional news items.

CJCM, 312 meters, Mont Joli, Que. 4.00–5.00 p.m., news, reports and short programme (language French); 7.30–9.00 p.m., musical programme, from studio, vocal numbers (language French); 10.30–12.00 p.m., studio programme, vocal and instrumental numbers (languages French and English).

CKAC, 425 meters, Montreal, Que. 12.45 p.m., Mount Royal Orchestra, luncheon concert from Mount Royal Hotel, news items of the day (languages, French and English); 3.00 p.m., afternoon broadcast, weather and stock reports, news items (languages French and English).

CKCD, 410 meters, Vancouver, B.C. 10.00–11.00 p.m., continuous dancing by Canary Cottage Orchestra from Hotel Vancouver, news items during intermission.

CKCK, 420 meters, Regina, Sask. 11.00–11.30 a.m., early morning broadcast, stock and market quotations, musical selections, early news of the day; 1.30–2.15 p.m., noon-time broadcast, stock and market quotations, music, news; 8.30–9.15 p.m., evening studio concert, vocal and instrumental numbers, news items.

CKLC, 400 meters, Calgary, Alta. 8.45–9.45 p.m., studio concert, short talk on topics of the day, vocal and instrumental selections, news items.

CKY, 450 meters, Winnipeg, Man. 12.30–1.15 p.m., noon-time broadcast, news items, stock, grain and market quotations, music; 4.00–5.00 p.m., afternoon broadcast, news items, children's stories.

Tuesday

CFAC, 430 meters, Calgary, Alta. 2.00–2.30 p.m., news, grain and market reports; 4.30–5.30 p.m., music; 8.45–9.45 p.m., vocal studio concert.

CFCH, 400 meters, Iroquois Falls, Ontario. 7.00–7.05 p.m., weather report; 7.05–7.15 p.m., forestry talk; 7.15–7.30 p.m., miscellaneous programme.

CFCN, 440 meters, Calgary, Alta.—12.30–2.30 a.m., studio concert, news crops, reports, dance music.

CFQC, 400 meters, Saskatoon, Sask.—1.15–2.00 p.m., livestock and grain prices, latest news, phonograph selections; 8.30–10.00 p.m., bedtime story, studio concert, vocal and instrumental.

CHBC, 410 meters, Calgary, Alta.—8.45–10.00 p.m., studio concert, news items.

CJCA, 450 meters, Edmonton, Alta.—1.30–2.15 p.m., crop and weather report, latest news items; 8.30–9.00 p.m., news items and short programme.

WHERE TO HEAR TALKS AND LECTURES

September 15–October 12

Monday—CFCH, CHNC, CKLC.

Tuesday—CFCH, CJCM, CKY, CNRR.

Wednesday— CFAC, CFCH, CHYC, CJCA, CNRO.

Thursday—CFCH, CJCM, CNRE, CNRM, CNRW.

Friday—CFCH, CKCK, CKLC, CKY, CNRT.

Saturday—CFCH.

CJCM, 312 meters, Mont Joli, Que.—4.00–5.00 p.m., news, reports and short afternoon programme (language French); 10.30–12.00 p.m., studio concert, vocal and instrumental, short talk, (languages French and English).

CKAC, 425 meters, Montreal, Que.—3.00 p.m., afternoon broadcast, weather and stock reports, news items of the day (languages, French and English); 6.00–6.30 p.m., kiddies' stories in French and English; 6.30–7.30 p.m., Rex Battle and his concert party; 7.30 p.m., special vocal and instrumental broadcast (language, English); 9.30 p.m., continuous dance programme by Joseph C. Smith and his Mount Royal Hotel Roof Garden Orchestra.

CKCD, 410 meters, Vancouver, B.C.—10.30–11.30 p.m., evening broadcast, studio concert, vocal and instrumental numbers, news items after first musical selection.

CKCK, 420 meters, Regina, Sask.—11.00–11.30 a.m., early morning broadcast, stock and market quotations, musical selections, early news items; 1.30–2.15 p.m., noon-time broadcast, stock and market quotations, music, news of the day.

Wednesday

CFAC, 430 meters, Calgary, Alta.—2.00–2.30 p.m., news, grain and market reports, music; 4.30–5.30 p.m., music, Red Cross lecture; 8–9 p.m., Twilight Organ Recital.

CFCH, 400 meters, Iroquois Falls, Ontario.—7.00–7.05 p.m., weather report; 7.05–7.15 p.m., forestry talk; 7.15–7.45 p.m., vocal selections; 7.45–8.00 p.m., miscellaneous items; 8.00–9.00 p.m., musical programme.

CFQC, 400 meters, Saskatoon, Sask.—1.15–2.00 p.m., grain and livestock prices, latest news items, phonograph selections.

CHBC, 410 meters, Calgary, Alta.—8.45–10.00 p.m., studio concert, instrumental and vocal, news items.

CHYC, 341.7 meters, Montreal, Que.—8.00–10.00 p.m., studio concert, vocal and instrumental numbers, short lecture, intermittent dance programme.

CJCA, 450 meters, Edmonton, Alta.—1.30–2.15 p.m., crop and weather report, latest news, etc.; 8.30–9.00 p.m., bedtime story, news items, short talk; 9.30–10.30 p.m., studio concert, vocal and instrumental numbers.

CJCM, 312 meters, Mont Joli, Que.—4.00–5.00 p.m., news, reports, items of interest, short afternoon programme (language, French); 7.30–9.00 p.m., musical programme from studio, vocal numbers (language, French); 10.30–12.00 p.m., studio programme, vocal and instrumental numbers (languages, French and English).

CKAC, 425 meters, Montreal, Que.—12.45 p.m., Mount Royal Orchestra, luncheon concert from Mount Royal Hotel, news items of the day (languages, French and English); 3.00 p.m., afternoon broadcast, weather and stock reports, late news of the day (languages, French and English).

CKCD, 410 meters, Vancouver, B.C.—10.00–11.00 p.m., continuous dancing by

CKCX, 440 meters, Calgary, Alta.—10.00–11.00 p.m., studio concert, vocal and instrumental programme, weather and market reports, dance music.

CKY, 450 meters, Winnipeg, Man.—12.30–1.15 p.m., noon-time broadcast, news items, stock, grain and market quotations, musical numbers; 4.00–5.00 p.m., afternoon broadcast, news items, children's stories; 8.15–10.30 p.m., studio concert, musical and instrumental selections, lecture.

CNRR, 420 meters, Regina, Sask.—8.35–8.45 p.m., children's bedtime story; 9.00–9.45 p.m., studio concert, part one, vocal and instrumental selections; 9.45–10.00 p.m., short talk on interesting subject; 10.00–10.30 p.m., studio concert, part two, vocal and musical selections, news items.

The Radio Bug, September, 1924.

POPULAR MECHANICS

Crippled Children Enjoy Radio Concerts; Right, Crystal Set on Pipe
© U. & U.

Children in This School Find Instruction in Radio Much More Interesting Than Three "R's"
© U. & U.

Small Crystal Set Mounted on Ring

Left, Broadcasting Heartbeats; Right, Elevator Man Listens In

Popular Mechanics, mid-1920s.

Sid Boyling

Earl and Joe came in and took down his pants and his underwear. McLean didn't stop. He went right on reading.

I got into broadcasting in 1931 in Moose Jaw, where they had a station called 10AB. It was a volunteer station owned by the community. The station had got its licence in 1922. The '10' was its designation as an amateur station. Each year they would advertise for people to become members by sending in a dollar. All the help was volunteer. It was a 'live' talent station and it came on the air at about five each day and stayed on until anywhere between eleven and midnight. It was entirely 'live' talent except for one record show which was put on by a local lawyer who collected music—the classics—and came on with a daily programme. Otherwise we only used records to allow one group to get out of the studio and another group to come in. We broadcast church services every Sunday morning and evening. The churches rotated.

Our programmes were amazing when you realize that the population of Moose Jaw was only about 20,000. The Women's Musical Club performed. There were two typesetters from the Moose Jaw *Times* who were excellent pianists; they had a weekly show. There were always dance orchestras who wanted to publicize themselves. Recitations came by the dozens. And in the twenties there were sufficient people who had come from Europe who had been performers in the old country and they came on to sing or play.

Carson Buchanan was secretary of the Moose Jaw Radio Club. In the early years of the Depression the club could no longer raise money from the listeners, who voted to close the station. But Carson Buchanan said he'd pay the debts, so they sold him the licence. The station became CHAB in 1935 when they got their commercial licence. The strange thing was that the government wouldn't give us network service. We held a rally and the whole city turned out. Speakers denounced the government for not providing Moose Jaw with radio service. But without network service, there was no way to continue and Carson Buchanan signed the station off. The reaction was so intense that the government got in touch and offered the network service, and CHAB was back on the air within a week.

I took over a request programme in 1935. Within a year it developed into a show where people just walked into the studio and performed. There were no appointments. You just walked up while the show was on and we talked a bit and then the performer sang or played. We had three national sponsors taking the programme, which was unusual, because in those days you rarely got sponsors in the afternoon at all. The show stayed with one sponsor for fourteen years and we were getting as much for it as for our primetime shows.

Before we became a member of the Dominion Network, what we did was this: One of the people in the city had a good radio and we hooked up with his radio by telephone and whatever stations he got were carried by us. We would get "Amos 'n' Andy," "Jack Benny" and all the other big shows. We did this for about a year, then the government stepped in and stopped us.

I opened the station at six in the morning and signed it off at night. Although I had part of the morning off, I'd always be at the

140

station, as we all would, because of our intense interest. I even made the Canadian Press one time by doing a commercial for Imperial Tobacco. I was supposed to say "pipe smoke" but I couldn't get the words out right and it came out as "smike pope." I was frantic, because it was a national sponsor, but I just couldn't get it right. I kept saying "smike pope," "pope smike." It just went on. Anyway, Canadian Press picked the story up and I was famous—briefly—for having a twisted tongue.

We had a sportscaster who was the Moose Jaw correspondent for the Regina *Star*. He did a sportscast once a week on our station but he always dashed into the studio just as the theme to introduce him was playing. We kept trying to get him to come in a little earlier. One day we decided to teach him a lesson. As soon as we spotted him coming, we moved all the clocks five minutes ahead. When he hit the top floor, the theme was on and we frantically waved him into the studio. As he began reading, one of the girls came over, sat on his lap and started talking about the wonderful time they'd had together the night before. But he never deviated from his script. About thirty seconds before it really was time for him to go on we all came in and laughed and he said, "You got me that time." We started the theme for real but all of a sudden it struck him that we were probably pulling something on him again. So he said, "You can't fool me again. You're all a bunch of dirty so-and-so's." Suddenly he realized from the looks on our faces that he really was on the air. He picked up his papers, walked out of the studio, went down the stairs and never came back to our station again.

Earl Cameron started his career with us. Earl, Joe Lawler and Bob McLean were three announcers we had at that time and the ten o'clock news was our programme at night. All the boys stood up to read the news in front of a lectern. One night Bob McLean was doing the news. Earl and Joe came in and took down his pants and his underwear. McLean didn't stop. He went right on reading, even though our studio could readily be seen through a big window in the hall of the hotel we were in. McLean, of course, had to get even. When Earl, whose turn it was the next week, began reading, McLean tip-toed into the studio and started to undo the buttons on his pants. Earl stopped in the middle of the news and shouted, "McLean, get your hands off me!" McLean ran out of the studio and the joke was on him again. All of this went out over the air, of course.

CHAB
MOOSE JAW SASK.
AN ALL-CANADA STATION

Walter Dales

I went into broadcasting out of sheer necessity. We weren't a very well-educated bunch. Usually it was guys like me who just came in off the streets. It was the early part of the Depression. I came to Prince Albert in 1932 or so because my brother, Peter, was managing CKBI. He was also writing a half-hour drama, "The Youngbloods of Beaver Bend," for the CRBC. I'd been doing a bit of writing for the *Free Press* but had left Winnipeg to ride the freight trains because all of my friends were doing it. I think I was about twenty.

When a few big merchants began to find that radio really could sell their merchandise the press became very jealous. That had a lot to do with the strangulating regulations that began to be applied. For example, a new kind of recording that we could make ourselves came along. It was a wax disc, a transcription, and immediately there was a regulation that if anything transcribed was broadcast, it had to be announced on the air that it was a transcription. So if we were in the middle of a drama and used transcribed sound effects we had to tell the audience that. This was ridiculous. There was a barrage of such regulations, all of which were fought by Hector Charlesworth, who said, "If the politicians left us alone, we'd be all right."

The press were encouraged in their lobbying by those who favoured government control of broadcasting. The Canadian Broadcasting League published a pamphlet titled "Radio Broadcasting: A Threat to the Press" saying that advertising on radio had increased by so many percentage points while advertising in the newspapers had decreased. They convinced a lot of editors that radio was a real threat to their survival and that they ought to favour radio becoming not an advertising medium but a public service. So the newspapers started to say radio was too important an educational vehicle to be in the hands of private exploiters. That's what they called us—exploiters.

The Canadian Broadcasting League published a pamphlet titled "Radio Broadcasting: A Threat to the Press."

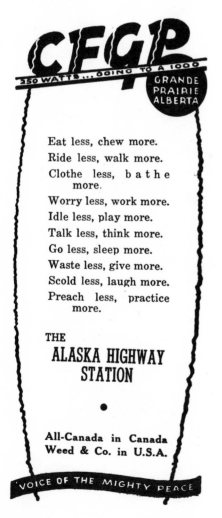

CFGP

250 WATTS ... GOING TO A 1000

GRANDE PRAIRIE ALBERTA

Eat less, chew more.

Ride less, walk more.

Clothe less, bathe more.

Worry less, work more.

Idle less, play more.

Talk less, think more.

Go less, sleep more.

Waste less, give more.

Scold less, laugh more.

Preach less, practice more.

THE
ALASKA HIGHWAY STATION

•

All-Canada in Canada
Weed & Co. in U.S.A.

VOICE OF THE MIGHTY PEACE

"MIGHTY MONARCH OF THE AIR"

So Easy To Tune Without Stooping

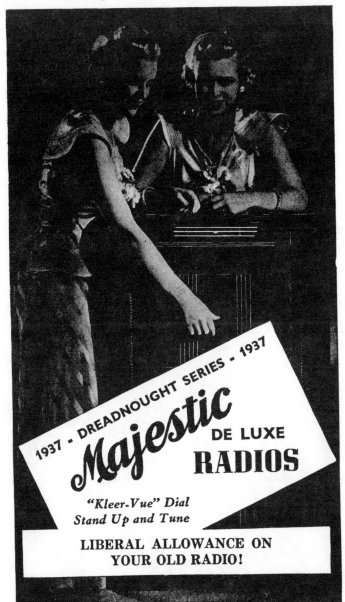

1937 - DREADNOUGHT SERIES - 1937
Majestic DE LUXE RADIOS

"Kleer-Vue" Dial
Stand Up and Tune

LIBERAL ALLOWANCE ON YOUR OLD RADIO!

Sensational New 1937 Colourful Tone

Majestic

"No Stoop, No Squint"
MODELS CIRCLE THE WORLD

No longer need you "Stoop and Squint" to tune-in, when you own a new De Luxe model MAJESTIC. The new simplified tuning dial (illustrated below) is so designed and set on an angle that it brings a new joy and convenience to short-wave and foreign station tuning. All of the latest major enginering improvements are built into the "QUEEN MARY" model illustrated, including NOISE SUPPRESSION Control, and also a locality interference reducer, thus giving quieter, clearer reception. The Mighty Majestic is famous for its "Colourful Tone".

A PRICE TO SUIT ANY PURSE

Trade-In Your Old Radio. Liberal Allowance.

Your Majestic dealer will explain the easy payment "Use-As-You-Pay" Plan. Terms as low as $5 Down.

ROGERS-MAJESTIC Corp. Ltd. Fleet St. Toronto

NEW "KLEER-VUE", "STRATE LINE" 1937 MAJESTIC 3-BAND TUNING DIAL

ASK YOUR LOCAL MAJESTIC DEALER FOR A DEMONSTRATION

G.R.A. Rice

The people there decided it was all a hoax and that we were really using a gramophone. They stormed the stage....

I received my early training in the British navy during the First World War and when, after the war, I came to Canada on family business, radio fever was in the air and I thought there might be some sort of opportunity in it for me. The Edmonton *Journal* had applied for, and received, a licence under the call letters CJCA. They bought a war surplus transmitter from the Marconi people in Montreal. The *Journal* needed someone to operate this equipment and since there was nobody else in Edmonton who knew anything about it, I became the sole operator of CJCA. The station was built on the roof of the *Journal* with a couple of towers and the usual horizontal antenna. On May 1, 1922, it was launched with just me and a staff of three others.

The original idea for CJCA was that it would be great promotion for the newspaper, which at the time had circulation problems, but I knew even then that radio would eventually be a commercial medium on its own. The Canadian National then came into the picture. They had radio receivers on trains and our station was part of their network. We functioned during weekdays

at certain hours as CNRE. They gave us a big locomotive bell which we had to ring on the air to provide CNR identification. And we had to ring it pretty hard too, because our microphones were simple telephones and didn't pick up all that well except for the voice.

We had a varied schedule because we had to share time with two or three other stations. Some were Bible stations, so there was a combination of some pretty peculiar things. You'd hear a religious sermon followed by a hockey match. Radio really meant something to people in those days because in the west women especially suffered from a peculiar kind of isolation. They lived on farms with neighbours who were four, five, ten miles away and they found that radio gave them something in common in their lives. They had new things to talk about that they had heard on radio. My wife, for example, did a one-hour show, "The Chatelaine of the Air," which was totally directed at women.

CJCA did one of the first remotes ever from McDougall United Church. This involved stringing a wire from the *Journal* over to the church roof. I had a young lad helping to drop the mikes in the organ. One Saturday he forgot to close the entry from the roof and the next day, which was Easter Sunday, the organist opened the service with a blast. Every pigeon that had got into the church came flying from every corner of the building. We had quite a time living that one down, to say nothing of getting the pigeons back outside.

To introduce radio to country people we put together a travelling display which we took around to different places so they could hear a broadcast. One time, in McComb, we put our display in a crowded hall. Halfway through, some of the people there decided it was all a hoax and that we were really using a gramophone. They stormed the stage and tried to find it. Radio was so new they were positive it was just another carnival trick.

One programme we developed was "Calling the North," which carried messages to the people who lived up there as well as messages for the Hudson Bay and the other old trading companies. A lot of these messages were in code because they gave prices on various furs and so on and were meant only for the ears of the businessmen.

I worked at CJCA for a long time during the pioneering years. Eventually I decided to apply for a licence of my own. That's when CFRN came into being. The R was my initial. The N was the initial of my original partner, Hans Neilson. We picked the roughest time to launch anything, the middle of the Depression. But we survived. It was tough because there was very little money available for local businesses to advertise and we didn't know what to charge as it was all so new.

Radio was a godsend to the prairie dwellers during the Depression. It was a life line between themselves and the outside world.

Dr. G.R.A. Rice.

T. J. Allard

Lives were less cluttered in those days. I suppose, in a way, radio was the beginning of clutter.

In the twenties and thirties, radio held a great fascination for people because it brought in the outside world. You could find families in northern Alberta driving fifty miles in forty below weather to hear perhaps three or four minutes of reception from KSL in Salt Lake City. (The Mormon Choir was the most popular feature.)

Another thing that built up listenership was a pride in reaching distant cities. If your set could bring in Denver, you bragged about it. I worked on mine until I could bring in Los Angeles so I could out-brag others. In those days the spectrum was so uncluttered it was not uncommon to pick up Russia, Australia, New Zealand—all manner of places—in northern Alberta. You would carefully note the time, the music and anything else that would give certain identification. Then you wrote that station which sent you back the DX postcard for verification. People collected these things the way they would collect rare coins today. Lives were less cluttered in those days. I suppose, in a way, radio was the beginning of clutter. Suddenly, there was all this stuff coming into their homes from the outside—some of it good; some of it not so good.

When broadcasting first started in Canada it was thought of primarily as a source of entertainment rather than information. News came later. That's because most of the people who went into broadcasting saw it as an extension of the theatre. That's partly why broadcasting was rigidly structured in hourly and half-hour and quarter-hour formats as distinct from today's rolling format. And of course, those we could draw on to do broadcasting were mostly people with theatrical experience of one kind or another. The impact of broadcasting was an explosion of entertainment. All of a sudden people in many parts of Canada had available to them the finest talent from the entire world. In an entertainment sense, these people had been isolated. They made their own entertainment at home or at the legion hall or at the community centre. They listened to amateurs. They had singsongs. That kind of thing. The movies were beginning to have an impact and that fed, I think, the desire for entertainment. You had visiting evangelists and Chautauquas, etc. When people found that by means of recordings and live broadcasts, radio allowed them to hear the finest entertainment from everywhere they went for that eagerly.

There was an incredible amount of live radio at first. Broadcasters didn't particularly like recordings. It was partly a matter of pride and partly that the recording equipment and the recordings weren't all that good. By today's standards the quality was incredibly bad. Nor was there a great supply. The record companies weren't that fussy at first about having their records used on air because they thought it might reduce sales. Only one or two of the more progressive companies encouraged the use of their records. In addition there was a reservoir of talent in most cities. Every city had a number of piano teachers, organ teachers, singing teachers who supplemented their income by performing in churches and at concerts. And there were bands all over the place. People went dancing then much more than they do now, especially on Saturday nights. Even a city like Edmonton, remote and isolated as it then was in the 1920s and 1930s, had two dozen places where one could go dancing on Saturday nights. So the talent was there, and broadcasting stations could draw on that, usually for no fee. Artists were more than anxious to get on. Tape was the thing that brought a lot of live radio to an end. Tape, you know, was developed primarily for military purposes. During a war there is no shortage of money for research and development, and there was a tremendous breakthrough in electronic equipment during World War Two. Before that we only had standard commercial recordings, the old seventy-eights. But the war introduced the beginnings of the modern day tape recorder, which brought about such great changes in broadcasting.

MIDNIGHT—And The International Radio Tests.

Gord Williamson

Behind me I had the whole Bentley family. I guess there'd be maybe fifteen or twenty of them. And their language was not always the best.

I started off writing sports. Dick Rice was the manager of CJCA when they were located in a corner of the newsroom of the Edmonton *Journal*. They wanted somebody to fill in between periods, the colour commentary and all that. So I started doing that. The man doing the play by play worked on display advertising for the *Journal*. One night something had gone wrong with the special Christmas page they were putting out. He had to do the page over again. So Mr. Rice asked me if I'd do the play by play. So I did and that started me. December 12, 1931. You didn't have any facilities in those days. You were right on the edge of the rink. You didn't sit, either, you stood. You had to duck flying pucks and hockey sticks and one thing and another. Those were the days of the old western Canada pro league. When Mr. Rice took over CFRN, I moved with him from CJCA. You might get five dollars a game. A little later, about 1935, I was doing it for Imperial Tobacco. They used to pay fifteen dollars a game, and expenses. I covered all of western Canada. You travelled by train or by car.

The weather was often a problem. Worst was in football when it got toward the end of the season. In those days you didn't have a broadcast booth. I used to go up and down the side of the field pulling the microphone cord behind me. It was okay if the weather was good, but if it happened to be a day when it was snowing or raining, then it got to be a nuisance pulling that ruddy cord. And the mud you got. And the dirt. Finally they began to get the broadcast booths, and that made all the difference.

When you're broadcasting from the wide open spaces, the crowd sometimes could distract your attention. I trained myself

to concentrate on the play and forget what was going on around me. I think the worst situation was in Drumheller, in the days when the Drumheller minor hockey club had all the Bentley brothers playing. I was broadcasting just from the seats. Behind me I had the whole Bentley family. I guess there'd be maybe fifteen or twenty of them. And their language was not always the best. And they never shut up. They kept yelling all the time and it made it a little difficult.

About 1934 Mr. Rice got a contract for newscasts from Texaco, and because I had experience I did news as well as all the sports. In those days, the one wire service was British United Press. All your international stuff came over BUP. We used to have four half-hour transmissions a day. From that you took what you needed to build your newscast. It meant an awful lot of rewrite. Your local stuff you just gathered yourself by telephone. And you scalped some from the newspapers. That picture changed when the war came in 1939. Then the teletypes started going steady.

We worked long hours. I'd go to work in the morning. Used to have to be at the station at half-past seven. I'd get there and do a sportscast and have another one at noon to prepare. I was also preparing newscasts. I'd go to work first thing in the morning and it would be around eleven-thirty at night before I got home because you went all the time. And you did everything. But it used to be fun. Now it's a job. One chap I worked with used to play jokes on me, so I never knew if the mike was going to be a stand mike on top of the grand piano or a desk mike on the floor without a chair in sight, and I'd just have to do my sports on my stomach. Those were really good days. But after the war it was strictly dollars and cents. You couldn't be fooling around. You had to be serious.

PATENT YOUR RADIO IDEAS

Consult—

THE RAMSAY CO.
PATENTS SEARCHES
TRADEMARKS COPYRIGHTS

273 BANK ST.   OTTAWA, CANADA
Six Years' Experience in Radio Research

THE ILL-FATED BUG WHO INVITES A COUPLE OF NEIGHBOURS TO LISTEN IN AND FINDS THAT, FOR THE FIRST TIME IN SIX MONTHS, THERE'S SOMETHING RADICALLY WRONG WITH THE SET.

THE BUG WHO USES A SIX-VOLT BATTERY ON HIS PEANUT TUBES AND THEN WONDERS WHY THEY BURN OUT.

STRANGE! THAT'S FIVE BULBS GONE THE SAME WAY!

HARRY D. WALLACE 1923

149

Kay Parkin

They gave me a script and I had to read commercials. Then I auditioned with another singing group. Then I had to take shorthand.

In high school two friends and I formed a trio and appeared around Saskatoon doing this and that. We entered an amateur contest on CFQC in Saskatoon and won first prize. One day, when the other two girls in the trio were away somewhere, the CRBC, who had just come into being, were in town holding auditions. A friend of my father came roaring up to our house in his car and said, "Get down there. They've been auditioning all afternoon and all they've been getting is classical, and they don't want classical." "But the other two girls aren't here," I explained. He said, "Go down anyway." So down I went to the Saskatoon Electric, where the studio was. There I sat, feeling more and more foolish, until all the people were finished and a man came out. I think it was Mr. Bushnell. He came over to me and said, "What can I do for you, little girl?" I said, "We have a trio." "Where?" he asked. I explained and I guess I looked so sad that he said, "Come on into the studio," and he asked me to sing without accompaniment. So I went to the microphone and sang "I Don't Stand a Ghost of a Chance With You." I thought that I really didn't stand a ghost of a chance, but Mr. Bushnell said, "Put this girl's trio on with the first programme." That's the way our trio got hired.

We stayed on first with an orchestra, but that was kind of expensive, so they had us sing with a trumpet and a violin, and eventually with just a violin. We were all terribly dedicated and we rehearsed every day. After about a year, the regional director said he had to give other people a try. Everyone was clamouring for a chance and people were saying things like, "Who are these young things from the Prairies?" When our lead girl left for Winnipeg to make her fortune I stayed on and sang with a local orchestra and later got in with four boys in a variety group to do local radio shows. I can't remember how much we were paid for that, a couple of dollars each, I think. The boys went out, sold the shows, and wrote copy, which they then showed to the sponsor. One was Intercontinental Packers, and another was Quaker Oats.

One day I got a call from CJCA in Edmonton. Evidently the manager there had asked the western regional director of the CRBC if he knew a girl who could work in the office and do on air work too. They phoned me and I was thrilled to pieces. I had to go up and audition. When I got to CJCA there was a small group rehearsing in one studio. The manager opened the door, shoved me in, and said to the boys, "I want this girl to sing with you." The musicians all looked at me as if I was something from Mars. But that went fine. Then they gave me a script and I had to read commercials. Then I auditioned with another singing group. Then I had to take shorthand. *Then* they said for me to go back to Saskatoon, as they had to get permission from the president to bring in an out-of-towner. It was two months before the word came to report. My parents wanted me to go to university but I was 'radio-struck' and nobody could change my mind.

When I moved to Edmonton I could have died a thousand times. They put me in the continuity department and gave me the list of accounts of a girl who was going on holidays. I'd never written commercials. So I went back nights and went to the files and cribbed. The manager came back one night and caught me. He said, "What's this? There must be something wrong with our system if a girl has to come here to work at night." I told him, "I'm a little homesick. I don't know many people here and I like to work." And the truth is, I could have gone back home a million times, but I knew my parents expected me to fail.

There were a lot of things I had to do in connection with my job. I was on air with the morning man. Then I worked all day in continuity. I relieved at the switchboard. I sang every night for the Hudson's Bay. Once a week I was on a half-hour Hawaiian show. And I had two programmes a week with children. Saturdays I sang at the McDonald Hotel on the network with the orchestra. When the Hawaiian show ended in one studio I'd be signing off and somebody would hold the door open for me. I'd rush into the next studio, put on the earphones, and sing "Blue Moon," the theme song for the Hudson's Bay show. The fellows were always trying to break you up while you were on the air. They'd unzipper your dress at the back, pull your stockings down, undo your collar. The only one who ever succeeded was Jackie Dawson. He had a newscast and in the middle of it I did a couple of minutes of women's news. This one time he reached over and grabbed my nose. That's something you can't ignore—someone holding your nose—and it really broke me up.

One time I was singing at the McDonald Hotel, on the floor level, and the band was on a little platform behind. We didn't rehearse very much. They'd give me my music and I stood holding it on one side of the mike. While I was singing a drunk dancer went by and seized the music out of my hand. I just reached out to the other side of the mike and grabbed it back as he danced by again. That was close. We had a girl named Dorothy who did a woman's programme in the afternoon. The control room was right beside the switchboard. One day when I was on the switchboard the door burst open during a musical selection and they carried Dorothy past me. I didn't know if she was dead or what. They told me to get in there and take her script. Talk about being jittery. I'd never seen the script, but the record was nearing the end, so I went in and didn't do too badly. Apparently Dorothy had given blood at the Red Cross, had come into the studio and fainted.

The fellows were always trying to break you up while you were on the air. They'd unzipper your dress.

RADIO RIBS.........by Harkley

And now, tripping daintily to the microphone, comes our glamorous Lady of the Dawn. In a moment she will pour forth a little of her exotic self in sweet song—it says here.

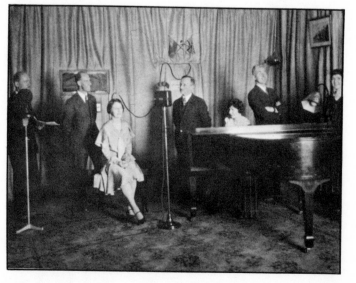

The CKUA players of Edmonton in 1928-29.

Norman A. Botterill

Red Deer, Alberta in itself didn't warrant having a radio station but its background explains why it did. The Alberta Pacific Grain Company of Calgary, one of the big elevator companies, had to send as many as five telegrams a day to all the elevators in the province stating the prices paid for each load of grain brought in according to grade and type. Somebody suggested that if they had a radio station that covered the province they could broadcast the prices instead of telegraphing them. So the Alberta Pacific Grain Company hired W.W. Grant, one of the early broadcasting pioneers. He built a radio station in Red Deer, a town in the centre of the province.

I was in high school and excited that there was going to be a radio station in Red Deer. I observed as much of its installation as I could. I played a little hookey to do that too. I hung around so much that I was finally allowed to appear on microphone and even to do some shifts. I didn't get paid, but I did a fair amount of on air work while finishing school. At the beginning the primary purpose of CKLC was to broadcast grain prices. They broadcast from Red Deer early in the morning, at noon, and in the evening. Of course, they had to be awfully careful because just one mistake meant that hundreds of elevators would buy the grain at the wrong price.

Then the company created a radio department at headquarters in Calgary and embarked on the kind of programming that was common in those days. They had a good amount of live and recorded material and it got to the point where it was operating full-time both in Calgary and subsequently at a studio in Edmonton.

I went to university for a year and did a little work at CKUA, the university station. But I didn't go back to school that fall. Instead I went to CKLC where they were looking for an assistant operator. I got the job—it was 1927—and I've been in the business ever since. Of course, the station in Red Deer was a great and wonderful thing. People were always coming around to see it. One time a farm family came in. Now the station wasn't a big place—it was just one room—so this family had to stand around and be quiet while the mike was open. Then while a record was playing you could explain what was happening. They were just about ready to go when the mother said, "When do you wind this thing?" She thought the whole station worked off a spring motor the way her gramophone did.

Everything went along fine until the crash, when, of course, the grain industry almost went broke. The grain exchanges became so slow that there was no need for them, so the AP Grain Company resolved that the radio station wasn't worth keeping. This decision coincided with the creation of the CRBC, which took our clear channel for themselves and offered to buy out CKLC. AP jumped at the chance to get what money they could and sold the thing. I stayed for a month or so, helping to dismantle and pack up the station. It was put in a boxcar and I don't know where it went. Frankly, once it was dismantled, I don't think it was worth reassembling.

I was footloose then. The manager of the station in Calgary,

At that time there was a flood of U.S. stations coming into Canada.

J.R. Foster, had created a publication listing all of the week's programmes—primarily American—because at that time there was a flood of U.S. stations coming into Canada. Foster invited me to join the magazine, which I did, and we published this thing for a year or so. I used to go to Edmonton and sell space in the magazine. That led me to Taylor-Pearson-Carson, the automotive people in Edmonton who were contemplating applying for a radio licence. They asked me if I'd be interested in joining them. The thought of getting back into radio was very appealing. I jumped at the chance, without even asking how much I would be paid. I think that was 1934.

It's empty now —
the room at the top of the stairs

Yes, but one of these days in the not too distant future the young Skipper will be taking it over again.

Just how soon that will be, depends upon the united efforts of all of us in this

FIFTH VICTORY LOAN CAMPAIGN

CFCN

CALGARY   ALBERTA

THE VOICE OF THE PRAIRIES

Francis Martin

My first brush with radio was in 1933. I started out singing on the air and I was called "Little Boy Blue." That was my theme song. In those days, a piano and a singer were the entertainment. I used to sing ballads and some semi-classics, but never anything 'heavy.' I got two-fifty a programme, which was paid in cash. In 1935 I joined the staff of CJCJ, which was owned by *The Albertan*. The manager wanted to create a new image for the station, which had been going downhill. He applied for a change in the call letters, and it became CKXL, which it's been ever since. Soon I was doing anything and everything. After a couple of years I started writing copy, although I'd been the worst English student in school.

I was nicknamed "Scoop" because I plagiarized the Canadian Press which had a bureau at *The Albertan*. I used to rewrite their news because there was no licensed news service for radio and the newspapers were very jealous of their news service. Still, you couldn't stop radio from stealing news. When they brought the first radio news service in, World War Two was warming up and getting a newscast together was hectic. I used to paste it up from local stories in *The Albertan* and world news off the machine. It wasn't too great a newscast. I was no news editor. I just rear-ranged the lead and let the rest of it go.

I used to sell spots for fifty and seventy-five cents each. If a man was going to spend a hundred dollars you bolted the doors and windows so he wouldn't get away. The fact is, it took a long time for radio to become recognized as a medium of advertising. People thought it was a novelty. In the West it wasn't until the 1940s that radio really started to move. When I think about it, I would say that World War Two had a lot to do with radio being recognized as a serious and valuable medium. People stayed glued to their sets for the latest news from the front and they developed habits of listening that stayed with them when the war was over.

I was nicknamed "Scoop" because I plagiarized the Canadian Press.

The Same, Soft, Natural Tones !

The voices of boy choristers possess an appealing quality— which is carried to you pefectly by MUSIC MASTER.

Through this wonderful Radio Reproducer you hear the clear, beautiful music that would delight you if you were listening to the choir itself, in some great cathedral.

The *wood* horn of MUSIC MASTER brings out the rich, full resonance of voices and musical instruments.

Hear MUSIC MASTER, the latest marvel of Radio. Ask your dealer to attach it to a good set and let it talk for itself.

Then take it home with you.

DEALERS EVERYWHERE

MUSIC MASTER is made in two sizes. The 14-inch model, for the home, may be obtained with spruce or mahogany finish horn. The 21-inch model for concerts and dancing, has the mahogany horn only.

THE MUSIC MASTER CORPORATION
(Formerly GENERAL RADIO CORPORATION)
Makers and Distributors of High Grade Radio Apparatus
PHILADELPHIA, Pa., U.S.A.

Montreal
John Millen & Son, Ltd.
321-23 St. James St.

Quebec
John Millen & Son, Ltd.
96 Crown St.

Toronto
John Millen & Son, Ltd.
71 Wellington St., West.

Ottawa
Whitcher & Co.,
197 Bank St.

Earl Connor

I first became aware of radio back in 1919. I was nine years old and my family was living in Kitsilano, B.C. One day I noticed a man who lived across the lane from us putting up a piece of wire from his house to a pole in his back yard. I knew it wasn't a clothesline; it was too high for that. I asked him what he was doing and he told me he was putting up an antenna for his wireless. He showed me all the bits and pieces that he'd put together—a spark coil from a Ford, an old windshield with tinfoil all over it to serve as a capacitator, and other things.

That got me interested. I collected some of these things myself and my dad and I put a wireless together too. After that we built others—small ones, big ones and some in between. Later I worked for a man at a garage who sold Sparton radios on the side, and I got involved with distributing these. Then I somehow got a job as chief engineer at CKMO Vancouver because the chap who had the job figured he could make more money as a wireless operator on the rumrunning boats which were active at that time. The station was owned by the Spratts, who also owned a broadcasting school. They didn't seem to take the radio station very seriously. In the summer they would go away on their yacht for a couple of months and none of us would get paid until they remembered to come back to sign our cheques. We'd manage to survive through contra. We got free meals and clothing in exchange for advertising on the station.

In those days there were several stations in the city sharing the same frequency—CKWX and CKMO, for example, split the day between them. In 1933 the CCF was coming on strong and there was a rabid CCFer named Lyle Telford in Vancouver. He was even more rabid than M.J. Coldwell or J.S. Woodsworth, the people who started the movement. Telford went around holding rallies and making remarks that upset a lot of people. At first he was content to gather a crowd in an auditorium but eventually he got the idea he could reach more people by broadcasting his message. He approached CKWX where I was working by this time. If there was anything the owner, Sparks Halstead, was against, it was the CCF. He lost no time showing Telford the door. So Telford trotted over to CKMO, whose owner couldn't see anything wrong with CCF money. He scheduled Telford to come on as soon as CKWX signed off. This really galled CKWX, not only because he was on but because it sounded as if Telford was broadcasting over CKWX.

By this time people were beginning to take Telford more seriously. One night he said something that got their hackles up in the provincial capital in Victoria. A radio inspector there got in touch with Ottawa. The next thing we knew a wire arrived at CKWX ordering us off the air. No reason given or anything. Sparks Halstead was beside himself. He asked Ross McIntyre, the chief engineer, "What will we do?" Ross said, "We'll do nothing. If they want to put us off the air, they'll have to do it physically because there's no way I'll turn us off. Get hold of your lawyer, get hold of your friends in Ottawa and find out what's going on." They still hadn't told us the reason they wanted us off the air. Anyway, we just stayed on until finally the wires stopped coming. We never did find out what was going on.

The chap who had the job figured he could make more money as a wireless operator on the rumrunning boats.

157

Don Laws

The press would scratch out the microphone call letters so readers couldn't see what station it was.

I went to school in Grand Forks, British Columbia. After that, I worked in a survey party. Then I joined the bank, got out of that, went into the stock business in 1928 and it crashed in 1929. So I trucked fruit up in Kelowna for two bits an hour. Then I came down to join my dad who had a bit of an agency that was going to specialize in radio programmes. Well, there wasn't enough volume. But I got to know George Chandler of CJOR and I went to work for him in 1933, selling time at a twenty percent commission. I can remember selling ads to an outfit that was teaching people how to sew. It took all morning to sell them on the idea of spending five dollars for an announcement. Then I went back to the station and wrote the copy. Eventually we got the five dollars, out of which I got a dollar. It was tough.

Sometimes there was enough money to pay the staff and sometimes there wasn't. We'd close down at two in the afternoon and everybody would go out and sell time. We'd open up again at five. We all doubled in brass. I operated the controls a lot and didn't announce much because I had a terrible voice. I used to do the old English football results because nobody could pronounce the names except me since I'd been born in England. Also, I used to do the stock quotations because I'd been in the business and knew the names of the stocks. If the station took a thousand dollars a month in, we were doing good. A lot of our business was contra.

The big trouble in selling advertising in the early days was that a merchant could put an ad in the newspaper and when he got home he could see it. He could say to his wife, "Look, dear, there's our ad; isn't it nice?" But when he bought a spot on the radio it was usually on when he was in his store so he didn't hear it. We were mostly on the air in the daytime hours then. Nighttime was dead in those days. Stations would shut down at nine, ten, eleven o'clock at night.

Finally, we started using personalities. When Vic Waters, for example, came on and said, "I'm going to tell you about a good product," they believed him. This is the key to advertising. It doesn't matter how many people read your ad, or hear your announcements. If they don't believe it, it's not worth anything. We pushed these personality programmes and we kept them balanced, so a guy wasn't pushing two competing products. It proved itself. People would say, "Well, if *he* recommends it, it *must* be good."

When the CRBC was formed at the behest of the Aird Report all the do-gooders flocked around and the newspapers, of course, were in there. They made sure that radio was going to be hamstrung as much as possible. One stupid thing was that you couldn't run an announcement after seven thirty at night. Another thing you couldn't do was quote prices. We used to get around that in a small way by saying, "Buy so-and-so's chocolate bars. They're less than a streetcar ticket." The street car ticket was five cents. If you were advertising a men's haberdashery you could talk for five minutes about how good a suit was and that you mustn't miss this bargain, and that the price was unbelievable. But you couldn't mention what the price was. It was a lot of baloney. The newspapers were afraid that radio was going to put them out of business, which was stupid. They were so anti-radio that if we were doing a remote broadcast and the press was there taking pictures they would scratch out the microphone call letters so readers couldn't see what station it was when the picture appeared.

CJOR started in 1922 as CKFX. It was owned by the Westminster Trust Company and became CJOR in 1926. George Chandler bought it for $600—half in cash, and twenty-five a month. The studio was in an apartment. He slept in the bedroom. The kitchen was the engineer's office. And they broadcast from the living room. Then they moved to space over the Alexandra Ballroom. Mart Kenney says he owes his success to CJOR. He was playing the Alexandra and the CPR was trying out bands in Calgary to go to Banff for the summer. Kenny wanted to audition, but he couldn't afford to go to Calgary. So we arranged things. After we went off the air at twelve o'clock we'd come back on the air at one, especially for Mart Kenney. He played a one-hour programme of music and because we were on a good frequency and all the stations were off they could pick us up in Calgary. The manager of the Palliser Hotel heard Mart, liked what he heard, and hired him. That's how he got his career started.

We also had a group at CJOR putting on live drama. We did historic dramatizations of all the big companies in this area—the CPR, the Powell River Company, MacMillan-Bloedel, for example. It made CJOR's name well known. We did the first Canadian Golf Championship carrying heavy remote equipment around on a stretcher. Nobody had any money but we'd work our guts out to do something because it was fun. We started "Town Meeting in Canada," a sort of a public forum. We did "Treasure Trail," a giveaway show. We gave away fifty silver dollars each week, and people had to send in their gum wrappers. We got thirty-five thousand letters in one week.

We were always playing tricks. One time we fitted a long tube to the microphone and when the announcer started his programme we started blowing smoke through this thing. He was going along and all of a sudden a puff of smoke came out of the microphone. He had no knowledge of mechanics and he thought it could blow up in his face. He tried desperately to get the operator's attention. The operator had been tipped-off and had his back to him. He was looking in the window of the other studio and could see what was happening. The announcer was waving his arms and trying to keep on with his broadcast. He went all the way through his fifteen minutes with this thing smoking all the time. He came out, perspiring and really shook up. Everybody was sitting around killing themselves laughing. We were always dreaming up things like that.

5000 WATTS   600 K.C.

CJOR

VANCOUVER

E. Ross MacIntyre

One day along came the radio inspector to look at his licence. Halstead asked, "Licence? What's that?"

I've messed around with radio ever since there was radio. Sometimes I wondered who knew the most—me or Marconi. I came to the Westminster station about 1926 and eventually I got to CKWX, a station that had really started in Nanaimo. This man Sparks Halstead had a store which sold radios and he needed something for his customers to listen to so he went to Seattle and bought a small transmitter. One day along came the radio inspector to look at his licence. Halstead asked, "Licence? What's that?" The inspector told him, "You've got to have a licence for these things." Halstead asked him how to get a licence and he then sent the money to Ottawa, and back came his licence. I think it cost $50.

When Halstead decided to move to Vancouver he just took his transmitter with him. The first thing he knows, the same radio inspector came around and asked, "How'd you get here?" "I moved," said Halstead. "Didn't you tell Ottawa?" asked the inspector. "I didn't know I had to," said Halstead. "Well," the inspector replied, "now that you're here, you're here." That's how CKWX came to Vancouver. Stations were assigned a certain frequency as they are today but if you could find a better spot on the band you'd just move to it. It drove the inspector crazy.

We did a lot of remotes at CKWX. Earl Connor and I would play leapfrog all over town with two remote units. He'd do thirty minutes in one place while I was moving and setting up somewhere else. Then I'd take the next programme while he'd run somewhere else and set up. Maybe 'run' isn't the right word, because the remote equipment weighed somewhere around eighty

SPECIAL LOW PRICES ON RADIO SUPPLIES

An Opportunity to get Complete Sets or Parts at Less than Actual Cost

In an effort to reduce a large stock to make room for the arrival of further shipments, we are sacrificing profits for turnover. We outline a few of the savings that can be made.

AMPLIFYING TRANSFORMERS

Very latest type, highest grade. SPECIAL PRICE $5.00 Bradley Stats. SPECIAL PRICE $2.25

HEAD PHONES—Best British Make—Type A

4,000 ohms. Regular price, $19.00. SPECIAL PRICE **$15.00**
3,000 ohms. Regular price, $17.75. SPECIAL PRICE **$15.50**
Holtzer-Cabot Head Phone, 2,000 ohms. SPECIAL PRICE **$8.75**
Dreyfus Concert Type. SPECIAL PRICE **$9.50**

SIGNAL CONDENSERS

.0001 Verbal Condenser Dial Knob, complete, guaranteed. SPECIAL PRICE ....$3.00 Bakelite Dials. SPECIAL PRICE 65c

Many other bargains we have not room to illustrate. Send for Special Price List to-day and get that set that you have been wanting, at a saving of 50%.

787 Queen St. W. **J. M. PAQUIN** Toronto ~ Ont.
"The Electrical Shop"

pounds. We would run a remote off a moonlight cruise, for example, which had an orchestra on board. We'd put a shortwave transmitter on the ship and pick it up on a receiver we had at the bowl in the middle of Stanley Park. We broadcast soapbox derbies. One time we even did a six-day bike race. I didn't know any more about six-day bike races than I did about running a submarine. In fact, I think I knew more about running a submarine.

We built most of our own stuff back then. The beauty of that was that every one of us knew every piece of equipment like the back of our hands. If something went wrong we knew how to fix it. When we first started we just used an ordinary hand-wound phonograph in front of a microphone. After a little scrounging we got a couple of magnetic pickups and two motors so we could go from one turntable to another. Until that time you had to stay quiet while the record was playing; otherwise, everything you said went over the air.

One time the inspectors blamed us for something that we didn't do and they were going to cancel our licence. They were coming to put us off the air so I barricaded myself in the transmitter building and told the inspector through an open window, "You can't get in here." I think R.B. Bennett was Prime Minister at the time and something derogatory had been said about him. The inspector jumped to conclusions without bothering to find out just what was said or who said it. It was another station and I wasn't about to have our licence cancelled. I hauled my meals in through that window and stayed put because if we'd gone off the air we'd have been off forever. Anyway, they finally straightened it out and we never lost a second of air time.

R~3 Magnavox Radio $62.50
with 14 inch Horn

R~2 Magnavox Radio 117.00
with 18 inch Horn

Model C Magnavox
Power Amplifier

3-Stage AC~3~C   ~ $150.00
2-Stage AC~2~C   ~   110.00

DISTRIBUTING
"MAGNAVOX"
To The Radio Trade

Did you receive our very complete revised Trade Price List ?

JOHN MILLEN & SON, LIMITED

"Wholesale Only"

71 Wellington St.   321-3 St. James St.   96 Crown St
TORONTO   MONTREAL   QUEBEC

Be progressive—enjoy wireless programs daily with the

MAGNAVOX
Radio
The Reproducer Supreme

No wireless receiving set is complete without it

Fred Bass

I don't know why he thought I'd make a good announcer by hearing me play the dulcimer.

I was working as a transmitter operator at CKWX in Vancouver in 1928 and although it wasn't what I wanted to do, it was a job and it was radio. I was a pretty good musician and had done a great deal of work in theatres playing piano at silent movies. One day at the transmitter I got a phone call from Harold Paulson, the station manager, asking me to come over to the studio and play the dulcimer on a children's programme, as the man who usually did it was ill. When I was finished Mr. Paulson asked me if I'd ever thought of becoming an announcer. I don't know why he thought I'd make a good announcer by hearing me play the dulcimer, but he gave me an audition and said, "OK, that's fine. Don't go to the transmitter on Monday. Come here instead as an announcer."

We were only a staff of seven at that time and it was a great way to learn the business. You did everything. For example, I'd go out and sell an idea to someone like B.C. Hydro. I'd go back to the station, write the commercial and select the music for the programme. Then I'd do the operating and the announcing for it when it went on the air. In the summer I did 'live' programmes with the Vancouver Symphony from Stanley Park. They went coast to coast on the network. I also did network programmes at Banff and Lake Louise with Mart Kenney's Seven Gentlemen and Murray Adaskin's Trio. There was no pay in this for me. The CP gave us guest rooms as a gift and we'd eat our meals with the staff there.

On Friday nights we did a one-hour show with a seven-piece balalaika orchestra and Russian singers. A husband and wife team wrote the show. I was the announcer and piano player and I also did comedy. That went on every Friday for a couple of years. Then I developed a comedy act with an old vaudeville man where we used dialects and we must have been OK, because that show went on for fifteen years. I developed another act using two pianos with a girl I knew and we called it "Knice 'n Knifty." And we had on all the famous artists who came to town—people like Gracie Fields. In the afternoons we had uninterrupted, live symphony music. Can you imagine the cost if we'd been paying for it? And radio attracted a lot of characters in those days. We had an old guy who looked like Kaiser Bill. He did a news programme called "Mr. Good Evening." He always came on the air that way and he always signed off by wishing all "our June brides a pleasant evening."

Our station was famous for opening things. We opened everything from bridges to YMCAs. It was a low-cost way of filling time. Church services fell into the same category. And we followed the fire engines. I could get right up close because the chief had been with me in the First World War and I had a pass. I'd get right up where the firemen had the nozzle and have the swish of the water in the background as I described the fire.

One time we had a blank spot in the schedule and the manager said, "What'll we put in there?" I told him I knew of a good quartet. Actually, I was thinking of some buddies in the Kiwanis Glee Club. Anyway, we knocked this thing together with me announcing, playing the piano and singing the bass parts. When the programme was over the manager called to say, "I don't know where you got that group, but it's great!" We were on the air every Sunday night for the next nine years.

Nobody made any money out of radio then, least of all the performers. You worked for what you could get. Leo Nicholson, for example, had a children's programme on CJOR during which he always mentioned a particular café. That meant he would get his meals free. The management went along with this because of the pay these guys were getting during the Depression. Eileen Robinson did a programme of piano music and she got paid in roasts and steaks by mentioning her butcher. Those were wonderful days and I thought I was the luckiest guy in the world to be a part of it all.

The Radio

Since Pa put in the radio we have a lot of fun,
We hustle to my room upstairs as soon as supper's done
And Pa he tinkers with the discs to get it loud and clear,
Then says: " Wait just a minute now, there's nothing yet to hear.
Oh, now it's coming! Silence there! Now don't you move a thing.
Says Ma, this is a marvellous age, a lady's going to sing!"

Then Ma she listens for a while, as pleased as she can be,
And when I want to hear it, too, she says, "Don't bother me!
Your turn comes next and sister's too; don't jump around that way,
I want to hear the orchestra—it's just begun to play.
I wish you children wouldn't fuss, I'm sure I cannot hear
While you are trying all the time to snatch it from my ear."

Then Pa takes up the thing awhile, and says: " Oh, that's just great!
A man is telling stories now. You kids will have to wait.
It's wonderful to think his voice is floating in the air
And people sitting in their homes can hear it everywhere—
All right, all right! It's your turn now. Perhaps this man will teach
You youngsters how you should behave. A parsons going to preach.

Pa put that radio in for me—at least he told me so,
But if it's really mine or not is something I don't know,
'Cos Pa wants it all himself, to hear the funny things,
An' Ma must hear the concerts through when some great artist sings,
But when the parson starts to talk on Selfishness an' Sin,
Pa says, "Now it has come the time time for you to listen in."

—Edgar A. Guest, in *The Vancouver Sun*.

Gerry Quinney

I started at CKWX, Vancouver in October 1930 with Sparks Halstead. We had the most inefficient antenna system that could possibly be imagined, yet it got us all over the world. When the boat would come in from Australia once or twice a month there was always a flock of mail from there. There were DX clubs all over the world and members would stay up all night trying to find radio stations to write to. It got to be a worldwide hobby.

I worked at CKWX for a year before the Depression caught up with us and, as low man on the totem pole, I was the first to go. When Jim Brown got a licence at CKOV in Kelowna I helped get that station going. It was 1931 and Jim couldn't pay me but he had a contra account with a hotel and a restaurant. That meant I had a place to sleep and a place to eat. After a while I went to Kamloops, another little one-man operation. I was the one man, in a shack on the side of a hill; rattlesnakes used to sun themselves on my steps. In 1934 I got back to CKWX.

There was no such thing as commercial equipment then and you had to build everything yourself. In Vancouver Earl Connor made our first disc-recording apparatus. He got an old machine that a movie house was throwing out and converted an electric pick up into a cutter. We made our discs by spraying a mixture of duco-black automobile paint on flat steel and when it reached the right viscosity we would cut the disc. That may have been the first acetate machine in Canada. We were making discs of various programmes and of spot announcements. We were also selling recordings to those who wanted them. During one election we got a contract from the CCF to do a series of recordings by J.S. Woodsworth to be circulated throughout western Canada. We told him he could get only fifteen minutes on each disc and that he'd better use a script. Halfway through the recording he got mad, threw his script in the air and said, "I can't do this. I'm not used to it." But he came back and said, "Give me a two-minute signal towards the end and I'll finish off." That's what we did. And he was so good he learned to wind up bang, right on the button. He was an amazing man and a great speaker.

We never did much in the way of news, except occasionally rob from the newspapers. I recall once we got a very big snowfall. There was about four feet of snow, which is an awful lot of snow for Vancouver. At this point I was sleeping at the station because I couldn't afford anything else. We were scheduled to be on the air at seven that morning. When I got up I didn't look outside before starting. I'd been broadcasting for about twenty minutes when phone calls began coming in. Apparently I was the only person at work in Vancouver. Nobody else could get out. I was able to put announcements on the air such as, "B.C. Electric employees don't have to come to work today because of the emergency." This was a tremendous service and it may have been the first big demonstration of the effectiveness of radio in Vancouver.

By this time broadcasting was finally becoming established but Sparks Halstead still subsidized CKWX. He'd take the profit out of his automotive service and put it into the station. He loved broadcasting. There were others like him. A.A. Murphy of CFQC in Saskatoon also had an automotive supply company. It's amaz-

After a while I went to Kamloops, another little one-man operation. I was the one man, in a shack on the side of a hill; rattlesnakes used to sun themselves on my steps.

CKOV
KELOWNA
B.C.
1000 WATTS

ing how much of the broadcasting industry in Canada grew out of the original automotive industry.

Back then you had to figure out everything yourself. You'd keep asking yourself questions: "How do you construct a programme?" "How do you announce?" "What is the pronunciation of this?" After 1936 we looked to the CBC as our model. When I got to Regina in 1936 I found myself saying, "If this is how the big boys do it, then this is how we'll do it." We all became professional announcers by the simple process of listening to the 'good' guys. We'd hear what they were doing and after the day was over we'd go to the beer parlour, have a drink and talk. If one of us made a mistake in pronunciation, another would say, "Gerry, I think the correct pronunciation is KORsakov, not KorSACKov." That's how we got to know how to say foreign names and places.

In 1936, the prairies had a news service—of sorts. An American company was transmitting by wireless. Bert Hooper would sit with his earphones on, listening to the code coming through and typing out the newscast. I believe the first responsible broadcasting of news to originate *within* a station may have happened at CFQC in Saskatoon. They were the first to say, "We're going to put in a news editor and give him a staff." After that, other stations started to follow suit.

The early audiences were very loyal and you got immediate reaction to whatever you did—particularly on the prairies. The isolation of the prairie farmer in the winter is something the world can really only imagine, especially in the thirties. The only communication these people had with the rest of the world was through their radios. They'd listen, believe everything you said. If you asked them to send in ten cents for a picture of the latest cowboy singer you got dimes by the hundreds.

I remember Don Wright announcing on a programme just before Christmas, "It doesn't look like the kids at the orphanage are going to have a very good Christmas dinner unless we get some turkeys." Well, you never saw so damn many turkeys in your life. We must have had about six tons of turkey, all of them plucked and frozen sitting in an alley behind the station. These turkeys were being sent in by people who had no money themselves. But all these poverty-stricken farmers had radios. And I think every farm home also had a guitar because every year, when spring came, we would have the damnedest influx of would-be cowboy singers knocking on our door for an audition.

Religion was very big on the prairies. We hopped from church to church because all these little churches would buy half an hour. While they were on the air they were soliciting funds so they could continue next week. They'd come in mid-week and lay their twenty dollars down in one dollar bills to pay for the programmes.

Well, you never saw so damn many turkeys in your life. We must have had about six tons of turkey, all of them plucked and frozen sitting in an alley behind the station.

Don Wilson

I started out in the technical end in 1930 at CKMO, Vancouver. I was a student at a school they were running and they made it part of the course that students worked without pay doing regular jobs at the station. In effect, I worked for them and paid twenty-five a month for the privilege. After a couple of months I told them I was resigning, so they hired me and gave me fifty a month for the same work I had been paying them to do. About a year later the guy who'd been manager got his fingers stuck in the till and disappeared before they could catch him. Since I was a convenient body they made me manager, although I was only nineteen.

The Depression was on but radio was booming. Somehow everybody seemed to find enough money for a radio even though they were expensive in relation to the times. Philco, for example, brought out little mantel models which sold by the carload for $80 to $120 each. They were quite good receivers and with uncluttered air waves you could bring in a lot of distant stations, especially after dark.

We did a terrific amount of live stuff in those days which made for lots of wonderful goofs. There's the story that's told everywhere about the guy who was doing the kiddies' show and who accidentally left his microphone open and said, "That should hold the little bastards for tonight." Well, it happened in Vancouver on CKWX and the announcer's name was Jerry Taggart. He later became an executive with the CBC. There was quite a big fuss over that because in those days you could lose your licence if someone said, "damn" on the air.

In other ways you could get away with almost anything. We had one guy who called himself "Professor Astro." He'd read a letter which was a fake in which Mrs. Z had written to say she'd lost a valuable wrist watch or whatever. He'd tell her to look under the paper in the right-hand drawer of her dresser and she'd find it. The next day he'd report that Mrs. Z had phoned to say she'd found it where he'd said it was. That got people interested and the 'sucker deal' was that they had to send in a dollar for their horoscope. Although those were Depression days the response was tremendous.

I started working for the CBC when they first began in 1936. They were opening a station in Vancouver and were looking for some local talent. I auditioned and was hired as an announcer. I stayed there for three years before being sent to Montreal as a producer of outside broadcasts. We did war-oriented shows from factories, shipyards, aircraft manufacturing plants. I did that until 1942 when I decided to get back to the west coast and private radio. I'll say this though; if it wasn't for the CBC, radio would be in a helluva mess. Radio was in pretty poor shape before the CBC came along.

After a couple of months I told them I was resigning, so they hired me and gave me fifty a month for the same work I had been paying them to do.

KELLOGG RADIO

P	C	OFFICIAL SCORE BOARD										
9	11	CHICAGO	0	0	0	2	1					
17	8	ST. LOUIS	0	1	0	0						
9	10	NEW YORK	0	0	0	0						
11	11	BROOKLYN	0	2	1	1						
11	9	CINCINNATI	0	0	0	0						
8	16	PHILADELPHIA	1	0	0	1						
8	10	BOSTON	0	4	0	0						
9	12	PITTSBURG	0	0								

BASEBALL SCORES BY RADIO

SAY THE RADIO BUGS

BASEBALL fans the country over will be counting on Radio this year more than ever before. Most Radio fans are baseball fans. Every one of them should see that his new set of Kellogg radio parts is ready in time for the baseball scores.

Get the Sport records and scores quickest by Radio—build your set of Kellogg radio parts for dependability and economy.

There is a certainty of satisfaction with Kellogg as shown by records of this equipment in use. Kellogg transformers rank among the best. To hear them in operation is to want them. Kellogg tube sockets give the utmost of service, while Kellogg switch arms and knobs are in a class by themselves for quick assembly, low resistance and satisfying operation.

Kellogg variable and fixed condensers, variometers and vario-couplers are all designed and built to give the satisfaction which the word Kellogg expresses in the electrical apparatus field. Kellogg rheostats have but one movable part. They come in six and twenty-five ohm resistances, easily interchangeable. They are simple, yet vary in control on the half turn of the resistance element. Kellogg DX head sets are known wherever radio is in the air. They are built mechanically and electrically for long service, sensitiveness, extreme lightness in wearing, and handling does not affect their tuning. They have Kellogg solid bakelite shells and are furnished with the Kellogg famous receiver cords of which many hundreds of thousands are in use to day in the telephone field. Kellogg radio parts are especially suitable in portable sets because of their strength and high class manufacture. They will stand rough handling as will no other radio equipment and yet have the range and afford the selectivity, in the limits of the circuits used, surpassed by none.

If you don't want to bother to pick out the parts for your favorite hookup buy one of our Radio Kits which include all the necessary and suitable parts including two stages of audio amplification; you can select the tuning units, as you desire.

This summer as never before radio will be heard in every summer resort and camp. See that your set is made of Kellogg radio parts.

Specify Kellogg Radio—

Use—Is the Test

KELLOGG SWITCHBOARD & SUPPLY COMPANY

1066 West Adams St., CHICAGO, ILL.

Laurie Irvine

In 1932 or 1933 I was working in the service shop of a wholesaler who sold Philcos. I was also a ham radio operator. I'd picked it all up as a hobby. A fellow named Ian Clark, whom I'd known for some time, said, "How would you like to be chief engineer at my radio station?" I said, "You haven't got a radio station." He said, "As of this afternoon I'm leasing the United Church of Canada's radio licence." The call letters were CKFC and the station had a hundred watt transmitter. A breadboard sort of thing right out of the *Radio Relay League Handbook* up in a tower room in Chalmers United Church. When I saw it I nearly went home. The station shared time with what was then CKMO but sharing time was hardly sharing. We had three to four-thirty in the afternoon and that was it. Except on Sunday when CKMO didn't do anything.

Around 1937 the company folded and I was out of work. I didn't do anything for a couple of months. Then a job cropped up at CKJC in Kamloops. We had wonderful working conditions there and we worked out a system whereby on Sunday the three-man staff could get by with two men simply by carrying CBC all day. That way we got every third Sunday off. We loved it and we did all this for the magnificent sum of about eighty dollars a month. I was there for four years, by which time the staff had grown to four people, so we got every second Sunday off. And my salary had grown to a hundred and five dollars a month.

Around 1941 I read that Taylor-Pearson-Carson had taken over CKWX in Vancouver and were going to build new studios in downtown Vancouver to replace an old set-up on top of the Georgia Hotel. I thought to myself, "They can't run a big operation like that with the staff they have now." So I auditioned and was offered a job as an announcer. After a short time I became chief announcer, then assistant to the programme manager, then the programme manager.

There was much more live programming in those days. The musicians' union hadn't yet priced live programming out of the business. Some people can't believe it when you tell them there was a regulation that you couldn't put records on the air between seven and eleven at night. We did a lot of live programming because of this regulation. Mostly it was music. Then we went into game shows.

When I arrived at CKWX I found a fellow named Fletcher Markle working in our 'continuity department.' That's a term that's gone from the business. Now it's 'copy department' because all they do now is write advertising copy. But in those days they wrote the programmes. Fletcher Markle had gathered around him a group of young radio actors and actresses and we did a forty-five-minute drama once a week. Our own "Lux Radio Theatre." They were mostly adaptations of movie scripts. Markle used to get the shooting scripts from film distributors and then I'd do an adaptation. What he was doing was probably illegal, but nobody worried too much. Among the people who worked with him on the series were Lister Sinclair, Peggy Hazard, Bernie Braden and Alan Young. I did some narration and bit parts.

Lots of funny things happened in that show. Like the time

A fellow I'd known for some time, said, "How would you like to be chief engineer at my radio station?" I said, "You haven't got a radio station."

There was a regulation that you couldn't put records on the air between seven and eleven at night.

168

Glen Robitaille, the chief engineer, got very mad at Fletcher because he had a habit of not giving him the script and music cues until the last minute. This particular day he got the show going and there was a part where there wasn't any music for about six or seven minutes. So Robitaille made a great show of getting out of his chair in the control room, walking out, and coming and sitting in the corner of the studio where Fletcher couldn't help seeing him. As it got closer and closer to the next musical cue, Fletch was climbing up the wall. At the same time, he was acting in the show. He was doing everything but scream at Robitaille which he couldn't do because the mikes were on. Finally, Robitaille got up, went around and hit the cue just in time.

All our shows, including all our record shows, were scripted. We didn't just run music. We ran a quarter-hour of waltz time or a half-hour of Guy Lombardo, or a slot called "The Big Bands." We'd do a half-hour with a big band. We'd use the theme of the band, pick the music, make it flow and then write copy to connect the pieces. Our criterion was that a record show didn't consist only of records. What you were to ask yourself when you finished was, "Did that sound like a live show?" And they did. We even put applause in. It wasn't easy for the audience to know that they weren't listening to a dance band remote from some big hotel somewhere. Early broadcasters really knew their music and it was no trick to run contests asking, "Who's playing tenor sax?" The thing wouldn't have gone sixteen bars before the phone was ringing off the hook with the right answer. Everyone knew musicians. And musicians were known for the sound they produced.

Soap operas were a real radio phenomenon. There were fifteen-minute serials Monday through Friday. Some stations started broadcasting those quarter-hours at nine-thirty in the morning and didn't finish until seven-thirty at night, except for maybe a half-hour at lunch time for news. Then they'd go back to the soaps. "Pepper Young's Family," "The Guiding Light," "Young Doctor Malone." One after another. The soaps were tremendously popular.

There was practically no news around in the early days. Even the CBC didn't have a news department until about 1940. News, actual news, was made by World War Two and all of a sudden people wanted to know what was going on overseas and newscasts became prime listening spots. More and more stations got hep to this. Everyone thought that when the war was over that would be the end of the interest in the news. They were wrong, of course, because the public had been educated into realizing how much they wanted to know what was going on, not just overseas, but at home. That, of course, meant news personnel.

The lack of decent recording equipment in those early days was a great drawback. There was no way of doing a quick recording. We would cut air checks and spot announcements on acetate discs with a very high wear factor because of the soft material used. Then along came the first tape machines. And everything changed. That was a revolution right there. And strangely enough, it came along when radio needed it most—about the same time that television came on the scene.

"I can't help it if Big Sister IS in love with Dr. Brent, whose heart beats faster for John's Other Wife, who Ma Perkins always says is trying to break up Pepper Young's Family. The meat's burning and I'm hungry."

A Listener

Who's that little chatter-box?
The one with pret-ty auburn-locks?
Who-oo can it be?
It's Little Orphan An-nie!

When I was a child we had our first radio, a Sparton Junior. This was around 1933. My father erected a tall cedar pole from which an aerial ran over to the house. Every Saturday morning my friends and I enjoyed "Let's Pretend," beautifully presented fairy tales. Each of us had the imagination to provide the video. "Little Orphan Annie" came on at about four-fifteen or four-thirty weekdays and I remember running up the steep hill to my house and hurling myself through the door and going over to the radio, my Orphan Annie special secret decoder in hand.

Ernie Rose

I wanted to be a radio operator on a ship, so in May, 1934 I came to Vancouver and joined the Sprott-Shaw School, which also owned CKMO and it was there that I learned commercial operating. I passed the exam in September, as did my buddy Bob Rennie. Unfortunately, the radio station needed only one operator and there wasn't a ship job available. We made an agreement that since this job paid sixty-five a month we would split the wages, split the work, and whoever got a job aboard a ship, the other one would take the job at the station. I didn't get a job on a ship, so in effect I was the loser, and that's how I got into radio.

The only real expenditure we had was tubes because we made or rebuilt all the other parts. We built our own consoles, transmitter—just about everything. When I came, the chief engineer said that if headphones were good enough for him in the control room they were good enough for the announcers too. Needless to say, our ears got a little soft after three or four hours with these things clamped on them. One chap, Tom Smalley, finally got fed up and bought a speaker from a wholesaler. When the invoice arrived the manager raised cain and told him to take it back. Later, Tom went out and picked it up again and asked the store not to invoice us for three or four months. He figured that by that time everybody would be so used to a speaker they wouldn't want to do without it. In the meantime, one of the kids at the school who came into the studio for training spilled paint all over it. We tried to remove it with paint remover, but in the process the speaker came off its pins. Now we couldn't take it back, and that's how CKMO got its first loudspeaker.

I would take my new wife and we'd sit in the back of the theatre and neck while the organist played.

Just before payday every month, we'd be called into the office and given a sheaf of invoices. We'd have to go around and bang on the doors of all of our customers and clients trying to collect money so that we could get paid. They always managed to pay us on Friday afternoon and our cheques would be issued about three-thirty—after the banks had closed. Whichever one of us had any money that weekend was the one we sponged off.

Part of my work that I especially enjoyed was an organ pick-up we did from the Orpheum Theatre every Sunday night. I would take my new wife and we'd sit in the back of the theatre and neck while the organist played. One time we had a chap named Hughie Walsh who wrote copy for us. Hughie had a sense of humour. He wrote a commercial for Fred Gibbard's Shirts that described them as "Shirts made in Canada's leading shirt houses." The announcer who read this commercial had a very English accent, so most of the time it didn't come out as "shirt houses" at all. Hughie was well aware of this; that's why he'd written it that way.

I left CKMO in 1940 and got myself a glorious job with the CBC. During the war we went out on special events with Model Y recorders, which were acetate disc things. They were very big, very heavy and very, very clumsy. We dragged these things all over the country. We boarded ships out beyond the straits of Juan de Fuca—ships such as The HMS *Glory*, which came in with prisoners from Hong Kong. I also travelled for two or three years through the prisoner-of-war camps in Medicine Hat. The prisoners had a simply delightful orchestra. One of them had been the assistant to the concertmaster of the Berlin State Orchestra and he'd put together one really beautiful symphony.

In those days those of us who worked together were like family. The day I got married we deliberately set the time for three o'clock as the station was off the air from two-thirty to four-thirty. The management closed the rest of the station down so everybody could attend. That kind of thing happened all of the time.

DON'T GET A DIVORCE

Few women want to go out because they hate their homes. It is because they need a change. Those wives who are in the home all day find the walls boring at night and they crave a glimpse of the outside world — but on the other hand, husbands after a hard day at the office are tired and wish to stay at home.

Get a
Rogers-Majestic
Radio

R. S. Williams Co.
F. A. TRESTRAIL
145 Yonge St.

COMPROMISE

Come to the nearest R. S. Williams store, select a Rogers or Majestic radio and have it sent home tomorrow, and from then on bring the outside world into your home and enjoy the comforts of your easy chair too.

Established Since 1849

Dick Batey

We were broadcasting this thing 'live' so I decided the best thing to do was carry on as if nothing had gone wrong.

I got into radio because I was stuck in hospital for a couple of years with a lot of time on my hands and my lifesaver was radio. I was listening constantly and logging stations from all over the world. This was in the mid-thirties. I thought the announcers on CFCT, which was what CJVI was called before it was bought out by the Taylor-Pearson-Carson chain of western stations, were pretty damn awful, and I thought I could do better. When I finally got out of the hospital in 1939 I went over to the station and told the owner, George Deaville, what I thought. "OK," he said, "you've got a chance." He was always on the lookout for people with that sort of ego, because he couldn't afford to pay much. "Pappy" Deaville didn't have much of a head for business. He was forever on the brink of disaster and didn't have any money to pay his staff. He had a whole succession of sales managers who would go out and sell a lot of business, collect the money and then disappear.

Radio's Funniest Show!

KORN KOBBLERS

the band of a thousand gadgets and a million gags!

a riot of fun

It's Fun for Young and Old Alike!

65-15 minute programs, featuring that King of Fun, Allan Courtney, comedy players, and guest vocalists, in a screaming riot of robust entertainment.

For Auditions Samples, Write, Wire or Phone

EXCLUSIVE RADIO FEATURES
COMPANY LIMITED

14 McCaul Street   Toronto

CFCT was perhaps the most haywire operation in the whole world when I joined. We were very run down. The record library consisted of stacks of seventy-eight r.p.m. records piled one on another with no covers. There were two turntables, only one of which could play thirty-three and a third records, and it had a broken motor. If you got a commercial recorded at thirty-three and a third you had to turn it with your finger. It was quite a trick to make sure the announcer on the commercial didn't sound like a soprano one minute and a bass the next. But it could be done.

In short, the place was falling apart when I got there. "Pappy" tried to keep it alive, but he fought a losing battle. Although it was the only station in Victoria it never managed to make any money under Mr. Deaville, so in 1941 he was forced to sell and it came under the direct control of Taylor-Pearson-Carson. They put in modern equipment, paid the staff regular salaries and turned the station into an efficient operation.

We started to do all kinds of things. For example, with the war on we did lots of war-related things. Every Wednesday night we'd broadcast an entertainment for soldiers from the YMCA recreation hut. I remember one time our local shipyard had built a minesweeper for the Royal Navy. It was to be manned by personnel who had escaped to Britain from the Dutch Navy. Princess Juliana of the Netherlands, who spent the war years in Canada, was in Victoria for a fancy 'do' to launch the ship. I was to broadcast it. When it came time for the Princess to release the champagne she reached out and released the gizmo that would send the bottle crashing into the ship. Meanwhile, the man below got the signal to knock out the blocks and the ship slid nice and gracefully into the water. However, the champagne bottle hadn't moved. Someone had put a pin in the gizmo as a safety precaution but had forgotten to take it out for the ceremony. I've never seen so many red faces in my life. We were broadcasting this thing 'live' so I decided the best thing to do was carry on as if nothing had gone wrong. After the ceremony was over someone tied the bottle to a long rope. The Princess walked down to the dock where the ship was and flung the bottle at its bow. The champagne smashed as it should and the boat was properly christened. That really was a better story, but by this time we were off the air.

Another time we had a young fellow with us who was short on experience but game to try anything. It so happened that Princess Elizabeth was visiting Victoria and it was a big deal for us. We had seven commentators along the route she was following. Because we were short of personnel we had this young fellow stationed up at the Department of Veterans' Affairs hospital, which was one of the places she was going to visit. Anyway, when the time came for him to come in with his report, we opened the lines and couldn't hear a thing except for the sound of feet walking in a corridor. After several attempts to bring him in we gave up and filled with other commentary. When he came back to the studio I lit into him and said, "What the hell happened?" He said, "I'm sorry, Dick, but when she walked through that door she was so doggoned pretty that I couldn't say a word." So all we got of her visit to the DVA hospital was the sound of her feet walking down the corridor.

John Ansell

In those years Decca didn't allow their records to be played on the air because they felt that if people heard their records for free on a radio station they wouldn't buy them.

I was still in uniform when I was hired by CJVI in Vancouver in 1945. The war was over but I hadn't been discharged. And I had no experience unless you count the set of lungs I'd developed as an instructor in the army. The criteria in those days seemed to be simply an ability to read the English language. If pronunciation was something you didn't have a great deal of difficulty with, they'd hire you. Because standards weren't high I got in as a junior announcer and had more fun than I ever had before, or since.

1945 and 1946 were the years of the musicians' strike in the U.S. and that meant, with few or no recordings available, that we did a lot of live musical broadcasting. Transcription services jumped in to help fill the gap by supplying programs on sixteen inch discs by non-union musicians. In those years Decca didn't allow their records to be played on the air because they felt that if people heard their records for free on a radio station they wouldn't buy them. Later, of course, they realized that the opposite was true. But the Decca ban meant we couldn't play some of the best artists such as Bing Crosby. Two or three other labels imposed similar restrictions. As a result, we had great chunks of live programming—things like quiz shows for housewives and Saturday night studio parties with audience participation. One show we did was, "So You Want To Be In Radio." People would come into CJVI and read scripts that we had prepared. We did all sorts of crazy things to fill time.

I was doing the morning show then and living about four miles from our studios which were in a penthouse in downtown Victoria. To get there by six-forty-five a.m. I had to catch the very first streetcar, grab a newspaper from the corner box, sign the station on at seven a.m., and launch into a newscast which I made up from the paper. We had a telex machine but it was turned off all night so the newspaper was absolutely essential. I'd be rushing down the street circling news items that I felt should go in the newscast while fumbling for the keys to the elevator which would take me to the penthouse. I had to have an elevator operator's licence to do this. When I got to the top, I had to run around throwing switches and phoning the transmitter to make sure the operator was awake and ready to go. By this time there'd be only seconds before sign on. It was all very tight but it worked fine as long as you got that first streetcar.

I followed that schedule for about six months, when Dick Batey, the program manager, called me in and told me we were going to start signing on at six-thirty a.m. to carry "Dr. Michaelson's Hebrew-Christian Hour" a programme every station in Canada and the U.S. that was short of money used. This "Hour" was a fifteen-minute show, on a sixteen inch transcription. I decided that the only way to get to work on time was to get a taxi and charge it to the station. This went along fine until at the end of the first thirty day period, the manager said to me, "Look at these bills! Your taxi rides cost more than we get for the programme!" I told him I was sorry, but I had to get to the station somehow. "Well", he said, "you go into the accounting office and get $50 and buy the station a bicycle." I rode that bike back and forth, six days a week, until I left the show and passed it on to the next man.

One morning the announcer who did the eight o'clock news had been out to party the night before and decided to sleep at the station to make sure he'd be on time. He was up at seven-thirty and for some reason had to go down to the lobby. He was in his bare feet, wearing nothing but his trousers. When he tried to come back up, he found he didn't have the keys to the elevator. The door to the stairway was locked. I was in the studio not knowing what was going on and as it got closer to eight I figured I'd better get some news together since there was no sign of the announcer. The phone rang and it was the police. They said they had a half-naked fellow they'd found climbing the fire escape who was claiming he worked at the station. They wanted to know what they should do with him. I said, "My God, get him back here fast. He's got a newscast in five minutes." They did and he went on the air as scheduled.

Another time we were to do a remote broadcast at the opening of a new bridge. When the time came to go there, there was no engineer available. We were in a panic. It turned out someone in scheduling had assigned all the engineers that day to bringing in the hay at the transmitter. Our transmitter was in the middle of a big field and that was a job that had to be done on fine summer days. That day happened to be one of those days. We managed to do the broadcast without an engineer. Those were days when all of us could turn our hands to just about anything that had to be done.

A Listener

The first radio that I can remember was one of those Philcos that sat on top of a cabinet. They were round on top. I had grown up listening to radio on the west coast and I didn't realize until I moved East a few years ago that there was a whole time difference in our culture. That is, we heard everything three hours earlier than people in the East. Easterners were hearing programmes in the evening and we, in the West, were hearing them in the afternoon. For example, we heard "Jack Benny" and "Fred Allen" and so on on Sunday afternoons while Easterners were getting them in the evening. We stayed home in the afternoons on Sundays while Easterners stayed home Sunday evenings. "The Happy Gang" came on at ten in the morning out west. Things like that made me realize the size of this country.

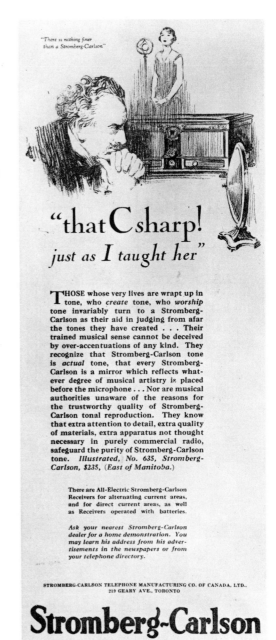

"There is nothing finer than a Stromberg-Carlson"

"that C sharp!
just as I taught her"

THOSE whose very lives are wrapt up in tone, who *create* tone, who *worship* tone invariably turn to a Stromberg-Carlson as their aid in judging from afar the tones they have created . . . Their trained musical sense cannot be deceived by over-accentuations of any kind. They recognize that Stromberg-Carlson tone is *actual* tone, that every Stromberg-Carlson is a mirror which reflects whatever degree of musical artistry is placed before the microphone . . . Nor are musical authorities unaware of the reasons for the trustworthy quality of Stromberg-Carlson tonal reproduction. They know that extra attention to detail, extra quality of materials, extra apparatus not thought necessary in purely commercial radio, safeguard the purity of Stromberg-Carlson tone. *Illustrated, No. 635, Stromberg-Carlson, $235, (East of Manitoba.)*

There are All-Electric Stromberg-Carlson Receivers for alternating current areas, and for direct current areas, as well as Receivers operated with batteries.

Ask your nearest Stromberg-Carlson dealer for a home demonstration. You may learn his address from his advertisements in the newspapers or from your telephone directory.

STROMBERG-CARLSON TELEPHONE MANUFACTURING CO. OF CANADA, LTD., 219 GEARY AVE., TORONTO

Stromberg-Carlson
MAKERS OF VOICE TRANSMISSION AND VOICE RECEPTION APPARATUS FOR MORE THAN 30 YEARS

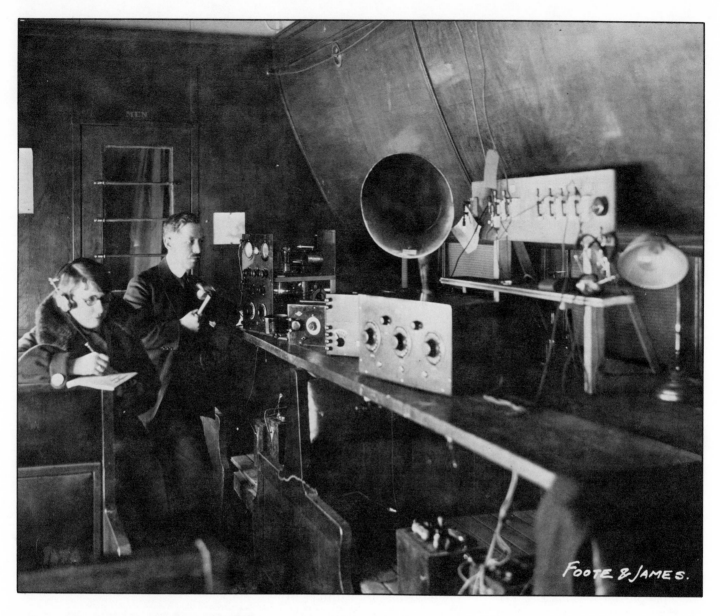

A test car used by the CNR for
checking equipment to be installed in
their passenger trains.

The CNR Network —Towards Public Broadcasting

J. T. Carlyle

I was working at the CNR office in Montreal when Sir Henry Thornton took over the Grand Trunk and other railways and called the whole system the Canadian National. It was at this time that Sir Henry decided we should have a radio department because radio was becoming quite popular and would be a good thing to have on trains. I was the first person hired by that department.

In late December 1923, we hooked up Ottawa and Montreal by telegraph wire for our first network programme. CNR rented the stations. There was only one station in each city allowed to go on at night. In Montreal, on Wednesday night, we'd hire the Northern Electric station; on Thursday it would be the *La Presse* station, CKAC; on Friday it was the Marconi station, CFCF. This went on for a while until we settled on one station, CKAC, and we broadcast from there on Thursday nights on a regular basis. That was CNR night. We would come on at seven and keep going until midnight but all the stations across the country wanted us to keep going. So we did—until three in the morning.

Donald Manson was head of the government radio department at that time. He had to enforce all the different rules that were in effect. For instance, you couldn't play recordings at night and you couldn't use commercials. The CNR had to get permission from him to use their own call letters instead of those of the stations in the various cities. They even had to get permission from the country of Morocco to use the letters CN on the air, because those letters had been assigned to Morocco by international agreement.

Radio became a big, big hit on the trains. Whenever I travelled across the country as part of my job, I'd hear complaints from dining car stewards that nobody was eating. They'd all be out in the observation car listening to radio. We used big Victor

I'd hear complaints from dining car stewards that nobody was eating. They'd all be out in the observation car listening to radio.

radios with loudspeakers but if anyone in the car objected to the radio being on, the operator could cut off the speaker and those who wanted to listen put on earphones.

Despite the fact that nobody knew much about radio in the 1920s, we did a lot of very good programmes. We put on orchestras and good singers. People such as John McCormack. (We paid him $500 and his train fare, which was a lot of money.) We had the Toronto Symphony once a week from Simpson's Arcadian Court. We also took programmes like "Amos 'n' Andy" from the American networks. We used about eleven stations across the country but the bulk of our programming was done from Toronto. On our first coast to coast broadcast we were all sitting there listening when some trainman came on saying, "How in heck am I supposed to get my train going with all that music filling up the lines?"

CN did a lot of things in radio. We had North America's very first coast to coast network. We did the first network broadcast from the deck of a ship. (That was about 1925 from the harbour in Montreal.) At our first birthday party in 1924 from Ottawa, we had a fellow from the Northern Electric station in Montreal doing some of the announcing. At one point he said, "We've got a telegram from someone in Chicago telling us they're listening." I said, "Aw, come on, you haven't really got a telegram." He replied, "Don't worry, we will." In fact, we got 5,800 telegrams that night from across Canada and the U.S. We also got thousands of letters. The boss insisted on hiring stenographers to answer them and he signed them all personally.

When CN got out of the radio business and the CRBC took over, most of us kept our jobs. I went to the station in Windsor and managed it for a while. I ran the Northern Messenger Service for a time. I did a lot of things and I wasn't immune to mistakes. One night when I was in Ottawa I got home and my wife asked, "How are things down at Spank and Barks Streets?" She told me I had said that instead of Bank and Sparks. I didn't believe her until I phoned the transmitter and they told me that indeed I had.

In the early days of the network one of the great things we did was gather choirs in Montreal, Quebec, Halifax, Toronto, Winnipeg and Vancouver. We'd get the choir from Halifax to start, then bring in the one from Vancouver and then one by one all the others would join in. It was fantastic. Nobody believed we were actually doing it that way. They said it was fake. It was a wonderful example of how radio brought the country together.

"How in heck am I supposed to get my train going with all that music filling up the lines?"

FARMERS KEEP POSTED ON MARKET NEWS

AS the Canadian National Railways has now complete arrangements for the Broadcasting of programs, etc., from the principal centres in the Dominion, Farmers will now be able to watch the market from their own fireside. The Dominion Livestock Branch of the Department of Agriculture has inaugurated an official market service and at 7.30 P.M., every Wednesday the stations at Montreal, Ottawa and Winnipeg will transmit market quotations and comments on the livestock and egg markets from the C.N.R. stations.

◀
Operator tuning receiver on radio car. Passengers were supplied with earphones if anyone objected to the sound of the loudspeaker.

◀
CNR radio car. 1920s.

Ernest Jackson

I did my first broadcast on May 15, 1924. The CN had just formed a radio department and I was one of the first employees. I'd learned how to make a crystal set and that started me in wireless, as it was then called. The only announcer before me in Toronto was Foster Hewitt. He'd just started with CFCA and CN used that station for one hour a week. We called it CNRT when we were on.

There was no training whatever. I just used my intelligence and scrambled around, picking up talent for our first broadcast. For example, we brought the King Edward Hotel Orchestra into the Star Building, where CFCA's studio was. The transmitter was in a bathroon. The tower was on top of the building. For that first broadcast, we paid them a little, but after that we paid nothing. The orchestra wanted the publicity and it was a novelty. We went along like that for years.

In Toronto we just borrowed facilities. We had our own CN transmitter in Ottawa and we got one in Moncton, and one in Vancouver. But in all the other places we just used phantom licences. That is, we used stations that belonged to someone else and simply inserted our call letters. CNRW was Winnipeg, for instance.

CNRT started with an hour a week. Then we built up to an evening a week. Sir Henry Thornton, the president of the CNR, was sold on radio for trains. So they built these radio stations and they put receivers on the Transcontinental and on the Montreal-Chicago run. There were receivers with headphones in the parlour cars. Then, of course, they wanted to do a little broadcasting themselves. I heard about it, so I applied and I got the job. I probably was the first one who did a regular network broadcast in this country. This would be about 1929. We had our station in Ottawa and phantom stations in Montreal and around, so I worked up a little network made up of Ottawa, Montreal, Toronto and Hamilton, and sometimes we brought in CFPL London. We traded programmes and kept things going over the CN telegraph lines. That was the beginning of network broadcasting.

The reason for these phantom licences where we would simply share time on someone else's station was that we couldn't afford stations in all of the centres. The CNR, after all, was a railway business and broadcasting was a sideline. They weren't making any money out of it. They *were* the sponsors. Advertising didn't come in until later. I did a lot of 'firsts.' I was the announcer on the first Royal Christmas Broadcast; George V spoke, and then I spoke for Canada. It was an ambitious job I had because you had to invent ways of doing just about everything in those days.

I probably was the first one who did a regular network broadcast in this country. This would be about 1929.

A Listener

My memories of radio go back to 1928, when I was still living in England. First we had a crystal set. Then we graduated to one that was built inside one of the wooden boxes that sugar came in. This set was in our downstairs bathroom and we had wires running from it to plugs in the living room and some of the other rooms in the house. You could plug in either the small speaker horn or the earphones. I guess a set-up like that was really something for those days.

When I came to Canada in 1930 one of the first programmes I heard was the Christmas broadcast of King George V. What a thrill for us, having just left home, to hear the King's voice. I believe that was the first time the King had broadcast one of these messages. During the war, we entertained some British children who'd been evacuated from England. We decided to give them a real North American Christmas which we copied directly from one of the episodes of a soap opera called "One Man's Family." It was a great success and we had radio to thank for that.

We listened to radio as a family and enjoyed programmes together—programmes like "Charlie McCarthy." I remember we missed all the fuss over the Orson Welles "War of the Worlds" because while it was on we were listening to something else. We didn't hear about it until the next day.

Rayphones

2000 Ohms

$4.50

Just real good 'phones; 'phones that will give you solid satisfaction; 'phones that you'll be glad to hand to your best friends to listen in on.

Don't judge Rayphones on a price basis only—in every respect they are well in the Eight Dollar grade. They look good—feel good—and *are* good.

Rayphones are manufactured in one style and resistance only—that which gives the best results under all conditions. Weak or strong signals are alike received with maximum audibility and clearness —free from distortion—whether used in conjunction with a valve or crystal receiver.

Buy a set today—you'll be more than pleased with your purchase.

THE MARCONI WIRELESS TELEGRAPH COMPANY
of CANADA Limited

VANCOUVER · TORONTO · MONTREAL · HALIFAX · ST. JOHN'S, NFL'D

Hotels of Distinction

CONSIDERING its population, Canada is probably better supplied with first-class hotels than any other country in the world. At Ottawa is the Chateau Laurier, which, architecturally, recalls visions of Old France, looking down on Major's Hill Park and far away through its turreted windows to the Gatineau and Ottawa Valleys and the blue line of the Laurentians. Practically adjoining it are the Parliament Buildings. The Higland Inn, Algonquin Park, Ont., in the Highlands of Ontario, combines the comfort of a city hotel with unlimited opportunity for sport and life in the wilds. At Port Arthur, the head of the Great Lakes, the Prince Arthur Hotel looks over a sea-port; only the sea is inland and the water is fresh, the shipping is oceanic in its size and importance. Minaki Inn, one hundred and fifteen miles East of Winnipeg, stands on a green promontary jutting out into the Winnipeg River, and one realizes why the Indians gave it its name, "Mee-Naw-Kee," which means "Beautiful Country." At Winnipeg itself, by the gateway of the old Hudson's Bay Fort, is the Fort Garry, a hotel that compares favorably with the best on the Continent. The Prince Edward at Brandon, Manitoba, makes it hard to realize that a generation ago buffalo were being hunted where motor cars are now running smoothly over the prairie trails. The Macdonald Hotel at Edmonton, Alberta, is another castellated building, where bright flower gardens are terraced high above the curves of the Saskatchewan River. Jasper Park Lodge is a glorified chalet, with a whole covey of little bungalows nestled around the main building, and a view of many mountains reflected in the lake where visitors are paddling and rowing.

Chateau Laurier..............................Ottawa, Ontario
The Fort Garry.........................Winnipeg, Manitoba
The Macdonald......................Edmonton, Alberta

are open all the year and are operated on the European plan.

The Prince Arthur..............Port Arthur, Ontario
The Prince Edward...................Brandon, Manitoba

are also open all the year and together with the tourist hotels, which are open during the summer season.

The Highland Inn...........Algonquin Park, Ontario
Nominigan Camp..............Algonquin Park, Ontario
The Minaki Inn................................Minaki, Ontario
Nipigon Lodge........ ....Orient Bay, Ontario
Grand Beach Hotel...........Grand Beach, Manitoba
Jasper Park Lodge................Jasper Park, Alberta

are operated on the American plan.

The greatest railway system in the world and the first railway in America to adopt "radio" broadcasting and equip its principal trains and hotels for the convenience and comfort of its patrons.

Canadian National Railways

Broadcast by The Four Porters on
CNRV, Vancouver. Late 1920s. ▶

Ottawa studio of CNR. ▶

Herb Roberts

In 1924, I was radio representative for the western region of CN in Winnipeg, which meant that I was in charge of Canadian National radio programmes in the West and in charge of the radio operators on the trains. CN owned three stations—CNRO in Ottawa, CNRA in Moncton and CNRV in Vancouver. In addition to that they bought time on private stations. In Winnipeg, where I was, we used CKY's facilities and the phantom call letters CNRW. In Regina it was CKCK's facilities and call letters CNRR. In Saskatoon, it was CFQC with call letters CNRS and in Calgary CFAC and call letters CNRC.

I would come to Regina, for example, as radio rep. At the time Bert Hooper had the most perfect system of broadcasting that I ever came across. His control room was never tidy, but it always worked. Wire—haywire—was all over the place as he was constantly improving things. He was an experimenter and a dedicated radio man; I don't think he lived for anything else. He was the most popular announcer in the West and at the same time the worst. Bert was "Mr. Radio" in Regina. Darby Coates was "Mr. Radio" in Winnipeg.

I broadcast supper dances on Saturday nights from the Fort Garry Hotel wearing white tie and tails. On Sunday nights we did "The Sunday Evening Musicale." In those early days all of our broadcasts originated in CN hotels. And to be invited to be on those radio shows was a heaven sent gift. The glamour of it all! People could hear you on the radio and that alone was payment enough.

Radio was so alive in those days and such a personal thing. It wasn't a matter of how much profit you made but a personal feeling about how much good you could do for the community. And because of the small number of people in the industry your name became a household word and you really *belonged* to the community. CN did some wonderful things in the development of radio. Austin Weir, the programme director, managed to get Tyrone Guthrie to produce radio shows. The scripts were written by Merrill Denison. The plays were produced in the CN studios on Sherbrooke Street in Montreal. Studio One was the speech studio; Studio Two was for orchestra; and Studio Three was for sound effects. We had a huge tank in Studio Three for water sounds and a marvellous tank it was too. Except there was no tap on it so it couldn't be drained. That caused some problems—including very stagnant water.

We had lots of other problems to overcome too. For instance, static created by feet. If you stood close to the microphone cord it would shoot sparks up the cord and into the carbon mike. That would pack the carbon granules together so that speech and music were distorted. The control room would then signal to 'cut.' As soon as you got this signal you'd lift the mike, shake it a few times to loosen the granules and then continue with the broadcast. We didn't have stop watches to get us off on the second but if we ran over, what difference did it make?

He was the most popular announcer in the West and at the same time the worst.

▲
Herb Roberts, western representative of CNR Radio.

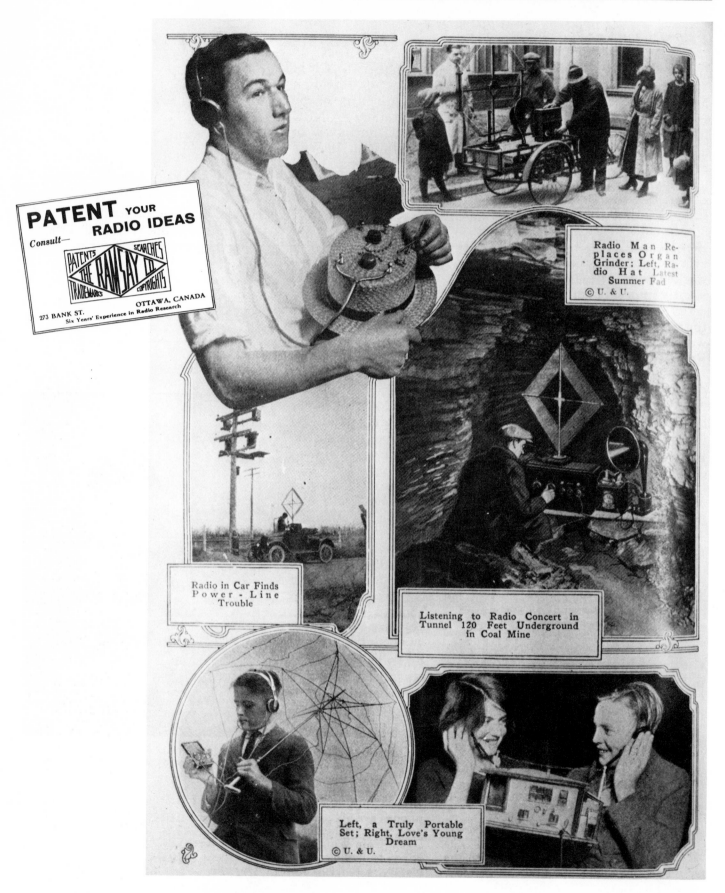

PATENT YOUR RADIO IDEAS

Consult—

THE RAMSAY CO.

PATENTS SEARCHES TRADEMARKS COPYRIGHTS

273 BANK ST.   OTTAWA, CANADA
Six Years' Experience in Radio Research

Radio Man Replaces Organ Grinder; Left, Radio Hat Latest Summer Fad
© U. & U.

Radio in Car Finds Power - Line Trouble

Listening to Radio Concert in Tunnel 120 Feet Underground in Coal Mine

Left, a Truly Portable Set; Right, Love's Young Dream
© U. & U.

Popular Mechanics, mid-1920s.

The ROYAL YORK
Another Milepost on the Right of Way of a Great Transportation System

Radio Reception in Every Room

AN interesting feature of the new Royal York Hotel is the installation of equipment for reproducing radio programmes.

While taking it easy in your bedroom you may put on the head set and listen to programmes picked up from eight different sources. If, during lunch or dinner, you glance around, you will notice here and there microphones picking up the musical programme. You may be dancing in the Ball Room, or attending a meeting in the Convention Hall, in fact, no matter where you are in the hotel, musical or other interesting programmes will be there to greet you.

Provision is being made for the showing of Sound Pictures, the latest combination talking and movie invention for the theatre, in the Banquet and Convention Halls. The future will see television also being used there.

The small children have not been forgotten. They, too, can have their radio programmes, for their play room is equipped with a loud speaker.

All this equipment, as well as a large proportion of the wires, cables and electrical supplies, was supplied by the Northern Electric Company Limited.

Northern Electric
COMPANY LIMITED
A National Electrical Service

Vic George

The motto was, "It has to be moral if it's oral."

I started with the CNR network. Like everybody at CNRO Ottawa, I learned about radio on the job. We were on the air only on Wednesday and Saturday evenings for twelve hours a week all told and a bit in the afternoons. Our job was to serve radio equipped trains which passed through our area. We did a wide variety of programmes out of Ottawa—everything from the prime minister to old-time fiddle contests. You'd be announcing the prime minister at nine o'clock and Jake's Old-Time Band at ten. And of course everything was live.

We had a hard time in Canada trying to compete with the programmes the Americans had on NBC and CBS. We had so little money. How do you compete with "The Metropolitan Opera" or "Jack Benny" or "Lux Radio Theatre?" The only way to compete was to exploit local talent. Our best singers and instrumentalists performed for small fees or no fee at all. And we did free programmes from night-clubs, although this could be risky as you never knew what kind of language would be used. The motto was, "It has to be moral if it's oral." We also did programmes by local choral societies and we had spelling bees and debates between local schools. Events of that nature made radio a part of family life.

We got into what we thought of as 'stunt' broadcasting as a reply to the great talent resources of the United States. In 1924, for example, the CNR, using Bell Telephone long distance circuits, linked their Ottawa station, CNRO, with their Montreal phantom station, CNRM, to create our first 'network'. Programmes flowed alternately in each direction and it's interesting to note that listeners in each city thought programmes from the other city were much better than their own.

The first national network broadcast was on July 1, 1927. It was a co-operative venture on the part of Canadian National Telegraphs, Bell Telephone and provincial telephone companies all across the country who hung wire on fence posts and did all sorts of things to make it happen. To our great joy and a little bit to our surprise—it worked. A great unifying force was now in existence, though at that moment it was rather makeshift. In the next few years the lines that linked the stations were brought up to high standards. The CNR opened three stations in Ottawa, Moncton and Vancouver and bought time in other major cities across the country. Initially, the purpose was to provide entertainment for passengers on CN trains equipped with radio sets. Artists were brought in from the U.S. and elsewhere to supplement Canadian talent. We had the Hart House String Quartet, The Toronto Symphony and Tyrone Guthrie's plays.

The Depression had a devastating effect on the radio industry which was still struggling for survival. There were lots of payrolls which were only partially met. Some not at all. One of the great heroes of early Canadian broadcasting was a Chinese restaurant owner in northern Ontario who was the only person in the town willing to cash the pay cheques of the employees of the local radio station. Nobody else would take them. Everyone was hit and in 1931 the CNR decided its radio department was something they could get along without.

186

I was lucky and moved to Canadian Marconi Company as manager of CFCF, which was then one of two stations in Montreal. It was clear that we needed more and better Canadian shows. I knew that the CNR stations in Moncton and Ottawa had exactly the same problem and was sure many others were no better off. I also knew that Canadian National Telegraphs had high quality carrier facilities linking most Canadian cities. Certainly everything east of Winnipeg. They were also underemployed after normal business hours—especially at that time. I went back to my old friends in the CNR and proposed that they provide network lines and a few programmes. Other stations would make good shows available, too, on a no-pay, no-charge basis. We'd all win that way. To my delight, the proposal was accepted. Soon after, stations from London, Ontario to Halifax became happy participants in a co-operative network that worked great for a couple of seasons. And it might still be working if the CRBC hadn't come along. Its first act was to expropriate our network without so much as a 'thank you.'

Some of the early sponsors did far more for radio than they're

The Hart House String Quartet was engaged exclusively by CNRT, Toronto. 1926.

given credit for. Imperial Tobacco had a birthday in 1936 and sponsored a national broadcast. It took the audience into the Connaught tunnel in the Rockies, to a lighthouse off Halifax, and to a similar spot off Vancouver, and so on and there was a large orchestra and choir to tie it all together. It went on for a couple of hours. In 1937 and 1938 Imperial Tobacco sponsored a weekly show of the same type. Commentator Walter Bowles contributed a story each week from a different Canadian city. There were two overseas commentators—one from London and the other from a European capital. And Lionel Shapiro spoke from New York each week mostly about show business.

Earlier, the first two-way Atlantic broadcasts had been sponsored by Imperial Tobacco. In 1934 we broadcast back to Canada every evening a summary of events at the British Empire Games with emphasis on the performance of Canadian athletes. Elmer Ferguson, then dean of Canadian sports writers, sat in Montreal and he and I had a transatlantic conversation each night about the Games.

In the early days the news service was poor. One reason for that was that the Canadian Press, as a result of newspaper pressure, wasn't anxious to allow radio stations to subscribe. Then the British United Press made their service available to us. Later the CP subsidiary Broadcast News came along. I brought Trans Radio News into Canada. We had it at CKAC on teletype. I remember when King George V died I arrived at the station ready to tear off their long, complete biography only to find that the paper had fed itself back into the machine and all I had was shredded wheat. This was to be the key to our commemorative broadcast, due to go on in half an hour. I phoned New York and explained my problem. They stopped everything else and fed the story through to me again.

CFCF was barely making money when I arrived in 1931. There were weird things that went on. One day I opened one of my desk drawers and came across some dirty laundry. An announcer said, "Excuse me, those are my shirts." Anyway, I began to clean things up. A year later there were about two people left who'd been on staff when I came in. I became known as the 'hatchet man.' However, we had a better and more profitable operation after that. I was also responsible for stopping the bilinguality of CFCF. The monolingual English were bored with the French, and the monolingual French were bored with the English. Bilingual people were bored with both because they heard everything twice. We finally said to CKAC, "You do all the French and we'll do all the English." And that's what we did.

For Only 10¢

THE Stations you hear—who are they? Where are they? Who operates them? What are their wave lengths?

This new Burgess Index of Broadcasting Stations, Record and Atlas answers those questions. It contains in part, a revised list of every broadcasting station in America. There are maps of the United States, Canada and the World, together with accurate charts showing time divisions of the world.

Keep A Record Of Every Station Tuned In

Several pages of this booklet are devoted to space for a record of the stations you tune in, the date, call number, location, time, distance and dial positions.

The Size Is Handy The Price Is Handy

This booklet fits the pocket—takes up little table space and the information you want is easy to find. It only costs a dime. This forty-eight page Index and Atlas was compiled to sell for 25 cents but in keeping with our policy of furthering the interests of radio enthusiasts, we are glad to distribute these booklets at cost. We believe you will be glad you secured your copy.

Mail this Coupon now

BURGESS BATTERY COMPANY,
169 Buttery, Niagara Falls, Ont

Enclosed is ...... cents for which send me....
copies of the new Burgess Index and Broadcasting Stations.

Name ....
Street ....
City .... State..................
Dealer's Name..
Street ....
City.. State..............

MAHOGANITE

has the beauty of polished mahogany

Mahoganite Radion Panels have a satin-like finish, comparable to that which age and a skilled cabinet maker give to mahogany. Radion Dials and Knobs are also made in Mahoganite, to match.

RADION

The Supreme Insulation

PANELS

18 Stock Sizes

Mahoganite and Black

6 x 10½	6 x 14	6 x 21	7 x 9
7 x 10	7 x 12	7 x 14	7 x 18
7 x 21	7 x 24	7 x 26	7 x 48
9 x 14	10 x 12	12 x 14	12 x 21
	14 x 18	20 x 24	

Look for this Stamp on every genuine RADION Panel. Beware of substitutes and imitations.

American Hard Rubber Co.
11 Mercer St. ~ New York

Representatives:
EASTERN CANADA: - DANIEL DEVIENNE, 251 ST. JAMES ST., MONTREAL, CANADA
WESTERN CANADA: - STERLING SPECIALTIES, 213 SOMERSET BLDG., WINNIPEG, MAN.

189

▶

Mackenzie King. First national broadcast. July 1, 1927.

▶

Partial text of speech delivered by Mackenzie King at the Canadian National Exhibition in August 1927.

Mackenzie King

There has been nothing comparable in its way to the nation-wide broadcasting of the proceedings on Parliament Hill on July 1, as effected through the co-operation of the railway, telegraph, telephone and radio companies, under the direction of the National Committee. For the first time in the history of Canada the word spoken on Parliament Hill and the sound of the chimes and bells were carried instantaneously in all parts of this vast Dominion. Never before was a national programme enjoyed by the citizens of any land over so vast an area. It is doubtful if ever before, at one and the same moment, the thoughts of so many of the citizens of any country were concentrated upon what was taking place at its capital, or whether those in authority were brought into such immediate and sympathetic personal touch with those from whom their authority was derived....

On the morning, afternoon and evening of July 1, all Canada became, for the time being, a single assemblage, swayed by a common emotion, within the sound of a single voice. Thus has modern science for the first time realized in the great nation-state of modern days, that condition which existed in the little city-states of ancient times and which was considered by the wisdom of the ancients as indispensable to free and democratic government—that all the citizens should be able to hear for themselves the living voice. To them it was the voice of a single orator—a Demosthenes or a Cicero—speaking on public questions in the Athenian Assembly or in the Roman Forum. Hitherto to most Canadians, Ottawa has seemed far off, a mere name to hundreds of thousands of our people, but henceforth all Canadians will stand within the sound of the carillon and within hearing of the speakers on Parliament Hill. May we not predict that as a result of this carrying of the living voice throughout the length and breadth of the Dominion, there will be aroused a more general interest in public affairs, and an increased devotion of the individual citizen to the commonweal?

◀
Crowd on Parliament Hill to see and hear first national broadcast. July, 1927.

The first *national* radio broadcast on July 1, 1927 was a great success.
▼

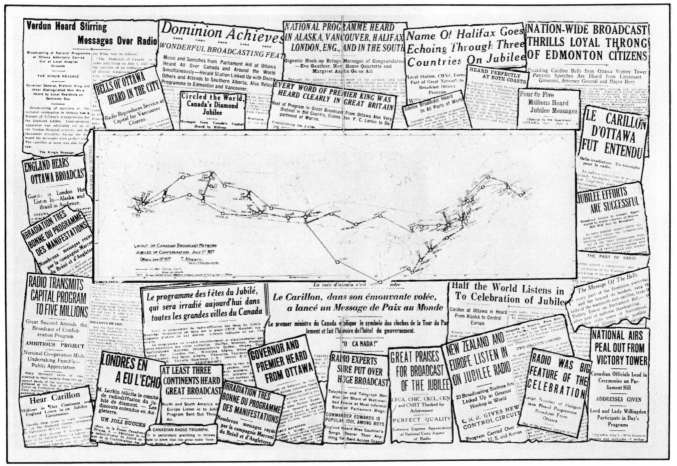

Tyrone Guthrie

It may seem odd that a railway company, however vast, should make offers of theatrical employment. However, in Canada at this period (1929) radio was operated by the railroads.

The head man of the Canadian National Railways' Radio Department, Mr. Austin Weir, had decided to produce a series of scripts dealing in dramatic form with Canadian history. Merrill Denison had been engaged as author. Since Canada had no indigenous radio drama it was decided to import a director from Britain.

More and more demands were placed, as is the way of weak radio writing, upon the effects department.

Even in Canada the sty where our radio plays were produced was called a studio. It was decorated in a cabbage green and everything in sight was made of basketwork, also in green, splotched with gold. There were no windows; even at nine of a midsummer morning we worked by electric light, shaded with green basketwork; there was no ventilation, conveniences were few and remote. It was a rather sissy version of the salt mines.

But we had good fun there. My colleagues were all railway workers rather surprised to find themselves drafted into this newfangled nonsense of radio, and very much surprised to be mixed up with play-acting. "The Romance of Canada" must have been one of the earliest radio serials. It certainly was the first dramatic effort of any scale on the Canadian air. For about twenty weeks we churned out a new historical episode every Tuesday, often with large casts and complicated effects. In those days there was no professional theatre in Canada. The talkies, newly and triumphantly emerged, had swept all before them. A few amateur groups bore the torch of drama. My first job was to recruit a company. In this my mainstay was Rupert Caplan.

Caplan introduced me to most of the principal amateur actors

Vic George and Herb Roberts creating sound effects for *Henry Hudson.* "The Romance of Canada" series was produced in Montreal for the CNR network.

in Montreal, Ottawa and Toronto. These formed a nucleus, to whom I added as occasion demanded Scots, where a Scottish accent was appropriate, Cockney, Irish, Yorkshire or Welsh. Dealing as they did with early days in Canada the scripts demanded mostly people from the Old Country, with marked regional accents to differentiate each character from the rest.

We unearthed some splendid talent. A bellhop from the Windsor Hotel was a first-rate Irish character. At the Y(MCA) a young man newly immigrated from Fife was doing the night shift on the elevator; he became our resident Scotsman. From time to time we did hire professional actors for leading parts. But mostly the players were amateurs who worked with great attention to duty and maintained a very creditable standard.

"The Romance of Canada" fell sick of a disease to which all serial undertakings are liable: the gradual exhaustion of the author. Merrill Denison began with *Henry Hudson*—an excellent script for which I was able to find an excellent cast. We got off to a flying start.

But gradually the pace began to tell. Halfway through the series, with about ten more scripts to write, poor Merrill was in trouble. He would deliver the current script just in time for the first rehearsal and then, exhausted, with no ideas, no enthusiasm, he would have to sit right down and beat his brains afresh. Furthermore, after the first ten or twelve installments he had used up the most familiar, as well as the most obviously 'radiogenic,' episodes in Canada's rather brief history. Each week entailed more and more research. More and more demands were placed, as is the way of weak radio writing, upon the effects department. The nadir was reached when we were asked to suggest, without benefit of dialogue or any descriptive build-up, that an elderly man was being gobbled up by rats.

From MY LIFE IN THE THEATRE, by Tyrone Guthrie. Copyright © 1959, Tyrone Guthrie. Used with the permission of McGraw-Hill Book Company.

Rehearsal for the radio play, *Henry Hudson* produced by Tyrone Guthrie for the CNR network. January, 1931.

The Aird Commission, 1928. Charles Bowman, John Aird, Donald Manson (secretary), Augustin Frigon. The Aird Report led to the establishment of the CRBC, The Canadian Radio Broadcasting Commission.

The CRBC

Graham Spry

My ambition during the First World War was to be either a gunner or a signaller. Wireless was then talked about in the army. It had been developed quite extensively for signalling and that fascinated me. But the war ended and I never got into signals. As a child when I lived in Toronto I had a friend on Walmer Road and we used to run strings across the yard and try and pass messages. You know, if you put a string in a circular piece of cardboard, or better still some sort of skin, you could pass sounds along the string to the other end.

After the war we old signallers and signallers *manqués* like myself formed the Winnipeg Radio Society, and we used to meet in one of the rooms in the old Arts Building on Kennedy Street. I don't know what happened to all those people, but certainly some went into radio. This was 1919, and we read of the experiments Marconi was doing in Montreal with stations called X2C or 2XC, now CFCF. By early 1920 it was on the air regularly, really much the same time as, or perhaps even earlier than, the Colchester station of Marconi in Great Britain or KDKA in Pittsburgh.

When I was at Oxford in the 1920s the British Broadcasting Company was already operating and the question was raised whether we introduce radios into the common rooms. Well, the common room at the college I was at, University College, had been Shelley's old room and the students were horrified at the idea of this gadget being put into the sacred rooms of Percy Bysshe Shelley. So we didn't have radio in the College. Even Christ Church, quite a scientific college, did the same thing. Although radio fascinated me, I didn't do much about it. I had lots to do.

In 1926, I became national secretary to the Association of Canadian Clubs. The executive asked me to draft a memo making

> My feeling was that broadcasting must not be treated as a business. That would be a disaster, except for the businessman. It had to be treated as a public service, like the school system.

<u>THE CANADIAN RADIO LEAGUE</u>
October 6, 1930
<u>Canadian Radio for Canadians</u>

Britannia rules the waves - shall Columbia rule the wave-lengths?

Brooke Claxton, Esq.,
742 Cote St.Antoine Rd.,
Montreal, Que.

Dear Brooke:

This is to invite you to become a member of a provisional executive of the Canadian Radio League, which has as its object
the protection of Canada from a radio system like that of the United
States. Our method of operation is, resolutions, delegations to the
Cabinet, articles in the press, and a highly reputable honorary
executive masking the machinations of a small, disreputable executive
consisting of yourself, myself, Alan Plaunt (he was appointed honorary secretary at a full provisional meeting last night) George
Smith, R.K. Finlayson, Margaret Southam, etc., I will not go into the
headliners for publicity purposes, but the list is thoroughly respectable. Those present at the meeting were not so respectable, they
were, Alan Plaunt, Graham Spry, and John Walker.

Alan is a gentleman of leisure and will do our dirty
work aided by Margaret Southam. Our principal object is to see that
the file Honourable R.B. will consult on his return is full of pro-
Canadian radio newspaper clippings. We will also see, by routes well
traced, that the various Ministers know that people throughout the
Dominion "are viewing with alarm" the American monopoly's invasion of
the sacred Canadian air. We are counting on the support of the
Southam and Sifton press and have included Dafoe and one of the
Southam's on our honorary executive. The president will probably be
some public spirited General, we have one in mind, who will be driven
into frequent expressions of "grave alarm", every palpitation of which
will be properly embalmed in the newspapers. We are raising a little
money and Alan has done some preliminary cantering in Toronto. We
have made a list of victims at $100 a stroke and want to raise about
$1000, for the costs of the agitation.

Will you join this executive? We plan to hold a meeting,
probably in Montreal, considering the dry character of Ottawa hotels.
In the meantime, keep the nefarious scheme dark. We wish to spring
full fledged into the ether and fear the chloroform of the powers
that be, if we spring too soon.

The Maple Leaf Forever.

Yours,

Letter sent by Graham Spry to Brooke Claxton. Spry and Alan Plaunt founded the Canadian Radio League; its goal was to persuade the government of R.B. Bennett to act on the recommendations of the Aird Commission.

suggestions about how to celebrate the sixtieth anniversary of Confederation. I suggested, among other things, a 'hook up' by telephone and telegraph of radio stations from coast to coast and this was accepted. So on July the first 1927, the sixtieth anniversary of Confederation, I stood on Parliament Hill and watched the Governor-General, followed by Mackenzie King and Ernest Lapointe, representing French Canada, speak to the whole of Canada. Now, this made an enormous impression on Mackenzie King. This is not just my imagination. Mackenzie King's private secretary, Norman Rogers, who was a great friend of mine, told me of the impression it had made. This was a turning point in thinking about broadcasting. Up to that point radio was a plaything. All the Canadian stations added together was about equal to the power of one American station in Chicago or New York. There wasn't very much to put together in this network, but it worked very well in a typical Canadian way, a mixture of public activity, public policy and private facility.

Mackenzie King saw that there was a means of communicating between the regions and building up Canadian unity. Shortly thereafter, the Liberal government appointed Sir John Aird to study the question of a national policy for radio. My feeling was that broadcasting must not be treated as a business. That would be a disaster, except for the businessman. It had to be treated as a public service, like the school system. Everyone in society required an education. Similarly everyone needed information. When Mackenzie King was defeated in 1930 the Aird Report had already been presented to the government. Bennett came in in the midst of the Depression. The job of the Canadian Radio League was to see that Mr. Bennett, *despite* the economic situation, would give expression to the demand, the undoubted demand, of Canadians of every class and occupation from coast to coast, for a decent broadcasting system that was Canadian in large part. I called the first meeting of the Radio League on the sixth of October, 1930. On December the eighth we held a meeting in the Chateau Laurier in Ottawa and almost every national organization you could think of was represented, so in roughly two months we had a great national organization. I went across Canada, once, twice, three times a year, and I knew there was this public opinion, but we had to convince R. B. Bennett and his immediate staff not only that this public opinion existed, but the way to give expression to it was through a publicly owned corporation, independent of day-to-day government, and financed by the audience. That we had to sell to Mr. Bennett. Bennett, an ardent Tory, was anti-public ownership traditionally. He was a corporation lawyer. But in many ways I think he has been misunderstood by those writing about him. He was also a great believer in Canada. It took a year or so, but once it was demonstrated to him that public broadcasting would be a valuable asset to the Canadian people, he supported, heart and soul, the idea of every home in Canada having a radio set which would bring them entertainment and information and that this information and entertainment would circulate from coast to coast.

Ernie Bushnell

In the early 1920s I was an entertainer travelling all over Canada and the U.S. on the old Chautauqua circuit. We had a professional male quartet and we were quite successful. I didn't know anything about radio back then—nothing at all—and especially I didn't know about artists and groups appearing on radio and not getting paid for it. We were always accustomed to picking up our cheques before we performed. Anyway, on a trip to Pittsburgh we were invited to appear on that big powerful station, KDKA, which at that time could be heard almost anywhere in the world. Certainly all over North America. We accepted the invitation but this time we failed to ask for our money before we performed. Afterwards when we went to collect we were told there was no fee because we had appeared on a 'sustaining' programme. I wanted to know what that was and was told it meant a programme that was put on almost entirely for the benefit of artists who needed publicity. I said, "We don't need any bloody publicity. What other kind of programme is there?" I was told that there was what was called a sponsored programme where the advertiser pays for the facilities at the station and for the talent which took part in it. "Well," I thought, "maybe there's something there for me."

This was 1926 and I could sense that the days of male quartets were coming to an end and that I would have to start looking around for a new career. So that December a pal of mine joined me in starting up a little broadcast service and by January of 1927 we had four or five rather large companies sponsoring what I still call some of the best programmes that have ever been put on the air. There were musical shows—Reginald Stewart conducting a twenty-six piece orchestra, sponsored by the Maple Leaf Milling Company. There was an hour with a great Canadian pianist, Ernest Sykes. That programme was sponsored by his father. We had a very good season with everybody happy, including the advertisers. Our contract with them was for thirteen weeks and when renewal time came in April, they all said they didn't want to be on the air in the summer but they'd be back in the fall. Well, good enough. I was launched into radio. We did these programmes out of CJYC, the old Bible students' station in Toronto.

CJYC at that time was sharing a frequency with the Toronto *Star* station, CFCA. The Reverend Bill Cameron, pastor of the Bloor Street Baptist Church, was an eloquent speaker with a very large following and this particular Sunday he was broadcasting a sermon on CFCA, which was on from seven to eight-thirty in the morning. Well, Bill was really going good when eight-thirty rolled around; he was nowhere near the end of his sermon. Normally on these shared frequencies things were pretty loose and one station would allow the other to finish before starting up. But not this time. The Bible students' station said, "It's our time," and they pulled the plug on Reverend Bill just as he was reaching the climax of his sermon and they put on their own programme. Well, there was hell to pay and the howls could be heard all over the continent. A chap named Cranston was editor of the Toronto *Star* at the time and a great friend of Prime Minister Mackenzie King. Cranston came roaring down to Ottawa raising Cain about what the Bible students had done. He got King's ear and it was he who

To prevent this kind of incident radio had to be nationalized and regulated by the government.

NO DULL EVENINGS

radio in every room

Throw a switch — and you have your choice of two programs. Press a valve — and you have ice-water. Select a book from the library catalog — and it's sent up to you. Wake in the morning, and find the newspaper under your door.

A Statler is your "home away from home".

The *organization of* Emstatler

There are Statler Hotels in:
BOSTON · BUFFALO (*Hotel Statler and Hotel Buffalo*)
CLEVELAND · DETROIT · ST. LOUIS
NEW YORK (*Hotel Pennsylvania, Statler-Operated*)

Hotels Statler
7,700 Rooms with bath and radio reception.
Fixed, unchanging rates posted in all rooms.

NO DULL SUNDAYS

first suggested that to prevent this kind of incident radio had to be nationalized and regulated by the government. The upshot was that the Bible students lost their licences. A friend of mine was at the old radio section of the Department of Marine and Fisheries. He told me they had over eighty bags of mail come in protesting the cancellation of the Bible stations, but the order stood. Eventually, of course, we did have nationalization through the CRBC and the CBC.

The staff of the CRBC with Chairman Hector Charlesworth.
Left to Right:
Stanley Maxted, Toronto
Horace Stovin, Western Canada
Chas. Shearer, Ottawa
E. L. Bushnell, Ottawa
J. Arthur Dupont, Ottawa
George Taggart, Ottawa
Hector Charlesworth, Ottawa
Jas. Houde, Quebec City
Frank Willis, Maritimes
Horace Brown, Ottawa
Rooney Pelletier, Quebec
George Wright, British Columbia

MEMORANDUM

Version française au verso

Aird Project Menaces the Trade and Commerce of Radio

On Guard Against the Nationalization of Radio

Not everyone wanted a public radio system.

MEMORANDUM

On Guard Against the Nationalization of Radio !

The Aird Project Menaces Trade and Commerce of Radio

BECAUSE the conclusions of the Report of the Aird Commission on Radio in Canada menace directly their interests, representatives of the industry and commerce throughout the Dominion owe it to themselves to prevent and oppose all attempts to put these conclusions into effect. Everyday experience shows that it is often too late to stop a movement once it is in motion.

FETTERS FOR COMMERCE

Even a summary examination of the document submitted by Sir John Aird and his colleagues to the Federal Government will not fail to open the eyes of our Canadian manufacturers and dealers. Thus, they will see the suggestion to increase the cost of licenses to radio owners — there is question of raising the fee from $1. to $3. — which will result in embarrassing trade by lessening demand and slowing up sales, because the increased license fee should tend to diminish the number of receivers. Likewise it will be noted that dealers will be charged with the onus of collecting the fees for the federal treasury and this situation would create all sorts of difficulties for dealers and cause recriminations amongst purchasers; since the dealers would be blamed for what would be believed to be an unwarranted increase in the prices of their merchandise. The door would open wide to all kinds of reclamations.

1

THE AIRD PROJECT

ADVERTISERS ILL-TREATED

In reading the Aird report it is noticeable that one of the principal aims of the Commissioners is to eliminate entirely, or, at least, to reduce advertising as much as possible in radio programs. If tolerated at the start, while the new system is being launched, the Commissioners have ever in mind the idea of suppressing radio advertising altogether. Result to Canadian trade: — Dominion advertisers, to their great loss, shall be deprived of a splendid medium of publicity, if they are prevented from using radio to advertise their goods; whereas American advertisers remain wholly free to take every advantage of the situation and thus reach all attainable Canadians.

INACCEPTABLE PROGRAMS

There is more involved. The attempt to follow, in Canada, the British radio system, as favoured by the Aird Commission, will still further injure the industry and trade in our land.

These State-controlled programs, prepared by persons independent of advertisers, are not addressed to all classes of society, but reach usually a restricted class of the community. Middle and Laboring classes lose interest in broadcasting because they dislike programs not prepared for them, but for altogether another audience. So, the largest section of the population buys fewer receivers. Here is another source of loss for manufacturer and dealer.

PROGRESS IN THE UNITED STATES AND CANADA

Finally, our men of business are best qualified to know that the country where radio has progressed most is the United States. Thanks to privately owned radio stations, trade and commerce are rapidly developing there. They may, with equal ease, satisfy themselves that, in our country, the prosperity of the radio industry is due to the healthy competition between station managers, who try ever harder to meet the wishes and needs of everybody.

State ownership would only weaken and paralyse a most remarkable expansion and Dominion trade and commerce would suffer thereby. Far better, indeed, to leave radio undisturbed and free, but under intelligent control. The success met with under private ownership warrants in every way the continuation of the present system in Canada. Latest federal figures show that for the first seven months of 1929

2

THE AIRD PROJECT

about 60,000 radio licenses more were issued than in the corresponding period of 1928 — an increase of about 30%. These statistics show that our present broadcasting stations are interesting and satisfactory to the public and trade has benefitted accordingly.

SUCCESS OF STATION C.K.A.C.

For example, since the inauguration of its new Radio Station, "La Presse" has received thousands of enthusiastic letters from Canadians and Americans, who stress the excellence of programs, the clarity of transmissions and who request a continuance of the good work. "La Presse" believes itself justified in declaring that, in so far as programs are concerned, the directors of privately-owned broadcasting stations can give real satisfaction to the public. Assuredly, the first requirement is to recognize the demands of the public. Naturally, some criticism is inevitable; especially from biased minds. It is, indeed, quite impossible to please everybody.

So, the best thing to do is to reward lovers of radio and the public generally for their approval and encouragement by a continuous improvement in program quality and delivery.

HEALTHY COMPETITION

Thus, the lesson to be learned from such popular favour is that the Broadcasting Station, the product of free, private ownership, can give in Canada entire satisfaction. Hence, the best system for Canada is private ownership ; allowing as it does fully for competition and the desire to furnish well-balanced programs. In no way is State-ownership desirable. Our country must fight that State-ownership of Radio, with which this Dominion is threatened in the report of the Aird Commission.

The splendid development of C.K.A.C. broadcasting station is due to private ownership and competition, those maintainers of healthy rivalry, which almost always lead to success. Like the Press, Radio must remain independent; for this instrument of dissemination shall become ever more powerful.

Radio broadcasting must be safeguarded, by every possible guarantee of freedom. Experience counsels prudence, at this time.

3

THE AIRD PROJECT

It is suggested that the control of radio programs be entrusted to provincial commissions, named by the Governments of each province. The triumphant conclusion is reached by some people that, in this way, Radio shall escape political interference. What a delusion ! As if any one could be certain that the nominees of the provincial governments shall not be political friends ! As these governments do not all share the same political views, it is not difficult to paint now the picture of the multiple colours that shall be spread over the radiophonic checkerboard of our Dominion.

A DANGEROUS SITUATION

And, how shall the Federal Government be treated by the various provincial commissions charged with the control of programs? In what difficult and dangerous situations will it not find itself ? In cases of abuse, it shall or shall not, have the power to interfere. If it has the right to intervene, the provincial commissions are not autonomous and, in this event, we are exposed to an even greater evil. If intervention be impossible, then probably the air shall be filled with a cacophony of all sorts of programs and abuses. Surely, such a situation is not practicable and is wholly dangerous.

The ideal, practical system for Canada is one permitting the free exercise of private ownership, while the Government polices the air; thus allowing listeners to enjoy radio's advantages, license-free and even without the payment of a dollar fee.

A DEFECTIVE SYSTEM

The Aird Commission wants the Government to establish 50 kilowatt stations, distributed over our territory. In Canada, stations of this power would cover the entire area, but listeners with weak sets might have difficulty in getting other stations. Consequently, these fans would be forced to listen to whatever programs this monster 50 k.w. station chose to supply. And, here, we would be in a fix similar, if not worse, to that now existent in Great Britain.

The "Saturday Evening Post", Philadelphia, dated November 9th, 1929, contained a carefully written article, in which was established the parallel between Radio broadcasting in Great Britain and in the United States. The author makes us feel the inferior situation of British fans, respecting quantity of programs. Contrariwise, the American stations seek to satisfy their clientèle by mass-broadcasts, comprising selections destined to please everybody; but the British Broadcasting Corporation spreads out programs over the day, or even over

4

THE AIRD PROJECT

the week, varying the selections to meet the likes of the different classes of the audience.

In other words, in the British system, broadcasts by advertisers being excluded, popular programs containing the varied features necessary to produce "balance inside the hour", are not usually supplied. It is not so in the case of broadcasts sponsored by American and Canadian advertisers who, within the time-limit, seek in general to reach and please as many classes as possible with varied and substantial programs. These are called "balanced-programs", which please everybody every hour.

THE NEED FOR POPULAR PROGRAMS

Effectively, in Great Britain, the commission charged with the preparation of programs is quite independent of advertisers and in its efforts to please the public, arranges programs to cover the day or the week, and to include a bit of everything, spread out accordingly. To hear any desired selection, the British fan must remain glued to his set, throughout the entire day, or week, or forego his pleasure. With such a system it is not surprising that many persons do not use their receivers as much as they might. As a matter of fact, it is asserted that never more than half the fans are listening-in.

Another result of the exclusion of British advertisers from the use of radio is seen in the neglect by stations to give insufficient popular programs and in the substitution of selected broadcasts of narrowed interest. Little wonder, then, that the middle and laboring classes in large numbers are losing interest in radio; that the number of receiving sets is much smaller than it should be. Meanwhile, the British radio industry loses through such a condition of affairs.

At no time has the average Briton more than a maximum of three programs to listen to ; while, in the United States, anybody may tune-in as many stations as desired, all of which stations are solicitous to furnish those thirty or sixty minute balanced programs, most likely to meet with public approval.

It will be seen that the British system, which some so thoughtlessly want to see in operation here, prevents the public from getting that quantity and quality which it desires, tends to do away with popular programs and ends by causing [...] to the radio industry.

5

THE AIRD PROJECT

THE HONOURABLE FERNAND RINFRET

The Hon. Fernand Rinfret, in an eloquent allocution, at the opening of the new C K A C station, emphasized the importance of the popular program and everybody should agree with him. There shall always exist certain groups demanding the same sort of broadcasts all the time. The role of a popular station is not to satisfy the wishes or fancies of such groups; although station directors will attempt to please even these special groups, from time to time. The director [of] a popular station must do his utmost to please everybo[dy] and, in order to do so, he must vary his programs to sati[sfy] all classes of the community.

We have shown that, in Great Britain, the State-suppl[ied] programs are sent forth to reach, virtually, a single class [of] people. This is true to such an extent that the great work[ing] class is mostly indifferent to radio. By ignoring advertis[ing] the directors of the British stations have largely effaced [the] popular portions of their programs. Let us not repeat [this] mistake !

The creation of 50 kilowatt stations would a[...] especially the owners of weak receiving sets, who might [...] to endure programs from these stations, for they woul[d be] unable to eliminate them and tune-in elsewhere. The prog[rams] thus imposed upon them may not please and, presently, [the] lack of variety will be born weariness, which, in turn, [will] damage the future of radio.

THE MIGHTY COST

In Great Britain, the advertiser vanished simultan[eously] with private ownership. The revenue previously earned [by] radio advertising is now replaced by a direct tax upon o[wners] of radio sets.

Has nobody given thought to the cost of running st[ations] such as those proposed by the Aird Commission? In [Great] Britain, with a population of forty millions and a te[rritory] to serve ten times smaller than our own, the public is m[ade to pay] yearly to the merry tune of $5,600,000. The annual lice[nse] is ten shillings. In Canada, with a population of bar[ely ten] millions, of four times less, and with a territory alm[ost ten] times greater, it is the easiest thing in the world to se[e where] this will lead us !

7

THE AIRD PROJECT

THE ALL-IMPORTANT CONSIDERATION

With the six wavelengths allotted to Canada, over our immense area, we may erect six stations with 20 kilowatt antenna power and perfect modulation. These six stations will cover easily our Canadian territory. The experience gained through the new C.K.A.C. station warrants this affirmation, respecting both power and range. So, with the remaining wavelengths, which Canadians share with Americans, our Government can allocate to each province, where needed, stations of lesser power. These 20 kilowatt stations will cost less than the proposed 50 kilowatt stations and will not drown out listeners in a sea of sound, as would certainly be the case with the 50 k.w. stations which are recommended.

Still, the most important point, the greatest problem of all to solve, is not to know whether future stations shall be of 50 or 20 kilowatts, (although the latter, as have been shown, offer many advantages). The question to decide is: Shall private-ownership or State-ownership — also, called State Socialism — dominate in our land?

Through the free station, wisely controlled, the public gets, of a necessity, the sort of programs it likes; each half-hour or hour broadcast being a balanced one. Besides, the free station, with its advertisers, is quite naturally obliged to give popular programs. Owners of radio stations and the advertisers who use them, insist absolutely upon the programs pleasing everybody, within the time limit of the broadcast. Therein lies the reason for the true popularity of such broadcasts.

TESTIMONY

The "Toronto Mail and Empire", issue of November 13th, 1929, said editorially:—

> "In the past two years or so, the Canadian radio programs have shown an improvement in quality. Canadians do not now need to tune in on an American broadcast to hear the best of music and the most important speeches of the day."

This citation merits mention, since it expresses the opinion of one of the principal newspapers of Ontario. Assuredly, a disinterested opinion, because the "Mail and Empire" owns no radio broadcasting station of its own; yet its offices are located near another important Toronto daily, ("The Star"), which owns its station.

Furthermore, letters pouring into "La Presse" testify to the happy results of the efforts made by directors of privately owned Canadian stations, furnishing listeners of the Dominion with programs more and more perfect.

6

THE AIRD PROJECT

The problem to be solved depends less upon the size of the population than upon the extent of the territory to be covered. In Canada, if the public is to receive both quantity and quality broadcasts, then the listeners must be taxed at least five or six times more than in Great Britain, if the cost of broadcasting is to be carried by them. Otherwise, the tax will fall upon other classes of society and be diverted from other governmental services.

DANGER AHEAD!

Remember, too, the danger of political influence, such as that experienced under the British system. Political interference, under State-ownership, immediately made itself felt during the last British general elections; when the Conservatives, who were in power, demanded and obtained twice as much broadcasting time as the Liberals and Laborites together. The adversaries protested vigorously and vainly, and certain voters even wanted to know if the Conservatives owned the stations ! But all these recriminations were useless!

You have been shown that broadcasting stations (born, nurtured, maintained by private-ownership) may and do in our country supply the popular programs demanded by the public; that 20 kilowatt-antenna stations are exactly what are needed in Canada and that such stations will allow everybody to receive desired stations, since nobody is slave to any one station.

PRACTICAL CONCLUSION

The sole practical conclusion for the public, then, is the privately-owned station, which supplies both quantity and popular quality. State-ownership of radio is a very great national danger and an attempt on individual liberty and freedom. It prevents the individual from exploiting an object which pertains strictly to the commercial domain. We might, also, refer to the wrong which, generally, political interference causes to trade. Henry Ford, the great American manufacturer, in an article on municipalization, published in "Contact" of November 1st, last, said: "Political action is always more potent to hinder development or to prohibit wrong practice than it is to encourage original development".

It would be unfortunate for our young country, where Liberty has flowered until now, to see implanted therein this new seed of State-ownership, which often means death to an industry; seizure by the State of what pertains to private concerns. Therefore, on guard against the nationalization of radio !

8

Fran McAuley

Women could do the work but it had to be a man who had the title and got the credit.

I was working with the civil service in Ottawa in 1932 when the CRBC was formed and my boss at the time said he thought this new radio commission might be a good thing and he advised me to apply. I took his advice, and was either the second or third person hired by the CRBC after the four Commission members. Hector Charlesworth, the chairman, was a colourful man who took great pride in everything about his appearance, including, and most especially, his beautiful flowing beard. But he was the boss and everybody knew it.

My job was to order the lines for the networks that we were establishing from coast to coast. There had been 'little' networks before this—one in the Maritimes, for example, and one on the west coast—but these were just regional. *Our* networks were meant to span the country. I remember asking my immediate boss one day to explain what it was we were trying to do and he said, "Oh, you don't have to know the reasons. Just fill the line orders and I'll look after the rest." I said, "But what if you get sick or something?" "Oh," he said, "I never get sick." Two weeks later he got sick and was away for five weeks, during which time I had to do his job and mine. Even after he came back I continued to do both jobs as he didn't have a clue what was going on. However, that was okay in those days because he was a man and I was *only* a woman. Women could do the work but it had to be a man who had the title and got the credit.

It was clear that the Commission was the beginning of something we all felt was going to be very important, and there was a lot of jockeying for position and power plays going on. Austin Weir, for instance, came to us from CN in 1933 but he didn't stay long. There was some kind of 'flare-up' and he either quit or was fired. He took some other job in Toronto before rejoining the network a few years later. Things didn't run very smoothly and I don't think the government knew what was going on. I remember Hector Charlesworth getting upset over the fact that even our paycheques weren't coming through on time. There was a young engineer named Al Ouimet who worked for us. His wife was expecting their first child. He'd come in trying to find out where his paycheque was because he needed the money. It was during the time the Dionne quints were born and he said, "If *my* wife has five, I'll be in real trouble." Ouimet later went on to become Chairman of the CBC.

Colonel Steel was another Commission member I had great respect for. He was inclined to run things in a military style but he was fair and played no favourites. The politicians didn't like him much because he refused to treat them differently from anyone else. If a clerk had an appointment at a certain hour but a senator showed up demanding to see him, he would keep the senator waiting while he kept his appointment with the clerk. You can imagine how much the senator liked that.

In 1936 the government changed. The Conservatives were out; the Liberals under Mackenzie King were in. The first thing they did was replace the CRBC with the CBC. This meant that Charlesworth and Steel and the others were out of jobs. They were given good pensions but there was a lot of bitterness, especially on the part of Charlesworth. And you can see that bitterness in what he wrote about the CRBC.

I was given a job with the CBC at their headquarters on Davenport Road in Toronto. That was a thrilling time too because there was so much excitement about network radio and here was I working with all these great artists—Percy Faith, Bob Farnon, Bert Pearl. Although they were big stars they never acted the part. They were just like the rest of us—excited about being a part of this great new thing. Those of us who worked for the CBC in those days felt like one big family. We not only worked together but we played together, partied together, and many of us married each other. We felt sort of united in this business of creating national radio.

I stayed with the CBC until the war was over. Then I had a chance to shift over and use my experience working for the United Nations, a challenge which held many of the same kinds of thrills as getting network radio off on the right foot in Canada.

The CRBC's four commissioners: Thomas Maher, Lt. Col. W. Arthur Steel, Col. R. Landry and Hector Charlesworth, Chairman.

French on Air Annoys West Members Told

Saskatchewan People Don't Want to Hear it, Moose Jaw Man Tells Committee

Ottawa, April 12 (Staff Special)—"There is no use of beating about the bush—there are objections to the use of French over the radio in Saskatchewan," H. C. Buchanan, of the Moose Jaw Radio Association, informed the House radio committee yesterday afternoon.

Mr. Buchanan was asked by W. A. Beynon, M.P., of Moose Jaw, for some of the complaints of the Saskatchewan people against the Commission.

"Is French a big cause of complaint," inquired Mr. Benyon. "Yes it is," replied Mr. Buchanan.

"Why is it?" asked F. A. Hearn, M.P. for Ottawa. "Is it because lot of the announcers don't know how to speak French?"

"That is not the reason," Mr. Beynon replied. "They don't want to hear French at all."

Mr. Buchanan said he was not expressing his own opinion, but the opinion of the public in his province when he criticized the use of French.

CLAIMS DISCRIMINATION

Mr. Buchanan outlined to the committee the treatment his station CHAB, has received from the Commission. He claimed he had been discriminated against in favor of other Saskatchewan stations.

At first the Commission had refused to allow CHAB to increase power. Later a suggestion was made that his station might be increased to 100 watts and an application for a 500-watt station was filed. Then rules were mentioned regarding the question as to whether available business would justify the expenditures.

Another station owned by Richardson was given authority to erect a station which, it was understood at the time, would be run by the commission.

"The people of Saskatchewan looking to this Parliamentary committee to clear up the situation there, which is unsatisfactory," declared Mr. Buchanan.

Mr. Buchanan severely criticized the Radio Act. "At no time in the history of radio broadcasting have the radio listeners of Saskatchewan had as much cause for complaint as at present." he declared.

Mr. Buchanan declared there had been a number of shuffles in the wave lengths in that province and each one was a little worse than the previous one.

"It has been said that the channel allotments in Saskatchewan have effected an improvement in reception in Saskatchewan. This is contrary to fact. Our station CHAB has been denied the use of the commission programs on the grounds of duplication of service."

CAN'T HEAR PROGRAMS

"A great many people in the Moosejaw area are also denied the opportunity of listening to programs they help pay for, and also other Canadian features. The present channel allotments would indicate that whoever is responsible for them was unaware of the [...]

"It is for and against commission programs," said Mr. Morand.

Thomas Ahearn, M.P., of Ottawa, asked the salaries of the radio commissioners.

The chairman said it was a question which should be discussed privately.

Mr. Ashcroft told the committee that there were 25 radio stations [...] his organization,

Legislation Coming, Bennett Confirms In First Radio Talk

Controlled Credit Assured Through New Organization — "Reasonable" Public Works Policy Will Stimulate Construction in Every Province

DOUBTS OLD BANKS WILL BE INJURED

(By WILLIAM MARCHINGTON.)
(Staff Correspondent of The Globe.)

OTTAWA, Nov. 20.—With the object of accelerating economic recovery, Prime Minister Bennett tonight announced that the Government of Canada would submit proposals at the approaching session of Parliament for the immediate establishment of a central bank and for the construction of public works in every Province of the Dominion next spring.

First of Broadcasts.

Following the example of the President of the United States, the Prime Minister spoke to the people of Canada over a nation-wide radio hook-up, and announced that he proposes from time to time to tell the people about the policies of his Government. The Radio Commission previously had announced that no charge would be made for the Prime Minister's half hour on the air, because the address would be of a non-partisan character, but it was stated tonight that Mr. Bennett personally insisted upon paying for the broadcast.

The Prime Minister alluded to the forthcoming revision of the Canadian Bank Act to remedy the defects in Canada's monetary machinery revealed by the stresses and strains of the trade depression, said that Canada had been committed at the recent World Conference to Imperial monetary co-operation through a system of central banks of the Empire, and spoke of the proposals which had been considered in London for the restoration of a satisfactory international gold standard and the stabilization of exchange rates.

Bankers' Fears Unwarranted.

He then declared that, notwithstanding the fears expressed by the two Canadian bankers on the Royal Commission headed by Lord Macmillan that a central bank might injuriously affect the existing commercial banks of Canada, he believed such fears were unwarranted, and the Government proposed to submit a bill to Parliament providing for the establishment of a central bank in Canada. He added that during the economic depression the banks of Canada had discharged their obligations in a manner that had won the admiration of the world, and, in his opinion, a central bank would afford them even greater opportunities and scope.

Coming to his second major point, Mr. Bennett announced that his Government had been giving serious consideration to proposals for a revival of the stagnant construction industry of Canada, and had decided to embark upon a reasonable policy of public works next spring. These would be undertaken in every Province of the Dominion with the idea of stimulating private enterprise, providing employment for a large number of artisans and thus increasing the purchasing power of many Canadians and hastening the return of normal conditions. He strongly urged those who have capital at their disposal to put it into productive use, and pointed out that the Canadian Government is necessarily restricted in the amount of money which it may spend.

Monetary Independence.

"It has become clearly imperative for Canada to exercise the greatest possible measure of monetary independence, and this it can do only if equipped for wise and timely action with other central banking institutions to lessen fluctuations in our external monetary transactions," Mr. Bennett declared, dealing with the Central Bank proposal.

"This, of course, does not exhaust the functions of a central bank," he continued. "It will place skilled and impartial financial advice at the disposal of the Government. The regulation of the volume of credit is important as a factor in influencing the level of economic activity, and, therefore, of prices, and this is a task which a central bank can most effectually and impartially undertake.

"There are the usual warnings against change. I avail myself of the opportunity to say that at the approaching session of Parliament, the Government will submit a bill providing for the establishment of a central bank in Canada.

"Fears have been expressed that a central bank may injuriously affect the established chartered banks. Such fears are unwarranted," Mr. Bennett declared

Prudent Program.

"We are charged by some with being overcautious," the Prime Minister said, explaining the Government's hesitancy about entering upon any extensive public works undertaking at the present time, "but when you consider that we in Canada, due to our geographical position and our large external debt, are subject to the play of great monetary world forces that we can very slightly influence, I think you will agree that it is a case where prudence should govern our operations."

The Prime Minister urged that "you who have capital available, turn it into productive use," to put productive machinery into action by increasing purchasing power.

"I am also asked, "What is the Government doing along similar lines?" May I remind you that the Government only has money to expend as it receives it from those who contribute to the revenues of the country as taxpayers, or lend to Canada in the confident belief that our borrower obligations will be honorably discharged.

"Universal depression has reduced revenues, and borrowing must be exercised with caution, unless improved conditions are apparent and the outlays are warranted by adequate returns.

"While at the present it is difficult to forecast with any degree of assurance what the future will be, the steady improvement of the last few months, in our opinion, warrants the view that we may be able, with the return of spring, to undertake a reasonable policy of public works in every Province of the Dominion that will substantially assist in stimulating private enterprise, increasing purchasing power, provide employment and hasten the return to prosperity."

Fortunate Canada.

Mr. Bennett referred to the position of Canada as "the most fortunate of any country in the world," but the times had imposed upon all Governments tremendous obligations and responsibilities.

"Inevitably a depression so universal as to disturb the whole fabric of civilization has resulted in sharp conflicts of public opinion as to the remedies that should be applied to restore prosperity.

"On the one hand I am beset by quack doctors of economy, theorists, harbingers of new and fanciful eras of peace and plenty for all; on the other hand, resisted by those who have comfortably and irrevocably settled their minds in grooves of nineteenth century political thinking.

"At the moment your Government conceives the situation to demand clear thinking and calm, dispassionate judgment in determining national policies. In that belief that they will continue to discharge their duties."

Thoughtful men could no longer believe that the production of primary commodities could go on unplanned and uncontrolled without regard to consuming capacity, Mr. Bennett said in touching briefly on the question of supply and demand. He referred to the recent World Economic Conference in London, where the representatives of sixty-four nations considered this problem.

204

Bilingual Programs Of Radio Commission Flayed by Orangemen

Chairman Criticized on Ground That in Book Published Some Time Ago He Initiated Prejudice Against Ideals of ~~Orange~~ Order, Says C.

ada, who pay the license fees and the salaries of the Commissioners," said C. M. Carrie of Toronto, Past Grand Master of the Grand Orange Lodge of Ontario West.

"The appointment of the Chairman was an unhappy choice," continued Mr. Carrie. "In a book he published a few years ago, he proved his prejudice against the ideals and principles which we, as Orangemen and Black Knights and Protestants, believe in and cherish. Quebec has more than a fair representation on the Commission, and the views of a large section of the people of Canada are not represented at all. The radio programs are apparently designed to promote the false claim that French is an official language in every department of life in this country. The pro-~~grams are not at all satisfactory, and~~

ARE YOU LISTENING?

Trenton Man Says He's Canada's Average Radio Listener— Charge Studio Audiences Are Crippling Movies—South African Taxis to Fight For Radio Sets

Claiming to be "Radio's Average Listener," Myron W. Snyder of Trenton, Ontario, writes to The Star: "I live in Trenton, Ontario, which has a population of about 5,000. This community is well served by American broadcasting networks as well as the Canadian radio commission network. We are so located that reception is good from Toronto, Montreal, Buffalo, Rochester, Boston, New York, Louisville, and Cleveland.

"I am 38 years old and of about average height and weight. My family consist of my wife and two girls, Eleanor 17, and Jean 14. I own a car and earn a salary of slightly less than $50 a week. My radio is a five-tube set. I am a true Amos and Andy fan but often give up this hour so the girls can listen to Myrt and Marge. I prefer good drama and always listen to Will Rogers, Eddie Cantor and Ed. Wynn. I listen occasionally to symphonic music and never to grand opera unless to be agreeable. My favorite orchestras are, Wayne King and Guy Lombardo.

"I buy very few products which are advertised on the air other than daily necessities. I buy sparingly of some featured articles purely for the interest I take in the programs which are advertising them! I certainly think that studio audiences are overdone, but I have always wanted to be present at the broadcast of one of my favorite programs.

"I very seldom listen to political speeches but I never miss one of President Roosevelt's talks. I do not like women speakers and with few exceptions, I do not enjoy women singers.

"I am fairly methodical about the programs to which I listen, and they form the greater part of my relaxation during the winter. In some instances I let radio programs interfere with social duties. As a family we are congenial regarding the radio and often give into each other, in order that everyone will be satisfied.

"I usually miss about two nights each week from the radio. Movies hold a great attraction for me and part of this is due to the fact that radio and movies have a close connection so to music. I ordinarily quit the radio at about eleven p.m. My wife has the radio tuned on about two-thirds of the day but I doubt if she hears it much. She has, however, three pet programs that draw her attention so closely that we sometimes have to eat slightly burned food."

Among the Week's Highlights

To-night: Guests for The Big Show will be Florence Reed, dramatic actress, and Charles Judels, Parisian comedian.

To-morrow: David Lloyd George in the afternoon, and Chief Justice Hughes in the evening.

Wednesday: Sally Eilers to be interviewed by Louella Parsons, and Nick Lucas opening a new series.

Thursday: Bobby Jones returning to the golfing wars; Frederick W~~arlock~~, noted actor; opens a series ~~of~~ "Raffles" broadcasts, and H~~elen~~ Morgan singing for the first time the air the hit song from her film "Frankie and Johnny."

Friday: The Grand National Aintree, England.

Saturday: Admiral Byrd from Antarctic and Abe Lyman's show "Bits From Broadway" with Helen Morgan, Tamar, Sargent and Woods Miller.

☆ ☆ ☆

From the Canadian Radio ~~Com~~mission Office:

Doris Scott will feature to ~~in~~ "Hour of Gaiety and Romance ~~with~~ Chester and the professor st~~ill go~~ing on.

Sid Lorraine is master ~~of cere~~monies for a program featur~~ing~~ Hamilton, Celia Huston, Eile~~en Ed~~dington and Eric Munding~~ton.~~

Charles Stainton you hea~~r on the~~ air now and then is reall~~y~~ Stainton Lucas.

Rachmaninoff's "In th~~e~~ Night" and "Eri Tu" from ~~the~~ Opera "Un Ballo in Masc~~ara" will~~ be presented by Anion ~~to-~~morrow night.

Rupert Caplan, Montrea~~l,~~ will present "Parade ~~of the~~ Provinces" to-morrow ni~~ght.~~

☆ ☆ ☆

This-and-that About Those:

Radio dial turners are ~~as~~ heavy squawkers as fil~~ms—~~ 400 times more critical than readers of newspapers, says Will Rogers, who writes, acts and broadcasts.

Radio has turned into a glorified medicine show, New York experts charge, with cosmetics and drugs occupying about 20 per cent. of the commercial air time.

Eighty-five thousand people are attending free radio studio performances each week, cutting into the movie business, charges Ed. Kuykendall, asking the NRA to do something about it.

Tuning In With Jim Hunter

Here Is Your Chance to Tell Ottawa What You Think of the Radio Commission

The Radio Commission has been functioning long enough now for us all to know if we believe that it should continue. The people pay the shot, therefore they have a perfect right to call the tune.

And with that in mind The Telegram feels that you, and you, and you, should have an opportunity to express your opinion. So far this chance has not been offered. Here it is.

These coupons as we receive them will be treated confidentially, and no one need fear that his or her name will be used in the columns of our paper. We are merely anxious to get at the root of what the public thinks about this subject.

Here is your chance to express your views in short order. You can depend on it that while your individual expression of opinion will be treated in strictest confidence, we shall see to it that they will be seen by those who should see them.

YOU'RE TELLING US

Are YOU in favor of Nationalized Radio? ....

Do YOU approve the present Radio Commission, and its operation? ....

Do YOU believe that the Canadian Radio Broadcasting has improved Canadian Radio? ....

Name ....

Address ....

City ....

The 1930s. The Toronto *Star*, *Telegram* and *Globe*. Radio still captures headlines. Issues of concern: the continuing controversy over publicly owned radio, bilingual programming, and 'just who is Canada's average radio listener?'

Colonel Steel

From the start our policy was to work with the private stations to create a network from coast-to-coast.

I had become interested in radio as a boy through the early work of Marconi and at university my training was in that direction. During the First World War, I was a technical officer in communications and when that was over we organized The Royal Canadian Corps of Signals, and did all the communications work for the RCAF and the Northwest Territories Radio System. We set up our first stations in Mayo and Dawson. Even with all the silver mining going on, there was no communication with the outside world. Later, we extended to the Mackenzie area with a base station down in Edmonton.

When the CRBC began in 1932 I was appointed commissioner in charge of technical development. Hector Charlesworth of Toronto, and Thomas Maher of Quebec City were the other two commissioners. Maher looked after the programme end and Mr. Charlesworth as Chairman supervised and looked after all dealings with government. Our first major task was to take over the five stations and staff members of CNR radio in Ottawa, Moncton, Montreal, Vancouver and Halifax. Then we got into arrangements with both the CPR and CNR to set up a network across the country. In the beginning we rented facilities on a per occasion basis but later we worked out a contract for a permanent network that would be available sixteen hours a day.

CRBC programming started off slowly with only a couple of hours a week. It took time to organize a programme department, to arrange for the necessary artists and for the stations which would carry the programmes. In the end we were doing about eight hours a day. Our aim was to have a number of CRBC-owned stations and to work out a full network by affiliating with privately owned stations. The original report envisaged all stations in the country being owned by the Commission as was the case with the BBC in England. But we quickly realized such a system would not work in Canada. The funds simply weren't available. So from the start our policy was to work with the private stations to create a network from coast-to-coast. I made a trip across the country and told station owners what we hoped to do and asked their advice on how best to do it. The stations were very co-operative and excited about taking part. The policy was that local stations would satisfy their own local requirements but would then make hours available to satisfy the Commission's needs for network programmes. I think we made a good start in establishing national radio. When we turned things over to the CBC in 1936 we owned seven stations and had two networks, one in the East, consisting of thirty-six stations and one in the West consisting of twenty-five. Our coverage stretched across the country and we were reaching from seventy to seventy-five percent of the population.

At the beginning we were much influenced by the Aird Report and it was our intention to have a purely public network. But when we realized we couldn't get the money we needed, we went into limited commercial sponsorship. Most of our money came from a government grant and the rest came from these commercials. The first year our grant was a mere $250,000 and throughout the four-year life of the CRBC, we never ever received more than

$750,000 in any one year. That paid for all of our network lines, our staff, and our programmes.

We did some excellent programmes. One of my favourites was "The Northern Messenger Service." That came about when Major Bill Borrett of Halifax told me he'd received a letter from the commander of a British expedition in Labrador asking if there was any way Canadian radio stations could be used to get messages to them. They were going to be there all winter and had no other means of contact with the outside world. I felt this was an idea that could be expanded to include trappers, traders, the staff of the Hudson's Bay Company and government people in the North. That became "The Northern Messenger Service" and every Saturday night we used as many stations as necessary to broadcast to the North. People would send messages in and we would broadcast them. The programme quickly became very popular and, before long, it ran several hours every Saturday night. We found that something like seventy-five percent of the messages were actually received by the people they were intended for. We sent out 20,000 messages between December 1933 and 1936 when we passed everything over to the CBC. They, of course, carried it on.

A Listener

I remember radio with great excitement but the greatest pleasure of all for me was the first time I heard a *car* radio. In 1935 I purchased an old wreck out of a junk yard and a radio came with it. I remember sitting in that old wreck with the radio on and did it ever sound great to listen to Shep Fields. I was in heaven.

Nairn Mogridge

My uncle said, "This thing radio is going somewhere. Let's set up a radio department. Will you join us?"

When wireless came along, I started to buy magazines on it and decided to try to make a set. A Quaker Oats box was, as I remember, about ten inches high and about five or six inches across—about the right size for the amount of wire you needed to tune in various stations. At that time, 1920, there wasn't broadcasting in the regular sense. KDKA didn't come on until later. NAA was the official station for the U.S. Navy and they sent out time signals every hour and it was beep, beep, beep. If you got that you knew you had NAA and *that* was an accomplishment. Refinements came mainly through amateurs. There were no engineers as such. The amateur news magazine was the trading post for information. Somebody found something, and somebody else tried it. To get your ham certificate you had to print out your circuit, explain it and read ten or twenty words a minute in Morse code. You practised by listening to the naval stations. A ham licence didn't cost anything, but then they introduced the two dollar fee, which covered both receiving and transmitting.

In 1924 I went to Detroit. My uncle had a furniture store, the A. G. Miller furniture store. His son was a ham radio operator like me and prior to my going to the States we used to communicate back and forth. He had about a hundred watt transmitter and I had about a five-watter. My uncle said, "This thing radio is going somewhere. Let's set up a radio department. Will you join us?" So I went to the States and was there until the crash of 1929. We sold sets in the store and built a broadcasting station, WAGM, for the A. G. Miller store. My cousin and I operated it after hours. We worked in the furniture store until six, and from six to one in the morning we did broadcasting. We put the transmitter in a two-car garage in my cousin's back yard. We had two hydro poles put up and the living room of my cousin's home was our broadcasting studio. We had fair success with it. My cousin and I took turns operating and announcing.

In 1929 when things got a little rough over there, I came back to Canada where I got involved in the manufacture of radios in Brantford. They had the Workrite franchise for Canada from Cleveland and were looking for somebody to run the plant. I happened to be the man at the right time. But we were too small to compete with RCA and GE and so on, and I recommended to the board that they get out of the business. They sold the franchise back to some company in Chicago. That left me unemployed.

About that time CKPC in Preston was purchased by Silas Galt and he was looking for somebody to run it. In Preston I did play-by-play hockey, and girls' softball and we had children's programming. We also had a line to Toronto, CKNC, which brought in programmes such as "The Cook-a-Noodle Club" and hockey. We'd just phone down and say, these are the programmes we want for this week, and they were on the line.

I joined the CRBC in 1933. It was operated by the Canadian National Carbon Company, who owned CKNC on Davenport Road in Toronto. It was an odd arrangement. The Carbon Company was paid a flat sum of money to run the operation for the Commission. So from 1933 to 1935 we were paid by the Canadian National Carbon Company. We had a piano programme for two hours that was ninety per cent spot announcements. We had "The Neilson Hour" with a forty-piece orchestra, Geoff Waddington conducting. We had "The Happy Gang." And "Melodic Strings." And "The Toronto Symphony." Simpson's were the first people to be allowed to sponsor the TSO. Charles Jennings was the announcer. It was all quite commercial. The *Star,* for example, bought the station twenty-four hours a day during the Moose River Mine disaster. I was on the board for the whole of it. I'd left the air when I came to the CRBC. I came as an operator and the only announcing I did was five-thirty in the morning when I put the station on the air with a guy from New York doing exercises.

During the war I was assigned to Maple Leaf Gardens as the CBC representative for the overseas hockey transmissions. The crew would go back to Davenport Road after the hockey game was over and Foster would put together highlights of the game. It started out as a half hour and by a couple of years later, it was down to about ten minutes. That was fed to the troops on Sunday morning. We would finish at maybe three or four o'clock Sunday morning and it was on its way overseas by six on glass discs.

One thing about broadcasting is that there are no two days alike. It's still unpredictable even though a lot of it's on tape. I often think how fortunate we were to have so few *faux pas.* The one I recall was Prime Minister King's declaration of the ceasefire, which we played an hour early. Just one of those things. The air was blue for a while.

A performer at the microphone of the Gooderham and Worts ("Cheerio") station CKGW in Toronto.

209

Harold Symes

I was working for the Canadian National Carbon Company in Toronto as an analytical chemist. CKCL had studios in the same building so I became interested in radio. When the CRBC came in I was invited to join them as an operator. We had some very good programmes, "The Neilson Chocolate Hour," "CIL Variety" and "Buckingham Theatre." Sunday nights we had "Forgotten Footsteps," a drama series based on events in history. We did a lot of remotes too. We would pile all of the equipment in a car and take off. We didn't have a truck until much later. There weren't too many frills and we worked very hard, although somehow it didn't seem like work.

After the CBC took over I was asked to set up a sound effects department. We had a storeroom in which we saved every bit of junk imaginable because we never knew when it could come in handy. We had old fire sirens, old machines of all kinds. Boxes of gravel. You had to be ready to improvise at any time. We built a 'glass' machine. It was four feet high, two feet wide and about a foot deep. We'd slide sheets of glass in at a forty-five degree angle. It was completely closed in with wire mesh so the glass wouldn't fly all over the place. A heavy ball was suspended on a chain. We pulled the ball, released it, and it broke the glass. To imitate the sound of creaking timbers on a ship, we had a 'creak' machine with cord around a drum with a little resin on it. That made good creaks. We used coconut shells for galloping horses. Crunching cellophane sounded like flames. There was always something that sounded like something else. That was the secret. And sometimes the invented sound was much better than a recording of the real thing.

I want you to fire this gun so that the audience will realize that Renwick doesn't mean to hit Grace — just teach her a lesson so that she'll stay home nights.

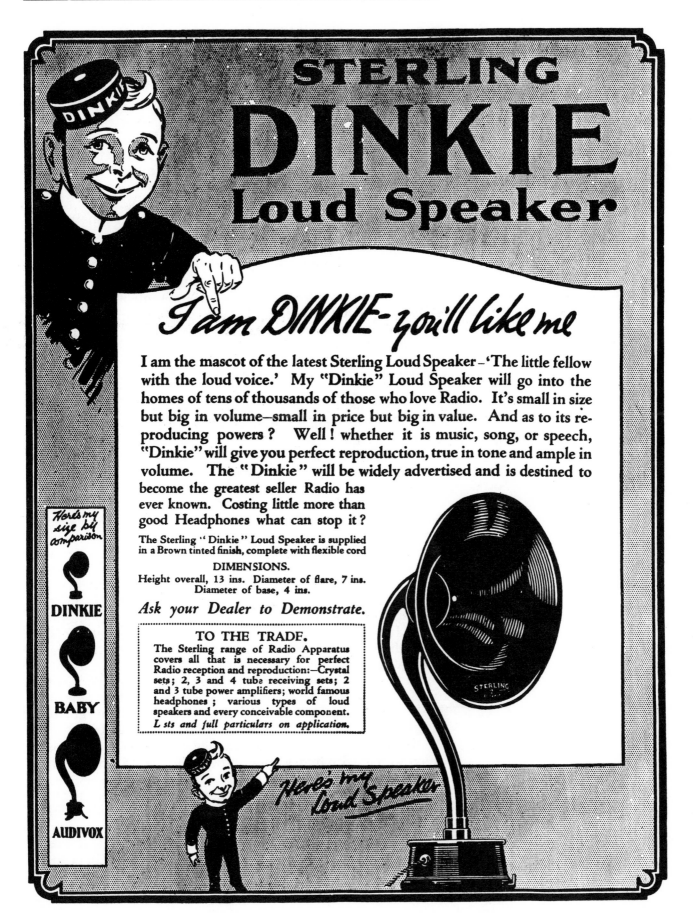

Montrose Werry

You had to delete the American commercials and cut in the Canadian ones.

I started in broadcasting about 1934, a year after I finished university. I was with the Canadian National Carbon Company, the original headquarters of the old CRBC. That was the place from which we fed the Canadian network, except, of course, for the province of Quebec. The old CNR network was turned over to the CRBC, and all their facilities became the property of the new chain. I started as an operator on the board and spent a couple of years at that. Eventually I became chief engineer in Toronto. I was there until 1939 when they moved me to engineering headquarters in Montreal where I was in charge of the construction and design of studio equipment. There was very little off the shelf in those days.

In the old days on Davenport Road the equipment was monstrous in more ways than one. A very low grade amplifier took a couple of cubic feet of space and a lot of power to drive. Equipment tended to be just a little bit cranky and you didn't have anything by way of recording or tape facilities as you do today. In the early days as an operator you did network shows. You brought the American network into Canada and you did commercial cut-ins and that sort of thing. You fed the network for each programme as it came up. In the early days it was always a problem to do remotes because the weight of the equipment was something to be considered. If you did a remote or 'actuality' from a flour mill or a bakery or a candy factory or something like that, you would do a complete interview that might take up forty-five minutes or an hour. Today, of course, they tend toward the five-minute clip or the one-minute clip.

It was all a bit more nerve wracking then than I think it is today. For example, take Sunday night when "Amos 'n' Andy" and some of the American programmes came through the board in Toronto—live—and had to be fed to the network. It was seven o'clock in Toronto, six o'clock in Winnipeg and so on. You had to delete the American commercials and cut in the Canadian ones. And the cue sheets we had weren't always accurate. If you got a song you were never quite sure how many verses they were going to sing. It might be five or six or seven and you'd be on tenterhooks as to whether the American announcer was going to come in before you had a chance to cut him. There was no cue out or anything. We used to get into the habit of fading quickly at the end of every verse to see if the announcer was going to come in. If the song came in again, we'd fade it up very quickly. You got to do things like that in a way that didn't sound too amateurish.

In the early days we used the old condenser microphones which were microphones about nine inches cubed that required special batteries and power supplies and were very, very heavy things to operate. The miniaturization of equipment is one of the big changes over the years. The reliability of equipment is another thing that has helped a lot. And so has the ability to delay and to edit. Now I think radio is a little bit cut and dried. It has a predictable format, whereas before people were forced to be more creative. Their delivery was a lot more spontaneous than it is today.

Technician Jack Barnaby in the transmitter room of CKNC, the National Carbon Company station in Toronto. CKNC was later taken over by the CRBC.

"The TONE and BALANCE of the

New MARCONI Radio
are equal to the best I
have heard," says

DR. ERNEST MacMILLAN

Distinguished composer, conductor and organist

Some of Canada's most brilliant artists and musicians have tested and approved the new Marconi radio for rich tone beauty and perfect reception.

"Excellent," says Boris Hambourg, internationally known 'cellist.

"Exceptionally clear," says Madame Jeanne Dusseau, internationally known Canadian soprano.

"Quite perfect," says the prominent Montreal organist and pianist, George Brewer.

In the New Marconi, a specially designed auditorium type dynamic speaker and audio amplifier reproduce voices and instruments faithfully, colorfully and with amazing clarity.

An automatic tone control, years in advance of hand control devices, featured on most sets, insures permanent tone reproduction of a quality chosen by these famous musical celebrities.

Twin models to the Marconi set, which Dr. Ernest MacMillan has in his own home, are on display at your dealer's store.

MARCONI A.C. "SENIOR"

A triumph of Marconi engineering, providing the finest in Radio entertainment. Perfected Automatic Volume Control. Silent meter tuning. Four completely isolated tuned circuits. Screen Grid Amplification and Power Detector. Special Auditorium Type Dynamic Speaker. This remarkable instrument of advanced design embodies the most modern developments in Radio. The rare artistry of this distinctive Cabinet creation will enhance the beauty of any home. Height-from floor 41". $285 with tubes.

"I am convinced," says this noted musical authority, "that the radio can become a most important factor in musical education. There are almost unlimited possibilities in this field."

The New MARCONI Radio

Canadian MARCONI Company, Montreal. Branches: Vancouver, Toronto, Halifax and St. John's, Nfld.

Wally Slatter

My parents were both involved in broadcasting. My father was president of Radio Representatives Limited, which represented stations from across the country for national advertising. He started in the very early days of radio as a musician. His group was called "Jack Slatter and His Canadian Aces." In those days people would stand in the middle of Yonge Street in Toronto and look up at this second storey window to watch the broadcasts on CKGW. Then came 1929 and the Slatter family had some lean years like everyone else. It was at that stage that Dad and another chap started the Toronto office of All-Canada Radio Facilities and from that came Radio Representatives Limited. My mother worked for the CRBC and later for the CBC.

My opportunity to go into the business came when I was eleven years old in 1934. There was a call for auditions for juvenile actors. I tried out and got the part and from then on I was a juvenile actor. I had several marvellous opportunities. The CRBC had a series written by Don Henshaw called "Forgotten Footsteps," hour long dramatic presentations with Geoffrey Waddington's orchestra. The series was about a museum whose caretaker told two kids, Wally and Peggy, stories about various objects. Then they would go into a dramatic portion. At the end they closed with the two kids and the caretaker again. When we did a CRBC drama we would start at ten in the morning. We would finish rehearsing at about four in the afternoon, and the show would go on the air at nine. Between four and nine you could polish up your own performance. They had some really professional producers like Robert Lucas and we worked with the best actors in Canada, so it was obviously a tremendous learning process. I especially remember Grace Matthews, Grace Webster and Jane Mallett. I used to get two dollars a show for some things and five dollars for others.

I kept on doing bits and pieces—commercials and so on—right up to when I entered the R.C.A.F. in 1942. After the war I went to work for my dad in the representation business. With Fred Metcalfe, a friend from school days, I applied for, and got, a radio licence for Guelph. We started on June 14, 1948.

"I tell you this Bloodstained Phantom is not going to get away with it. The law will catch up with him, you mark my words, Grigsby."

215

Frank Willis

In those days the inside of a radio studio was much like the inside of a coffin, lined with plush and satin.

Radio was not my original idea of a career, although I found myself on the air at an early age. My first appearance in a radio station was at the opening of CHNS at the old Carleton Hotel studios. I was playing a banjo in a Hawaiian group. In those days the inside of a radio studio was much like the inside of a coffin, lined with plush and satin.

When I was twenty I set my mind on commercial art and went to New York to study. My family operated the Willis Piano Company in Halifax and wanted me in the business but I couldn't face up to collections and repossessing pianos. After protracted negotiations they gave me a small allowance to live on in New York. For a while after these studies were over I worked at the Long Island Studios of Paramount, but it was 1930 and I could see the signs of deepening depression. I returned to Halifax and hung out my shingle. One of my clients was Mills Brothers, a women's wear store.

About this time I began to work as a freelancer for CHNS producing, writing and announcing radio shows. We produced two plays by Merrill Denison, *The Weather Breeders* and *Brothers in Arms,* in the latter of which I made my first radio appearance as an actor. Major Bill Borrett, the managing director of CHNS, was taken with a series of Sherlock Holmes stories I adapted and acted in. I don't recall that I got permission from Conan Doyle, but radio and I were both very young and the practice of hijacking material was commonplace. I also began my slumber hour of poetry reading and organ music, then called "Harbour Lights" and later "Nocturne." I also produced the "Ampico Program," a Sunday afternoon show of piano music. The money was pouring in. I received two dollars per week for "Harbour Lights," ten dollars a week for writing, producing and acting in the Sherlock Holmes series, and three dollars a week for the Ampico Show.

In 1933, when the Canadian Radio Broadcasting Commission was formed, Hector Charlesworth offered me a job as regional director for the Maritimes. I was very interested in the new concept of national radio, whose philosophy, as I understood it, was to use the influence of radio to draw this sprawling nation together. So for the next few years I functioned as Maritime regional representative, producing and announcing shows and scouring the provinces for talent.

One person I found in that early search was Don Messer. Later, Messer added Charlie Chamberlain, "The Singing Lumberjack," which he really was. From Sydney we had "Cotter's Saturday Night" and from Halifax a string programme, "From A Rose Garden," and a concert hour, "Acadian Serenade." I wasn't infallible as a judge of potential talent. I turned down Mary Grannan (of "Maggie Muggins" and "Just Mary" fame) when she first auditioned for me.

In 1936 came the Moose River Mine Disaster. I take no special credit for my part on the story as I was the only CRBC staffer east of Montreal when the story broke. Three men were trapped underground by a rock fall in an abandoned mine at Moose River. On the Monday when I arrived at the rescue site the story was already several days old—because there had been

From J. FRANK WILLIS: My Life on the Air, by Jock Carroll. Originally published in *Weekend* magazine. Copyright © 1961, Jock Carroll. Used with permission.

The Moose River mine disaster in April, 1936 had the whole world tuned in to Canadian radio. Aleister Bowman of the Maritime Telegraph and Telephone Company uses earphones to listen for word from the trapped miners.

Excerpt from Frank Willis's broadcasts from Moose River.

Ladies and gentlemen, once again the Canadian Radio Commission calling Canada and associated networks in the United States, from Moose River, Nova Scotia. We have nothing further to add to what has already gone before except to contradict an erroneous impression that is being created in the U.S. that the mine is in danger of caving in. This is *absolutely not true. This is an official statement. There is no danger of any such thing happening. The pit, the shaft that these men have dug and have timbered and re-timbered, is just as safe as is humanly possible to make it. This statement has been published in some Canadian newspapers and has been broadcast in the United States. Don't believe it for one moment. I have it from officials here with whom I am working in closest co-operation and that is absolutely untrue, I repeat, work is going forward just as quickly as it possibly can. These conflicting statements are being issued from far distant points. We're standing here; we can spit into this pit and yet from thousands of miles away people are contradicting what we have to say. This must stop. I'm stopping these broadcasts now until something definite happens. I don't care to go on the air anymore and be contradicted from thousands of miles distance. We have given you the official word from the government officials working here and we can no longer carry on under these circumstances and I want to tell you that there is no danger here to the miners or to the buried men. Everything is safe and that is the final word and this is the Canadian Radio Commission.*

some question as to whether or not the CRBC should cover the story in competition with the print media. On Saturday and Sunday I had talked on the phone with Ernie Bushnell, Arthur Dupont and Hector Charlesworth at CRBC headquarters in Ottawa, urging that we do so. At nine o'clock Monday morning in Halifax I received the green light. We had no such thing as remote broadcasting equipment, so I picked up an old banquet microphone, borrowed an engineer named Cecil Landry from Halifax Station CHNS, an amplifier from CP Telegraphs, a Graham-Paige car with the newfangled mud tires, and set out for Moose River with CRBC engineer Arleigh Canning.

When I arrived shortly after noon on Monday I was an unwelcome addition to the swarm of newspapermen already on the spot and their first instinct was to prevent me, by force if need be, from having the use of the single iron-wire telephone line which connected us to the outside world. Happily, just before the fists started flying, the dispute was arbitrated by the Maritime Telephone and Telegraph Co. whose land line we were squabbling over. They ruled that as the only radio man on the job I was entitled to two five-minute spots in every sixty. It was now known that there was life below because smoke had seeped through to the surface from old dynamite boxes the trapped men had set on fire.

But before I could get any sort of story out louder than a thin inaudible whisper each of the parties along the eighteen-mile rural telephone circuit had to be persuaded to break a lifetime habit and refrain from listening to others on the line. Each telephone lifted from the hook weakened the signal and we had to persuade the subscribers to listen to my broadcast on their radios rather than on their telephones. Having negotiated an agreement with this host of eavesdroppers, I began at four p.m. on Monday, broadcasts that were to continue for three days and three nights. At that time the CRBC was spread so thin that my nearest relief man was in Montreal, twenty-four hours by rail from a story that might be over at any moment.

Not until two days later—when I lost my temper for the first and last time on the air, and spoke out harshly about false news flashes which had appeared in print outside—was there an interruption. At this point the CRBC felt my nerves were getting bad—they were—and that they would force me to take a two-hour rest by refusing to take my broadcasts. Though well intentioned, this had exactly the opposite effect. I spent the two hours dancing up and down, afraid that the rescue would be made during this enforced radio silence.

Moose River was a stiff test of my CRBC career intentions. I was swamped with offers to cash in on the continent-wide publicity. U.S. theatre chains and radio networks wanted me to make personal appearance tours. Manufacturers wanted me to endorse their products. But I felt there was something wrong about capitalizing on a thing like the Moose River disaster.

For the next few years I busied myself with the Maritimes coverage of the CBC. We produced "The Lunenburg Choir" programmes, "Pierhead Yarns," and an inter-city bridge contest which aroused wide interest. I almost made a hash of the bridge contest one week because I was leaving town in a hurry to cover the International Schooner Races. It was my job to deal the bridge hands for the contest, which were then sealed and opened on the air as the programme began. I had made a misdeal and the unfortunate announcer did not discover the mistake until the programme was on the air. One hand had fourteen cards, another twelve. Somehow the announcer turned the bridge contest into a discussion of bridge in general.

In 1939 I went on an exchange with the Australian Broadcasting Commission where I learned much, until called home to help set up arrangements for the first royal tour. Then came the war. In the years following the war I believe Canadian radio had its finest hours. Writers like Len Peterson and Joseph Schull had returned from service. Andrew Allan launched his famous "Stage" series. Our school broadcasts, forums, farm and public-affairs programmes were acclaimed internationally.

The broadcast crew at the Moose River disaster returned to a heroes' welcome in Halifax. Major Bill Borrett of CHNS welcomes home engineers Arleigh Canning and Cecil Landry, newsman Frank Willis and driver Lou Murphy.

Mart Kenney

We were no better nor worse than a lot of these orchestras and we knew that the best way to make it was to 'have a wire.'

▶

Radio made Mart Kenney and his Western Gentlemen, Canada's most popular big band.

I had been playing professionally, since I was eighteen, around Vancouver and making very good money for the time—around $125 a week, but a good friend convinced me that music was so insecure I should get into the selling end of the business—selling instruments. He said if one could learn to sell, he'd always have something to fall back on. He offered me twenty-five a week and a move to their new branch in Regina. I thought about that and finally agreed and made the move. That was in 1929. I got married right away and we settled in, but immediately after that the stock market collapsed and the bottom fell out of everything, including the market for musical instruments.

There was nothing to do but head back to Vancouver. I had no job, and none to look forward to, so I did different things, including running an appliance shop and writing a few musical arrangements. This led to filling-in for the leader of the band, and eventually being asked to form my own band to play at The Alexandra Ballroom in Vancouver. That was really the start of the Western Gentlemen. I was very fortunate to get a break like that. However, it was nip and tuck for the next couple of years, barnstorming all over the place and barely making ends meet. We were just another small orchestra, trying to get along and of course, competing with other orchestras for whatever work was available.

We were no better nor worse than a lot of these orchestras, and we knew that the best way to make it was to 'have a wire.' This meant if you could be connected to a radio station while you were doing a 'date,' you would be heard by a much wider audience and become better known. Well, by great fortune, in 1934, along came the man who is known as the 'father of radio' in Western Canada, Horace Stovin. He was the director of radio for the CRBC, in the West and he offered me a job on the network. This meant being heard all the way across Canada.

That's what made all the Big Bands in the States, including Glenn Miller who got a network spot about the same time we did. You couldn't help being famous because your music and your name were constantly being heard at a time when everybody was listening to nighttime radio. There were lots of good bands around playing great music, but they never got heard outside their immediate areas.

Once we got established on the network, we realized that this was very different from playing for a dance. You had to arrange your music in a way that it would *sound good on radio* and we would practise, and change things around for hours before a broadcast, until we could get exactly what we wanted coming out of that speaker. We were doing those first broadcasts in 1934, from Waterton Park, and we were worried as we approached the end of the series, because we had no further work lined up. I think it was the second last week that we got a telegram from the Saskatchewan Hotel wanting to book us because they had heard us on radio.

The next year, in 1935, the network decided to put us on Sunday nights, which was taking a bit of a chance because of the sacred nature of the Sabbath in those days. However, it worked out and became extremely popular. The programme was called, "Sweet and Low," and it went on for years. We got bushels of mail from all over the country and there isn't any doubt at all that it was radio that was responsible for the success of The Western Gentlemen. The power of that medium was tremendous.

Frank Deaville

The show was called "Woodhouse and Hawkins in Nitwit Court."

In 1931 the Calgary *Albertan* had a radio station, CJCJ. My partner and I were working in a hardware store. We had an act that we'd been taking around to banquets to make a couple of bucks on the side. The manager of the station used to come in and we'd say, what's the matter with your programmes, they're not much good. He said, what have you got to offer? So we went up and auditioned and he sold us for thirteen weeks. And we only had *one* act. Then we had to get busy. Of course, there was no money for hiring other actors. We had our setting in an apartment building. My partner was the star tenant and I was the caretaker. That's how it all started. And every time we used a new voice, we had to make one up. This is how all the different voices came into being. The show was called "Woodhouse and Hawkins in Nitwit Court." We had a retired major and his son who'd just come out from England. They had a Scotchman living there. And there was Hawkins the janitor. And we had a Mortimer Snerd type of fellow. Mortimer Snerd came along *after* our character.

We were still working and got paid five dollars a show for doing this on the side. Of course, once we got on the network there was more money. We were making about fifty, sixty dollars a week, and we were getting guest shots and dramatic parts on the side. We were doing quite well for the times. The network put us into a half-hour show in Winnipeg with a twenty-piece band and a sound effects man. In those days you used to have a big door with latches, chains, bolts. After dress rehearsal the boys in the band would lock the door. In the middle of the show the sound effects man would go over and grab the door and the whole thing would come over on top of him. We did the show in the old Walker Theatre and the place would be packed. Radio was fun in those days. Today it's all push-button stuff. If you wanted to break a window in those days, you'd actually break a pane of glass. For a fire scene, you'd crackle cellophane. Walking on snow would be cornflakes. Now you can get sound for everything you want on discs.

We had about twelve years on the network. We carried on during the war, also did some work on the BBC and the U.S. networks. After we left the CBC we did a variety show on CFRB. We started our own ad agency on the side and did game shows like "Spin to Win" and "Double or Nothing."

for
successful

RADIO PROGRAMS

it's

Woodhouse & Hawkins
1175 Bay St., Toronto, Ont.
KI. 4864

Art McGregor and Frank Deaville were "Woodhouse and Hawkins." They and their many zany characters became regular features of CRBC and CBC radio in the late 1930s and early 1940s.

WOODHOUSE AND HAWKINS

A few, short weeks ago two nitwits of the networks, namely Art McGregor and Frank Deaville, left the West to come to Toronto to star in "Marching in Swingtime", a new series of variety programmes. Already they have endeared themselves to their new air audience and to Canada's fledgling birdmen at R.C.A.F. Manning Pool where the programme originates every Monday at 8.00 p.m. EDST. Here they are along with an artist's idea of their various mike personalities.

How to Get the Most from Your Radio

1 Have your antenna installed by a competent service man.

2 Use a good ground. A cold water pipe makes the best ground. Solder the lead to it or use a standard ground clamp. If you cannot use a cold water pipe, a sheet of copper, approximately three feet square, buried in moist ground makes an excellent one. Hot water or steam radiator pipes usually will give satisfactory results.

3 Place the set so that the antenna and ground leads are as short as possible. If the lead-in comes through the window, place the set near the window, not on the other side of the room.

4 A shielded lead-in will sometimes eliminate objectionable noises.

Felt pads under a set will often aid in minimizing unpleasant noises.

5 See that all connections are tightly made.

6 Allow several inches clearance between the back of the set and the wall.

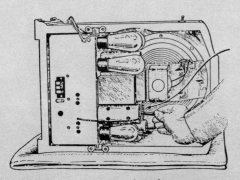

The proper adjustment of a radio receiver requires full technical knowledge. If something goes wrong with your set, call in a trained service man.

From *RCA Victor Catalogue,* 1931.

7 If possible, make the set face a doorway or drapes of some kind.

8 More pleasing tone quality can often be obtained by insulating the set from the base floor with small felt pads.

9 Sometimes reversing the plug on an a.c. set will improve reception and reduce noise. Never reverse the plug on a d.c. set.

10 Static and electrical disturbances can be reduced by turning the tone control to the extreme bass position.

11 Do not attempt to make adjustments on your set unless you are thoroughly competent to do so. The skill of a good service man is available at a reasonable cost.

12 If your set employs batteries, see that they are always up to the required voltages. Worn-out batteries cause noise, reduced volume, and lack of sensitivity.

13 If your set uses a storage battery, see that distilled water is added at regular intervals so that the liquid never falls below the top of the plates.

14 Do not play the set too loudly. It is less disturbing to the neighbors and you get more life-like reproduction.

15 Have your tubes tested at least once a year.

Charles Jennings

There were no actual commercials for liquor, of course, but the 'G' and 'W' and the "Cheerio" were an indirect way of describing their wares.

I started as an announcer in 1928 on the Gooderham and Worts station in Toronto, CKGW. They called themselves, "Canada's Cheerio Station." CKGW was said to be the most technically modern station in the world. It was owned by a distillery and I don't suppose it bothered them that their distillery message was being heard loud and clear in the United States where prohibition was in full flower. There were no actual commercials for liquor, of course, but the 'G' and 'W' and the "Cheerio" were an indirect way of describing their wares.

There was a good deal of glamour about radio then and I

suppose that's what attracted me. I had just finished my second year at the University of Toronto when I heard about an announcing job at CKGW. I auditioned, got the job and never left the business for the rest of my working life. In 1933 I became the first news announcer for the CRBC. Our news, which was written especially for us by Canadian Press, came to us on what's called 'flimsy' paper. I had to take great care while I was on the air not to crackle the sheets as I turned them.

Although my main job was to read the National News, I did some remotes too. One of the great stories I covered was the arrival of the dirigible, R-100. We did it from the CPR Telegraph offices in Montreal. We couldn't get access to the airfield so we had to do a tremendous amount of faking. We went on the air at six-thirty in the evening and didn't sign off until seven-thirty the next morning. The airship had run into bad weather and was about twelve hours late arriving and during those hours we had to keep talking or switching to the Royal York Hotel where Fred Cully's band was playing. When he stopped at one o'clock someone brought in a hand-wound gramophone. And there was all sorts of material being dug up for me to read between records. When the R-100 finally did come we were the first to see it. So, as it turned out, we were fortunate in not being permitted on the airfield.

I continued to read the national news when the CBC took over from the CRBC. However, I wasn't totally in news. I was also the announcer for many of the classical music programmes including the broadcasts of the Toronto Symphony Orchestra. When I finally left the news in 1938, it was to come to Ottawa as assistant to Ernie Bushnell, who was Programme Supervisor. It was our job to organize a National Programme Office, which had responsibility for all programmes on the CBC. Twice a year we had supervisors come in from all the regions for planning sessions as we changed our schedules twice a year. There was one schedule for Standard Time and another for Daylight Saving Time. Everyone would come to these meetings full of ideas for programmes they wanted on the network and we'd try to fit everything together like a giant jigsaw puzzle. Some programmes would fall by the wayside when new ones were fitted in and, of course, not everyone was happy. But there were only so many hours available.

Then, too, you had all the special things that keep happening. Transatlantic solo flights were a big thing at the time, for example. You'd have to fit those into the schedule. When something like Munich came along you'd suspend regular programming. Our job was to do the best we could in balancing what was happening in the country and in the world. When something happened outside Canada that we felt merited special coverage we'd have to find reporters and commentators because those were the days before we had our own. We'd somehow figure out how best to get these reports back to Canada and then we'd get them on the air.

The outbreak of the war was a particularly tumultuous time because we had to change all our schedules to a wartime basis. We had to find correspondents in Canada to go over and we had to find a way of getting them over and of providing them with what they needed while they were there and of getting their reports fed back to Canada.

▲
"This is Charles Jennings announcing...."

◄
The arrival in Montreal of the R-100, one of the world's largest dirigibles. This newsworthy event was covered by a network of fifteen Canadian stations and the full CBS network.

FIVE YEARS OF ACHIEVEMENT • 1936-1941

A series of illustrated pamphlets describing the work of the CBC, in its principal aspects, since November, 1936. The complete titles in the series are:

MUSIC • DRAMA AND FEATURES • NEWS • TALKS • SPECIAL EVENTS
SCHOOL RADIO • WAR EFFORT • AGRICULTURE • ENGINEERING
FINANCE AND ADMINISTRATION

Copies are obtainable on application to Dept. of Press and Information, CBC, 55 York St., Toronto

CANADIAN BROADCASTING CORPORATION

THE WORLD SERIES

———

WEDNESDAY OCTOBER 2
1.15 p.m. E.S.T.

———

CBC COAST-TO-COAST

Bette Davis brings her great dramatic talent to listeners of the CBS-CBC network on Sunday, October 20 in the "Silver Theatre" broadcast from Hollywood at 7.00 p.m. EDST. She will be heard in the leading role of "The Hour Shall Come", a two-part radio drama. (Photograph courtesy CBS.)

WARTIME CENSORSHIP OF NEWS

Listeners sometimes ask whether the CBC censors the news.

Emphatically, the CBC does not exercise any function of censorship. The news bulletins prepared by the CBC National News Service give a full and unbiased account of the day's important news events, in Canada and abroad, without any effort to suppress or modify the news in any way; even when—as may at times be the case with the war news—it happens to be of an unfavourable or disturbing nature. It is taken for granted that intelligent listeners are prepared to accept the bad news along with the good, and prefer a realistic picture of the day's happenings to news that has been sugar-coated as a sop to wishful thinkers. At the outset of the Balkan Campaign last spring, for instance, CBC News Editors refrained from misleading listeners with false optimism that was not justified by events.

Foreign news is censored at the source and not in Canada. The CBC News Service is subject only to the general wartime censorship which applies to all newspapers and radio stations. The restrictions imposed by the Chief Radio Censor deal not with the suppression of news, but the withholding of information that would be of obvious value to the enemy — information of troop movements, ship sailings, location of war industries, and so on.

The CBC

Bob Bowman

My father, C. A. Bowman, was editor of the Ottawa *Citizen* and he had a newspaperman's disdain for broadcasting. But he caught me listening to radio a couple of times on a crystal set I'd built using a Quaker Oats box. I'd say, "Dad, listen to this." Then, by gosh, one night he heard Chicago and he too began to take an interest. He saw that Canadian radio stations were becoming affiliated with American stations and he appreciated the danger. All our movie theatres were owned by Canadian Players and he could see the day coming when all our radio stations, especially in the big centres, would be owned by American interests too. He began writing editorials in the Ottawa *Citizen* not only against the Americanization of broadcasting but against broadcasting generally. My father's editorials, and lobbying by people like Graham Spry and Allan Plaunt, led to the appointment by Mackenzie King of the Aird Commission, of which Dad was a member. They recommended that there be national broadcasting in Canada. Then the government changed hands. The new Prime Minister, R. B. Bennett, agreed with the principle of national broadcasting. He created the Canadian Radio Broadcasting Commission.

I graduated from McGill in accountancy in 1932. However, in 1932 there was nothing to count. I was damn lucky to get a job on the *Citizen* as a reporter at fifteen dollars a week and part of my job was to cover the CRBC. I dropped in to see Hector Charlesworth practically every day. I could see that things weren't working out properly and that they needed somebody with a knowledge of broadcasting. The government realized this too and they brought Gladstone Murray over from Britain in an advisory capacity.

In 1934 I went to Britain and dropped in on the BBC. They

He could see the day coming when all our radio stations, especially in the big centres, would be owned by American interests too.

were just starting to broadcast news to various parts of the British Empire. They offered me a job for six months. Of course, I was thrilled to get into broadcasting, even though I wasn't on air. I wrote newscasts. And I didn't stay six months; I stayed three years. The reason was that hockey was becoming popular in Britain in those days and the British commentators couldn't handle it. Which got me into actually broadcasting on air. I was the first so-called American to broadcast regularly in Britain.

Around that time, the government again changed hands in Canada. The CRBC was scrapped, the Canadian Broadcasting Corporation was created and Gladstone Murray was invited to come back to Canada as the first general manager. Murray and I had spent the three years I was in London discussing that very possibility. I followed Murray back to Canada as quickly as I could. I arrived just in time to take part in the Christmas Day Show, 1936. They sent me up to Callander, Ontario, to do an interview with Dr. Alan Dafoe who'd delivered the Dionne Quintuplets. It was the loneliest Christmas I ever had. I spent practically all of Christmas Day at Dr. Dafoe's home, out on his verandah, while he had a big Christmas dinner inside.

Early in 1937 I did a series of half-hour programmes called "Night Shift" about places where people worked at night. We started in the Caledonia coal mine at Glace Bay. I should say here that we were introducing a new actuality broadcasting technique to Canada and perhaps North America with "Night Shift." Until then the usual practice was for a commentator to write a script and read it from a more or less fixed position near the scene being described. Often these broadcasts were faked. Commentators would say they were speaking from a position three thousand feet below the ground when they were near the surface. Sound effects were often used to take the place of real sounds. I didn't believe in that technique because while it might fool listeners, it didn't fool people in the broadcasting area and eventually word spread that programmes were faked. So in "Night Shift" we actually went to where we said we were, spoke extemporaneously, and dragged our heavy equipment with us. Preventing our microphone cables from getting caught in machinery was often a problem. So was the noise level in big factories.

We did the programme all across the country for weeks. They were live, right on the spot, and had the usual technical problems. But it was great fun and went over well. When that series was over in the spring of 1937 Ernie Bushnell made me his assistant and one of my jobs was to attempt to arrange reciprocal programmes with the United States. We were getting plenty of shows from them such as "The New York Philharmonic" and other first-class programmes, but we wanted them to take something from us too. It wasn't easy to convince them that we had anything good in Canada.

When I began, the CBC only broadcast at night. But when we moved into daytime we had to find new programmes, which wasn't easy. We were scraping the bottom of the barrel searching for ideas of any kind. I remember George Taggart, who was in charge of the Ontario region, saying, "Look, we've got a group on our station in Toronto doing a local show, but they're pretty good and I think they could go on the network." They were called "The

---

CBC NEWS POLICY
(General Directives)

To give this basic policy more exact definition and meaning, the following directives have been given to all CBC News Editors—

1. Accurate news must be the first consideration. Stories must be faithful to source material in facts, emphasis, and general purport.

2. CBC News Bulletins must be based on source material supplied by the authorized news agencies, or secured by members of CBC News Staff under the authority of the Senior Editor in each newsroom. No outside source of news may be given payment for news, either direct or indirect.

3. News should not be treated in a sensational manner. Crime stories, where they have sufficient general interest to be used at all, should be handled with discretion. Remember that they go into the home and may be heard at unsuitable times.

4. News should be handled so as not to create alarm or panic. Flash stories about fires, accidents, etc., should not be used until the news is entirely dependable.

5. CBC Editors should not editorialize, speculate, or predict into factual news items. Speculative comment should be used only if it comes in the body of a news story and is quoted from an authoritative source.

6. Domestic political news must be treated with absolute impartiality. In controversial stories, both sides of the issue must be given equal emphasis.

7. No libelous or scandalous news should be permitted in News Bulletins, nor should voice inflection be allowed in any way to colour the news.

8. No suicide stories—unless about prominent figures; and even these should be very carefully handled.

9. In all writing the canons of good taste should apply, particularly in referring to physical handicaps or deformities.

10. No stories about lotteries, gambling odds, or any reference to any sport news that would cause people to gamble or bet on the outcome.

Happy Gang" and that's how they got their start on the network.

After we'd moved into daytime broadcasting Bushnell realized that it was cheaper to broadcast actuality stuff than it was to put on studio programmes, so he made me Director of Special Events. My job was to get actuality daytime programmes. I bought the rights to regular Big Four football games for $400 a broadcast and to the Grey Cup for $600. CFRB had the rights up to that time. Boy, were they mad! I fired Harry Foster, the football commentator, and tried out all kinds of people, including Foster Hewitt. We finally hired a fellow named Roy Dilworth as our football commentator. Then I got the rights to the Canadian Open. And we created the first documentary programmes using mobile units to go out and record and then bring the material back to the studios to combine the sound with the music. CBC Mobile Unit No. 1 was a Dodge pulling a trailer full of equipment. We did a documentary about Banff. We did fishing broadcasts. The first one about trout fishing was broadcast live from Buckingham, Quebec. We actually caught a trout while we were on the air and fried it during the programme. We did bass fishing from the French River and salmon fishing from the Miramichi.

Early in December of 1939 Ernie Bushnell asked me to get to Halifax as quickly as possible. I was to see General Constantine and say "Constantinople." The moment I arrived in Halifax, I could see what was up. There were five ocean liners on the wharves and a big battleship out in the stream. I went up to Constantine and said "Constantinople" and he explained that the First Canadian Division was sailing. He didn't say where. He wanted me to record our troops going on board. After they'd arrived at their destination, I'd be able to broadcast their departure. I did what I was told. But then I heard that the Canadian Press was sending a man *with* the troops. I thought, "If CP can send a man, so can the CBC." I got on a secret line to Gladstone Murray and explained the situation.

CBC PROGRAMME SCHEDULE

ISSUED BY PRESS AND INFORMATION SERVICE, CANADIAN BROADCASTING CORPORATION

| ONTARIO REGIONAL | WEEK OF JANUARY 5, 1941 | DAVENPORT ROAD, TORONTO |

CBC NATIONAL NEWS SERVICE

"This is the national news bulletin brought to you by the CBC".

Since Wednesday, January 1, 1941, this has been the introduction to the National News period, formerly provided through the courtesy of the Canadian Press. The CBC has established news bureaux in its five programme regions at Halifax, Montreal, Toronto, Winnipeg and Vancouver. It has staffed these bureaux with writers qualified, through long service in handling news, for the exacting and important task of providing listeners in Canada with up-to-the-minute reports on the war, world affairs in general and items of particular interest to Canadians.

Since the inception of the CBC National News Service, four fifteen-minute bulletins and two shorter bulletins have been presented each day over the nine stations owned by the CBC and, in addition, over a network of 25 privately-owned stations. The CBC News is, and will continue to be, a sustaining service and it will be written by the news staffs in the five regional centres and announced by staff announcers of the CBC.

The aim of the CBC in establishing its own news service is to provide bulletins which are dependable, authoritative and unbiased. The bureaux will write their news from the services provided by the Canadian Press and the British United Press, such as is supplied to the daily newspapers throughout the country.

The establishment of its own news department is in keeping with the CBC's policy of providing an adequate broadcast service to Canadian listeners and to be responsible for that service from creation to presentation.

I'll never forget a cable from some lady in Canada. It read, "I heard my son's voice tonight. God bless you."

Within a day I was assigned to the Aquitania. The CBC rushed Art Holmes, a sound man, down to Halifax with all of our heavy equipment and we got to Britain with some recordings we made with General McNaughton on the way across. I only had a suitcase with enough clothes for five days in Halifax but there I was in Britain for what looked like the rest of the war. Art Holmes went back to Canada to design a mobile unit and he was away for several months while they built it. One of our first broadcasts was done from the opening of British Columbia House, a canteen for Canadian soldiers where they could get hot dogs, pork and beans, and apple pie—the kinds of food they were missing in Britain. We booked the transatlantic circuit for half an hour. The formal part of the opening took about ten minutes and there I was with twenty minutes to fill. I was desperate. So as the troops were filing in to get their food I asked each man to identify himself and send a message home. My God, the reaction to that was just fantastic. I'll never forget a cable from some lady in Canada. It read, "I heard my son's voice tonight. God bless you." That was the beginning of broadcasts of troops coming on the air and sending messages home. It was the most popular thing we did.

I stayed over there and we got great material like the bombing of London. Our chief engineer, Art Holmes, spent his nights

Radio helped bridge the distance between soldiers and their loved ones.

The CBC Presents

"WINGS OF THE EMPIRE"

A feature broadcast in commemoration of the first anniversary of the Commonwealth Air Training Scheme.

TUESDAY, DECEMBER 17
8.00-8.55 p.m. EDST

CBC NATIONAL NETWORK

BEAVER CLUB BROADCAST

Now I have heard your voice again. So tense
    I listened as you spoke from overseas
And when you called my name, the stubborn rents
    That parting tore, a moment were at ease.
Has memory played me false, or radio?
    Your voice seemed deeper, born of courage stern,
And still it rang with cheer I used to know,
    And hinted eagerness to soon return.

Some other voice . . . another heard a brother;
    A sweetheart felt a surge of rapture rise.
And, back at home, tears flowed at sound of "Mother",
    And "Father" smiled with pride—and wiped his eyes!
And heads bowed low in thanks for miracles
That span the seas to England's citadels.

—Reprinted by permission of the writer, Howard S. Ernst,
of Toronto, Canada.

Keeping in touch with the news from home.

getting the sounds of war. He'd park our big recording van in Hyde Park and record the sounds of bombs and gunfire. I'd see him the next day and say, "It was terrible last night." He'd say, "Yeah, but wait until you hear the bomb I got." One night I said, "Look, Art, don't spend every evening recording bombs. Stay home some nights, and take it easy." He promised he would. The first night he stayed home his apartment house was hit and he spent the night digging himself out. Luckily he wasn't hurt.

After Dieppe the CBC brought me back home. By this time they'd changed general managers and the new general manager and I just didn't get along. He wouldn't let me do any more broadcasting. So when Southam offered me a job as their Washington correspondent I accepted, reluctantly, even though it was for twice the salary I'd been getting from the CBC. I went to Washington where I spent three years. Then I came back to Canada and went into private radio.

LIFE IN THE BLITZ DESCRIBED IN NEW BBC SERIAL DRAMA

The front-line life of a typical London family of five—the normal and not-so-normal incidents of their wartime days — their hopes and fears—alarms and excursions; these are the material of a remarkable series of programmes broadcast last spring in the BBC's North American Transmission. "Front Line Family" will be broadcast from Ottawa to CBC's National Network each weekday morning at 11.00 a.m. EDST, beginning Monday, September 1.

Robinson is the family's name. Mr. Robinson runs his own small business and keeps it going despite Nazi efforts to wreck it. He is a keen and purposeful Home Guard. His wife tackles the by-no-means easy task of running the home and relieves the loneliness of the evenings when her family is out on the job by helping at the local canteen.

There are three children; Dick, twenty-six years of age, is in the Auxiliary Fire Service; Kay, twenty-two, is going to it in a munitions works; and Andy, twenty, is a ground mechanic in the R.A.F. who is determined to rise. The family's life is shared by Bill McKenna, a Canadian soldier billetted with them.

Alan Melville is the author of the series, and has founded the episodes on his observations of real life. He has written and produced revue sketches for the stage and broadcasting, and had already gained considerable reputation as a writer of thrillers before joining the BBC four years ago.

Ethelwyn Hobbes Presents
"WARTIME SHOPPING"
10.00-10.15 A.M., EDT
A brief review of
Consumer Information
CBC ONTARIO NETWORK
Mondays to Fridays, Inclusive

NEW VICTORY LOAN SERIES OFFERS ELOQUENT COMMENT ON HITLER'S NEW ORDER

One of the most artistic and eloquent comments on the process of persecution employed by Hitler was contributed by the motion picture screen when "So Ends Our Night" received its premiere.

Now radio has arranged to present its message to audiences who are following the Victory Loan Series on Friday nights. An adaptation by the Canadian writers, Kay and E. W. Edge, will provide a cast of dramatic artists with one of their most important assignments of the season. Rai Purdy, prominent Toronto actor-director, will be in charge of the radio version of "So Ends Our Night". The play will be produced Friday, June 13, at 10.00 to 11.00 p.m. EDST, and will be heard over the National Network of the CBC.

While famous radio conductors and singers have been travelling to Canada each week to donate their services to the Dominion's War Loan, others have gathered in studios in the United States to do their part for the same cause. Now the dramatic artists are swinging into the campaign to add their bit and Mr. Purdy is assured of a group of leading actors, surrounded by a competent supporting cast. It will be their task to interpret one of the most graphic stories of the "new order" of tyranny and treachery that has been written in the past few years.

5.45 to 6.00
★ **WOMEN IN A WAR WORLD**
Talk by Byrne Sanders. From Toronto to CBL CBO CBY
Miss Sanders, Editor of the Chatelaine, was the only Canadian woman invited to attend the Tenth Annual Forum of Current Problems held in New York last week. This meeting was attended by 5,000 representative women from all parts of the United States, and was presided over by Mrs. Ogden Reid, President of the New York Herald Tribune.

7.45-8.00
8.45-9.00 ADT
★ **JAMES M. MINIFIE**
Commentary on recent news in the United States. Delayed broadcast. From Toronto to CBA CBO CBL CBY
James M. Minifie discusses recent events in the United States. Appointed White House Correspondent for the New York Herald-Tribune last year, he has been CBC's Washington correspondent since November, 1941. As Foreign Correspondent for the Herald Tribune, Minifie covered the Spanish Civil War and was head of the Rome and London bureaus of the paper.

10.15-10.45
11.15-11.45 ADT
★ **VOICES OF VICTORY**
Actuality broadcast describing Canada's war industries. From Toronto to CBA CBO CBL
T. W. Wiklund of the CBC, and Moray "Spook" Sinclair, of Winnipeg, are visiting the war plants of the Dominion, describing the work being done in each place, and bringing individual workers to the microphone to introduce themselves to the people of Canada. These programmes are under the sponsorship of the Department of Munitions and Supply.

4.03-4.15
5.03-5.15 ADT
★ **THANKS CANADIAN MOTHERS**
Anonymous talk. From Toronto to CBA CBO CBL
The mother of a young Canadian airman, speaking anonymously, offers her thanks to other Canadian mothers who, through their sewing groups, canteens and money-raising organizations, are doing so much for her son and his friends who are away from home in the service of their country.

Bob Bowman, Art Holmes and "Betsy," the CBC's recording unit.

Correspondent Bob Bowman talks with one of the casualties of the ill-fated raid on Dieppe. August 1942.

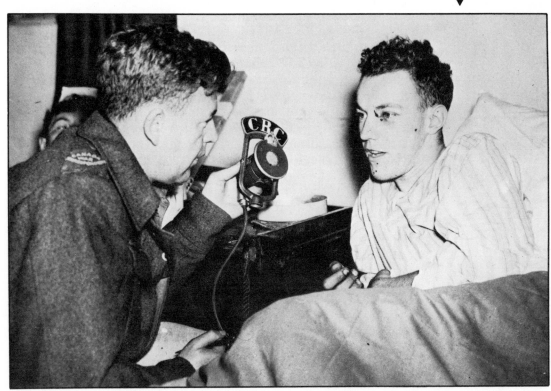

Art Holmes

When the bombing of London was going on, I got the idea that it was important, historically, to get those sounds recorded.

I was in high school in Toronto when radio was getting started. That would be 1920-21 and I was lucky enough to get part-time work as an operator/announcer at a little station that the Marconi Company had in their offices on King Street. It only operated at night so it fit in with my school work and the course I was taking in commercial radio operating. I wanted to become an operator on ships and see the world. And that's what I did. I worked as a radio man on Great Lakes ships during school vacations and after I had finished school, I was able to get jobs on some of the great transatlantic liners out of New York.

I went directly from the transatlantic liners to public broadcasting with the old CRBC. Those were trial and error days. When you came upon a new situation you had to invent your way out of it; there was nobody else's experience to fall back on. We'd make up a piece of equipment for the job. Then someone would improve on that for the next job and so on. So-called 'portable' equipment wasn't really portable at all. It was just very heavy equipment that was called 'portable' because they put handles on it.

Around 1934 they came out with a radical new microphone called a "condenser." It was better than the old carbon mikes but it was big and bulky—eight or nine inches square. It had the amplifier and everything in there. You had to lug a big battery along just for the mikes alone when going on a remote. As well, the condenser mike was very sensitive. The least little jar would knock it out. But even at that it was a great improvement. One of the biggest problems with remote broadcasts was the wind blowing into the mikes. It could ruin what was otherwise a perfect broadcast. Trying to solve that problem took years.

One of the most interesting and challenging jobs I had before the war was the Royal Tour of 1939. It was something that had never been done before and we had to figure out how to do it. That wasn't easy, especially when you arrived in little towns with no facilities for handling broadcasts. We had two teams each carrying its own equipment by train. While one team was setting up and overcoming problems in one place, the other team did the same thing in the next town. And we were always working against the deadline of being ready when the train arrived with the King and Queen on board.

The war, of course, was the biggest challenge of all. There was no tape at the time. All we had were these big disc recorders which were heavy and awkward and had to be kept level at all times. On land you could do this by means of jacks but on the ocean it was a different story because of the roll of the ship. That's what I found when Bob Bowman and I were suddenly put on board a troop ship in 1940 and told to interview the troops on the way over. We had no time to figure things out in advance and when we did record, we were afraid to test the recording because the same rolling of the ship might ruin what we had. It was a soft disc and if the needle came out of the groove, it could cut the record all to pieces.

When we got to London, we found the BBC didn't have facilities to play back what we had recorded. We had been operating at sixty cycles, while they used fifty. Everything seemed to work against us but by trying this and that we solved the problems and got the interviews on the air back to Canada. Bob Bowman then got the idea that we should stay there but we both knew we would need special equipment for this. We visited the Maginot Line to get an idea of the kind of thing we'd need and I drew up some specifications for a mobile unit which would hold all our equipment and I went back to Canada to have it built. I was back in London in May or June 1940 and we immediately began recording all the activities of the Canadian troops.

Even with our special equipment, recording under wartime conditions was extremely difficult; we soon found out what you could or couldn't do. Some of those big explosions would knock everything out of kilter. When the bombing of London was going on, I got the idea that it was important, historically, to get those sounds recorded. I knew no one else was doing it, so when air raids were on, I'd go out with the mobile unit and race around to get closer to the falling bombs. I wasn't trying to be heroic; it was just something I felt I should be doing. Some nights the bombs fell so close that my recordings were ruined. After a time, I learned to gauge how loud an explosion was going to be by the amount of noise the bomb made as it was falling. Then you could cut the volume down on the recorder. I always figured you could be hit by a bomb wherever you were so it didn't bother me that while people were running away from an area, I was driving into it. As a matter of fact, one night I didn't go out recording and a bomb fell on the building I was living in and destroyed my apartment. The whole place fell all around me and I lost the hearing in one ear.

Arthur Holmes inside "Betsy," the CBC recording unit.

We were aware that this was the first time a war was being reported complete with sound. Even the BBC wasn't doing it that way and they later got in touch with us to get copies of our recordings so they could use them on their own broadcasts. We did that all through the Battle of Britain and we went down to Dover to record sounds of the 'dogfights' going on there. The equipment we had developed was unique; nobody else had anything nearly as good. We did recordings for just about everybody— American, British, Polish, you name it. Canada really led the way. The BBC had developed some good equipment—in fact they'd overdeveloped it, made it too good, so that it was too heavy to be portable enough for war.

We also went to the battlefields in Europe—to Italy and Normandy and all over. At the time of Normandy, Marcel Ouimet, Matthew Halton and I were the first three people in Canadian uniforms to enter Germany. Three CBC guys. I suppose you could say we were where the action was. It's funny, you know, but those recordings I made during the war have been used in countless movies and TV shows all over the world. It's strange to be listening to something on the radio or watching a movie and suddenly hear one of 'my' bombs. I can recognize almost every one.

Marcel Ouimet, Matthew Halton and I were the first three people in Canadian uniforms to enter Germany. Three CBC guys.

CBC correspondent Marcel Ouimet, Ortona, Italy. 1943.

236

Many British children spent the war years as guests of Canada. The CBC had a regular programme for them, "Children Calling Home." The BBC had a similar programme titled "Hello Children."

NAZI EYES ON CANADA

Orson Welles, who is coming to Canada to put his sturdy and flamboyant shoulder to the war finance wheel, has one great problem. That's keeping up with the Orson Welles legend. Ever since Orson burst upon the American stage with the erratic effulgence of a meteor, he has been trying to keep up with his own reputation. He has been regarded with mingled alarm, admiration and disbelief as a sort of baby Gargantua; he has been hailed as the white hope of the languishing American theatre. "Orson Welles," said one critic after watching him romp through a rehearsal of Native Son, with which he returned to the New York stage after two years in Hollywood, "Orson Welles is a very noisy young man, but he is no phony."

George Orson Welles was born in Kenosha, Wisconsin, in 1915. Right from the start he met painters, writers, actors and all sorts of talented personalities in the arts, who treated him as if he were an adult, and soon he believed he was. At 27 he is a very old man indeed, old in experience and accomplishment, that is, but far too young for the beard which he wore briefly in Hollywood.

He was a guest star at the Abbey Theatre, Dublin, when he was only 16 (he had gone to Ireland on a sketching tour), and his production of Citizen Kane last year climaxed the first stage of a career which promises to go right on being more spectacular than any of the characters he portrays.

Mr. Welles' role in Canada will be that of Sam J. Dornan, editor of the weekly newspaper in Alameda, Saskatchewan, and hero of the sixth play in the war finance series, "Nazi Eyes on Canada". The broadcast will be heard coast-to-coast from the Toronto studios of the CBC on Sunday, October 25 at 7.30 p.m. EDT, 8.30 p.m. ADT.

1.00 to 1.15

HELLO CHILDREN

★ Messages from parents in Britain to "war-guest" children in Canada and United States. Rebroadcast of BBC Empire Transmission. From Ottawa to CBL CBO

CANADIANS OF GERMAN ORIGIN TO PRESENT BROADCAST OVER CBC

Canada's citizens of German lineage will speak to their fellow-Canadians over CBC's National Network on Wednesday, May 7, from Winnipeg, in the eleventh broadcast of the series "Canadians All", heard at 10.30 p.m. EDST.

The programme will include music by a German Canadian choir, with Victor Klassen, tenor, as soloist. Mr. Klassen has been heard frequently on CBC networks. A German Canadian member of the Canadian armed forces will speak for his compatriots, and on behalf of the Dominion at large, the spokesman will be Dr. J. W. Clarke, M.C., of Winnipeg.

It is not generally known that many of Canada's early pioneers, the United Empire Loyalists, were of German origin. There were also many Germans from the Hanoverian regiments of King George III who settled in Eastern Canada when their regiments were disbanded or withdrawn. These settlers have become completely integrated as citizens of the Dominion, and many prominent Canadians have come from their ranks. German Canadians constitute the largest national group in the Dominion, apart from the British and French. Seventy percent are Canadian born, and a further ten percent were born in the United States. Ninety-eight per cent are English-speaking.

FIRST NEWS OF CASUALTIES NOT GIVEN IN RADIO BULLETINS

Relatives and friends of Canadians who are on active service in the Army, Navy, or Royal Air Force, need have no apprehension that in listening to Canadian Press news bulletins presented by the Canadian Broadcasting Corporation, they may receive the first news of casualties over the air. No names of casualties are made public through The Canadian Press, either in press dispatches or radio bulletins, until after relatives have been officially notified.

While it is not considered desirable that radio should be used as a means of publishing general information regarding casualties, there are times when Canadians have lost their lives or suffered injuries while playing a distinguished part in some military, naval or air engagement. If names are mentioned in such cases, as a fitting tribute to their valour, this will not be done until relatives have been notified by the Government.

ROGERS MAJESTIC
LIMITED

Manufacturers & Distributors of Radio Sets • Tubes • Radio Apparatus • Electrical Appliances

Head Office, 622 Fleet St. W.
TORONTO, CANADA

Gentlemen:-

Now that Italy has capitulated, and in view of the general conditions of the war, it would seem wise to focus our attention even more sharply on our post war set-up. Many of our dealers have not been frankly and completely informed regarding our post war policies, and as a consequence, have become justifiably concerned about their future and our distribution picture. Just so there will not be any misunderstanding regarding Rogers Majestic's position, here are a few important facts which you will want to keep in mind.

Will Rogers and DeForest radio sets be sold after the war? The answer is definitely, yes. Just as soon as our facilities permit.

Plans relating to both engineering and production are already under way. From a study of these plans I am confident that Rogers Majestic will be a very strong factor for both the early and later markets in the radio and electronic field.

You will not be used as a guinea pig in launching an untried and unproven line of products. We intend to build our reputation on quality and outstanding merchandise.

Great strength has been added to the Rogers Majestic organization during these war years to enable us to be a leading post-war producer as well as one of the leading producers of vital war equipment. Men of the highest reputation have been engaged to operate and direct the engineering, production, and sales staffs. We have increased our floor space since the war started from 80,000 square feet to 170,000 square feet.

Many new products that we will offer to the public cannot at present be revealed. Our designing activities are being directed by an outstanding engineer, and we plan on a program which will be mutually for the benefit of all concerned, modern and aggressive.

War production naturally ties us down in our factory tasks and we regret that we cannot get around to see you at the present time, but I want to let you know that we are thinking about our dealers and jobbers, and that we are ready and will be ready to serve you in the post-war era.

With the above remarks, I ask your continued patience and support. Please feel free to write me any time regarding any phase of our business.

Yours sincerely,

H. P. Mackechnie

H. P. Mackechnie, President,
Rogers Majestic Limited.

An Open Letter to Our Radio Dealers and Jobbers

HPM-FM

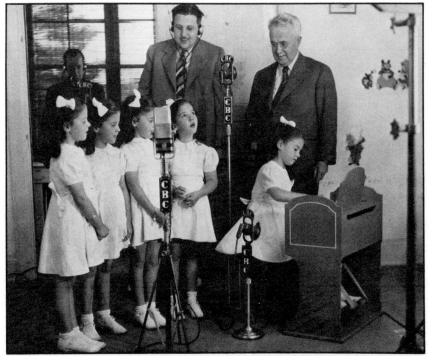

Are You Listening to
THE ARMY SHOW
staged and produced by
Canadian Army Members
under the direction of
CAPTAIN
GEOFFREY WADDINGTON
Sundays at 9.00 p.m. EDT
CBC NATIONAL NETWORK

◄

The Dionne quintuplets singing "There'll Always Be an England." A Red Cross fund-raising programme, 1941.

◄

German prisoners of war in Canada broadcasting to Germans in Europe over the CBC's International Service. For security reasons their faces were obliterated.

SPORTS FROM HOME

Canadian and American baseball fans now serving their countries in Britain were able to follow their favorite teams in the World Series just concluded. A special fifteen-minute summary of the game was broadcast daily at the end of the final innings, through arrangements made by the Mutual Broadcasting System and the BBC.

Don Dunphy, famous to sports enthusiasts for his blow-by-blow accounts of boxing championships, prepared and delivered the summaries, which were timed to include a play-by-play description of the thrilling last moments of each baseball battle. These summaries were broadcast by the BBC in the regular "Forces" programme.

Short-wave stations in Schenectady and San Francisco also beamed the actual play-by-play descriptions of the games to troops in Europe, Africa, South America and the Pacific arens.

Listen to
"SOLDIER'S WIFE"
MONDAY TO FRIDAY
at 11.30 a.m.
CBM   CBO   CBL

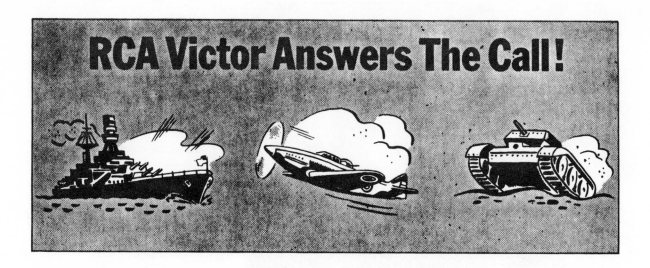

RCA Victor Answers The Call!

Keeping Faith With Our Fighting Forces...

For the duration of the war RCA Victor gives full priority to manufacture and development of war radio equipment for the Army, Navy and Air Forces.

Out of the wealth of its past experience and research . . . out of new extensions to its great Montreal plant . . . comes RCA Victor's ability to meet war needs *on time and in quantity.*

Keeping Faith With YOU...

RCA Victor, after satisfying every front line need for your defence, will continue to devote its remaining capacity to the domestic requirements of your customers. As the tempo of war production speeds up, domestic production must of necessity decrease.

There will be fewer home receiving sets for you to sell. But you may be assured that every RCA Victor radio will continue to be of the highest quality and value.

RCA Victor will continue to advertise regardless of merchandise shortages. RCA Victor has planned an institutional campaign to run concurrently with its present merchandise advertising. The institutional drive will increase in scope and intensity as product promotion decreases.

As a dealer, your RCA Victor franchise will take on an added value, for when victorious peace comes, the RCA Victor name will have been kept before the public and its present position of leadership maintained.

Military Transmitters and Receivers · Laboratory and Test Equipment · Transoceanic and Broadcast Radio Equipment · Home Radio Receivers · RCA Victrolas · Victor Records

RCA VICTOR COMPANY LIMITED - Halifax - Montreal - Ottawa - Toronto - Winnipeg - Calgary - Vancouver

Lorne Greene

I got into radio in the late thirties. Things were tough all over and I needed a job. Someone suggested I should audition at CBC as an announcer. I had some acting experience but none as an announcer so I was pretty dubious. But I decided to try anyway. Steve Brodie was the man who gave me the audition, and when it was over he said, "Thank you very much, Mr. Greene. We'll let you know in three or four days." I thought, "Sure you will." But, by gosh, Mr. Brodie did call and told me I was accepted and that I would be starting in Ottawa. I was flabbergasted. The first person I met was Byng Whitteker and the second was Alan McFee, who was Chief Announcer in Ottawa at the time.

Three months later I was delighted to be transferred to Toronto and have my salary boosted to $25 a week. I wasn't there long before they had me doing the national news and that's what brought about the appellation "the voice of doom." It was started by one of the newspapers in Winnipeg during the Battle of Britain. London was being destroyed by bombs. So when I was reading these bad news reports, I just naturally started giving it everything I had. As far as I was concerned, bad news was bad news and I wanted the listeners to know it. Most of my news during those years was bad news and I suppose "the voice of doom" tag came naturally. However, I remember one night later in the war, I looked over the newscast and saw that most of what I had to report was good news about the Battle of Libya, which was then raging. On my own, I decided to preface things by saying, "Ladies and gentlemen, for a change, most of the news tonight, is good." The result was that I was called in and chastized for editorializing. I felt pretty badly about this until a few days later when hundreds of letters came in from listeners saying they were tired of bad news and that it had been so good to hear my comment that night.

The appellation "The Voice of Doom"...was started by one of the newspapers in Winnipeg during the Battle of Britain.

▲

After the war, Lorne Greene started a radio school.

◄

CBC's national news reader, Lorne Greene. 1941.

241

The CBC's mobile unit visiting an R.C.A.F. training school. 1942.

EMPIRE DOMINIONS UNITE
FOR CHRISTMAS BROADCAST

A young air pilot in training in Canada, a New Zealand farmer, an Australian woman munitions worker and a naval rating from Malaya will be heard describing their work in defence of the Empire on the "Empire Chistmas" broadcast to be heard over the CBC National Network on Monday, December 25 at 9.15 a.m. EST.

This special broadcast which will precede the Christmas message by His Majesty the King, will also bring to listeners throughout the Empire an actuality broadcast from a hospital behind the lines of the western front. An exchange of greetings with French troops and loyal greetings from the British Expeditionary Forces to the King will be a highlight of the broadcast. After the visit to France the BBC microphone will pay a brief call to the Royal Navy and the Royal Air Force before starting westward around the world.

After leaving Europe the first stop will be Canada, where one of the pilots in training under the Empire scheme will speak before a CBC microphone on Canada's war effort. Next, a New Zealand farmer will describe that Dominion's work in helping to feed the Empire in war time. The Australian munitions worker will follow the tribute to merchant seamen, and then the naval rating will speak. Next on the programme will be India's greeting to the King-Emperor and from South Africa a member of the coastal defence will broadcast in English and Africaans. The message of His Majesty at 10.00 a.m. EST will culminate this Empire-wide event.

DON'T BE A NUISANCE — TUNE RADIOS DOWN

It's a truism that Radio cannot please all its listeners all the time. It is equally true that what pleases you on your radio may catch your neighbour in the wrong mood. While you hunger for talks, he may be a chamber music addict and when you settle down for a feast of symphony, he may feel in the mood for "Perfidia". The portend of this preamble is clear. Summer zephyrs are just around the corner and when they reach your neighbourhood don't add deafening sound effects to their perfumed burden. When windows are wide open, keep your radio tuned softly so that your neighbourliness may be clothed in consideration for the other fellow's tastes.

There is nothing which can fan a mild antagonism like a blaring radio. Apartment-dwellers are particularly susceptible to this irritation and as temperatures rise, tempers go with them unless everybody in the block remembers the folks next door.

This summer more than ever, with war industries employing men and women in increasing numbers at night, war news keeping others in anxious vigil and war endeavour on every hand taxing the nerves of the nation, the rest hours of the populace are precious. It is the responsibility of every patriotic Canadian to help his fellows meet the new and heavier strain in good health, good spirits and good humour. A softly-tuned radio turneth away wrath. Make this your listening guide for the summer of 1941.

8.45-9.00 ADT
★   WHAT IS MORALE
A talk by Professor J. D. Ketchum. From Toronto to CBA CBO CBL CBY.

J. D. Ketchum, a member of the Department of Psychology at the University of Toronto and one of the Dominion's leading authorities on social psychology, is presenting a series of talks on national morale in war time. Today's title is "Emotions in Morale", and Professor Ketchum will point out the importance of a controlled and practical, rather than an emotional outlook.

CBC OPENS TO CANADA
A WINDOW ON THE WORLD
Canadians are served today by news that is authentic, unsensational, complete

TODAY, in the exciting time of war, Canadians enjoy through the CBC News Service bulletins that are dependable, authentic and presented in a clear and unambiguous style.

Here truly is a window on the world...a window that gives Canadians everywhere an accurate and impartial view of the world in action. Five CBC News Bureaux in Toronto, Halifax, Montreal, Winnipeg and Vancouver provide both national and regional services of news bulletins, based on the full newspaper wire services of The Canadian Press (which includes the international dispatches of Associated Press) and the British United Press (which includes the foreign service of the United Press). To 95% of the whole Canadian population...four CBC news bulletins are broadcast daily in each Time Zone. In the preparation of news, accuracy and conciseness are the guiding principles. There is no sensationalism, no false emphasis, no glorification of minor successes, no belittling or overstressing of enemy victories—a balanced picture of the day's significant events.

CANADIAN BROADCASTING CORPORATION

A Listener

We could tell how bad the foreign news was by looking at how bloodshot his eyes were.

Ours was a pioneer family in Kirkland Lake and my father, who was mechanically inclined, was able to make his own crystal set as did many other young people. But living where they were they were unable to receive much except static, and what they could receive, faded in and out.

My first contact with radio occurred when at the age of four I came in from playing to hear two worried parents tell me that Germany had just invaded Belgium and Holland. My father, opened a crate that had been used as a door stop. Lo and behold, the crate brought forth a brand new radio in perfect condition.

Of course, the war news took precedence and how well I remember the announcer, Lorne Greene, "the voice of doom" and Matthew Halton reporting from somewhere in Europe with the forces. In those days, one had to have a licence to own a radio and the poor guy who came to the door for that money wasn't loved much. As I recall, the fee was expensive, even for those times. My father worked as a projectionist and would not only see the newsreel in the theatre but when he came home about ten o'clock would immediately go to the radio to hear the CBC news. After that, the fun would begin. From midnight on, this radio, which had a short wave knob on it, would be tuned in all over the world. The fact that my Dad could both speak and understand the majority of the European languages was to his advantage and he would sit by the hour hunched over, smoking endless roll-your-own cigarettes and drinking pots of hot, strong tea until the early hours of the morning. In the morning, huddled in the kitchen which was the only warm room in the house, drinking hot chocolate before facing the icy blasts on our long walk to school, we could tell how bad the foreign news was by looking at how blood shot his eyes were.

When I was old enough to go to school, a whole new vista opened up for me via radio. I still have an envelope containing reproductions of paintings which were sent by the CBC to accompany an Art Gallery of Ontario art appreciation course given during school broadcast time. To this day, I credit my love of Tom Thomson and the Group of Seven and earlier Canadian artists to school broadcasts. Living in Kirkland Lake was like being in a cultural desert and only through radio could we find out about the rest of the world. Occasionally our announcers paused from a diet of country and western music to give us, courtesy of the CBC, a live symphony concert from Massey Hall. What a treat!

I had other favourites. There was "Penny's Diary," "John and Judy," the "Lux Radio Theatre." Dinah Shore had a fifteen-minute spot. There was a young man called "Tony the Troubador," who I imagined, crooned wearing a Spanish costume. "The Stamp Club" was informative and enjoyable as was "Sunday Morning Concert" which usually featured the Hart House Orchestra or Quartet or another equally well known group. Of course, one could not forget the soaps, or "The Happy Gang," or "Singing Stars of Tomorrow." Wayne and Shuster brought humour to our dreary, dark winters and "Saturday Night Hockey" was a must.

We had to cheer on our native Kirkland Laker, Ted Lindsay, even though he played for Detroit.

You must forgive my rambling but you opened up a Pandora's box of memories. I left Kirkland Lake to come to Toronto for university. It was pretty hostile in a strange new city but shortly after my sister and I arrived, she won a radio in a bingo game. I eagerly turned the dial and when I heard the one o'clock time signal on CBC, I knew I had found my friend again. Of course, the first places we frequented in Toronto were the Art Gallery and Massey Hall.

My son David has inherited my father's original radio. He's stripped the varnish off the wooden cabinet, restained it, and now it has travelled with him to its new home in Nanaimo where it occupies a special place of honour. It is still in perfect working condition.

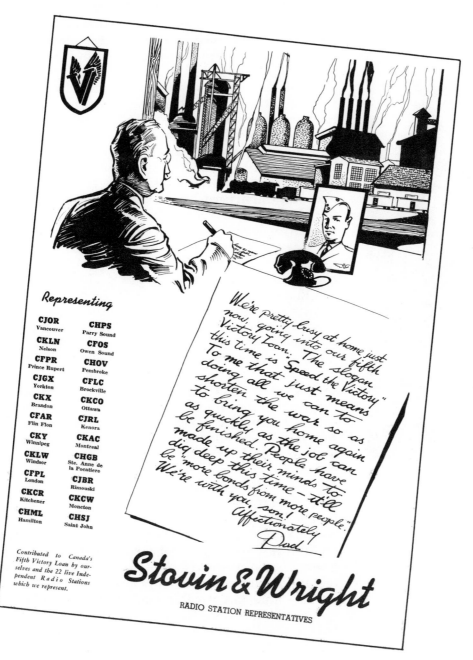

Jack Brickenden

After the war I went into newspaper work in Western Canada but in 1949 I had a chance to shift to the CBC, whose news service was now well-established. I started in Toronto, which was the hub of it all, and it was exciting to work with some of the top news people in the country. Bill Hogg and Charlie Gunning were in charge and we had a network of correspondents. In London there was Matthew Halton. In Paris, Douglas La Chance. In Washington, James M. Minifie. In Ottawa, Blair Fraser, and so many others. They supplied on-the-spot pieces for "News Roundup," a fifteen-minute programme that followed the "National News." Practically everybody in the country listened to this half-hour package, which was indeed the news Bible for many years. Norman Depoe was the editor of "News Roundup" and I became his assistant. We'd meet every morning in Bill Hogg's office and line up the stories to be covered, and it was my job along with Norman Depoe, to get in touch with our correspondents, brief them, and then arrange to bring in their reports from London, Paris or wherever.

Earl Cameron was the national news reader. He had a believability and an authority that couldn't be matched. When he read a newscast it was like it was carved in granite. I remember when I first met Earl. I expected to meet somebody nine feet tall and thought he would look like Moses on the Mount, because that's the way he sounded. But he turned out to be Mr. Nice Guy, totally lacking in affectation or ego. He liked open-collar sports shirts and often needed a shave but when he took hold of a script I felt I hadn't done a good job on, he made it come across like the world's greatest writing.

Even at that time, in the late 1940s and early 1950s, the newspapers were still fighting radio. In their eyes, radio was the competition. If they had a picture of a news story they wanted to run, and the picture included a radio reporter with his microphone showing the call letters of the station, they would remove all traces of radio from the pictures. I know that for a fact because of my time at newspapers. I was ordered by the editor of the Winnipeg *Tribune* not to give any free publicity to radio.

Radio was at its height at that time. When I tell my children that we used to sit around the living room listening to a radio programme they find it hard to believe. But we did. We not only sat but we actually looked at the radio as the sound came out. The first time I was allowed to stay up all night, when I was about nine, was to listen to Frank Willis at the Moose River Mine disaster.

The Farm Broadcast department became one of the CBC's most important units. It produced some great radio and some tremendous personalities. For example, Peter Whittall, who later became famous as "Mr. Fix-It," was an extremely funny man. One day he took his wife, who was about to give birth, to hospital and then continued to the CBC to do his broadcast. While he was on the air someone passed him a note saying the baby was born; it was a small girl, weighing only five pounds. Pete read the note on the air and ended with the comment, "I hardly got my seed back," which is a farm expression for a poor crop. It almost cost him his job.

I was ordered by the editor of the Winnipeg <u>Tribune</u> not to give any free publicity to radio.

1941

▶

All-Canada was one of the first media-buying agencies.

246

Don't wait till Surrender Day...
start talking to your customers NOW!

RIGHT NOW, while factories are furiously turning out the war materials needed to bring victory, publicity programmes should be paving the way for successful resumption of peacetime business.

For peacetime industry must run in full gear if private enterprise is to cope with the gigantic process of demobilizing armed forces and war work. And peace industry means the requirements of Mr. Watts the retailer and Mr. and Mrs. Jones the consumer.

Don't wait till Surrender Day to rush out to them with your merchandizing plans. Avoid the rush. *Start talking to them now!*

Keep them thinking about your name—your products. Talk about your plans, your improvements, your part in peace as well as in war. But *talk* to them—NOW!

Tell them through the medium of a friendly, human voice—through radio. Through the facilities of **27** "All-Canada" stations from coast to coast you can pick your territory, your time, your type of programme. A *key* station in any market you wish to reach.

Check with your nearest "All-Canada" office. Your "All-Canada" man can give competent advice on any problem affecting radio. He can help plan your programme or help you select from the most complete transcription library in Canada. Ask your agency for a recommendation.

Call the ALL-CANADA MAN

 ALL-CANADA RADIO FACILITIES *Limited*

MONTREAL · TORONTO · WINNIPEG · CALGARY · VANCOUVER

THE CRAIGS HELP TOO

The Craig's, like most other Canadian folk have had the ordinary everyday life of the family ruffled a bit by the demands of war. For the next two weeks the whole household will be so busy with other things it is simply out of the question to be ready for the daily broadcasts. So radio fans will please understand and give Roland Todd a welcome. He is the Canadian organist who will play familiar and favourite tunes while the Craig's are catching up with the tasks which have accumulated these last few weeks.

Janice is going to Niagara to help with the fruit picking. Thomas hasn't a thought for a thing but the safe harvesting of his crops; Martha says she won't have her face out of a canning kettle for ages and Nora isn't going to let Martha do it all by herself. Bill has plenty to do managing the farm across the road for its city owner and giving Dad a hand. Well, there it is.

The Craig's will be back August 17 and in the meantime they hope that none of their regular fans will miss this "blessing in disguise" for Roland Todd's music should prove a happy substitute these busy weeks when every man wants a song in his heart.

Health Insurance

The Canadian farmer is one of the defenders of democracy. His job is to feed the fighters and the civilian workers of the United Nations, and someday he will help to build up the young bodies of those who will work in peace for the new world.

To face the rigours of his task the farmer must have health as well as spirit. He can only make a contribution worthy of his brothers in arms and his fellow workers in industry if he is fit, and free from the worries of an ailing wife or son.

Here on this page is the story of how one Saskatchewan community took practical means to insure the health of not one family, but a whole community. The next broadcast in the National Farm Radio Forum, Monday, August 17 (8.30 p.m. EDT, 9.30 p.m. ADT, in Eastern Canada, and for Western listeners at 10.30 p.m. EDT) will tell the story of the Municipal Health Service which is in operation in the municipality of McKillop, Saskatchewan.

6.00-6.15 ADT
7.00-7.15 ADT
★ DON MESSER AND HIS ISLANDERS

Old-time music directed by Don Messer. From Charlottetown to CBA CBO CBY

Don Messer's band, well-known in the Maritimes and other parts of Canada, has chosen 'Ragtime Annie', "Old Resin the Beau", "Ricketts", "Second Reel" for this evening's performance. Vocalist Charlie Chamberlain will present "Jingle-Jangle-Jingle' and "Dear Old Girl".

RELAX AND ENJOY
Transcribed musical programme. Commercial. From Toronto to CBL.

8.30-8.55
9.30-9.55 ADT
★ NATIONAL FARM RADIO FORUM

A dramatized discussion of farm problems in wartime, arranged in co-operation with the Canadian Federation of Agriculture, and the Canadain Association for Adult Education. From Toronto to CBA CBO CBL CBY

Continuing its broadcast series devoted to the problems of food production in wartime, the National Farm Radio Forum tonight deals with the relationship between the country's manpower and agriculture, and discusses ways and means of securing the farm labour needed to meet our food objectives.

The CBC's farm family serial, "The Craigs" was written by Dean Hughes and featured actors Grace Webster, Doug Masters, Alice Hill and Frank Peddie.

Orville Shugg

In December 1938 I got a wire from E. L. Bushnell saying they were going to try an experimental fifteen-minute broadcast of farm news on the CBC's Toronto station, CBL, and that they would pay me for my ideas. I had submitted a document to Gladstone Murray in 1936 outlining a mid-day farm broadcast, so it was a simple thing for me to submit the ideas again and collect fifty bucks. In January 1939 I was called in and asked to set the whole thing up. Although I had never been inside a radio station in my life I figured that there would be lots of people around who could put any ideas I had into effect.

I joined the CBC on the sixth of February, 1939, with the title of Supervisor of Farm Broadcasts and two weeks later, on the twentieth the first farm broadcast went on the air. It was a fifteen-minute programme from twelve-thirty to twelve-forty-five Monday to Friday. My thesis was that if you could bring accurate up-to-the-minute information to the farmer, he would clamour for it and more. Don Fairbairn was the first commentator. The programme was so successful that by May 1939 I was able to extend it to a half-hour and start the first of the "farm family" dramas, "The Craigs." The idea was to provide entertainment *and* information in a framework farm people would understand. To do this we hired Dean Hughes, a professional writer who had been born on a farm and had lived there until he was thirteen. He became so involved in "The Craigs" that he bought and moved back to a farm. He called it "Briarwood," the name of the Craigs's farm. Soon the programme branched out all across the country. The Maritime farm broadcast went on the air at the end of June 1939, The Prairie farm broadcast in September 1939, and the British Columbia farm broadcast in September of 1940.

Our idea with these noon broadcasts was to help put more dollars in the farmer's pocket, but there was another side we wanted to develop as did the different farm organizations which had pressured the CBC for such programming. That was the social lot of farmers. We felt radio was much better than print in accomplishing this and so it was that "National Farm Radio Forum" came into being. Neil Morrison and myself worked on this. The first year of "Farm Radio Forum" was done with dramatized scripts but after that it evolved into discussions by individuals from various communities across the country. I had been travelling back and forth across Canada for many years and the one thing that struck me was the insularity of the various communities. Radio—and particularly the farm programmes—helped change that through the exchange of information.

Our idea with these noon broadcasts was to help put more dollars in the farmer's pocket.

FIVE YEARS OF ACHIEVEMENT

CBC AGRICULTURE

Radio Column

FRANK CHAMBERLAIN

Today we are happy to announce the results of Simpson's Radio Column "Listeners' Popularity Poll." Every questionnaire that bore a signature and an address was turned over to Elliott-Haynes Ltd., an independent research organization, and several days were required to tabulate the many hundreds of entries. All American programs and artists were, of course, weeded out, because it was a poll of your favorite Canadian programs and artists.

❖ ❖ ❖

Listeners named "The Happy Gang," with Bert Pearl as master of ceremonies, as their favorite program. There was no uncertainty about their choice. This program, long popular right across Canada, stood ahead of all others in this general classification. The program is heard on CBL, Mon. to Fri., at 1.15 p.m., and George Temple and John Adaskin are producers.

❖ ❖ ❖

The Toronto Symphony Orchestra, under Sir Ernest MacMillan, was named the listeners' favorite orchestra program. This may surprise those who look upon the Symphony as a "classical" orchestra, playing to the "highbrows." While Toronto's musical taste is known to be high, some people will wonder why orchestras playing more "popular" music did not come first in this classification. The program is heard on alternate Tuesdays, CJBC, at 9.

❖ ❖ ❖

St. Stephen's Anglican Church broadcast, heard on CFRB Sundays at 7 p.m., was named the favorite religious program. Rev. Canon J. E. Ward is the rector.

❖ ❖ ❖

When it came to naming their favorite dance orchestra, the fans picked Mart Kenney and His Western Gentlemen without hesitation. This is the group of musicians, with Norma Locke as their singer, who have entertained thousands of servicemen and women and war workers all over Canada. They are heard on "Music Club," Mondays at 8, CBL.

❖ ❖ ❖

Of the quiz programs, they chose "Treasure Trail," a natural thing to do, because this program has held first place in Canadian audience ratings (evening programs) for many years, and is fifth among all Canadian and American programs heard in the evening in Canada. It's heard Wednesdays at 8.30, CFRB, and Jack Murray is the originator and producer.

❖ ❖ ❖

Listeners had no trouble in naming their favorite "variety" program. They came right out and named "The Happy Gang" for a second win.

❖ ❖ ❖

It didn't take a Nostradamus to predict that the N.H.L. Hockey Broadcast, with Foster Hewitt, would win the favorite sports program classification. Hockey is Canada's favorite sport and Hewitt is the public's star sports broadcaster. The program is heard Saturdays at 9.05 p.m. on CBL and CFRB, and on some week nights over CKEY.

❖ ❖ ❖

Over the years, first on CFRB and now on CBL, Claire Wallace has built up a large and devoted following. Listeners name Claire's "They Tell Me" their favorite in the "women's interest" category. It is heard Mon., Wed. and Fri., at 1.45 p.m., CBL.

❖ ❖ ❖

"Just Mary," written and told by Mary Grannan, who also writes "Children's Scrapbook" and other children's broadcasts, won "hands down" in the children's program group. Heard Sundays at 1.15, CBL.

❖ ❖ ❖

Understandably, Simpson's is pleased that "Simpson's Musical Clock," with Stu Kenney, won honors in the "Morning Wake-up Program" classification. The program is heard on CKEY, Mon. to Sat., from 7 to 9 a.m.

❖ ❖ ❖

"Stage '45," most discussed dramatic show on the Canadian air-waves today, was named as the listeners' favorite in this class. Andrew Allan is producer. Program is heard Sunday at 9, over CBL.

❖ ❖ ❖

The listeners named Grace Matthews as their "favorite dramatic artist." She is Carrie Murdock in "Soldier's Wife," and is heard on many other top programs.

❖ ❖ ❖

A shy, slim little fellow was named "favorite singer." He is Eddie Allen, who has been heard with "The Happy Gang" for many years and now is also heard on "Dream Time" every Tuesday, CJBC, at 10.30 p.m., with John Adaskin producer.

❖ ❖ ❖

Centre of much public discussion these days are the news broadcasters. Jim Hunter won the most votes. He is heard on CFRB, Mon. to Sat., at 8 a.m. and 6.30 p.m.

❖ ❖ ❖

Joe Chrysdale's "Club 580" on CKEY was named by the young bloods as their "favorite 'teenage program." The program features hot recordings of popular dance bands, and is heard at 4.05 p.m., Mon. to Sat.

❖ ❖ ❖

The Robert Simpson Co. Ltd., and its radio editor congratulate the winning artists and programs. The Listeners' Popularity Poll was created for fun, but the results have helped promote interest in Canadian radio and its personalities. Listeners are now invited to express their comments on the results of the poll. Confine all letters to 50 words or less, and mail them to Frank Chamberlain, care of Simpson's Radio Column, the Robert Simpson Co. Ltd., Toronto.

◄

"Court of Opinions" was a popular panel discussion. Alan Savage, Kate Aitken, moderator Neil LeRoy, Lister Sinclair and an unidentified guest.

◄

"Citizens' Forum" originated from many points in Canada and featured debates on controversial issues of the day.

New Liberty, December, 1949.

▼

CANADIANS OPPOSE FEE BOOST			
Results of nationwide survey conducted by Elliott-Haynes Survey Organization			
Question: There is a possibility that the radio licence fee in Canada will be increased from $2.50 to $5.00 a year to provide the C.B.C. with increased revenues to defray rising costs of broadcasting; to provide better programs; and to give more extensive service. Would you say you are *for* or *against* this increase in licence fees?			
	For	Against	No Opinion
CANADA	**4.4**	**84.0**	**11.6**
ZONES Maritimes	1.0	93.0	6.0
Quebec	6.0	82.7	11.3
Ontario	5.3	90.7	4.0
Prairies	2.0	96.0	2.0
British Columbia	4.0	74.0	22.0
SEX Men	2.8	87.1	10.1
Women	5.9	81.0	13.1
AGE Under 30	6.9	75.7	17.4
30—50	2.8	88.4	8.8
Over 50	5.6	83.1	11.3
December, 1949			

Harry Boyle

You had the feeling that come ten o'clock every evening every radio in the country was tuned in to the CBC.

Harry Boyle at age twenty-nine.

When the CRBC came into effect in 1932, it was the result of a lot of people agitating for a national broadcasting system. The CRBC wasn't properly funded and it didn't quite know what it was doing but it formed a nucleus that the CBC could build on when it came into existence in 1936 as a result of people like Alan Plaunt and Graham Spry lobbying for public broadcasting. The original intention was that the CBC would be a self-contained system with its own means of distribution but that has never been accomplished. To attain a full national system there had to be an intermeshing of the private stations *and* the CBC. The private stations became what are called 'affiliates' and in the early days many of these stations resisted the CBC because they were inclined towards the American system. In fact this co-ordination of the private and the public is suited to Canada's purposes. We have a large population along our border and small populations in remote areas—areas which would never have received service from private broadcasters since there weren't enough people to support it from an advertising viewpoint.

Ironically, the biggest impetus to our system came around 1936 when shades of war were beginning to form in Europe and there was the abdication of Edward VIII. All the private stations in the country were plugged into the CBC and the CBC was getting service from the BBC. All of us working in private radio at that time had our eyes opened to the fact that broadcasting wasn't just a parochial thing in a small town or even a large city. It was a national and international thing and that's what attracted many of us away from private radio to the CBC.

I left CKNX in Wingham in 1941 and went to work for a newspaper. I had done everything in private radio that I wanted to—from collecting bills to writing a local soap opera—and it was invaluable training. When the CBC offered me a job in 1942, I jumped at the chance because I saw it as a kind of intellectual mecca and this was reinforced by the fact that the CBC had had enough vision to form an overseas unit to report directly from Europe on the war. You had the feeling that come ten o'clock every evening every radio in the country was tuned in to the CBC to find out what was going on. The CBC brought all of us to the front lines.

A lot of us who went to work for the CBC at that time had gone through a depression, had drifted around the country seeing people in abject poverty trying to find jobs and on relief. Then suddenly in 1939, there was lots of money for everything. Quite a number of us in the CBC in various departments were certain there had to be a better way. So while the CBC played its part in helping the country as far as our war priorities were concerned, we also made sure other issues were discussed from health insurance to co-operatives and from grain marketing to transportation. These things, along with the war, formed a high percentage of the broadcasts the CBC carried. Then, too, we had plays—many of which were really social documents. I remember one in Andrew Allan's series—*Burlap Bags* by Len Peterson—about the unionization of department stores. We weren't ideological in the sense of proposing one particular kind of a state but we wanted the CBC to be in the forefront, to be the one national institution that could discuss these issues. That was what sustained the CBC and carried it along until it became involved in television. When TV arrived you not only had the whole overlay of entertainment, you also had prosperity. People were less concerned with social issues.

There's no doubt that this country is a better place today because of the influence of CBC radio. Many people who didn't work for the CBC became involved in exploring social issues in magazines and elsewhere because of the CBC. The CBC had connections with all kinds of organizations: the Canadian Association for Adult Education, the wheat pools in the west, the co-operative movement in Antigonish, N.S. All of those organizations had a direct stake in the CBC and when it was in trouble with the politicians they responded.

The country wasn't exactly a cultural wasteland before the CBC arrived. There were drama groups and things of that nature from the Atlantic to the Pacific, all doing their own thing. But there was no way for them to hear what others were doing until public broadcasting came along. And there were bright young people in small communities starving for good drama and good music and it wasn't until the CBC came along that they satisfied their thirst. The CBC tied the country together and became a mecca for anyone who wanted to write or create. They drifted towards it from all over the country.

In 1947 I created a programme called "CBC Wednesday Night." I was Programme Director for the network and we had scattered through our schedule a number of commercial Canadian and American shows. The result was that I couldn't get the sweep of time needed to put on lengthy productions that were really worthwhile. I appealed to Davey Dunton, the CBC Chairman at the time, for one night a week in which we could do these things. That's how "CBC Wednesday Night" came about. James Bannerman, whose real name was Jack McNaught, was chosen to do an introduction to each programme because he had a wonderfully intimate style and the common touch. People got into the habit of tuning in for Bannerman's introduction just to hear his announcements. He was wonderful. I used to call him "an intellectual 'con' man." He often admitted that what was coming up didn't appeal to him very much but when he went on to describe it he made it sound so intriguing that listeners stayed tuned. That programme was responsible for introducing thousands of Canadians to opera, classical drama and music and many other things they would never have heard anywhere else.

Dick Halhed

She was a competent lady who usually wore a flowered hat in the control room and rolled her own cigarettes.

I got into radio in 1938 and my first three years were spent in private stations. The next thirty-five years were spent at the CBC. Not everyone in private radio aspired to join the CBC, but I did. After several auditions over a couple of years I finally received a letter from Colonel R.P. Landry at CBC headquarters in Ottawa advising me there was a vacancy on the announcing staff in Vancouver and that I could report for work on August 1, 1941.

In Vancouver I delighted in working with some of the real professionals. Bill Herbert was the chief announcer. One of his customs was to cup a hand around one ear so that he could hear his voice externally and not simply through bone conductivity inside his head. He claimed it helped him to control his modulation. Before long, several of us did the same thing, *especially* when we performed before live audiences. I must confess I didn't find it helpful. I suspect most of us did it more as an affectation than anything else.

Andrew Allan was there at the time and he was greatly respected as probably the best radio drama producer in North America. Culture fairly oozed out of this tall man who was always faultlessly groomed. What Andrew said was law and he struck fear into the hearts of all beginning announcers. He always addressed his actors as "Mr.," "Mrs." or "Miss." He could bear no sloppiness or wasting of time and he rehearsed until he got exactly what he wanted. He may have been fussy but he was respected like God.

Another producer at the time was Ada McGeer, who did recitals and talk programmes. She was a competent lady who usually wore a flowered hat in the control room and rolled her own cigarettes, though rather sloppily. There were usually shreds of tobacco sticking out all over the place. Once, just before her programme was to go on air she was lighting up; the loose tobacco went up in a puff of flame and so did the half-veil on her hat. Ada was a bit shaken but fortunately only her eyebrows were singed and her show went on on time.

Ira Dilworth, a former English professor, was the head man in Vancouver when I got there. He was regarded as remote and austere by those who didn't know him well. Actually he was a gentle and cultured man who could be as hard as nails to any staffer guilty of a misdemeanor. Nobody ever called him anything but Mr. Dilworth or "Sir." In December 1942, Mr. Dilworth summoned operator Jim Gilmore and me to his office and told us he had an assignment that would take us away for three or four months. We were being sent to CFPR in Prince Rupert. CFPR had just been leased by the CBC to provide better service to an area where 20,000 American troops were stationed. He said it was a small operation but important to Canadian-American relations. Our job was to increase the station's programming from six hours a day to seventeen. The CBC would record all major network programmes in Vancouver and ship them by boat to Prince Rupert once a week. This meant that in addition to any productions we could do ourselves with the troops, we would get all the American Armed Forces shows such as "Jack Benny," "Lux Radio Theatre" and "Charlie McCarthy."

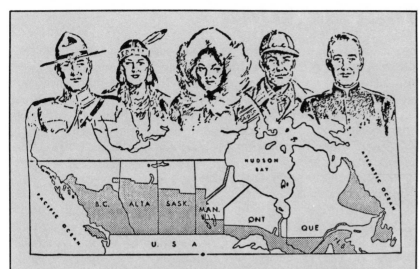

PRIVILEGED CITIZENS OF THE NORTH

Here are five handsome Canadians who never use a ration card—and never miss a Friday night broadcast of CBC's Northern Messenger. Mounted police, Indian maid, Esquimo chatelain, trapper and priest all play their eager roles in the life of the North country and because they carry out their respective tasks in months of bitter weather they purchase their supplies in advance and have no ration card worries. But they do get lonely for news of the folk back home and that is where their long-time friend, The Northern Messenger, comes in. On Friday, March 26, CBC will bring to a close the ninth year of these greeting broadcasts to Canada's men and women stationed at the outposts. So it's "au revoir and good hunting" to all our friends until next fall.

Life at CFPR was never dull during our three-month stay. The American pilots were constantly buzzing the station and if our microphone happened to be open the racket drowned out whatever was being said on the air. Another daily hazard was the vibration of the gargantuan trucks roaring by loaded with boulders from the building of a new link to the Alaska highway. Our news came up by Morse code from the Canadian Army Signals Corps. It was converted into type for us and delivered by dispatch rider. It wasn't always up to date but we got it on the air three times a day except for the morning of January 1, 1943, when the signals people had obviously been celebrating the New Year to excess. The copy handed to me was so incomprehensible that we simply announced that "due to circumstances beyond our control" there would be no news that morning.

Our three months in Prince Rupert ended in March 1943 when Jim Gilmore and I boarded a ship going south. We left behind a nicely balanced seventeen-hour daily schedule of CBC and American programmes and, I believe, a lot of good will.

Andrew Allan

I began to read books because of your plays—all kinds of books I never thought I'd be interested in.

The girl in the club car, as we pulled west out of Calgary, had that look of freshness that can move a man, even when he is still young. It will move him close to tears when he is older. Since the only vacant chair was beside her, I sat beside her with the pretext of my morning paper. The car was lively with the new people that had come aboard during the forty-minute wait at Calgary. One of the joys of the transcontinental trains was the way the atmosphere changed as you passed through the various regions, new people boarding to replace the old. It was the way to appreciate the horizontal mosaic, which is the real Canada.

In my compartment, since Toronto, between vague tries at reading and writing I had been considering the winter just past and how my life was going. On my way to Vancouver for a holiday I had decided that the endless tussle to keep the Sunday night "Stage" on the air was pointless—at least, to continue trying to keep them on the air in any form and with any content that made sense to me. Several seasons of guerilla warfare had brought me, despite our reputed success, to the draft of a letter to the CBC management recommending that the "Stage" be discontinued. The draft was in my briefcase and I would have a fair copy of it made in Vancouver and send it back East. It would be a relief.

10.00 to 10.30
WHO'S JOHNNY CANUCK?

★ Feature broadcast. From Toronto to CBL CBY CBO
Two Canadians, Anne Marriott and Margaret Kennedy, are the authors of this "definition" in verse of the average Canadian. The script will be presented by a dramatic cast directed by J. Frank Willis, and Samuel Hersenhoren's orchestra will play special musical settings by Godfrey Ridout.

11.00-11.15
12.00-12.15 ADT
★ **CANADIAN CANTERBURY TALES**
Drama. From Winnipeg to CBO CBL
From "The Flying Bull and Other Tales", by Watson Kirkconnell of McMaster University, Ben Lepkin and Tommy Tweed have adapted these Canadian stories for radio. Stormbound in a little hotel at Manitou, Manitoba, a group of men while away the time by telling stories. Tonight is the Sergeant's turn, and so listeners will hear the Sergeant's Tale of the Manitoba Stonehenge, a story of gold and crime in Canada's northland.

10.00-11.00
11.00-12.00 ADT
★ **THE WHITEOAKS OF JALNA**
Radio drama. From Toronto to CBA CBO CBL CBY
Maza de La Roche's classic stories of the Whiteoaks clan come to life from CBC's Toronto studios. The distinguished British character actress, Barbara Everest, is coming to Canada to play the Grandmother, and other leading roles will be taken by Courtney Benson, Ivor Lewis, and Rupert Lucas, Head of CBC's Drama Department, who is directing the series. This is the first in a series of nine broadcasts.

Actors running through their lines at a rehearsal for the "Stage" series. In the control room, technician Bruce Armstrong and producer Andrew Allan.

The girl in the club car was as devoted to her book as I was to my newspaper, which was not at all. The foothill country began to slide past the windows—light enough and free enough to lift the weight off any man, even a man with a lump of lead in his briefcase. A horseman rode up to a fence and waved his big hand at us. As we rose to wave back the girl and I were smiling at each other. "You're Andrew Allan, aren't you?" she said. I was. "You're the reason I'm here," she said. This was enough to seize the attention—especially an attention already more than half seized. I made a suitable noise.

"We live on a farm, away up north of Edmonton," said the girl. "We're just plain people, I guess. We haven't got any books to speak of, or pictures, or music, or anything. But I have a little radio in my room. Every Sunday night I go up there to listen to your plays. All week I wait for that time. It's wonderful. It's a whole new world for me. I began to read books because of your plays—all kinds of books I never thought I'd be interested in. And now I'm on my way to Vancouver to stay with my aunt and in the fall I'm starting at the university. And it's all because of you and your plays. What do you think of that?"

What I thought of that was too deep to be said. But what I did about it was to go to my compartment and tear up the draft of the letter. We had seven more years of "Stage" after that.

SIR CEDRIC AND LADY HARDWICKE
Pictured at the CBC microphone are Britain's famous actor knight and his delightful and gifted wife, professionally known as Helena Pickard. The study was made last winter when Sir Cedric and Lady Hardwicke came to take part in CBC's Theatre of Freedom.
Lady Hardwicke will return to Canada soon again to render yet another service to the Empire at war. She will enact the role of the courageous mother in a new British war drama, "Mrs. Brown Had Five Sons", and she is making this trip to Canada at her own suggestion. The CBC will present Lady Hardwicke and the play over the National network on Friday, September 26 at 10.00 to 11.00 p.m. EDST.

ALDRICH FAMILY LISTED TO APPEAR ON SPECIAL BROADCAST OVER CBC

One of radio's first families is coming to Canada. With famous stars of the stage and screen paying weekly visits to CBC studios to participate in the "Theatre of Freedom", it was only natural that fellow radio artists should wish to do their bit for Canada, too. So Henry Aldrich is coming up — yes, young Henry, America's most famous "enfant terrible", and all the family with him. They will appear as stars of a special CBC Variety Show on Friday, March 7, at 8.00 to 9.00 p.m. EDST, and it is expected that the broadcast will be staged from one of Toronto's larger auditoriums so that the Aldrich fans, whose name is legion, can be represented at the broadcast.

Henry Aldrich is really Ezra Stone, and Ezra Stone is the young man who, more than any other actor of stage, screen or radio, has interpreted the hectic 'teens of his generation. Henry, or rather, Ezra, was a fugitive from a college education, an incorrigible youngster who almost fell into fame, they met so quickly. His first step in the entertainment world was as the frequently-chastized chap in "Brother Rat", one of George Abbott's many stage successes.

The Aldrich Family was part of another Abbott success, "What A Life". First Ezra just helped Abbott in the casting, reading Henry's lines while the others tried out, but all the time knowing that Henry was being kept for a young actor, then on tour. Ezra got the part, though, as Ezra gets most things he wants. Among them this trip to Canada.

Sir Cedric and Lady Hardwicke broadcasting for the CBC on "The Theatre of Freedom."

From ANDREW ALLAN: A Self Portrait, by Andrew Allan. Copyright © 1974, Garry Allan. Used with permission.

So you want to BREAK into RADIO!

By FRANK CHAMBERLAIN

ANDREW ALLAN was the leading light in Dramatics at the University. Started in CFRB. Went to England and worked for radio agency. He is now drama chief of Canadian Broadcasting Co.

GABRIELLE: Singing Star on "Music for Canadians" was born in France and came to Canada as a child. Returned to France for schooling. In 1939 she came back to this continent and made her way to Hollywood. Was invited to sing on the air. Has sung in N.Y. and Mexico.

FOR DECEMBER, 1944

What to do . . . .
Whom to see . . .
How to begin . . .
Where to go . . .

IN Truro there's a little girl in a church choir who knows beyond a shadow of doubt that if she could only break into radio, Gabrielle, the new singing star of "Music for Canadians", wouldn't stand a chance of holding her job.

There's an eighteen-year-old reporter on a French daily in Montreal who is perfectly sure he could outshine John Collingwood Reade, Rex Frost and Willson Woodside as a news commentator, if someone would give him a microphone.

Across this country of ours, in towns and cities, there are anywhere from 50,000 to 100,000 men, women and children who have been told they "ought to be in radio". Why? Goodness knows. But there they are, housemaids, nurses, policemen, lawyers, doctors, janitors, elevator operators . . . dreaming of the day they can talk, or sing, or play, or act before a nation-wide audience, on a coast-to-coast hook-up.

They see the pot of gold there is to be made in radio. They see fan mail pouring in. They see themselves the centre of national acclaim. They visualize the National Broadcasting Company or Columbia offering them contracts to go to New York. From New York it's just a step to Hollywood and movies.

Well now, let's get down to cases. What chance has this little girl in Woodstock who has just spent three years at a Boston School of Expression and now wants to break into radio? Just because Willy Shanks is handy at telling jokes to the Elks, has he any prospects of becoming the Canadian Jack Benny? What chance has Johnny Jones, winner of a gold cup for violin playing at the Yorkville music festival, of crashing radio's national networks?

For the answer I went to Elizabeth Long, supervisor of women's programmes for the CBC; Lieut. Austin Willis, radio actor, announcer, narrator, now with the Canadian Navy; Bernard Braden, one of Canada's best radio actors and script-writers; and half a dozen more. Tell me, I said,

47

what Joe Doakes and Susie Shaver ought to do to break into this broadcasting business?

This is what they said: First of all, take a look at the different kinds of jobs radio offers: (1) vocal artist, (2) musical artist, (3) actor, (4) script-writer, (5) producer, (6) director, (7) reporter-writer, (8) announcer, (9) sound effects man, (10) engineer, (11) operator, (12) linesman.

Now take a look at yourself, and ask yourself these questions: (1) Can I sing as well or better than people already on the air? (2) Can I play as well or better? (3) Can I act? (4) Can I write? You finish it.

Supposing the answer is "yes", what then? Where do I go? Whom do I see about a job on the air? This is the $64 question And the answer, my ambitious one, lies in your own backyard. Miss Long, Lieut. Willis, Mr. Braden and all the others I interviewed agreed that the ultimate goal of singing or acting or writing for the big network shows begins in doing a job well in your own home town of Oshkosh.

"Me? I broke into radio by singing on a small radio station". Al Savage, star of "Treasure Trail" for many years, and now producer of half a dozen national network shows, said when he was asked how he broke into radio. "Then I became an announcer. When I learned what radio was all about I became a master of ceremonies, and now I'm a producer".

Bernard Braden said he started in radio as a singer, too. It was on a private radio station in Vancouver. Soon he was announcing. Then he was given parts in plays. Then he moved to Toronto, centre of radio production in Canada, and it wasn't long before he was writing drama for "Stage '44" and "Stage '45", and acting lead parts in many of them.

Do you suppose that Mary Grannan started broadcasting her "Just Mary" stories for children on the national network all of a sudden? No, indeed. She broadcast a thousand stories on a little Fredericton station, for practically nothing, before she broke into the big time.

Sometimes it's a question of luck. Like Estelle Fox, of Toronto, for instance. "I wanted to sing on the radio, so walked into CFRB in Toronto, and told Andrew Allan I wanted to get on the air. He had just lost one of

his singers to a Montreal station, so gave me a chance, and there I was on the radio", she said. What she didn't tell me was that he had been singing for five years before that, waiting for a chance to broadcast.

Some people get into radio like Elspeth Chisholm did, but not many. She didn't have any idea about broadcasting until a man she didn't know spoke to her on a street-car. "Pardon me", he said, "but would you mind telling me where you learned to speak with such a lovely tone?" That started it. Some weeks later when somebody asked her to "ghost" for a broadcaster who had written a good script but couldn't broadcast it, Elspeth got the job. She did so well, she was given assignments of her own. Today she is in the talks department of the CBC. But I should tell you that long before all this happened, Elspeth acted, produced and wrote in amateur dramatics at school.

Andrew Allan didn't step into Rupert Lucas' shoes as supervisor of drama for the CBC in one fell swoop. Oh no. In college Andrew loved drama. He played in Hart House Theatre. He joined CFRB in his early twenties. He went to England where he worked for a radio agency. Then he produced and directed radio drama in Vancouver. Suddenly Lucas was asked to take over a job in Hollywood, and Allan was offered his job.

Alan Young didn't get a contract with the Blue network all at once, either. First, a small station job at $14 a week. Then a move to a larger city, and a larger station. Then a chance to broadcast on a national network. And an agent happened to hear him. An agent from New York. Now that doesn't happen very often, but it did happen to Alan Young.

I was amazed to find so many of our radio stars had their training in the Little Theatre movement. Babs Hitchman, Grace Matthews, Wis McQuillan, Esse Ljungh, Judith Evelyn, Peggy Hassard, Bud Knapp, Frank Willis, Frank Peddie are only a few. Some, like Doug Masters, Rupert Caplan, Joe Carr and Rupert Lucas came from the stage. Percy Faith worked his way up from a pianist in a movie theatre, to arranger, orchestra director on a local station, on to national network and then to Chicago, where he is said to get 1,000 a week. Some get on the

NEW WORLD *Illu*

. . . and help your Smile!

Never ignore "Pink Tooth Brush." Let Ipana and Massage help keep your gums firmer, your smile brighter.

TODAY AND every day, proper home care of your teeth and gums is most important. So be extra careful in choosing your dentifrice. And consider Ipana —the modern tooth paste designed not only to clean teeth thoroughly but, with massage, to help the health of the gums.

It's a good thing to remember that gums as well as teeth need regular care. The beauty of your smile—the bright gleam of your teeth—depend so much on firm, healthy gums.

If your tooth brush ever "shows pink," *see your dentist right away!* He may say your gums have become tender

—denied sufficient exercise by today's soft foods. And, like so many dentists, he may suggest "the helpful stimulation of Ipana Tooth Paste and massage."

For massage with Ipana speeds up circulation within the gum tissues— helping gums to become stronger, firmer, healthier. So, each time you brush your teeth, remember to massage a little extra Ipana onto your gums.

Help your dentist help your smile. At home, give your teeth and gums the modern care of Ipana and massage.

A Product of Bristol-Myers Made in Canada

Start today with *Ipana and Massage*

48

SHORTY KNOCKS THE GALS FOR A LOOP
WITH HIS MARMALADE SANDWICHES

● THERE ARE WAYS, *and* ways to acquire
popularity—but Sh...

Kissin's always fun!
WHEN BREATH IS SWEET AND FRESH!

76% of all adults have bad *breath!* Play safe—use
COLGATE'S TOOTH POWDER

Scientific tests prove conclusively that in seven out of ten cases COLGATE'S TOOTH POWDER instantly stops oral bad breath.

SAVES YOU MONEY! Compared to other leading brands, a large tin of Colgate's gives you up to *30 more brushings*, a giant tin up to *46 more brushings*—for not a penny more!

TIP TO SMOKERS! Colgate's Tooth Powder is one of the quickest, easiest ways to guard against tobacco stain and tobacco breath! Get Colgate's today.

COLGATE'S TOOTH POWDER
25c   40c
CLEANS YOUR BREATH AS IT CLEANS YOUR TEETH

Colgate's Nylon Toothbrush
Colgate Nylon bristles can't get soggy.   Special Value **29c**

WALK ON *Happy feet*

● Why put up with stabbing pain at every ... t a Blue-Jay ... Plaster on that ... now. Makes it ... ...ier right away, ... corn is cush... ...dand the Blue-Jay medication starts to work. Best of all, Blue-Jay helps get rid of the ...orn—helps soften it ... so you can lift it ...t, core and all.

BLUE-JAY FOR CORNS

FRANK WILLIS: C.B.C. producer and assistant Grace Athersich. He started in high school dramatics, and went on to the Little Theatre. He might be called the "voice of poetry". Ladies swoon when he reads it over the air.

his instruments. I know announcers and musicians who pay out as much as $15 a week for taxi-cab fares, hurrying from one studio to another to keep appointments. They will never live to be as old as the late Sir William Mulock. And no matter how hard they work Mr. Ilsley will take off a slice of their pay cheque.

AUDITION: every day across the country newcomers seek an audition in the radio. Stations are always looking for fresh talent. But before you go, make sure that you can act as well, or better than people on the air.

THE JUDGES: they sit in a room by themselves away from person being auditioned. Usually they are unknown to contestant. They are not infallible and make mistakes, but they are willing to give a newcomer a break.

IF SANTA SHAVED
HE'D CHOOSE A **RUBBERSET**

A Genuine Rubberset Shaving Brush, the original set-in-rubber brush, makes an ideal gift for men of any age. Sold everywhere from **50c** to **$15.00**

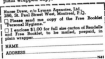

Genuine **RUBBERSET** SHAVING BRUSHES
44-27

FEMININE HYGIENE

Happy married women thank RENDELLS

Rendells solve simply the intimate problem of Feminine Hygiene. Send for Nurse Drew's booklet as thousands of other women have done. Benefit by her clear and honest information on this delicate subject. It explains how the Rendell method assures the complete, antiseptic protection so necessary to your well-being and happiness. No more doubts—no more fears. You can depend on Rendells. The coupon will bring your plain wrapped copy.

Nurse Drew, c/o Lyman Agencies, Ltd. 386, St. Paul Street West, Montreal, P.Q.
☐ Please send me copy of the Free Booklet "Personal Hygiene."
☐ I enclose $1.00 for full size carton of Rendells and Free Booklet, to be mailed, prepaid, in plain wrapper.
NAME
ADDRESS   N41

Now made to the **NEW IMPROVED FORMULA** Foil wrapped in boxes of 12
— *Ask Your Druggist* —   N-41

RENDELLS

SAMUEL HERSENHORN: who has been twenty years in radio. He began his career as a violinist in a small orchestra, and is now one of the top conductors on the C.B.C.'s list. Musicians earn up to $200.00 per week.

air because of a special knowledge of something. I heard Stuart Thomson on the air the other day, and I'm sure he was there just because he knows more about birds than anyone else in Canada.

So you want to break into radio? All right, break into radio locally, on a small station first. Do you want to write the great Canadian novel, or the great Canadian radio script? Start writing new stories for the local newspaper. And while you're breaking into radio on a small scale, my experts advise this: (1) go to your local library and study every book published about radio. There's quite a collection of them, by Norman Corwin, Arch Oboler, Earl McGill, Alice Keith and others. (2) Go to a good radio transcription studio and have a recording made of your voice (or your piano playing, or whatever you do) (3) visit your local radio manager and talk things over with him. (4) There are regional directors of the CBC

at Vancouver, Winnipeg, Toronto, Montreal, Ottawa and Halifax, but don't for heaven's sake, bother them unless you have something worth-while to offer.

How much money can you make in radio? Now there's a question. For scripts of plays the CBC pays $50 to $125. Announcers get $25 to $35 on a small station, and free-lance announcers in Toronto earn (or rather, they make anywhere from $100 to $300 a week). Singers on a small station make $15 to $20 a week, but singers who appear on half a dozen programs a week in larger centres might earn $50 to $100 a week. Musicians in small centres might earn $25 a week; and in the larger cities anywhere from $75 to $200 a week.

John Duncan, harpist, for instance, is so busy broadcasting he keeps nine harps located at various radio studios and concert halls, so that he can race from one place to another without the bother and delay of transporting

JOAN BAIRD, assumed name of a banker's daughter, interviewing Mac Evans at Royal Aleandra. Applied to Elizabeth Long of C.B.C. for job. Was sent to work in a laundry for a week and to write script on...

NEW WORLD Illustrat...

51

From *New World Illustrated*, December, 1944.

259

▲ CBC school broadcasts began in the 1940s. A class stops to listen.

◄ A production of *Macbeth* was one such broadcast.

Jane Mallett

I did some amateur acting at university and then got married to my one and only husband (fifty-five years) and continued amateur acting with him at Hart House.

I was doing professional stage acting at about the same time as I began radio acting in the late 1920s. I was getting $60 per week as a regular member of an American stock company, resident here in Toronto, and playing at the Empire Theatre (a new show each week) on Temperance St. It was a vast sum then and seemed even vaster in retrospect through the Depression.

We did many of the early radio shows "for peanuts" or less. It was a great day when Andrew Allan wangled two dollars for us on a half-hour show he had written for CFRB where he was on the staff. CFRB was on Bloor West then. I did solo pieces I wrote myself for a series there for Roy Cocksley. I played in "Out of the Night" for Rai Purdy in various roles from innocent ingenue to the Devil himself (or herself let's not be sexist). Commercially, for Phillips, I told the ladies "How to be Charming" at four o'clock every Monday, Wednesday, and Friday for two years (all our scripts were written in New York). It certainly began to seem piffling when I did the last broadcast in 1940 when France fell. Also at CFRB, I did Pat Joudry's "Sweet Sixteen" serial and "Bijou Theatre," a melodrama with a radio audience, and many other shows. CFRB was great for Canadian talent in those days.

In the 1930s, I worked at CRGW (Gooderham and Worts) on the top floor of the King Edward Hotel. The studios were carpeted and draped throughout yet the windows could still be opened for air. There was usually only one circular microphone, in front of which the actors crowded, clutching their scripts and sound effects. I remember Jack McLaren, the singing comedian, dropping to the floor to make way for the next two performers. In one of the Canadian history plays (we did dozens) when the Indians were attacking, I, as heroine had to speak lines on mike while carefully rotating a sieve full of beans to simulate rain—*and* in the same scene, at the same time, scream *off* mike as another character.

It was at CKGW I had a part in a series called "The Musical Crusaders," playing the daughter of a couple who sang. In 1930 we did what I am told was the very first hook-up for drama, seventeen independent stations right across the country. I still have the poster with the photo of the cast and Charles Jennings, the announcer. My mother, living in Regina at the time, told me she was on her way downstairs to join my father at the radio when she heard my voice say "Hello Mother, hello Dad!" and was so startled, she thought for a moment I'd come in the front door.

How slapdash it was sometimes. In a very early play, I found myself talking to myself as mother, grandmother and child. Someone had forgotten to cast the other two parts and I was the only female in the show.

During the war I had fine roles in a fine CBC series "Theatre of Freedom." Many big stars came up from the U.S.A. to work with us. They felt that their country too should be in the struggle for freedom against Hitler. Rupert Lucas was the director and the plays all dealt with some aspect of the struggle for freedom.

I, as heroine, had to speak lines on mike while carefully rotating a sieve full of beans to simulate rain—and in the same scene at the same time, scream off mike as another character.

262

Bud Knapp and Jane Mallett

Walter Huston, Henry Hull, Florence Reed and Herbert Marshall were the actors I worked with. In another series I did Shakespeare with Eva Le Gallienne, Katherine Proctor and Margaret Anglin. Other CBC wartime programmes I was involved in are too numerous to list. I also performed in many serials, "John and Judy" for six years, "Brave Voyage," "Jake and the Kid," and I had two separate roles in "The Craigs" for years.

Then in 1944 Andrew Allan began his stellar Sunday night "Stage" series which Esse Llungh took over eventually. We had Lucio Agostini at first then Morris Surdin composing and performing the music. It was most satisfactory to have the music in the same room with us. It all became a *unit*.

Over the years I have noticed that many fine performers from stage and film think and have said that radio is easy. Many of the public share this view. "All you have to do is read your lines." If that were all, it would result in non-acting. In radio you have to have even greater concentration than in other media. You have to *believe* that you are in a given situation so you can bring the listener into it with you. You have to *listen*.

It is the theatre of the mind and imagination and is in many ways more difficult than stage or television, because you have only your voice going for you.

263

Bob Christie

That was the pinnacle. When you got an acting stint on "Stage" you had arrived, you were at the top of your profession.

I started in radio drama back in 1933 or 1934, while at the University of Toronto. Edgar Stone had set up a studio in the basement of Hart House and actors were encouraged to come and work with him. He was an experienced stage director but he wanted to become a radio director and he needed people to work with. It was all very experimental. After his days as Director of Hart House were over, Stone opened Radio Hall in a big house on Spadina Avenue. That would have been about the time of my graduation in 1935 because I recall going around to see if I could get work there. The Eaton's Santa Claus show was produced there.

Radio had been a great attraction for me since about 1928 when I was still in high school. I had a radio set which I'd made myself and through my earphones I could hear people talking in Philadelphia and New York and all sorts of marvellous places. I tuned into the dance bands at The Casa Loma. Radio was such an exciting thing I could never bring myself to go to bed.

Andrew Allan, who had taken a job at CFRB as an announcer, became perhaps the first disc-jockey in Canada. He had a programme on Saturday afternoons where he put together highly varied music. He would play a symphony and then talk about what it meant. He was put in charge of the CFRB library and went to London every year to buy British records. He used his Canadian experience to get jobs in London. I was living in England for a time, doing commercials, and Andrew hired me to be on a series which featured Gracie Fields. I was the announcer for Oxydol, Gracie Fields sang and Andrew was in the booth. Andrew did many radio shows in England in which I had a few parts but that stands out as the best. Back in Canada Andrew was given some time on CFRB at eleven-thirty on Saturday nights, and of course, all of us who were amateurs and friends besieged him for parts. He didn't pay, but he was doing drama! He was supposed to have only a half-hour, but if he had a good play, it could be extended.

Those were wonderful days. Of course, we were all beginners. We weren't by any means blasé. You need to be a little bored by a job before you're relaxed enough to do it well. You have to be blunted a bit in your intensities. None of us were blunted then. We were all into this thing up to our ears and our performances were often exaggerated. If you listen to some of those old broadcasts you can hear the stilted delivery and the strained voices. Except for the soap operas which were always done in a low-key manner and seemed much more real. I think that was the secret of their success.

During World War Two I was chosen with five or six others to form a radio unit under Bob Keston, who was our commanding officer. The BBC gave us technicians and we were a broadcasting unit behind the Canadian lines to counteract German propaganda. Every day at noon we rebroadcast the farm broadcast from the CBC, and we had a great collection of records plus a lot of recorded remote broadcasts. For instance, we had dance bands from the King Edward Hotel in Toronto to bring a touch of home to our guys.

When I came back to Canada, Andrew Allan's "Stage" series

was well established. On the day of my discharge I had a lunch date with Andrew and I came to the CBC still wearing my uniform. In the corridor I met Grace Matthews and Jane Mallett each of whom took me by an arm and said, "Come with us." It turned out that auditions were being held for the part of George in a series to be called "George's Wife." Now that the war was over they decided that a new title was needed for the programme "Soldier's Wife." I got the part of George. Here I was not yet out of the army and I was a radio actor in Canada.

At that time, right after the war, probably the best radio drama being done anywhere was done here in Canada. The Americans were doing good work but they were doing commercial plays—plays that were slick and easier to do. Stuff like "Lux Radio Theatre." 'Starry' things. The authors here were writing tougher and more serious scripts. And people stayed home on Sunday nights to hear "Stage." That was the pinnacle. When you got an acting stint on "Stage" you had arrived, you were at the top of your profession. We did plays such as Hugh MacLennan's "Barometer Rising." It was gripping, solid drama. It was done 'live' and we had to be very much on our toes. We couldn't make the slightest mistake.

One time we did "Murder In The Cathedral." The pronunciation of one of the characters' names had been discussed at great length. Our rehearsals had gone badly and we were all very tense. However, things seemed to be going just beautifully when suddenly an actor mispronounced the name. When he realized what he'd done, he was aghast. Without looking at Andrew, he took his script and threw it in the air. Here we were, on the air, live, with his script all over the floor. The actor was shattered. We all were. But after a moment, we were back to our professional selves with someone sharing their script with the unfortunate actor.

The Soldier's Return

Listeners interested in the return of service men and women to civilian life are invited to hear a new CBC series

THE SOLDIER'S RETURN

now broadcast each Wednesday at 10.15 p.m. EDT over the CBC Trans-Canada network.

This series deals with the many problems attendant upon the return to civilian life of men and women of the forces. Psychologists and men from the services, whose personal experience and knowledge of army, navy and air force personnel have led them to study these questions, have been invited by the CBC to participate in these programs.

At the conclusion of the series, CBC will publish a digest of the talks. A limited edition will be made available at 25c per copy to listeners writing to "The Soldier's Return," Canadian Broadcasting Corporation, Box 500, Toronto 1. Postal note, money order or stamps should be enclosed with the order.

George Waight

When radio drama began in Winnipeg, radio producers naturally drifted to the Little Theatre to get actresses and actors to play the parts. This was in the late twenties and early thirties, and I was in there right at the beginning. I think I've done from a thousand to two thousand appearances in radio dramas, all in my spare time. I was also a banker, you see.

Andrew Allan and Esse Llungh were in Winnipeg then. I used to leave the bank at lunch time and go over to the Farm Broadcast Department to pick up my script and we'd go right on the air—live—for the fifteen-minute farm broadcast. Then I'd have a little bit of lunch and go back to the bank.

We created our own sound effects on these programmes, which was fun. Nowadays, if they want the sound of anything they go to the library and pick out a sound. We'd stage a fight, hitting each other to make the sounds while reading the script. Slapping a face and so on. This sort of thing went on all the time. For a shot sound we used a flat ruler on a cushion. It was very good too. One time we wanted the sound of reverberation from up in the hills. We came up with a football bladder with loose buckshot inside. Blown up tight it made a perfect sound of thunder coming nearer and nearer all the time. I remember we had King Charles the First galloping to get out of the country, and we had to have him galloping in a stage coach down a gravel road. So we came up with a saucer with gravel in it and an egg beater just barely touching it. I worked half the night at home dreaming that one up. Another fellow stood by with a piece of belt and a chain—creaking the harness, you see. It worked wonderfully well. The listeners supplied the rest with their own imaginations. They built pictures in their minds if we gave them enough authentic sound. Then we'd meet them afterwards and say, "You know how we did that?" They didn't want to know. They didn't want to spoil their memories. It was all brand new, and we were inventing the techniques as we went along.

Esse W. Llungh.

JOE SCHULL: Has written dramas for "Stage 44" and "Stage 45," CBC Sunday night show. Is now overseas.

GERALD NOXON: Authored first feature program series produced by BBC in 1934; has done much writing.

BABS HITCHMAN: Mother of two boys, she's written 1,092,000 words for Pond's "John and Judy" broadcasts.

DON HENSHAW: Vacationing here, he stayed on to become Canadian citizen, write Canadian radio shows.

ARCHIE MacCORKINDALE: Originally studied to be concert pianist, now combines radio and magazine writing.

DON BASSETT: Man behind popular "L for Lanky," which is now in its second year, and still going strong.

TOMMY TWEED: Good at scripts, good at acting. Author of "Hidden Enemy," "A Roof Over your Head."

JEFF HURLEY: Writes new program "Servicemen's Forum." Got his early training as reporter; now with WIB.

BERNARD BRADEN: "Fool's Paradise" took a day to write; "Brief for Incoherence," a gruelling two weeks.

WILLIAM STRANGE: Commander in RCNVR; writes "Fighting Navy," has had plays on "Carry on, Canada."

22

RADIO'S UNKNOWNS...

By FRANK CHAMBERLAIN

LEN PETERSON: His is radio classic.

A new Canadian profession has sprung up in the past half dozen years, and scarcely anybody has noticed it. It's writing for radio. Script writers are pounding out millions of words destined to make their imprint on Canadian thought and life. For every thousand words journalists or authors turn out for dailies, weeklies or monthlies, these writers for the air grind out ten to fifty thousand words. For every dollar writers of published words earn, radio's script writers are earning three dollars.

When Merrill Denison wrote dramatic scripts for a series of CNR broadcasts 15 years ago, he didn't realize he was pioneering in a field that today is paying scrip writers $5,000 to $15,000 a year. Three or four are making $20,000, although those making big money writing also broadcast the stuff they write.

There are script writers of plays, soap operas, news, spot announcements, continuity — script writers of every other kind of program. Let's look at the play writers first. Tops in the class are Len Peterson, Fletcher Markle, Bernard Braden.

A western Canadian, Len Peterson won international fame when his "They're All Afraid" was given first prize at the University of Ohio's annual exhibit of educational radio programs. Not only did it win first prize award in its own class, it came first in 16 classes, and the play is now being used by the University of Wisconsin as a model of what a good radio play should be.

Nobody seemed to think that Canadian radio could produce anything original in drama — at least nothing so good as Norman Corwin or Arch Oboler — until 23-year-old Fletcher Markle wrote 13 plays Andrew Allen produced from Vancouver under the title "Baker's Dozen." Canada sat up and took notice.

Bernard Braden threatens to become a script writer of importance. He has written 10 plays for radio. Every one has or is being produced. His colleagues in radio accuse him of writing plays with a view to his playing the leading role.

In between writing for radio, Mary Grannan writes books. One has sold 75,000 copies. If Mary Grannan lived in United States she would be earning $20,000 a year, but as a salaried employee of the CBC she doesn't earn anything like that.

If you want to look at the money-raising possibilities of writing script for radio, we'd better cite Kay and Ernie Edge, Toronto husband and wife, who do the writing for "Soldiers Wife," "Canadian Cavalcade," "Out of the Night" and other programs. Ernie says that when he and Kay start writing, anything can happen, from hair-pulling to breaking chair legs. "We have to forget to be polite," he says. Kay does the love scenes, Ernie the documentary stuff.

Gordon Sinclair is one of radio's busiest writers today. The glamorous Claire Wallace is another. Willson Woodside, news commentator, says radio pays him two and a half times as much as publications.

The CBC has done more for Canadian radio script writers than anybody else. In a nine-month period they bought and produced 226 half-hour English-language plays. Of these, 193 were written by Canadians. They pay anywhere from $50 to $125 for a script. Producer Maurice Rosenfeld has been offering $200 a script.

Of this I am sure: radio writing, the new profession, is growing up. And there's money in it.

John Drainie

Radio acting is one of the most difficult things, if not the most difficult thing, that an actor has to do.

In the 1930s, when I was about eighteen, I hadn't really found myself. I was on the verge of being a dropout. But I was rehearsing in a play, "The Queen" by Maxwell Anderson, and I was entranced by it. It had a fine sound; it had a ring to it. I had a very small part but I knew everybody's lines. I could have done the whole play myself. I was walking home at three one morning saying all these lines out loud in a ringing voice and suddenly it was as if I were seized by the Furies. I was in a paroxysm. I realized that there was something here—the power of the spoken word—the spoken word as it could come out of me. And I knew that from then on, this was what I wanted to do.

At that time the CBC was doing its share of dramas, comedies and musical shows. But the private stations were putting on a lot of these things too, and I did a great many productions at CJOR in Vancouver. That's where I first worked with Alan Young. It was in a comedy show directed by Andrew Allan; Fletcher Markle was in it, and Bernie Braden. We all worked on each other's shows and we were all ready to descend on Toronto which, eventually, we all did. Radio was just coming to its crest in the late 1930s and I was in there like a duck.

One of the things I had was what all actors need—the inspiration of other actors. You look at them during a rehearsal or a performance and if they're doing what they should be doing and working as hard with their lines as you are with yours, you get what you need back from them. If, on the other hand, they are *not* working as hard as I am, I'm afraid I have no patience with them and am inclined to lose my temper. I have a very bad temper in situations like that.

I remember one time I went to New York in about 1946 to do a Mercury Theatre, and Orson Welles, who is only about a year older than I am, said, "I don't know where to go from here. There isn't anybody in the world I respect." I thought, "You poor fellow." I had gods I worshipped all around me. They were the great voices from England—Charles Laughton, Ralph Richardson and others. That's what I looked for in an actor—primarily, a powerful respect for the spoken word. That's the actor's main job. He is the guardian of the spoken word.

I find that the best way to work is to try and solve the immediate problems: Where do you have to move? Who are you talking to? What is the sense of what you are saying? What is the playwright getting at? What does the director want? Get all those things going so you don't have to be doing seventeen things at once. You must get them to the point where they are automatic and when that happens something magical occurs. You then have a sense of truth which comes down on you and, as Stanislavski says, "The gates of inspiration gently open." This is the way it's done. You do it as a tradesman—solving all the problems first.

Radio acting is one of the most difficult things, if not *the* most difficult thing, that an actor has to do. There is no stage with all the accompanying scenery and effects. There is nothing but the voice and that little microphone. The voice is everything and I always depended greatly on my own ear. I could listen to my voice

"John Drainie is in the extremely rare category of an answer to a director's dream. He is one of the top ten actors in my entire radio experience and I congratulate Canadian Radio on having developed him."

Norman Corwin.

JOHN DRAINIE
114 BELSIZE DRIVE
TORONTO
HY. 3303

actor • announcer • producer • writer

and tell whether it was right or wrong. I didn't have a great voice as voices go, but I worked on what I had to make the audience *see* the character I was depicting. The imagination of the listener is terribly important in radio drama and it is up to the radio actor to feed that imagination. A good actor should be able to create characters so listeners can 'picture' them the way they want to see them. The trick is to make the listener believe he is hearing the 'real' character you are portraying. You have to spend a lot of time on the character and the transfer of this from the page to an oral concept which you hope is a real expression of what the writer is after. You have little to worry about except getting it across with your vocal tones, your phrasing and so on.

That's where radio is superior to films and television, as far as the actor is concerned. The actor is the *last* thing considered in TV and films. Lights and scenery come first. In radio, all the technicalities are out of the way and the radio actor is able to concentrate on the character he is trying to portray. Radio is an actor's medium; the other two are the province of the producer.

A promotional sketch for "Jake and the Kid." John Drainie was Jake.

Gordon Keeble

He was to bring the sub up to the surface. But he had turned the wrong dial. There was a great clang followed by the sound of a car driving away.

I started as a freelance performer, an actor mostly, and a singer to some degree, and that took me into announcing. During that period, just after I'd left school in the early 1930s, I was deeply involved in little theatre. Everybody was in those days. And naturally enough, the people who worked in little theatre were also the people who worked in radio. The old CRBC only rehearsed and produced after six p.m. as everyone had to have a daytime job. We'd leave work, have a quick bite, and be up at the Davenport Road studios at six and ready to go on the air at nine. I think we got something like twenty-five dollars a show. That included three hours of rehearsal and the performance, so it wasn't that bad. But it was sporadic and you certainly didn't live on it. Nobody could live on what they made from radio at the time.

The big thing in those years was a series that O'Keefe's ran. This is back in the days before beer could be advertised. They had a soft drink called O'Keefe's Stone Ginger Beer, so naturally, as announcer I managed to lose "stone ginger" pretty quickly in reading the line.

O'Keefe's decided in 1938 to have a talent contest. The prize was a screen test in England. We broadcast from the Uptown Theatre. We were the show between the movie features. This was all great fun, but I wasn't really making a living, so one day I read an ad for an announcer in Northern Ontario. They auditioned me on a Tuesday and I was working in North Bay on a Thursday.

The North Bay experience was supposed to last a couple of weeks while one of the local announcers went on holidays. He didn't come back which was par for the course in those days. The station broadcast eighteen hours a day. As announcer-copy writer, I wrote every damned word that went out over that station. Shifts in those days would be from seven in the morning to seven at night or eleven in the morning to one in the morning. You didn't think anything of it. They never hired local people because if they did, that meant you had other things to do with your life. If they hired a guy in Timmins, for example, they'd move him to North Bay. That way they could get these hours out of him.

My two weeks in North Bay lasted five months. Eventually, after a lot of different stations and experience, I ended up as chief CBC announcer in Toronto. We did a lot of propaganda stuff during the war. During one dramatic show, about a submarine patrol, Alan King was playing the part of the commander of the submarine. He was to bring the sub up to the surface. The sound effects man gave us great bubblings and noises. But he had turned the wrong dial or something. There was a great clang followed by the sound of a car driving away.

The announcing staff consisted of some people who were celebrated in later years. We had Elwood Glover, Lorne Greene, John Drainie and so on. We got the idea one day that it would be nice if we got a half-hour on air to ourselves so the announcers could do what *they* wanted to do. The station manager gave us the go-ahead and mostly we did dramatic works. I guess every announcer is a frustrated actor. We came on one night to do a play about espionage. In the course of the script, the spy arrives at a gate in a taxi. The sound of the taxi driving up is heard and he climbs out with all the appropriate door noises. He pays the driver, gives him a tip, and the driver thanks him. During rehearsal nobody was ever given the line "Thank you," but somebody standing near the microphone always said it. When we came to do the show on air, the cab drives up, the door opens and so on, but this time nobody said, "Thank you." There was a brief, but pregnant silence. The fellow who was playing the spy somehow wasn't prepared just to leave it alone and walk off. Instead, he said a second time, "And here's something for you." With that, thirteen voices answered, "THANK YOU."

The Music is *there*. . . .

But it takes FREEDOM FROM INTERFERENCE to bring it out

Millions of dollars are right now being invested in radio broadcasting. Never before have you been afforded the wealth of diversified entertainment, amusement and instruction now offered with such a lavish hand by *radio*.

Byrd, Lindbergh, King George, President Hoover . . . such are the notables who in endless procession pass before the microphone, whose living voices thrill, entertain, educate. And don't forget the great singers and musicians; the famous bands and orchestras; the opera, symphony, the big games and sports!

The music is *there*. It's in your home, in every home. And it's all *hearable* at a cost so small that the most economical "evening out" becomes a comparative *extravagance*.

But no singer can sing effectively when his mouth is gagged. Just as it takes freedom from interference to bring out the full rich tones of the voice, so does it take properly equipped radio to reproduce those tones when put on the air. And that is why you should be sure your

The St. James Model

A rich reproduction of Elizabethan design. Top, sides and front are of walnut, the front being richly embellished with real wood carving. One of four exquisite new Period models priced from $158.50 to $237.50 in Eastern Canada. From $175.00 to $260.00 in Western Canada. (Less tubes).

Licensed by Canadian Radio Patents, Ltd.

radio is a Stewart-Warner. For here is the radio that brings in all programs true to life—with nothing added, nothing taken away. Gone is the distracting interference, the mumble and the mutter of nearby stations. Gone are distorted tones and hum. What you *hear*, is what you *want* to hear—just that and no more!

Embodied in these sets is every fundamental essential for championship performance, *clear across the dial*.

Behind them is a quarter of a century's experience in the making of fine electrical precision instruments. No radio you can buy will give you more for your money.

Stewart-Warner Radio is as pleasing to the eye as to the ear. You may choose from four authentic Period cabinet designs with genuine carved decorations and exquisite finish. But see them—hear them. They are now being displayed and demonstrated by authorized dealers everywhere at extremely low prices. Easy terms too.

Remember! The Music is *there*! But to get it without interruption and interference, just as it truly *is*—get it with a Stewart-Warner! Let a demonstration prove it. Stewart-Warner-Alemite Corp., Ltd., Belleville, Ontario.

STEWART-WARNER *Radio*
A Great Radio Backed By A Great Name

Frank Willis.

Frank Willis

In my opinion radio was better when everything was 'live.' We got better performances from actors when they knew the words they were speaking were the final product. The problem with tape is that they know mistakes can be corrected and that a poor performance can be done over again. Before tape, an actor had to get 'up' for a performance and stay there because, unlike live theatre, you knew you couldn't come back and do a better job the next night.

There was a degree of concentration in earlier days that slipped away in the era of tape. Actors then, were able to overcome any emergency. One time during a play there was a four-way bit of dialogue and one of the actors, Tommy Tweed, somehow got locked out of the studio. Without missing a beat, the three others took over his part and nobody noticed anything wrong. Another time the sound effects recordings didn't work and Tommy Tweed, without blinking an eye, took over and imitated the sound of a dog pursuing Huckleberry Finn through a swamp.

Ruth Springford forgetting she had one more scene to play, once left the studio and went home. It was a play about a retiring locomotive engineer called *Hoghead's Last Run.* At the end of the play he comes home to talk of his retirement with his missus. But the missus wasn't there. John Drainie, who was playing the engineer, calmly improvised. He said, "Oh, I guess she's gone to the store." Later he added, "Well, I know what she'd say anyway," and he just said the lines she would have said. The thing was it sounded exactly right. Nobody caught on. The other thing was that Ruth suddenly remembered having to do that last scene while in her car less than a block away. She left her car in the middle of traffic and ran back to the studio. She arrived out of breath and terribly upset but we assured her that everything had turned out fine.

Another time Tommy Tweed, who was talented in many directions, wrote *Secret Treaty,* a play about giving the country back to the Indians. It was supposed to open with John Drainie up on a ladder. Someone comes along and asks "What are you doing up there?" When the show began there was no John in sight. He was in the men's room still rehearsing his part. So when the question was asked, out of nowhere came a voice sounding remarkably like Drainie's. It was Fletcher Markle who knew John so well, he could sound like him. It worked out perfectly and when John appeared, he just picked up his next line and carried on. The radio audience was unaware of any of this. That whole troupe was totally professional and could handle any situation that came along.

There was a lot of practical joking too. I remember one time when "The Happy Gang" crew set all the studio clocks ahead twenty minutes. The only person who didn't know this was Bert Pearl. When the clock showed it was time to begin, Blaine Mathe knocked on his violin and they carried on with "Who's there?" and all the rest of their opening. After the opening the gang launched into the bluest stories you can imagine and poor Bert, who was an extremely high-strung fellow anyway, almost had a breakdown. I must say that not all practical jokes were as cruel as that one. The joking around was a way of relieving the tension of 'live' broadcasting.

The joking around was a way of relieving the tension of 'live' broadcasting.

273

Steve Brodie

The announcer on the CBC represents, or should represent, the standard of near perfection that we look for.

Gladstone Murray gave me the job of training the speech of announcers and, of improving the standards of English on the CBC. I had gone to him looking for a job of any kind really. He gave me an audition, and from that came the job which I gratefully accepted and did for twenty-five years.

Broadcast language and the language spoken in the streets differ greatly. The truth of the matter is that most people do not speak well. That's not meant to be a criticism. It just happens to be a fact. Ordinary conversation is full of errors—in grammar, pronunciation, sentence structure and so on. That kind of thing is not acceptable as a standard for broadcasting. The announcer on the CBC represents, or should represent, the standard of near perfection that we look for. If an announcer mispronounces a word, chances are that those listening to him will accept his pronunciation as proper and the error will multiply. The same applies to grammar. Therefore, there is a great responsibility vested in broadcasters to be correct.

My job wasn't meant to make all CBC announcers sound the same. It was to make sure that they understood the English language and knew how to use it. It was my job to help them improve where necessary and to assist in any way I could with problems they were having. I travelled back and forth across the country visiting each of our stations at least once a year, talking with announcers and listening to them. In the early days of the CBC, in 1936 and 1937 and 1938, I also visited the private stations affiliated with us. I would sit down with each announcer for a couple of hours and have him read. Then, together, we would listen to the recording and I would make criticisms and we would discuss them. I can't remember one occasion when an announcer resented anything I might have to say. I do remember how scared I was when I started having to speak to extremely experienced announcers—men like Charles Jennings.

There were great regional differences in the sound of English across the country. In Newfoundland, where people had been cut off for three hundred years from the rest of the world, the language had become what linguists call a "relic area." In the English used there you could hear Dorset dialects which hadn't been in use in England for three centuries. There were other examples of regional differences all across the country but Newfoundland presented the most marked example.

Settling on a standard pronunciation, even for commonly used English words, was part of my responsibility, and I might say, one had to be careful in this; people tend to become a bit hot-under-the-collar when they are told that the way they've been pronouncing a word for years is not acceptable. For example, take the word schedule. Do you say "sked-ule" or "shed-ule." I maintain that they both are correct although "shed-ule" seems to indicate you're from England while "sked-ule" indicates you're Canadian—or one of us. However, if you go back to the time of Shakespeare you'll find they're both wrong. In that era, it was "sed-ule."

My job also was to inform announcers by Telex across the country of the proper pronunciation of any foreign names or places that might occur in the news. This was something the announcers appreciated greatly as it can be very unsettling to appear on the air and 'take a run' at some word you've never seen before and not be at all sure that you are pronouncing it properly.

In the selection of announcers I always felt that although quality of voice was important it was one of the least important qualifications as long as it wasn't objectionable. I've always felt that intelligence and interest in the things that the announcer was dealing with were the most important requirements along with the ability to make something written sound like ordinary conversation. I felt that an announcer should never sound as if he were reading, as that is not his job. If he's doing his job right he is trying to explain and make clear the subject he's *talking* about, not *reading* about. The truth is that most people cannot read aloud and make it sound right. The job of an announcer is to do just that.

I've always had a great love for the language and more than anything else, I've tried to instill that love in others.

Your Announcer Is . . Allan McFee

Allan McFee enjoys life. He has always believed it was meant to be enjoyed and he has done his best in 27 crowded years. His motto—"good friends, good food and good fun"—should not be taken as evidence that Mr. McFee has jumped aboard a perpetual round-about of dining, wining and making merry. But he has cultivated, besides his mind, his senses and his sinews too. Still looking like the college star athlete he was seven years ago, he can act like one if circumstances require it.

His zest for living commenced at an early age in Belleville, Ontario, and grew apace at Upper Canada College where he took an active interest in everything from football to part singing. In fact, he was a member of the U.C.C. Boys' Choir which performed with the Mendelssohn at Convocation Hall in 1927 That was when Allan was 14. For the next two or three years he engaged in a full school curriculum in the winters and coached in dramatics and lifesaving at Ridley College camp in summer.

It was during the first year at Onondaga Camp that he wrote and produced a play that should have been the black-out of his enthusiasm for the drama. The young producer was asked to take the production of "The Spider" to a near-by town. Mr. McFee, in addition to writing and staging the show, played the title role. Besides a grisly make-up, the actor-manager wore protruding false teeth which, early in Act I, proceeded to pop out whenever he spoke a line. To this embarrassment was added the fact that he should have been shot in Act II, and the gun refused to fire. So instead of a corpse as the curtain fell, the audience beheld a slightly stunned creature, (his brother actor had fetched him a clout over the head with the butt as a last resort) crawling around in the footlights in search of a set of false teeth.

Next Allan McFee perfected his physical education. He paddled with the Parkdale Canoe Club in 1934-5, representing the club both years at the Canadian Canoeing Association meet, at Montreal. He rowed with the Argonaut Eight in 1936-7, racing at Henley Regatta those two seasons. After that he had the thrill of his life; he was accepted on the CBC announce staff at Ottawa in September, 1937. Transferred to Toronto in the spring of this year, he is one of the regular news announcers and is frequently assigned to musical and feature presentations.

McFee does not think that everything worth mentioning has happened since 1900. He likes good literature, the plays of Ibsen, gentlemanly virtues, the primeval forests; he believes in parental respect, the golden rule; despises pettiness, delights in generosity, ignores taboos, loves parchesi and aquamarines. He is five foot eight, weighs 178 pounds, has dark olive skin, black hair and flashing brown eyes. When he saw his newest picture he was delighted, thought it flattered him. Nobody else thought it even did him justice.

Alan McFee

My father would say, "Go to bed, you rotten little swine. You'll never get into radio."

It was a consuming ambition of mine to be a broadcaster. I wanted to get in, right from the start. But I was interested in announcing and not in the technical side of things. In those early days there weren't that many good announcers. I'd practise in my room with my hand cupped to my ear. "Hello, this is Alan McFee." And then I'd try it again *sotto voce.* "Hello, this is Alan McFee." In those days there were no tape recorders to let you hear how you sounded, so you had to rely on your cupped hand.

I don't remember when I first became interested in radio. I can remember my father with those "cat's whiskers," they were called, made from a round salt box with those precious earphones held to the ears. To me it was such a magic thing. I remember listening to programmes from the States—I didn't know where any of those places were—where dance orchestras broadcast for four or five hours at a time. I used to think that I'd love to be sitting there saying, "And now, here's lovely Marjorie Main stepping front and centre to sing the beautiful song, 'I'm in the Mood For Love.'" I used to practise that sort of thing all the time. My father would say, "Go to bed, you rotten little swine. You'll never get into radio." I remember saying to him one time, "Gee, Dad, I'd like to be a radio announcer." And he said, "I suppose the next thing you'll want is to put lipstick and rouge on and do your hair up." I talked about radio all the time.

He wasn't a stupid man, but he couldn't understand me. Before he died, though, he was terribly thrilled with his son. He'd tell people, "My son's going to be on tonight. You listen to him." But that strange prejudice existed in him. His grandfather had come from Scotland. They were hard, hard working people, and to him broadcasting was too ephemeral. Surely one didn't get *paid* for it! He'd say to me after I started out in Ottawa, "After you put those records on, what do you do?" He could never understand, you see, that between records we had to scurry around preparing for the next programme. He'd hear me say, "Now here's such and such a record." Then he'd listen to the record being played and think, "What's that boy doing now?" He didn't see how that could be man's work. He thought I should be mending shoes or whatever in my spare time.

I remember the old acetate recordings of commercials. We'd do eight commercials on one side of the disc and then turn it over and do eight more. If you made a mistake, say, on the eighth commercial, well, the whole thing had to be done over again. This made it very, very tough. Especially when you were with five or six other people. Somebody was bound to make an error. If it happened in the first or second commercial, it wasn't so bad, but when it got to the eighth, tension would start to build. It was worse than being on the air live because it meant everything had to be done over. That's the way you learn, of course. I mean, today broadcasting is so easy in comparison. Of course, we've been at it a long time, haven't we? I think that the tape recorder solved an awful lot of the problems. That was probably the most important development in my kind of work in broadcasting. Oh, gosh, the immediacy. I like errors to happen because then you can sort of cover—not fly for cover, just cover up. At the present time I tape five of my own programmes a week and I do one 'live.' The one I do 'live' is my favourite because I'm on my own, and then I just fly. At least I think that I do. I hope I do.

My parents moved to Ottawa from Belleville, Ontario. But first we came to Toronto, and when my parents went on to Ottawa I stayed on as I had a job with Imperial Tobacco in their warehouse. The warehouse job started at seven-thirty in the morning and went until six at night, and on Saturdays it was from seven-thirty in the morning until one in the afternoon. But I still had that urge to get into radio. Of course, it was a difficult thing to do as the only experience I had was my work at Imperial Tobacco, which hardly qualified me for announcing. But I tried to get into radio. I had an audition with the CBC in the old building on Davenport. George Taggart and Charles Jennings auditioned me. They told me I had quite a lot to learn, but they kept my audition. When I was home in Ottawa I also did an audition there. They seemed to like it, so I told them that I'd also done one in Toronto, and they sent for it. The next time I was in Ottawa, Gladstone Murray—which shows what a small corporation it was then—auditioned me at head office. He was the President of the CBC, and a magnificent man. A gentleman of the old school. And charming in every way. I remember sitting in his office and he said, "McFee, how would you pronounce 'master of ceremonies?'" and he caught me on it. The CBC in those days was modelled on the British Broadcasting Corporation and all of our pronunciations were taken from the BBC handbook for announcers. And remember, we had three hours of direct transmission from the BBC every day on Canadian radio. Anyway, I got a job in Ottawa with CBO.

All programmes in those days came from Toronto or the BBC. The BBC programmes were terribly dull. Things like "Beekeeping in the North." Of course, we were feeling our way and weren't sure what we should put on. I replaced Herb May in Ottawa when he was transferred to Toronto. I was a very bad announcer, by the way, when I first started. It takes an awfully long time to become a broadcaster. In the early days there was an apprenticeship to be served, in Ottawa, or Sydney, Nova Scotia, or wherever. What you hoped for was some day to get to Toronto. That was the place to be. When I was in Ottawa I received a hundred dollars a month. That was a good wage. Friends in other jobs were making around fifteen dollars a week. When I got to Toronto just before the war I got $125 a month. Having served my apprenticeship I was now considered a professional. Announcing then was a matter of lifting the words off the page. No ad-libbing was done. Everything was scripted. We had no writers, of course. We wrote all our own scripts. We had no researchers then either. Now, writers and researchers are the backbone of the business.

Byng Whitteker
C.B.C. TORONTO

On the Air for

C.B.C. SUSTAINERS
&
CAMPBELL SOUP CO. LTD.
FORD OF CANADA
HOUSEHOLD FINANCE CORP.

Mary Grannan

I would have Maggie meet her friends in the woods. There was Fitzgerald Fieldmouse, Grandmother Frog, Petunia Possum, Benny Bear and Greta Grub.

I read stories over the CBC for twenty-three years on Sundays and the only Sunday I can remember being off was when President Roosevelt died. I started with CBC in October 1939, but I had begun doing the "Just Mary" stories in Fredericton a couple of years earlier. I was a primary school teacher and I had been making up plays and stories for my classes for several years. I put together the idea for "Just Mary" and took it to CFNB. They gave me a spot on Sunday nights where listeners couldn't miss me— right between two very popular programmes, "Dr. Stewart's News" show from Halifax at seven-thirty and "The Jack Benny Show" at eight. The following summer Gladstone Murray came to Fredericton and offered me a CBC network spot in Toronto.

I made my stories up from little things I noticed every day. For example, I was walking on Yonge Street in Toronto and noticed that the rooster was missing from the weathervane on a church steeple, so I wrote "The Wandering Weathercock." Having been a schoolteacher, I noticed that children seemed to like my stories best when I told them in the way they spoke and using words they would have used themselves, I transferred this to broadcasting. The children wrote me tons of fan mail and asked me to tell certain stories or to make up stories about some idea they had. As a matter of fact, a great deal of my story ideas came from their letters.

Later I introduced "Maggie Muggins." I would have Maggie meet her friends in the woods. There was Fitzgerald Fieldmouse, Grandmother Frog, Petunia Possum, Benny Bear and Greta

Mary Grannan.

Grub. They all had different voices and I played all these animal characters. This meant a lot of nature study for me because I had to be right about these creatures. Once I said Maggie Muggins liked this little dog and had saved all her chicken bones for him. I was deluged with letters saying that dogs should never be given chicken bones because of the harm they could do to their stomachs. I had to be very careful.

The reaction of the children themselves was the most satisfying thing. One little girl wrote from Vancouver telling me she had been planning to go to the circus with her father but she'd caught measles and couldn't go. She told me how unhappy she was. I wrote back and told her I was sorry as I too liked the circus but I said that in a couple of weeks I'd write a story for her with her name in it. Her name was Penny Webb. So I thought of spider and web and I had the spider come and tell her that since she couldn't go to the circus she could come instead to the spider fair, which was better than the circus. Later, a woman named Ivy Webb wrote to ask for a copy of the story. She changed the name of the little girl from Penny Webb to Patti Webb, the name of a niece who lived in England and had been so affected by the War that she wasn't interested in anything and had been hospitalized. Not long after I got a letter saying that Patti was running around showing the nurses this story about her. Then I got a letter from Patti's doctor saying that Patti had been released from hospital and how wonderful it was that a spider had saved her. That really impressed me with the tremendous power radio had—how a letter from a little girl in Vancouver helped another little girl in the south of England.

Maggie Muggins is fun, and she has freckles on her nose, and it's turned up, and she has two pigtails, the colour of brand new carrots. She has a friend named Mr. McGarrity. He gardens in a garden, and days when Maggie can't think of things to do, he always thinks of something. He knows where raspberries get their thorns. And I'll never forget the day he showed Maggie the robin having a feast in the cherry tree. Maggie talked about that the whole of the day. Now here comes Maggie Muggins herself. She's dancing down the garden path and she's singing, Tra la la la la la la lee. Here comes Maggie Muggins, me.

MORE JUST MARY STORIES

street. A little girl who had been rude and naughty every day of her six years, was at breakfast. She had just brushed her cornflakes to the floor. The dish had crashed into many pieces and the milk was running over the tiles.

"Pamela," cried her mother. "Why on earth did you do that?"

"Because," said Pamela, "I hate cornflakes. I told you yesterday I hated cornflakes. I've always hated cornflakes, and porridge too! I want chocolate cake."

"Pamela, you are not going to have chocolate cake

100

Lou Snider

"The Happy Gang" caught the imagination of radio listeners.

In 1934 I was musical director of "Ken Sobel's Amateur Hour." We used to hold auditions in the CKCL studios on University Avenue in Toronto and later at CFRB's studios. Ken Sobel was a wonderful man who pushed Canadian talent when nobody else was doing it. Oscar Peterson, for example, came up through that amateur show. I can vividly remember Oscar winning a watch— that's what the prizes were—and he was about sixteen at the time. He played "Chinatown" with a boogie woogie beat in the left hand. We all thought, "Boy, this kid's great!" Another one who came up that way was Phyllis Marshall. So did Joan Fairfax. A lot of talent came out of "Ken Sobel's Amateur Hour." It provided one of the few ways for youngsters to get started on the professional road in the thirties. Even people who didn't win got their starts because of that show. Harry Mannis, the CBC announcer, sang on the show.

When my partner, Murray Ross, and I started at CFRB we used to do fifteen-minute shows, and we split the fifteen dollars' fee between us. It was the same on CBC; that was union scale. For that we also wrote our own scripts and timed our own shows. Those were the days before producers. I can remember when they began using producers at the CBC. A chap came up to me and after introducing himself said, "I'm your producer, and I'm going to be frank with you. I've never done this before. But I'm going to sit in the booth and look wise. You and Murray keep on doing what you've been doing. Play your music; time your shows. Just do what you've been doing." And that's the way it went. We did our thing, and he sat there looking wise and enjoying the music.

A high point in my life was my association with "The Happy Gang." They had been on the air for quite a few years before I got involved as a regular. I was flying small planes as a hobby until I cracked up and landed in hospital with some very serious injuries. Bert Pearl came to visit me and asked if I would like to join "The Happy Gang." There I was, wondering if I'd ever get out of hospital, and Bert was offering me a job. I was delighted. But I said, "Bert, I don't want to take someone else's place." He said, "No. You won't replace anybody. We'll use you as a kind of utility man. Kathleen Stokes on the organ and Blaine Mathe on violin do the serious music, but when we do pop tunes, we'd like you on the Hammond organ. Once in a while we'll feature you on piano because Jimmy Namarro, who plays piano and xylophone, should get a break." It was late in 1947 when I started with them as a regular. I had played with them before that, of course, including one time when I was home on furlough from the air force during the war.

"The Happy Gang" caught the imagination of radio listeners because the show had fine musicianship, sincerity, and a great sense of fun. I'll tell you how we worked musically. There were very few written arrangements. We would pick up stock arrangements and everybody would fiddle with them until we had a Happy Gang sound. It was odd instrumentation, but it worked. We never had drums, and we didn't have a bass until late. Mainly there was a violin, piano, organ and xylophone, and Bert was the man who welded it all together. The "Knock-knock. Who's there?"

It's the Happy Gang. Bert Pearl (left), is shown with Bob Farnon, Blaine Mathe, Kathleen Stokes, George Temple.

that opened the show was done by Blaine Mathe, who rapped his knuckles on his violin.

"The Happy Gang" was one of Canada's longest running radio shows, starting around 1937 with just Blaine, Kathleen, Bert and Bob Farnon, who played trumpet in those days. Hugh Bartlett was the announcer. Bert Pearl had been a studio pianist around the CBC in Toronto at the time. They asked him to fill a programming hole for the summer months. The show caught fire and stayed on air until 1959. Herb May and Barry Woods were two well-known announcers who followed Hugh Bartlett and the list of musicians and singers who guested on the show is long.

Live radio days kept us on our toes all the time. We made few mistakes because we knew there was no second chance. I remember one close call I had. We were doing a CBC programme called "Children's Scrapbook." Paul Sherman was the conductor. Mary Grannan wrote the script and Peggy Loder was the child star. We did our rehearsal this day and had a break, so I jumped in my car and drove to a restaurant for a cheeseburger. I figured I had lots of time, but unfortunately I got caught in heavy traffic on the way back. I had the car radio on and as I drove through the gate at the CBC the show had begun without me. Since we only had five musicians in the band, my presence was sorely missed. I had a lump in my throat as I bounded up three flights of stairs to the studios. Worst of all were the dirty looks I got from the conductor when I sat down at the piano. For me it was a nightmare coming true. All performers in radio have these terrible dreams of being on the other side of town as the second hand on the clock ticks away to starting time.

I mentioned Mary Grannan, who did such wonderful children's programmes on the CBC. I played piano for her for twenty-three years on "Just Mary." She was a wonderful lady, an ex-school teacher who had a great understanding of how to use radio. She never spoke down to children and all of her tales had a little moral but without being preachy. She did the same thing on "Maggie Muggins." She was a big comfortable-looking lady who was famous around the CBC for her big hats. We had a great rapport. She only had to indicate with a few words in the script what she wanted at a particular moment and I was able to hit it for her. We only had one read-through for each show and then we would go live to the network. People used to think that we'd rehearsed all week.

1.00 to 1.30
★ THE HAPPY GANG
Variety programme with Bert Pearl master of ceremonies; Kathleen Stokes, organ; Blain Mathe, violin; Bob Farnon, trumpet; and Eddie Allen, accordion. CBC-MBS ex-change from Toronto to CBI. CBY

"Opportunity Knocks" a CBC talent
show. The contestant is Marthe
Létourneau.

6 30-6.45
7.30-7.45 ADT

★   ARTISTS AT HOME

Ronald Hambleton, art critic and commentator, interviews F/O Carl Schaefer and F/O Goodridge Roberts, leading Canadian artists. From Toronto to CBA CBM CBO CBL

6.45-7.00
7.45-8.00 ADT

★ BBC NEWS AND COMMENTARY

From BBC to CBA CBM CBO CBL

7.00-7.30
8.00-8.30 ADT

★   JACK BENNY

Variety program. Commercial. From Vancouver to CBA CBM CBO CBL

7.30-8.00
8.30-9.00 ADT

★   "L" FOR LANKY

R.C.A.F. drama. Commercial. From Toronto to CBA CBM CBO CBL

8.00-8.30
9.00-9.30 ADT

★   CHARLIE McCARTHY

Variety program.   Commercial. From NBC to CBA CBM CBO CBL

8.30-8.45
9.30-9.45 ADT

★   WEEK-END REVIEW

A review of the week's war news by Elmore Philpott. From Vancouver to CBA CBM CBO CBL

8.45-9.00
9.45-10.00 ADT

★   OUR SPECIAL SPEAKER

Address by Graham Towers, Governor of the Bank of Canada and Lieut.-General A. G. L. McNaughton, on the Sixth Victory Loan. From Halifax to CBA CBM CBO CBL

9.00-9.30
10.00-10.30 ADT

★   "STAGE 44"

"The Dragon's Tail," a play for St. George's Day, by Comdr. William Strange.   From Toronto to CBA CBM CBO CBL

9.30-10.00
10.30-11.00 ADT

★ ALBUM OF FAMILIAR MUSIC

Frank Munn, tenor; Jean Dickenson, soprano, and Evelyn MacGregor, contralto. Commercial. From NBC to CBA CBM CBO CBL

10.00-10.15
11.00-11.15 ADT

★   CBC NATIONAL NEWS

Toronto to CBA CBM CBO CBL

10.15-11.00
11.15-12.00 ADT

★   SONGS OF EMPIRE

Orchestra and chorus. From Vancouver to CBA CBM CBO CBL

11.00-11.15
12.00-12.15 ADT

★   BBC RADIO NEWSREEL

Direct from London. From BBC to CBM CBO CBL

11.15-11.30
12.15-12.30 ADT

★   J. B. McGEACHY

Talk. From BBC to CBM CBO CBL

Charlie McCarthy returns to the CBC network on Sunday, September 7th, at 8.00 p.m. EDST. As last year, his guest on the first programme of the new season will be Deanna Durbin, shown here with Charlie. (Photo courtesy NBC).

BREAKFAST CLUBBER

Don McNeill, master of ceremonies on Blue Network's Breakfast Club, who was voted Star of Stars in a U.S. annual popularity poll, is an easy-going, nimble-witted man about a microphone who started in radio as a spare time radio announcer back in 1928, while a student at Marquette University.

After graduation in 1930, Don journeyed to Louisville, Ky., where he announced programmes on another station until his sense of humour began seeping into his routine. There he met Van Fleming, a popular singer, and the team of McNeill and Fleming were born. Five months later they were on a Pacific coast network as Don and Van, the Two Professors, and a year later they landed in Chicago.

McNeill was born December 23, 1907, in Galena, Ill. He stands six feet two inches, weighs 187 pounds, and his likeable personality and infectious smile make him a true "emcee". The Breakfast Club is heard on the CBC Network every morning, Mondays to Fridays inclusive.

6.00-6.15
7.00-7.15 ADT

★   DON MESSER AND HIS ISLANDERS

Old-time music with Don Messer's orchestra. From Moncton to CBA CBO CBY

Another quarter-hour of hoe-downing with Don Messer and His Islanders and Charlie Chamberlain, vocalist. On this evening's broadcast Charlie Chamberlain lends his voice to "Carry Me Back to the Mountains", and "I'll Be With You in Apple Blossom Time", while the Islanders dust off and fiddle five ancient favourites including "Mrs. McLeod's Reel", "John McNeill", "Kerry Dance", "Nellie Gray" and "White Cockade Reel."

9.00 to 9.30
MART KENNEY'S MUSICAL GRAB BAG

★   Variety programme. From Toronto to CBL CBY CBO

"Musical Grab Bag" is a good name for the new type of entertainment Mart Kenney and His Western Gentlemen are presenting for members of the Forces at the CBC Playhouse in Toronto. This evening it is the turn of the R.C.A.F. to pick numbers out of a hat for the orchestra to play. The man who chooses the selections can also dictate which instrument is to be featured in their presentation. Judy Richards, Art Hallman and the vocal quintet are the starring vocalists.

◄ A typical Sunday evening on CBC radio.

IT'S THE "JOHNNY HOME SHOW!"

Frank Shuster and Johnny Wayne, who write the "Johnny Home Show."

The comedy story of that lad from Beaversville, **Johnny Home**, and his Pal **Sam Lightfoot** who have returned from overseas and are trying to re-establish themselves in civilian Life.

Written by Shuster and Wayne
Produced by J. Frank Willis

EVERY FRIDAY NIGHT

10.00 p.m. AST; 9.00 p.m. EST; 8.00 p.m. CST;
7.00 p.m. MST; 6.00 p.m. PST.

STATIONS OF THE CBC TRANS-CANADA NETWORK

Wayne and Shuster with Foster Hewitt for a Mimico Mice/Toronto Maple Leaf game.

Wayne and Shuster

Our first radio show was on CFRB. A man named Maurice Rosenfelt from MacLaren's Advertising happened to catch one of our college shows and felt we were "not bad." We bothered the life out of him for a year until he got us a little morning show three times a week. It was called "The Wife Preservers" and was sponsored by Javex, which was just a little local product at the time. Javex's business expanded by 100 percent within three months. It wasn't us that did it; it was radio. It was the first time Javex had advertised on radio. It could also have been that we gave household hints with a slight sense of humour. In those days there was no humour in commercials.

Radio was a magical thing. Sets and costumes were built in the imagination. We did a skit where we went to the moon and there we were, on the moon—on radio. We couldn't do that on television nearly as well because the audience would see it was a painted set. There are no painted sets in the imagination. You close your eyes and if there's a director who knows how to manipulate the magic, you find yourself in a vastly more beautiful world, even though you can't actually see a thing.

Our first evening programme was a show on CBC for Buckingham Cigarettes called "Blended Rhythm." It had Eric Wilde and a forty-piece orchestra. Bob Farnon was on trumpet, Bert Pearl was at the piano, and Samuel Hershenhorn was one of the violinists. The producers decided we should do short sketches in the middle of the show and we said that would be fine, but what about an audience? They told us the orchestra would supply the laughter. We wondered if that would be good enough. We had listened to Jack Benny, Fred Allen and all those comedians; we heard lots of laughs and they sounded marvellous. But we did two shows with just the members of the orchestra supplying laughs. Although we were just two kids starting out we knew enough to go to MacLaren's and tell them it wouldn't work out without lots of laughs. We were prepared to step out of the show but they put us in a studio with an audience. Those shows did as well as any of the American ones. Here we were—two Canadians—being funny! Instead of hearing jokes about smog on the San Fernando freeway or about Brooklyn, here we were doing jokes about Vancouver, Toronto and Prince Edward Island. The audience had a sense of identification with us. We'd joke about hockey. They'd never heard hockey jokes from the United States. This, then, was theirs and it was Canadian. At first we were called "Shuster and Wayne," but when we got back from the service in 1945 Bill Byles of the Spencer and Mills agency thought that "Wayne and Shuster" sounded better. We didn't care one way or the other.

Sometimes we'd sit down and think of what would be really funny. For instance, "Hockey Night in Canada." We used to listen to Foster Hewitt every Saturday night and we hit on the idea of getting him to come on our show. We got crowd noises from Maple Leaf Gardens and did a game between the Toronto Maple Leafs—using the names of the real players and getting the effect of a genuine hockey game. Anyone just tuning in would swear that a real game was on. Our team was the Mimico Mice. It was great, and got to be an annual event. That skit was uniquely

They'd never heard hockey jokes from the United States. This, then, was theirs and it was Canadian. Our team was the Mimico Mice.

Canadian. Many of our sketches could have been transposed to American radio and the audience would have understood what we were doing. But the hockey game could only have been done in Canada. We think people loved it for that very reason.

When we were in the armed forces the army decided to do a radio show and they asked us to participate. Jack Benny was invited to appear on the programme and we wrote a half-hour script for "The Canadian Army Show" with Jack Benny as a guest. Benny really liked our script and we were thrilled, of course. The "Army Show" began in Montreal and from that we built a half-hour radio show called "This Is the Army."

Then a bunch of us were brought together and told that since we could do a successful radio show, we should try our hands at a stage show. Jack Arthur was the civilian producer. The other producer was Vic George, a broadcaster from Montreal. Rai Purdy of CFRB was second-in-command and there were also a lot of CBC types. Geoff Waddington became musical conductor. Bob Farnon was the arranger. We did the book and lyrics and played the leads. "This is the Army" toured Canada. When the time came to go overseas the decision was made that, rather than take the show to London, England—as had been done with "Meet the Navy"—it would be better to play for the troops in the field. So when we went over in 1943, we split into five compact units each with its own trucks, lighting system and generator. We could go into any town and set up in a field or anywhere we wanted. Our show was in the tradition of The Dumbells of the First World War. Most importantly, sitting and talking to soldiers from all across the country gave us a glimpse of Canada we would not have gained any other way.

When we came back to Canada we were approached by the CBC to do a show which would explain rehabilitation credits to veterans. "Johnny Home" ran for fifty-two weeks. Its producer was Frank Willis; his brother Austin played the lead.

Later we became the first Canadians in radio to have our own names in the title of the programme. In the States it was "The Jack Benny Show" or "The Fred Allen Show" and so on. But here it was "Fun For Three" or "Yakking it Up." We thought this was because of money. If stars were built up they would ask for more money. But what the powers that be didn't realize was that stars attracted more of an audience. Bert Pearl was not permitted to have his own show. It was "The Happy Gang" with Bert Pearl. But the fact is, it was his show. He put the whole thing together.

◄
The Army Show. Johnny Wayne is in the second row with a star on his chest. Frank Shuster is in top row, second from the left. In soldier's uniform to the left is tenor Jimmy Shields.

Max Ferguson.

Max Ferguson

I came on the air with Rawhide late in the year of 1946. I had taken my audition with the CBC and was told to get a little experience and they would call me. I went with a local station in London, Ontario, my home town, and worked there through the summer, and to my surprise the CBC were true to their word. They contacted me and offered me an opening which was available in their Halifax studios as an announcer. That was in December and in that first week I did just about everything that an announcer does—putting the women commentators on the air, doing the fish broadcasts. All the chores.

The following Saturday morning I came in to see what my schedule for the next week would be and I noticed that I was to start off at eight-thirty with a morning programme called "After Breakfast Breakdown," a half-hour of cowboy music. I'd never been overly fond of cowboy music. I liked the legitimate stuff, like the Sons of the Pioneers, but the drugstore cowboy music drove me up the wall, and it still does. I wondered how I'd ever get through the half-hour without going insane. I was around twenty-one or twenty-two at the time, and I was impressed with the fact that I was an announcer with the illustrious CBC, but I was appalled that my friends would hear me doing this crummy cowboy show, so I changed my voice by dropping it way down. I pulled this name "Rawhide" out of the air. It had some connotation of old untanned leather. I did the programme and insulted all the cowboy singers such as Hank Snow, who came from Halifax and was idolized in the Maritimes. I didn't know him from a hole in the ground. Instead of introducing him as "Hank Snow, the Yodelling Ranger," I went on and said, "And now, here's Hank Snow, the yodelling Mongolian idiot." Sid Kennedy, the manager, said, "If you want to get out of this place alive, you get back on the air and offer a retraction." I came on again with the weakest apology in radio history, saying, "I'm awfully sorry about that slip of the tongue when I referred to Hank as the yodelling Mongolian idiot. I was thinking of another yodelling Mongolian idiot I knew out West." Apparently the Maritime listeners bought that.

I thought the programme was a 'one-shot' affair, but on the basis of that one show Sid Kennedy thought it was a far-out idea and a tremendous way of doing a cowboy show. I told him that I didn't want to do that kind of show, it just wasn't my cup of tea. However, over the weekend he was in touch with CBC Toronto, and the following Monday I was told that I would be doing the show on the Maritime network. It went to the Maritime network for a year. Nobody knew who Rawhide was in those days. My identity was kept nicely concealed and listeners began writing in; the show was really catching on. I got some interesting letters, including marriage proposals from elderly ladies in Newfoundland. Finally my identity was announced. An officious announcer-type had to come on at the end of the show and announce, "The role of Rawhide is played by Max Ferguson." It [made me] sad, because I immediately started getting letters saying, [I feel l]ike an idiot. I was the one who wrote you so-and-so. I [thought yo]u were a nice old man and now I feel so silly."

I went on and said, "And now, here's Hank Snow, the yodelling Mongolian idiot."

After my identity was released the show went on for about another year to the Maritime network. By Valentine's Day 1949, I was transferred to Toronto. They asked me if, in addition to my announcing chores in Toronto, I would donate (and I do mean donate) the "Rawhide Show?" My announcing duties consisted of everything from the seven o'clock news in the mornings to the dance band remotes at night. Somewhere in between, I was supposed to have this half-hour show ready—writing skits, etc. I did that for about five or six years as a staff announcer before I went free lance in 1954. Of course, the show had more characters than Rawhide. I did a voice called "Granny," and one called "Marvin Mellobell." I developed these voices out of a sense of boredom and frustration. I *hated* the show. Just to help make the half-hour pass I started to make my own sound effects. This was before the unions came in and one could still make one's own sound effects. I'd just sit there and open a little door and have Granny chat with Rawhide. Then I devised the Goomer Brothers who were always selling their illegal apple cider. Then there was Marvin Mellobell, the synthesis of all the rotten objectionable faults that announcers have, like adenoids, pomposity, and so on. All of these voices developed, but it was just for my own amusement. At that stage I didn't know if anybody was listening.

I've been asked if my characters were based on real people that I've known, or knew. The only one based on a real character was Marvin Mellobell. Philip J. Buster, my politician, was based on the bombastic type who would come out with absolute banalities. His favourite line was, "But never lose sight of the fact that the boys and girls of today are gonna be the men and women of tomorrow!" said, of course, as if he were announcing the end of the world. There was a fellow in Toronto I used to hear and I built Marvin around this man's voice. When I was transferred to Toronto this chap actually came up to me and told me how much of a kick he got out of my 'voices.' He said, "The one I like the best is Marvin Mellobell." He went on to say that he knew the announcer that I was taking-off and mentioned another announcer on the staff.

I received a lot of flak when I first started "The Rawhide Show" in the Maritimes. I remember one time being called on the carpet over the cowboy music and the way I was introducing it. By this time I had learned that Hank Snow was, or had been, a Halifax boy, and that Wilf Carter was also well liked down there. The two were almost neck and neck in popularity. I was advised when I was playing cowboy music to make sure I put one of each of their records on every day. Apparently one day I put *two* Wilf Carter records on, and only *one* Hank Snow, and a brother and sister from Mahone Bay got through to their Member of Parliament, who was astute enough to see that there was more here than just a trivial matter of one artist being played more than another. He saw it as a way of getting at the CBC. It got right to the floor of the House of Commons. Wilf Carter's mother wrote me one time and almost made a little trouble. Wilf Carter woul[d] always open his records with a little spoken monologue [that] went, "Well, boys, kinda nice sittin' around the old campfir[e], throw another log on the fire and I'll tell you all about [the Straw]berry Roan." Then he'd sing "The Strawberry Roan with an impersonation of Wilf and say awful things. For instance, Wilf had another song titled "My Silvery Gray-Haired Mother in the West." I'd say something like, "Throw my silvery gray-haired mother on the fire, Tex, and I'll tell you the story about such and such." I had no idea that Wilf's own mother was living in New Brunswick. She naturally was a little put out. Those were the little controversies. The big ones didn't happen until I moved to Toronto. I guess by then, I'd gotten a bit stronger with my satire. The skits in the Maritime days were not as politically oriented as they later became going out to the full network. In the Maritimes I'd have the Goomer Brothers pestering the CBC. In addition to the weather reports, they wanted a "Mountie Report," because when they were making hard cider down on Gasper Road, they wanted to know where the mounties were. There weren't that many political happenings down there that I could satirize.

I vilified the CBC on my shows, but I'll give credit where credit is due. The CBC gave me carte blanche. As a matter of fact, Ted Briggs, the Regional Director, once called me in and said, "Look, we don't mind if you knock us, but for God's sake don't ever get on the air and sing the praises of the CBC because then you'll appear as a paid flak for us." So I *did* criticize the CBC and hit fairly close to the bone, telling of goofs and of cases of mismanagement and, much to the CBC's credit, they never did tell me that I mustn't dare say this or that. Mind you, the other interpretation of that could be they just weren't listening.

Much later in my career I remember being embarrased when some columnist said I was "the conscience of Canada." That certainly was not my intention. It sounded so pretentious. My connection with my audience was through the mail, and the letters that I would get—which is the most satisfying part of any show—would be things like some guy telling of listening to a certain skit in his car and having to pull over because he was laughing so much and of a policeman coming over to ask why he was parked on the side of the road. Or letters saying that someone would always be indebted to the programme because during their father's last illness it was the only thing that he was able to enjoy. These were the things that made it all worthwhile, really. Any network programme becomes a unifying thing to Canadians. If they are transferred from West to East they know they can still hear a favourite programme in whatever part of Canada they are living. I've heard so many times that some person left home to go to university in another part of the country and still could hear my programme, and knew that his family was also hearing it so many miles away.

I did a fair amount of television, and still do. But generally the "Rawhide" series on radio was great and far more satisfying. I could do a skit with just the help of a sound man. To do the same thing on television would literally take a week! I did a skit one time where there was supposed to be about sixteen nationalities on board a destroyer. A skit like that done on television would take such a vast amount of set-building, fussing over lighting, costumes, and all the rest of it. It would drive me up the wall! In radio, though, with just sound effects, it would be done with about five minutes to get ready.

"Look, we don't mind if you knock us, but for God's sake don't ever get on the air and sing the praises of the CBC.

Bill McNeil

Radio holds a special place in the hearts of Cape Bretoners. That's because Marconi himself did many of his early experiments there. First at Table Head, about a mile from my parents' home in Glace Bay, and later, a few miles inland, but still within the town limits of Glace Bay. He erected his huge wooden radio towers and built a home and a great steel barn to house the radio station called VAS, the Voice of the Atlantic Seaboard. He lived there with his family, hired local men to help him, and fascinated everyone with daily broadcasts of the weather.

Everyone talked about this "mysterious little foreigner" with the dark clothes and the moustache, and about the magical things he was doing "over there at Tower Road," which was what the area was named in honour of Marconi's radio towers. Nobody saw him much, as he seldom left his property or his experiments, but you could hear what he was doing on the crystal sets everyone was building or on the more sophisticated receivers that were coming on the market. If you tuned carefully, there it was: "This is VAS, the Voice of the Atlantic Seaboard. Here is the marine weather forecast." Three or four times a day it would come in and Cape Bretoners would gather around their radios. It may not have been the greatest programming in the world, but for us at that time it was the most exciting.

I was born in 1924 and I grew up with those call letters and that early voice in my ears. I think I could say "VAS" before I could say "Mama." My father was an early 'radio bug' and from the time he came home from work until he went to bed, he never stopped twirling dials and trying to find new stations from all over the world. His eyes would gleam and he'd shout with excitement when he'd pull in a voice from somewhere, speaking a language he didn't (but pretended to) understand. The nighttime air in our house was filled with French and Russian, German and static. In the daytime VAS was the only station we could get.

Then Nate Nathanson came along in 1929 and got CJCB going. We began hearing all sorts of things, day and night, including the network offerings of the old CNR. Through the 1930s CJCB kept getting better and Nate kept his station going from morning to night. As an affiliate first of the CRBC and then of the CBC, we got it all on CJCB—from "Amos 'n' Andy," to championship fights. I can still hear the voice of Clem McCarthy, the greatest sportscaster of them all: "The winner, and still heavyweight champion of the world...Joe Louis."

People talked about radio constantly. If Betty Brown, our local women's commentator gave a recipe for raisin cookies on her morning show, every miner's lunch box would have raisin cookies for weeks. Had Ann Terry, another women's commentator, wanted to run for Premier of Nova Scotia, she would have won in a landslide. When CJCB ran a contest to choose "Miss Cape Breton"—the winner would travel to the 1937 Coronation of King George VI—there were so many Surprise Soap wrappers sent in that the post office had to hire extra staff to handle the mail.

Radio personalities—local *or* international—were equivalent to the 'rock' heroes of today. Unlike the rest of us who in the

VACANCY

FOR

EXPERIENCED ANNOUNCER

on 5 kw. Maritime Station

Send disc and full particulars

to

MALCOLM NEILL

STATION CFNB FREDERICTON, N.B.

Depression had nothing, and never expected more, *they* were glamourous. If a local fiddle player or singer displayed their talents over CJCB, they instantly became the talk of the town: "He must be good. He played on CJCB."

This was the world I had the audacity to try to become part of in 1944, the year I took my first audition as an announcer at CJCB. I was an amateur actor with Father Bob Donnelly's youth group at our parish church. Nobody ever said I was a great actor, but they did say I had a fair voice and "should be in radio." I was at the time, a reluctant miner, who had been able to complete high school and one year of university before money ran out. I was desperate to get out of the mine and I grasped at radio as a remote possibility of escape. My CJCB audition didn't get me in and neither did the countless auditions I took at radio stations all over the province during the next six years during which time I tied myself even more to the mines through the acquisition of a wife, a house, and a son. My desperation didn't help the auditions, nor did my "Cape Breton accent," and my meagre knowledge of radio.

In 1949, the CBC put a radio station in Cape Breton to act as a relay point for the programmes that would be going across the water to our new province of Newfoundland. As usual, I was there trying to get in. But when CBI went on the air, its staff didn't include my name. I kept auditioning until one day in 1950, when a job came open and I was invited to audition along with seventy-six other hopefuls from across Canada. Two weeks later I was informed I had made it onto a short list of three and would have to take another audition. Convinced that I would never make it, I shook my way through another audition (including French, German and Italian pronunciations) and I went back to my nice cool coal mine to await the announcement of failure. Two weeks later I received a phone call asking, "When can you start work?"

The remainder of that conversation and the rest of that day remains a blur. Two days later, I was sitting in front of a CBC microphone. It's hard to describe the excitement I felt and the amazement of the people of my community. I had kept my ambitions—and auditions—to myself, as I felt it would be easier to explain success than failure. Many years later, Ken Bagnell of Glace Bay, who had become a well-known writer, wrote in the *Globe and Mail,* "When the news spread through the community that Bill McNeil, a Glace Bay miner, had been hired by the CBC, it couldn't have produced more shock than if a Protestant had been made Pope." I felt much the same way. More than thirty years later, it's still a thrill to sign on.

Bill McNeil.

When the news spread through the community that Bill McNeil, a Glace Bay miner, had been hired by the CBC, it couldn't have produced more shock than if a Protestant had been made Pope.

Television . . .
Will Canada be ready when it comes?

Canadian television is expected to make its debut in September, 1951, when CBC-TV programs will be broadcast from Toronto. Already some 23,500 Canadian set-owners are viewing TV broadcasts from the United States.

The potential of television's pulling-power is not surprising. For only in television does the advertiser have a medium which can demonstrate the promise of his product . . . in sight, in sound . . . in motion, in use . . . *all in the viewer's home.* Here are examples: —

An appliance manufacturer introduced a new product to audiences in a single city of medium size. From just one program orders came in for a total of $1,650. in sales. Advertising cost: $1.78 for every $30 appliance sold!

A cook book offer on an afternoon cooking show produced 11,000 requests — accompanied by cash — in three days.

A dairy offered a seasonal novelty through local 20-second TV announcements. Within two weeks more than 50,000 orders came in — a 500% increase from pre-TV days.

But to make use of television's

potential is no easy, last-minute job! To solve problems of programming and selling you need intimate experience with this new medium.

The J. Walter Thompson Company has worked closely with television for twenty years. In September, 1930, our Chicago office directed the first commercial TV program ever put on the air. Today the J. Walter Thompson Company supervises the production of 20 national network and local TV programs. Spot announcements for 225 stations. For one client alone, more than 200 personalized TV film announcements.

When television comes into its own in Canada, will you be ready with your TV plans? If your program is to be among Canada's first in September, planning it NOW is none too soon.

In helping you to make your plans and program successful, the J. Walter Thompson Company Limited can call upon the skills and experience developed over the years by our offices in the United States.

Since its first TV Show in 1930, the J. Walter Thompson Company was also —

- First to produce a full variety show (1940)

- First to present a regular weekly *hour-long* sponsored program (1946)

- First to produce and direct a regular weekly *hour-long dramatic program* (1947)

- First agency to employ its own TV set designer

J. Walter Thompson Company, Limited,
Dominion Square Building, Montreal, and
80 Richmond St. W., Toronto

The Coming of Television

A Listener

We looked on our radio as a member of the family. Mom always joked about it. She'd say to dad, "Well, we're all home tonight; you and I, the three boys, one girl and Marconi." We really depended on our radio, especially during the Depression when there was no money for any other kind of entertainment. Radio gave us the first good music we ever heard and it introduced us to drama. I think we learned more from the talk programmes on radio than we learned in school. Then when the Second World War came along it was our Marconi in the corner that we depended on to keep us informed about what was happening.

The radio could make us laugh and it could make us cry. It could be the best companion you'd ever want on a lonely winter night. Best of all, I think, was the "Stage" series on the CBC. I used to shut my eyes and listen to those plays from beginning to end without saying a word or moving an inch. I learned to paint the most beautiful mind pictures to match the words I was hearing and for that one hour I would be transported wherever the playwright wanted me to go. It was truly magical.

When the War was over we started to hear about the coming of television and like everybody I was excited by the prospect. The idea of having pictures to go along with the sound of radio seemed like the ultimate dream. I figured that if I loved radio, I would love television a thousand times more. When TV did come in 1952, my husband and I were ready. We had bought a set and were tuned in for the first broadcast. For weeks we spent every free hour in front of the set. We even watched the test pattern. But mostly it was the novelty of it that we were thrilled with more than anything else.

Before long we were listening to radio again. There were nights the TV wasn't turned on at all. I think my imagination was better at building sets for plays than the people who were

TV has a place in our home but it hasn't become a member of the family like the radio was in my parents' home.

"The Craigs" attempted to adapt to TV.

"I don't care if you are playing television. You put your clothes back on . . . and you stop saying: 'I'm the sponsor and what I say goes'."

▶
The Massey Commission. Arthur Surveyor, Georges-Henri Lévesque, Vincent Massey, Hilda Neatby, Norman Mackenzie. Its report urged the CBC to move into television broadcasting.

▶
CBC technician George Lovatt at work during first experimental telecast of a hockey game.

"It's perfect. You can close your eyes and you'd swear you were listening to the radio."

paid to do it. My skies were always bluer, my heroes were always handsomer, and my mountains didn't look painted on a bedsheet. I found I could enjoy music better if I wasn't distracted by pictures of the orchestra.

Thirty years later I still feel that way. TV has a place in our home but it hasn't become a member of the family the way the radio was in my parents' home. That place is still reserved for "the wireless." Now that our own children have moved away there's just me and Dad and Marconi.

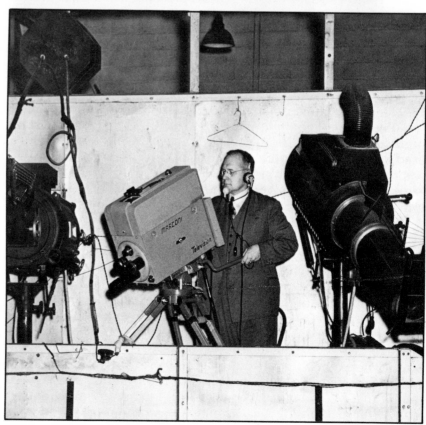

The Globe and Mail

Final Edition   TORONTO, SATURDAY, MAY 27, 1950.   5 Cents Per Copy

Toronto TV Programs To Start Sept. 1, 1951

▲

In fact, CBC television didn't come on the air until September, 1952.

Little Money At Outset, CBC Notes

By FRANK FLAHERTY

Ottawa, May 26 (Staff).—Owners of television sets in the Toronto area may be able to tune in on programs from a Toronto station about Sept. 1, 1951, A. D. Dunton, chairman of the CBC board of governors, said today.

Answering a question from Charles Henry (L, Toronto-Rosedale), Mr. Dunton said that was the earliest date on which the proposed CBC television station could be operating.

Canadian television would have to do a good job with little money, Mr. Dunton said. Television planners had to start with the assumption that they would not have anything like the funds available that are at the disposal of television producers in the United States or the United Kingdom.

Reinforcing this point, Ernest Bushnell, CBC director of programs, said the CBC would never have $30,000 or $40,000 to spend on a show. If it could spend $2,000 on a single production it would be lucky.

"We hope to be able to put together a limited program service that will be first class despite that," said Mr. Bushnell.

He added that as a start the Toronto station would be on the air for one, two or three hours a day. Programs would include some brought in from the United States but also a good proportion of Canadian programs. There would be one or two good children's programs each week as well as special Canadian events. Many things in the arts and sciences were fit subjects for television.

Television was a new art, he said, and new methods had to be created.

Generally speaking it was not satisfactory to train a television camera on a stage play. The talents of Canadian dramatic groups would be used but they would have to perform especially for television in the studio.

W. A. Robinson (L, Simcoe East) questioned whether television development should have priority over the provision of radio service to areas which did not now get proper service.

"It is very hard to say," said Mr. Dunton. "I think both should proceed together. There are some outstanding examples of unserved radio areas. On the other hand there is very strong pressure for at least a start on television."

The CBC expects it will pile up deficits during the first five years in the field of television, Mr. Dunton said he believed that by the end of five years revenues would be sufficient to balance expenditures.

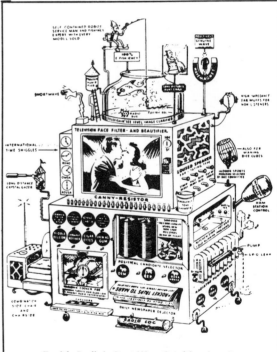

Zenith Radio's Post-War Combination Set

This Rube Goldbergian cartoon is Zenith Radio Corp.'s satire on post-war television promises. It was sent to thousands of Zenith dealers as a warning not to "kid the public into believing that it is going to have a combination radio-phonograph-F.M.-facsimile set for $14.92, with 40% off for cash." Zenith named the contraption the Great Christopher Model. One Zenith dealer in Wisconsin missed the point, sent in his check for the new instrument. General Motors' Dr. Charles Kettering received a copy of the cartoon and remarked: "We have the same people designing automobiles."

The key to the lower St. Lawrence

CJBR
RIMOUSKI

CFPA
PORT ARTHUR ONT.   250 WATTS

CHNS
THE VOICE OF HALIFAX
THE CHOICE OF HALIFAX

15,000 WATTS
CKY
WINNIPEG

CJRL
COVERING NORTH WESTERN ONTARIO
KENORA

CKCW
MONCTON   NEW BRUNSWICK
The Hub of the Maritimes
REPS: STOVIN IN CANADA; McGILLVRA IN U.S.A.

CJCH
"The Friendly Voice of Halifax"
Representatives: NATIONAL BROADCAST SALES, TORONTO, MONTREAL
JOSEPH HERSHEY McGILLVRA, NEW YORK CITY, U.S.A.

CJGX
Yorkton
SASKATCHEWAN
940 ON YOUR RADIO DIAL
Representatives:
HORACE N. STOVIN & CO. — Toronto, Montreal
INLAND BROADCASTING SERVICE — Winnipeg
ADAM YOUNG, JR., INC. — U.S.A.

920 KC   CKNX   1000 WATTS
The WESTERN ONTARIO FARM STATION
Representatives J. L. ALEXANDER TORONTO & MONTREAL
AN INDEPENDENTLY OPERATED STATION

Covers
THE RICH
FRUIT BELT
of
BRITISH COLUMBIA
CBC BASIC ★ 1000 WATTS
CKOV
KELOWNA ★ *Okanagan* BROADCASTERS LTD.

Index

Picture Credits

Page 34   Reproduced from the Smallwood collection with the permission of Joseph Smallwood and Newfoundland Book Publishers, St. John's.

Page 36   PA-128024/ Public Archives Canada

Page 50   Top of page. PA-122243/ Public Archives Canada

Page 83   From the collection of Foster Hewitt. Used with permission.

Page 85   From the collection of Foster Hewitt. Used with permission.

Page 102   PA-66452/ Public Archives Canada

Page 103   PA-66500/ Public Archives Canada

Page 113   PA-101350/ Public Archives Canada

Page 134   PA-66478/ Public Archives Canada

Page 182   Top of Page. PA-66621/ Public Archives Canada

Page 182   Bottom of page. PA-79116/ Public Archives Canada

Page 192   PA-92386/ Public Archives Canada

Page 194   PA-122227/ Public Archives Canada

Page 209   PA-68128/ Public Archives Canada

Page 217   PA-70770/ Public Archives Canada

Page 230   PA-115176/ Public Archives Canada

Page 233   PA-6862/ Public Archives Canada

Page 236   PA-66238/ Public Archives Canada

Page 251   PA-6858/ Public Archives Canada

Page 256   PA-111573/ Public Archives Canada

Page 261   PA-6860/ Public Archives Canada

Page 263   PA-6863/ Public Archives Canada

Page 269   PA-6856/ Public Archives Canada

Page 282   PA-112532/ Public Archives Canada

Page 288   PA-111381/ Public Archives Canada

Page 295   PA-6861/ Public Archives Canada